THE PROFLIGATE SON

THE PROFLIGATE SON

Or, *A True Story of Family Conflict,*
Fashionable Vice, and Financial Ruin
in Regency Britain

NICOLA PHILLIPS

OXFORD
UNIVERSITY PRESS

OXFORD
UNIVERSITY PRESS

Great Clarendon Street, Oxford, OX2 6DP,
United Kingdom

Oxford University Press is a department of the University of Oxford.
It furthers the University's objective of excellence in research, scholarship,
and education by publishing worldwide. Oxford is a registered trade mark of
Oxford University Press in the UK and in certain other countries

© Nicola Phillips 2013

The moral rights of the author have been asserted

First Edition published in 2013

Impression: 1

Published in the United States of America by Oxford University Press
198 Madison Avenue, New York, NY 10016, United States of America

British Library Cataloguing in Publication Data

Data available

ISBN 978-0-19-968753-4

As printed and bound by
CPI Group (UK) Ltd, Croydon, CR0 4YY

For my son, Sam

One would hope that it would not be so with Friends and Relations. . . . Their natural ties of love should lay restraint upon their passions, and keep them in better order. But 'tis rather all the contrary. . . . They quickly fly out into excess, recriminate, complain of, and reproach each other, with more sharpness and ill-will, than other People.

— William Fleetwood, *The Relative Duties of Parents and Children,* 16th ed. (1811)

CONTENTS

ILLUSTRATIONS
AND CREDITS

Map 1. London, c. 1809. *Kat Bennett.*

Map 2. The Voyage of *The Surry*, c. 1814. *Mike Morgenfeld.*

Figure 1. William Collins Jackson, *Filial Ingratitude; Or, The Profligate Son*, 1:1. © The National Archives.

Figure 2. I. R. and G. Cruikshank, *The Corinthian Capital*, frontispiece to Pierce Egan, *Tom & Jerry: Life in London* (1821). © The Mary Evans Picture Library.

Figure 3. Sir Martin Archer Shee, *John Evelyn of Wotton* (1821). Courtesy of Sotheby's Picture Library.

Figure 4. Charles Turner (after James Ramsey), *Thomas Potter Macqueen* (mid-nineteenth century). © National Portrait Gallery, London.

Figure 5. *New Roads to the Temple of Fortune*, frontispiece to *The Scourge*, vol. 1 (1811). © Trustees of the British Museum.

Figure 6. I. R. and G. Cruikshank, *A whistling shop: Tom & Jerry visiting Logic, "on board the Fleet,"* illustration from Pierce Egan, *Tom & Jerry: Life in London* (1821). © The Mary Evans Picture Library.

Figure 7. Augustus Pugin and Thomas Rowlandson, *The Bow Street Office* (1808). © City of London, London Metropolitan Archives.

Figure 8. *A Barristerial Duel, or Who's Sent to Coventry Now* (1816). © Trustees of the British Museum.

Figure 9. Augustus Charles Pugin and Thomas Rowlandson, *Interior view of the Sessions House, Old Bailey, with a court in session* (1809). © City of London, London Metropolitan Archives.

Figure 10. James Miller, *Newgate* (1800). © City of London, London Metropolitan Archives.

Figure 11. George Dance, *Ground Plan of Newgate* (1780). © The British Library Board, Crace Maps, VIII.83.

Figure 12. The *Discovery* convict ship (1829). © The National Maritime Museum, Greenwich, UK.

Figure 13. Luke Clennell, *Frost Fair on the River Thames* (1814). © City of London, London Metropolitan Archives.

Figure 14. Major James Taylor, *View of the entrance of Port Jackson and part of the town of Sydney* (1823). © National Library of Australia.

A NOTE ABOUT MONEY
AND FINANCIAL VALUES

English Currency, ca. 1790–1820

12 pennies (12d.) = 1 shilling (1s.)

20 shillings = 1 pound (£1, bank note and after 1816 1 gold sovereign coin)

21 shillings = 1 guinea (a gold coin with a fixed value of 21s. in general use until 1816)

The impact of the French revolutionary wars (1792–1799) and the Napoleonic Wars (1799–1815) led to a scarcity of gold, which consequently rose in value, and also to a shortage of silver and copper coins. Parliament passed an act to make paper money (banknotes) legal tender in 1797 and in 1816 initiated a "Great Recoinage" to stabilize the currency, but a paper money economy had been growing throughout the eighteenth century. City banks commonly issued notes as "promises to pay," and these along with bills of exchange and other forms of creditworthy paper effectively became negotiable instruments and therefore passed into circulation. The shortage of circulating coin contributed to a culture of commercial transactions based on (often long-term) credit.

Social Class and Standards of Living

Based on the estimates (1801–1803) of contemporary statistician Patrick Colquhoun, the titled aristocracy had an average annual income of £4,000–8,000; eminent merchants and bankers, around £2,600; and gentlemen, £700. The minimum necessary to support upper-middle-class gentility was £300 per annum, but less-well-off middle-class families—shopkeepers, tradesmen, farmers, military officers, and clergymen—lived fairly comfortably on about £120 a year. The majority of the working population subsisted (or struggled in times of scarcity) on £10–40 a year or less.

Modern Values and Exchange Rates, ca. 1800–1830

Assessing the worth or converting the value of old money to modern prices is at best an inexact science—the prices of goods constantly fluctuated and were always relative to incomes of different social groups—and the task is made more complex by the difficulty of finding directly comparable data to use. In this book, I have therefore not attempted to make direct comparisons, which, even if roughly indicative at the time of publication, would quickly become outdated because of the rapid rate of inflation. There is a website that readers may find useful to understand the relative value of money past and present: www.measuringworth.com was set up by US academics and enables comparisons between multiple sets of data to compute changing values over time in both British pounds and US dollars. It is considerably easier, however, to be more accurate about the historical rate of exchange between the two countries. Between 1800 and 1830 the average exchange rate varied from $4 to $5 for each British pound, but it was at its lowest in 1812 at $3.62 and highest in 1816 at $5.22.

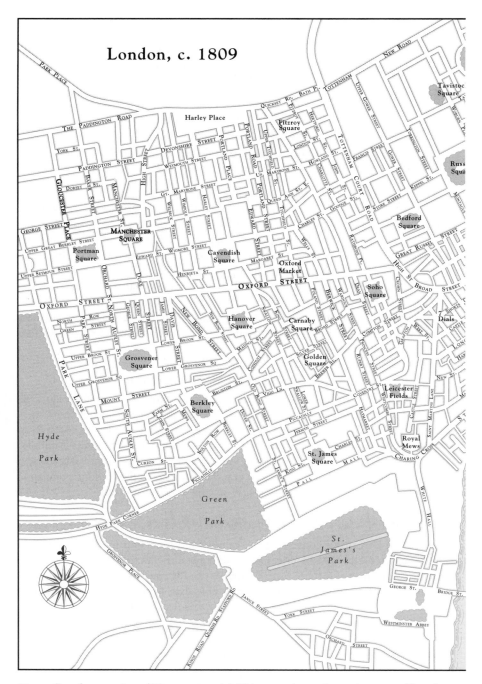

MAP 1. **London, c. 1809.** (*Map not to scale.*) This map shows the main areas of London that William Jackson frequented. The Jacksons and the Evelyns lived near the western edge of the capital at numbers 30 and 80 Gloucester Place, respectively. Sir George Shee lived at 24 Manchester Square. William had easy access to the shops of Oxford Street and the surrounding area, but he also sought entertainment around St. James' Square and

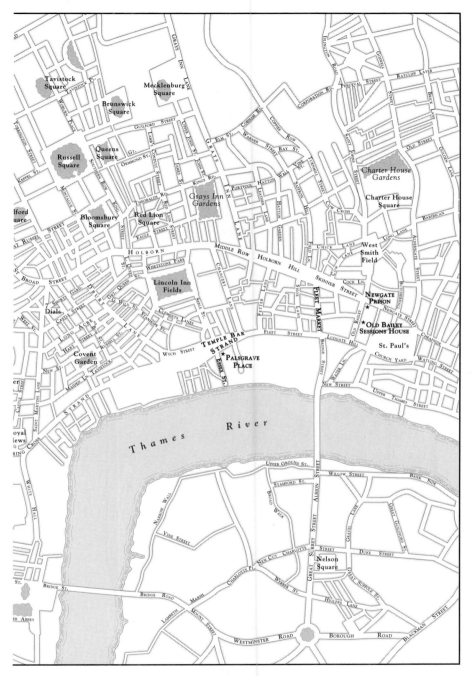

Covent Garden. The Fleet debtors' prison was at number 9 Fleet Market. The Old Bailey Sessions House and Newgate Prison are just to the east, bordered by Old Bailey and Newgate Street. The sponging house where William was twice confined for debt stood in Palsgrave Place, on the southern side of The Strand between Essex Street and Temple Bar.

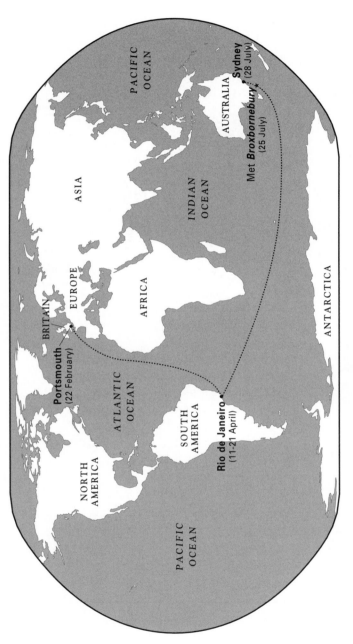

MAP 2. *Voyage of The Surry*, c. 1814.

INTRODUCTION

The Profligate Heir

*'He's such an infernal character—he's a gambler—he's
a drunkard—he's a profligate in every way. He's shot a
man in a duel—he's head and ears in debt, and he's
robbed me and mine of the best part of . . . [a] fortune.'*

—William Thackeray, *Vanity Fair* (1847)

On the night of October 27, 1812, howling gales tore through
the streets of London, whipped up the surface of the Thames,
and battered against doors and windows. The massive walls
of Newgate Prison remained impervious to such assaults of nature, yet
for those prisoners awaiting trial, the night was no less disturbed. The
October sessions at the Old Bailey, London's central criminal court,
would start the following morning, at the end of which many would
find themselves facing transportation to Australia or the hangman's
noose. In an apartment separated from the majority of filthy,
verminous prisoners sat a slim young man with hazel eyes and brown
hair. He occupied privileged accommodation in the prison because his
family had the ability to pay for it, and in Regency Britain even the

penal system recognized the claims of superior social status. The son of a wealthy East India Company merchant, William Jackson had been born a gentleman, but on this bleak night at just twenty years of age he had to confront the demise of all his once bright prospects. His lawyers had warned him there was little hope of avoiding conviction for forgery, a capital crime for which the death sentence was rarely respited. William did not lack courage: he had dreamed of a brilliant career in the army and had fought duels to defend his honor. But he had begged his father to save him "from death and ignominy," for the shame such an end would bring was as bad as death itself.

William had once been the apple of his fond father's eye and a popular, fun-loving boy, but his plea made little impact on Mr. Jackson now. He agreed only to pay sufficient funds to separate William from the ranks of common prisoners and to supply him with legal counsel. He would not visit his son in jail and forbade any other relatives from doing so. Although he hoped William might be saved from death for his mother's sake, he was equally desirous that the law remove the errant youth from society permanently. For Mr. Jackson believed his only son and heir was exactly where he ought to be and had even sketched the outline of a gallows on the back of one letter. He sent William a "mourning suit" so that he could appear clean and respectable in the Old Bailey courtroom, and be laid out decently in his coffin should the verdict go against him. In his father's eyes, William was a profligate son and "transportation or the drop at Newgate" was, as he had warned several years earlier, the fate of all profligates.

A PROFLIGATE SON was every Georgian father's nightmare. He was a stock character in art and literature and a symbol of the failure of respectable parents to instill the virtues of moral, sexual, and financial self-control in their sons. Samuel Johnson's dictionary defined a profligate as an abandoned, shameless person, lost to virtue and decency. The dire consequences of such behavior were vividly illustrated in William Hogarth's *A Rake's Progress* (1733), which depicted the descent into vice, debt, and mental destruction of a young man who had inherited a fortune from his miserly father. Pamphlets containing salacious accounts of the lives of convicted felons, which blamed their fall into criminality on a profligate youth spent on prostitutes, drinking, and sartorial excess, were often sold at public hangings. This was also a scene depicted as the fate of the idle apprentice in Hogarth's *Industry and Idleness* (1747), which, the artist declared, was "calculated for the use & Instruction of Youth."[1]

Evangelical reformers determined to improve the morals and manners of what they saw as a degenerate society continued this theme from the late eighteenth century into the early nineteenth century. Hannah More's popular and prolific *Cheap Repository tracts* were chiefly designed to "promote good morals among the poor," but her sister Sarah, who also wrote some of these pamphlets, discussed the dire effects of inheriting a large sum in *The Cheapside Apprentice: or, The History of Mr. Francis H* (1796). Young Francis inherited £3,000 from his uncle and indulged in such profligacy that his fortune rapidly disappeared and he turned to forgery to cover his debts, a path that led inevitably to the gallows. The subtitle to this tract therefore warned readers that "a gay life may prove a short one." Like the other morally instructive tracts, *The Cheapside Apprentice* would have been circulated to prisoners, soldiers, and sailors, but these short stories also proved surprisingly popular among the gentry. It was this kind of didactic literature about the dangers of a misspent youth that most clearly contributed to Mr. Jackson's understanding of, and therefore his reaction to, what he saw as his teenage son's depraved and potentially dangerous behavior.[2]

William Jackson was born in 1791, and public debate about profligate sons during that decade was fueled by the excessive prodigality and massive debts (of more than £500,000) contracted by George, Prince of Wales. Newspaper commentators and satirists alike portrayed George III as a thrifty, bourgeois father and his son as an immoral, aristocratic libertine. Such depictions replicated a rather stereotypical division of class values, but the middle classes commonly associated profligacy with aristocratic vice. Yet then, as now, many men who had enthusiastically pursued the pleasures of wine, women, and fashion in their youth did not grow up to become dissipated or criminally inclined adults. During a parliamentary debate over the prince's debts in 1795, one member questioned, "How many Members of that House were wild in their youth? Had they not been forgiven and had their debts paid?"[3]

Contemporary fears of the degenerative effects of vicious pleasures and uncontrolled indulgence were greatly heightened by the French Revolution. The appalling bloodshed of Robespierre's Terror and the growth of Napoleon's power were seen as direct consequences of the immorality of the French people. Ideas about the dangers of profligate behavior bringing about the ruin of individual families thus spread to fears about the moral destruction of the whole of British society, leading to similarly terrifying consequences. Indeed, in 1798 one bishop told the House of Commons that the French might struggle to overcome British military might, but they were also "endeavouring to enforce the influence of their example, in order to taint and undermine the morals of our youth" by exporting a number of particularly alluring female dancers skilled in "wanton theatrical exhibitions." The widespread reaction to all of this was a call for a reformation of manners, a revival of religious morality, and an emphasis on rational self-restraint. What might once have been viewed as pardonable vice or passed over as youthful indulgence became increasingly unacceptable to "respectable" citizens.[4]

Not everyone subscribed to the outpouring of intolerant moral sentiment. Some, like the poet Lord Byron, believed it lacked real sincerity and functioned merely as a badge of propriety. Pierce Egan, an author and sports journalist, penned a popular antidote in the form of a comic guide to the "pleasures of the town" that vividly portrayed the manners, morals, and pleasurable pursuits of Regency London's bucks and beaus. Published in 1821, *Tom & Jerry: Life in London* followed the exploits of Corinthian Tom, who takes his friends on a journey of drinking, dancing, gambling, theatergoing, rioting, cockfighting, and sexual conquest from the richest to the poorest parts of London. Tom was not, Egan insisted, "vicious from principle; although it might be urged his morals would not bear the strictest investigation." He had merely fallen into "the general error of youth, that his own opinion was equally as good as the experience of his parents," for which minor sin he was punished neither by imprisonment nor by death, but continued to live life in great style.[5]

The wealthy young-men-about-town who people Egan's pages reflected the lifestyles and values of William Jackson and his young friends—to them (and others from the ranks of both elite and lower orders) the accusation of profligacy was just hypocritical cant. In his youth, the author William Makepeace Thackeray described Egan's book as "a school-boys delight. . . . We firmly believed the three heroes . . . to be the most elegant fashionable young fellows the town afforded, and thought their occupations and amusements were those of all high-bred English gentlemen."[6]

MR. JACKSON'S UNDERSTANDING of profligacy as a vice is clearly visible in his three volumes of *Filial Ingratitude; Or, The Profligate Son*, written between 1807 and 1814, which form the central source for this book. These are an account of William's descent from educated young gentleman to convicted felon between the ages of fifteen and twenty-one. Each volume of carefully copied family and official letters, interspersed with Jackson's explanation of events, begins with the same two quotations. The first, taken from Dr. John Moore's popular Gothic novel *Zeluco* (1786), describes how "tracing the windings of vice and delineating the disgusting features of depravity are unpleasant tasks." Although almost unheard of now, the novel would have been immediately recognizable to contemporaries and was widely admired in the late eighteenth and early nineteenth centuries. It chronicles the exploits of an "irredeemably wicked," selfish, and profligate son from childhood to violent death. The second quotation is from William Shakespeare's *King Lear*, from which the title phrase "filial ingratitude" is also drawn. Mr. Jackson sympathized with Lear's lament about his daughters' cruelty and shared his hopes for his own child's reformation:

> *Is it not as this mouth should tear this hand for lifting*
>   *food to it? But I shall not chide thee:*
> *Let shame come when it will, I do not call it. . . .*
> *Mend when thou canst, be better, at thy leisure;*
> *I can be patient.*[7]

Young William's story was thus presented as both a tragedy of parental care betrayed and a classic rake's progress in which the immoral and the illegal were conflated. Jackson wrote initially with retributive intent—in 1811, he threatened to publish his account if

William did not reform his behavior—but the narrative contains a strong element of self-justification. The letters and comments in *Filial Ingratitude* present a robust defense of Mr. Jackson's actions as a "good" father to a profligate son. In Georgian England, being seen to be a good father was considered evidence of a virtuous public man. Demonstrable affection for his wife and children, combined with obvious authority over their behavior, was an essential component of a man's public reputation, which underpinned his whole career. As we will see in Chapter 1, when Jackson's career in the East India Company came under threat, both his professional and his private reputation took on a new importance and so therefore did the consequences of his son's behavior.[8]

After his return to England, Jackson published two versions of his *Memoir* (in 1809 and 1812) of his service in India, which were designed to clear his name by detailing a cruel miscarriage of justice that he believed had robbed him of his position in the East India Company. Even after he was cleared of all charges and reinstated to his original position, his experience in India continued to have a profound impact on the rest of his life, on his family, and, particularly, on the life of his young son. When William showed signs of teenage rebellion and immoral behavior, Jackson took up his pen to justify his actions once more and started to write *Filial Ingratitude*.[9]

MR. JACKSON'S UNFINISHED narrative was never published, and the volumes have lain largely undisturbed, along with hundreds of aging and unseen letters, for nearly two hundred years. At his death, all Jackson's papers were transferred to the court of Chancery (where civil law disputes were heard), and his estate became the subject of an interminable lawsuit. In these boxes of Chancery documents, William's side of the story survives too, and his voice is raised frequently to challenge his father's account. William's correspondence with his friends—kept by his father in carefully marked paper packets sealed with unbroken wax but not copied into the narrative—serve to provide a very different perspective. After the elder Jackson's death, fewer of William's letters survive, so his voice becomes fainter and less frequent in later chapters. There are also bundles of filthy letters bound in tattered ribbons deposited to the court by William's mother after Jackson's death, in which, occasionally, her voice—one that appears only to agree with her husband in *Filial Ingratitude*—resurfaces to support her son.[10]

Yet more voices do not necessarily mean more truth. Letters are written to inform, to persuade, to chastise, to plead, or to mislead, and for many other purposes besides. In them, family members also play roles (consciously or unconsciously) as responsible parents, dutiful children, and supportive relatives, or as the injured father, the abandoned son, the disappointed mother. Letters are also written according to prevalent cultural codes and conventions; they are more or less formal types of correspondence that shape and limit expressions of thoughts and emotions. Today those different conventions are seen most clearly in the language and topics we address when writing letters, e-mails, and texts that broadly correspond to the formal letters, brief communications, and hurried notes carried across London by runners in the Jacksons' day.[11]

This book is the extraordinarily dramatic story of an imperfect boy who grew up to become a flawed man—in one sense, a typical Regency rake's progress. But at its heart, this is about the tragic relationship between a father and a son and about the generation gap they failed to bridge. In the past, expressions of emotion, accepted codes of behavior, and areas of parental responsibility were governed by very different social and cultural attitudes, but these feelings and family roles are still familiar to us today. The ways they shape our family life and mold our individual characters are still the subject of frequent discussion and numerous advice books, as they were in the eighteenth and early nineteenth centuries. William's story also works as a microhistory—a means of exploring past attitudes toward consumer culture, credit, and particularly debt, as well as the ways a wealthy family used the judicial system to control its son's delinquency. As such, this story sheds light on many modern concerns about raising children and dealing with undesirable youthful behavior. Today we still debate the impact of sexual images, fashion, and peer pressure on teenagers, and the recent economic crisis has left a new generation of young people facing a future of debt. The profligate son remains a character who can illustrate parental fears for their offspring's futures in different ways at different times.

THE SINS OF THE FATHERS

India and England, 1798–1805

*The Office given to a young man going to India is of
trifling consequence, but he that goes out a trifling
boy, in a few years returns a great Nabob.*

— Edmund Burke, "Speech on Fox's East
India Bill" (1783)

One typically hot and humid day in 1798, the weavers of
Coongaycoorchy, a small village in the Tirunelveli district of
southern India, were going about their daily business making
cloth to fulfill an order from the East India Company's official head-
quarters in Madras. It was a good order, for the company had paid in
advance, thus providing a much-needed measure of financial security
for the villagers. But this peaceful scene of rural industry was suddenly
disturbed when a force of two hundred armed pikemen appeared on
the outskirts of the village. The soldiers, paid retainers of the poligar
(a local warrior-king) Kattobomma Nayakar, of Panjalamkurichi, demanded immediate payment of a large sum of money. The villagers
were accustomed to paying regular taxes to their overlord, but this was
different—a surprise request for a much higher amount. Perhaps fool-
ishly, given the poligar's reputation for violent retribution, the weavers
refused to pay.[1]

In response, the pikemen began to ransack the village and soon found money the weavers had hidden in their turbans, but that was not enough to satisfy the poligar's demands. The pikemen seized and flogged the male weavers, then ritually violated their womenfolk by stuffing mud into their mouths. The soldiers departed, dragging with them seventeen weavers, whom they continued to beat periodically on a journey through the hill country. When the party halted, the orgy of violence reached a climax in the treatment meted out to the most eminent weaver. The unfortunate man was stripped naked, whipped, and thrown to the ground, where bloodsucking leeches were applied to his flesh and the poisonous sap of the milk hedge was poured into his eyes. Once the leeches had gorged themselves enough to become firmly attached to the man's flesh, his tormentors tore them off, leaving gaping wounds on his body. They then wound a necklace of milk hedge round his neck, beat him with slippers, ripped out his beard—another form of ritual humiliation—and finished by pulling out his teeth. This grotesque torture proved effective, for the remaining weavers pledged bonds to supply the poligar with seventy *chakrams* (circular throwing weapons).[2]

Their ordeal over, the weavers scrabbled in the dust to retrieve their friend's teeth and sent them, as proof of the wicked oppression they had suffered from their overlord, to William Collins Jackson, the East India Company's representative and tax collector at Ramnad. For the unfortunate collector, whose duty it was to dispense justice as well as to collect taxes in the area, the arrival of this packet of teeth triggered a confrontation with the warrior poligar that would end his illustrious career with the company—a disaster that would haunt him and his young son for the rest of their lives.

NEW ARRIVALS TO MADRAS were often disconcerted to discover that their long voyage from England was not the most perilous part of their journey to India. Their ships were forced to moor some way out to sea to avoid being crushed by the huge waves that crashed against the shoreline. William Collins Jackson had first braved that boiling surf in 1782 at the age of nineteen, balanced precariously in one of a fleet of small wooden boats that ferried terrified passengers to the burning sandy beach. The eldest son of a respectable "middling sort" of merchant family, Jackson had left his home in Exeter to seek his fortune in India more than a year earlier. He had little money apart from a small bequest from his uncle, but he held great hopes of becoming one of the many young men who joined the Honourable East India Company as lowly clerks (known as writers) but returned to England as wealthy gentlemen. Many of these men used their frequently unscrupulously acquired fortunes to buy themselves a large country estate and a seat in Parliament. They were commonly called "nabobs," which was originally a distortion of "nawab" (the official title of rulers of Indian states), but the term was soon used in a derogatory sense to describe returning company employees. In 1771, *Town and Country Magazine* described a nabob as a man who had "obtained the fortune of an Asiatic prince and returned to England to display his folly and vanity and ambition."[3]

The company had originally been set up by merchants as a trading venture under a royal charter in 1600, managed by a Court of Directors in London, and financed by public shareholders. From the mid-eighteenth century, as the company's private armies defeated French and local nawabs' forces in battles over trade and imperial territories, its role was transformed from simply trading to primarily governing large areas of India. Military successes bought the East India Company substantial rights to collect taxes, but rapid expansion also proved financially ruinous. Beginning in the 1770s, the British government stepped in to regulate the company's financial affairs, and in 1784 Parliament set up a Board of Control to oversee company dealings with native rulers. The East India Company effectively became a subsidiary arm of the British state and India a jewel in its expanding empire.[4]

The town of Madras had grown up around Fort St. George, which protected one of the company's earliest trading posts. It was one of three presidency (or territorial) capitals through which the East India Company administered its growing interests in India. Calcutta had become the capital city and home of the English governor general of India in 1772, but the governor of Madras continued to oversee most of southern India. Madras itself was divided into White Town, the European sector that was home to company employees and their families, and Black Town, a coalescence of indigenous Indian villages in which

Portuguese, Armenian, and Jewish merchants also resided. The appropriately named White Town was then a city with neat streets and squares lined with handsome houses and gleaming public buildings all painted brilliant white and set off with colonnades and porticoes. It was surrounded by an arid plain speckled with elegant country residences set in classical gardens and inhabited by wealthy senior company employees seeking to replicate the landed status of an English country gentleman in temperatures that often topped 100° Fahrenheit. During the late eighteenth century, the presidency towns had become increasingly European in outlook and less permeable to Indian culture and customs. In 1769, Alexander Dalrymple (a former writer at Madras) described how Englishmen were known to be "much attached to their customs and opinions," and writers, such as Jackson, were recruited at a young age in the hope they were not yet "much warped by national prejudices." Yet these writers could live cocooned within a web of British values that were unlikely to be greatly challenged unless they traveled far beyond the boundaries of the company compound and away from the fellowship of its British servants (the term for employees). Writers spent the early years of their careers copying accounts and reams of correspondence to learn about company affairs. Indeed, all company servants were encouraged to record every event in great detail in order to keep the English directors in London well informed—a habit Jackson never lost. As a result, he acquired vast amounts of knowledge but little understanding of the people in whose country he lived and worked.[5]

THE EARLY YEARS in India proved hard for young Jackson. He had a fierce sense of moral probity and, since his family had suffered because of his father's mismanagement of its finances, a horror of getting into debt. The company was experiencing severe financial constraints at that time, so it withheld Jackson's pay for a whole year. To avoid borrowing at exorbitant rates of interest and becoming entangled with financial arrangements "which [had] so often . . . been the bane of the younger servants of the company," he used up his small capital.[6]

Yet this personal financial probity did not extend to a full rejection of the prevalent Indian custom of giving presents (or *nuzzers*)—often objects or jewelry of great value—as a normal part of any negotiations. In explaining the use of presents within Indian culture in 1788, Governor General Warren Hastings claimed that "the Company's servants have ever been accustomed to receive presents . . . and I shall venture to say, there is not an Officer commanding His Majesty's army . . . who has not received presents." In Britain, however, there had been a backlash against what was widely viewed as cold-hearted exploitation, bribery, and corruption by officials, which caused the company to crack down on the practice. Jackson therefore resented, but ultimately accepted, the company's refusal to allow him to keep the value of presents bestowed upon him by the Indian ruler Tipu Sultan for his role in helping to negotiate the Treaty of Mangalore in 1784. For the struggling twenty-year-old, the injustice of seeing his senior colleagues handsomely rewarded for their services while his own efforts went financially unrecognized by the company continued to rankle for years to come.[7]

Although his financial gains were more moderate than he had hoped, Jackson nevertheless made good progress up the company ladder, and by 1787 he had been promoted to deputy secretary in the Military and Political Department at Madras. This gave him the status he needed to propose to an attractive young widow whom he had met on board ship to India when returning from one of his periods of leave. Jane Stuart (née Shee) was sailing to India with her younger sister, Anne, to join their brother, George Shee, in Calcutta, unaware that he had hopes of making good marriages for both women. Jane was already connected to the East India Company and was well acquainted with the way of life expected from the wife of a company servant: her late husband, by whom she had had a daughter, had been a company employee. Her brother, George, was an extremely promising member of the Calcutta presidency staff, and his kinsman and patron was the esteemed politician, orator, and outspoken expert on Indian affairs Edmund Burke. The Shees were a well-respected and long-established Anglo-Irish gentry family from County Mayo, and the family's Catholic beliefs do not seem to have blighted Jackson's affections or blinded him to the manifold advantages of marrying a woman with excellent connections and considerable wealth. Through his marriage to Jane, Jackson gained two supportive and important lifelong friends,

George Shee and John Evelyn, both of whom would play key roles in his family life and especially that of his son.

When George Shee learned of Jackson's marriage to his sister in 1787, he declared himself delighted to have acquired a brother-in-law "such as your friends describe you" and at "my dear Jane having a fair Prospect of Happiness open to her for life." Shee had joined the East India Company at just sixteen years of age in 1770, three years before Warren Hastings became the first governor general of India. Shee was a highly intelligent man known for his "uprightness and integrity," but he was less rigid in his moral outlook than his brother-in-law. He possessed a more passionate and fun-loving nature than Jackson, and he enjoyed amorous adventures, music, and riding fine horses. Shee was also a political idealist; he strongly supported the beliefs of his benefactor Edmund Burke, who was an implacable opponent of Governor Hastings and criticized the "geographical morality" practiced by company employees who reset their moral compass as they approached the equator.[8]

This potent combination of political beliefs and impulsive, occasionally rash behavior had almost ruined Shee's promising career in 1778. He was caught aiding a friend (and more senior company official) in seducing a writer's wife by procuring a ladder and dark clothing to help him climb into her bedroom at night. When the seducer was discovered and detained by Indian servants, Shee broke into the house to free his friend. The enraged husband sued the official for damages, and at the subsequent trial Shee's reputation was severely damaged for his part in the plot. The judge declared that Shee's behavior "had been as reprehensible as it was derogatory to the character of a gentleman." He was obliged to remove himself from polite society and take up a less visible post as collector at Farruckabad, where he proceeded to make a great deal of money by trading on his own to supplement the salary he gained from trading on the company's behalf.[9]

When Shee returned to Calcutta—in around 1782 as Jackson was first arriving in Madras—he sought to shore up his reputation and respectability through marriage to the daughter of a well-connected, much-traveled, but financially insecure widow with an unconventional past. The daughter, Elizabeth Maria Crisp, was by all accounts a very attractive, accomplished young woman. Although this may not have been the glittering social match that Shee could once have hoped for, his initially practical pursuit of Elizabeth grew into a genuinely emotional bond, and their marriage in 1783 turned out to be a successful and prosperous union. Just a year later the couple had a son, named George, and the whole family went back to Ireland in 1788, where Shee used the wealth he had acquired in India to purchase property, power, and position in the manner of many returning nabobs before him. Shee bought Dunmore estate in County Galway in 1791 and three years later was created a baronet—a matter of great pride to the Jacksons. In 1797 he secured a seat in the Irish Parliament and that same year was made Surveyor General of Ordnance for Ireland. The family also had a London home in Manchester Square and acquired a large country estate, Lockleys, in Hertfordshire.[10]

By the 1790s the fear and furor over nabobs upsetting the social order, by buying political power that should belong to traditionally landed families, had begun to subside. Yet it was Shee's patron, Edmund Burke, who did the most to keep the danger of despotism and corruption in Asia alive in the minds of English citizens. Indeed, Shee himself provided Burke with some of the material he needed as chairman of the Commons Select Committee on East Indian Affairs to impeach Warren Hastings for corruption in 1788. A leading light in the Whig Party, which both Shee and Jackson supported, and a former East India Company shareholder, Burke had been appointed to a parliamentary select committee to investigate "injustices" committed by the company in India. During Hasting's trial, Burke painted a picture of India as having been pillaged by unscrupulous nabobs, men who made staggering profits by ignoring the universal laws of British justice and morality when they worked in foreign lands. It would become known as the trial of the century, and at its start people lined up for hours or slept overnight in nearby coffee houses to hear Burke's great orations. But the trial dragged on for seven years, and eventually Hastings was acquitted in 1795. Both Shee and Jackson, however, retained their admiration for Burke and, more importantly, considered themselves to be just, honorable men to whom the appellation of nabob did not apply.[11]

The man George Shee had originally intended one of his sisters to marry was John Evelyn, a descendant of the famous seventeenth-century diarist and gardener of the same name, whose estate at Wotton he eventually inherited in 1817. Like Shee, John Evelyn was of Anglo-Irish stock and had grown up in Ireland, where his father was a pastor and dean of Emly. He had joined the Calcutta establishment as a writer at the same time as Shee in 1770, but at the more mature age of twenty-seven. When the Shee sisters arrived in 1782, Evelyn was a respected senior merchant and member of the Calcutta Board of Revenue nearing his fortieth birthday and in need of an English wife. He was a gentle and liberal-minded man who had, like many of his fellow company servants at the time, formed a stable relationship with a half-caste Indian woman. Such relationships were often very affectionate, and nearly one-third of British wills in Bengal between 1780 and 1785 contained bequests to the mixed-race children resulting from these unions. Evelyn was no exception—he had a son with his *bibi* named George Nyleve (a reversal of his own surname) to whom he bequeathed a small property in England on his death.[12]

Some Indian *bibis* lived openly with their white lovers and were accepted by their friends, but for a company man with an eye to his career and a return to England, marriage with a mixed-race woman was not an option. There was a shortage of suitable English women in Calcutta, so when the newly arrived Jane Shee announced her betrothal to Jackson, Evelyn's matrimonial hopes naturally focused on her younger sister, Anne, even though the girl was only eleven years old when she arrived. They were married five years later in George Shee's house at Dacca when Evelyn was forty-four and Anne, who converted to Protestantism, was just sixteen. With the marriage to Anne, the Evelyns became family relations and close friends with the Shees and the Jacksons—a friendship that would last all their lives. The Evelyns left India in 1790, taking their two young sons, John and William, with them. Like Sir George Shee, John Evelyn returned a very wealthy man and purchased an estate in County Mayo, but a few years later he moved his official family to Bath in England.[13]

The year before the Evelyns left India, Jane and William Jackson celebrated the birth of a baby son, but tragically he died before his first birthday. It may have been a small measure of consolation, but

Mr. Jackson's career continued to progress, and he was promoted to become secretary of military, political, and secret matters in Madras. The arrival of another son in November 1791 was a cause of great joy. Filled with paternal pride and hopes for an illustrious future for his son, Jackson named the baby William Collins Burke Jackson, thus combining the names of both his own parents with that of his hero, Edmund Burke. Anxious that this precious child should not succumb to the dangers of disease and the Indian climate, Jackson sent his wife and young son back to England, where he knew they would find support from the Shees and the Evelyns. As William grew older, there were many occasions on which he would be grateful for the assistance of his maternal uncles, whose experiences in India seem to have contributed toward a less judgmental assessment of their nephew's youthful follies. The proud father remained in Madras alone, but the tough climate and long hours of work took a severe toll on Jackson's health. In 1796 he asked to be transferred to the less onerous post of collector, which entailed overseeing the collection of company revenue and acting as a district magistrate. The following year he was given the post of collector at Ramnad, more than three hundred miles south of Madras.

Jackson knew that the position of collector had long been one of the most lucrative available, but times had changed since George Shee had occupied a similar position at Farruckabad and used it for such financial advantage. Lord Cornwallis, the new governor general, had implemented measures to combat accusations of corruption against company collectors, who were now barred from trading on their own account in the districts under their control but were guaranteed a higher fixed salary and a pension. Yet the wording of the company's Board of Revenue Regulations remained open to interpretation: for new collectors like Jackson, there were still ways to continue the profitable sale of cloth (a staple of commerce). Rules against the acceptance of *nuzzers* were also brought in, but these made little impact; as Jackson would soon discover, gifts were still offered to company officials. Nevertheless, he prided himself on being an honest man, impervious to the financial incentives that had so dramatically enriched his predecessors. The trial of Warren Hastings had made a huge impact on Jackson, whose family ties as well as his personal and political beliefs bound him to Burke's prosecution case.

In his desire to perform his public duty honorably, Jackson worked tirelessly in Ramnad to stamp out the practice of Europeans and Indians loaning money at extortionate rates of interest; such loans had entangled nawabs, poligars, and civil and military servants of the East India Company in a disastrous web of corruption across the whole southern region. But the price of Jackson's moral crusade was high; it made him dangerous enemies both within and outside the East India Company. Although the company officially praised his vigor, shortly after his appointment and just days after taking action against usurers in Panjalamkurichi, anonymous papers accusing him of bribery and corruption against the poligars were circulated throughout his district.[14]

THERE ARE MEN for whom the upholding of an honorable principle is of paramount importance, no matter what the cost to themselves or others. Mr. Jackson was such a man. Yet his moral certainty meant that he was largely blind to cultural differences. Thus, without a trace of irony, Jackson's head assistant could later assure his superior that he was invariably governed "by the dictates of your own judgement" and that "no native upon earth could induce you to adopt a measure which you yourself considered to be wrong." Jackson drew a clear distinction between the legitimate authority he exercised on behalf of the East India Company and the kind of arbitrary power wielded by Kattobomma Nayakar with such shocking violence against the Coongaycoorchy weavers. As one of a growing number of company servants imbued with a sense of British superiority, in Jackson's eyes the poligar was just a particularly bothersome minor chieftain—one of fifty-one "licentious and unruly tributaries" under his jurisdiction. In the company's view, poligars were merely military garrison commanders who held the right to collect dues from local villages to fund their military service, but in return they owed taxes to the company.[15]

Poligars like Kattobomma Nayakar saw their position in Indian society and their relationship with the company rather differently. According to local custom, the poligars were warrior-kings who expected to expand their petty empires by attacking neighboring poligar lands and building up resources by withholding payment of taxes to higher-ranking rulers. The usual strategy was to send numerous excuses for nonpayment, so as not to alarm their overlord, and to cooperate with him in battle only when necessary to obscure their longer-term goals. Kattobomma had sent many messages to Jackson expressing regret that he could not come to pay his taxes because of his own, or his mother's, ill health. He claimed that the previous collector had accepted that it was the custom of the poligars "not to pay obedience at the first or second summons but to put it off to the third."[16]

Company collectors were well aware of the point-scoring nature of this exercise. What they failed to understand was that the poligars' use of extreme violence was a necessary and expected demonstration of increasing power, part of a deadly serious game that had been played out in southern India for centuries. To the company, violence such as that meted out on the unfortunate Coongaycoorchy weavers was proof positive that poligars were "ruthless and powerful brigands" rather than the "venerable little kings" they believed themselves to be. To Kattobomma, the attack was no more than the political practice of coercive negotiation—he had visibly demonstrated his power by carrying out his threats in a manner that had painfully humiliated the weavers without rendering them economically useless.[17]

During a tour of the southern pollams (districts ruled by poligars) in the summer of 1798, Jackson and Kattobomma Nayakar engaged in a carefully orchestrated clash of wills as each sought to maintain or increase his status. After many months of fruitless correspondence between collector and poligar, the Madras Board of Revenue instructed Jackson to insist that Kattobomma come to Ramnad to pay his long overdue taxes. Hence, when Kattobomma approached Jackson's *dubash* (a personal secretary and interpreter) and asked for a meeting to settle the accounts before the collector returned to Ramnad, Jackson decided to stick to the letter of his instructions in order to publicly enforce the poligar's obedience to company policy. This competition for status dragged on through the exhausting heat of August into September, as the collector continually refused to meet the poligar, thus forcing the Indian ruler to follow him for twenty-three days over a distance of four hundred miles back to Ramnad.

Both players knew that the prize for victory was power and personal authority, but neither had any understanding of the intellectual and cultural beliefs that informed the other's strategy. The collector appeared to have gained the upper hand when Kattobomma and his followers finally arrived outside the city walls of Ramnad on September 19, but the duel continued the following day when Jackson received the now visibly nervous poligar at his cutcherry (a courthouse and an administrative office) within the splendid Ramalingavisam Palace at Fort Ramnad. Jackson remained seated as the poligar approached and laid a handkerchief containing a few gold pagodas (coins) in front of him. This was a *nuzzer*, the customary gift from an inferior to a superior that the company had attempted to ban, although it was still accepted by some collectors provided that the giver remained in the room (presumably to prove transparency). During the meeting Jackson chose not to offer Kattobomma a chair, so the poligar and his party were forced to stand before the collector for a full three hours. Then, in the manner of a schoolmaster pointing out to a wayward pupil the errors of his ways, Jackson proceeded to have all the letters he had written to the poligar over the preceding months read out in public.[18]

The contents of Jackson's letters could not have made comfortable listening for a proud leader, and even though Jackson consistently claimed he had wanted the poligar to hear them to ensure he understood their contents, his actions were later construed as, at best, tactless. In one letter Jackson complained that Kattobomma owed revenue to the company when it was well known that his income was four times higher than his tax assessment. The reason the poligar could not pay, Jackson insisted, was because

> instead of attending to the duties of your station . . . you have given yourself up to dissipation and debauchery. Instead of endeavouring to make your Pollam prosperous and the people under you happy you have delivered over the management of public affairs to men, who are incompetent to transact it . . . [while you] constantly indulged yourself in weak and vicious pursuits.[19]

Initially, Jackson had magnanimously agreed to "make large allowances for a young man like you, but vicious habits once acquired, are not easily shaken off." If Kattobomma were to "persist in such folly, after your eyes have been opened to the danger, [it] would betray a weakness so criminal, that it would not be possible to excuse." Kattobomma was at least thirty years old when he received this communication, and Jackson just four years older; although the tone of condescending fatherly advice adopted by the collector appears offensive to modern ears, it was not inconsistent with that used by other senior company officials. When Jackson wrote to the Madras Board of Revenue seeking permission to send a military force to punish the poligar "in the most exemplary manner" because he had "trifled with my authority and disobeyed my orders," the board replied in a similarly paternal tone, expressing the hope that "this last serious warning might save this young man from ruin." The responses of both collector and company were informed by the belief that profligate behavior in a young man was a sure path to self-destruction and criminal prosecution. Indeed, Jackson's response to his own son's rebellious behavior years later would be exactly the same.[20]

The effect on the poligar of this humiliating process was electrifying and, for both men, ultimately disastrous. Feigning illness, Kattobomma went to get some fresh air in the garden, but on seeing a detachment of armed guards near the palace and fearing arrest, the poligar and his party made a dash for the main gates of the fort. In the confusion that followed, a British adjutant, leading two guards of sepoys (Indian soldiers), attempted to block the escape. Hoping to prevent the situation from escalating into violence, the adjutant ordered his men to hold back and he stepped forward alone to confront Kattobomma. Without thinking, the adjutant stretched out his arms toward the poligar, whose pikemen, appalled to see a foreign soldier about to touch the royal person, moved to stop him. In the melee, observers saw only a brief glint of sun on steel as a dagger was raised and plunged into the adjutant's chest. Poligar and pikemen surged forward as the surprised officer stepped back, before suddenly staggering and falling to the ground dead. During the ensuing scuffle, two sepoys and several of the poligar's men were wounded or killed and his chief advisor was captured. The others ran through Ramnad, looting the town's bazaar and escaping with rich rewards. As the poligar emerged unscathed onto the plains around Ramnad, Jackson saw thousands of armed men appear, as if from nowhere, then melt once more into the distance with their leader. Convinced that the presence of such large numbers of soldiers meant that the whole escape had been preplanned, Jackson sent urgent requests to Madras for a battalion of sepoys, half a regiment of cavalry, and two "battering guns" to be sent to Ramnad. He planned to pursue and recapture the poligar, but the troops never arrived, and the poligar plundered every government village on his journey from Ramnad to his fort at Panjalamkurichi.[21]

Nine weeks later Mr. Jackson stood on the walls of the fort looking at a white, pagoda-shaped tent pitched some distance away on the scorched plain. Inside the tent sat a committee of inquiry headed by Lieutenant Colonel Brown and including two other eminent members of the East India Company. The committee had been appointed to investigate the incidents at Ramnad, which, it was feared, would spark a poligar war across the southern pollams. Jackson's head assistant, James Balfour, sat with the committee and took notes while it examined a series of European and native witnesses, all under oath. Humiliated and facing the destruction of his honorable career, the collector himself was excluded from the proceedings. The night before he had heard the local tom-tom drummer spread the news that the collector of Ramnad would have no power over the committee or over Kattobomma Nayakar, whose person was "to be considered sacred" by all. The poligar, dressed in his finest robes and, according to Jackson, still carrying "the very dagger he had employed in the assassination" of the adjutant, came before the committee attended by an armed guard and a large group of advisors and followers who continually chanted his titles and greatness. His legal representative, Captain Davison, was an old enemy of Jackson's to whom the latter had refused to grant a clandestine share of profits from a local fishery. Davison was also clearly in the poligar's pay: at the start of the proceedings, he felt it necessary to present the committee with five hundred pagodas, on account of the gift of a horse from the poligar, which he now understood had been improper for him to receive. The collector suspected other malign influences at work too—particularly from the Europeans he had expelled from Panjalamkurichi for making extortionate loans to the poligars—but he could prove nothing.

The hearings continued into late December, when the Ramnad committee ordered the arrest of Jackson's long-serving *dubash* on suspicion of taking bribes. Kattobomma claimed his manager had offered the *dubash* 2,000 pagodas for an interview with the collector during the journey through the southern pollams, but the *dubash* had been offended and demanded 5,000. Even more damaging, Kattobomma insisted that Jackson had demanded a *nuzzer* of 15,000 *chuckrums* (small coins) from the poligar of Shevigheny and that both collector and *dubash* had refused a counteroffer of 10,000 *chuckrums*. It was this kind of corrupt extortion that Kattobomma insisted would happen to him if he paid his own taxes.

Jackson demanded a right to reply to these accusations, but he was refused on the grounds that he was not on trial. He wrote despairingly to the governor of Madras, enclosing the proof that he was not allowed to present to the committee, but he knew his position was becoming untenable. In Jackson's eyes, the Ramnad committee's investigation into Kattobomma Nayakar's actions was a flagrant breach of all the principles of British justice—he cited evidence from Warren Hastings's trial and checked points of law in William Blackstone's definitive *Commentaries on the Laws of England* (1765–1769) to prove his assertions. He was therefore furious but not surprised that the committee acquitted the poligar of Panjalamkurichi of the charge of murdering the adjutant and declared that the officer had been killed by an unknown pikeman. The inquiry decided that the poligar had not unduly delayed his attendance at the collector's cutcherry and that by compelling Kattobomma "to follow him for twenty-three days [Jackson] was subjecting him to a mortifying degradation in the eyes of the inferior Poligars through whose pollams he was passing." The committee's report concluded that Kattobomma's escape from the city had not been premeditated, but rather had been precipitated by the humiliating treatment imposed on him by collector Jackson, who should have asked the poligar to produce the letters he had written as proof of receipt rather than having them publicly read out.[22]

Jackson was dismissed from his post, and two weeks later he set sail for England. In 1799 Kattobomma Nayakar organized a rebel alliance to fight against the British in what became known as the last poligar war. He was defeated and so ended his life at the end of a hangman's noose. To Jackson, this was predictable, for such was the inevitable fate of all profligate young men, and he had long ago warned the poligar that he would one day have to "take the consequences of your own fatal follies."[23]

DESPITE HIS DISASTROUS dismissal from the East India Company, Jackson returned to England in 1800 a rich man, with the ability to claim the status of gentleman on the same terms as John Evelyn, if not quite Sir George Shee. To many eyes, he must have appeared little different from any other nabob, but he remained a man wedded to prudent economy rather than ostentatious display, and even without the damage to his reputation, he never showed any desire (unlike other nabobs) to enter Parliament. He placed many thousands of pounds on deposit in the hallowed halls of Coutts & Co, bankers to the wealthiest and most elite families in England, and he counted Thomas Coutts a personal and particularly useful friend. Coutts & Co was one of a new breed of fashionable West End banks, which usually preferred to lend money to titled or landed clients than do business with newly enriched merchants. Jackson was wealthy enough to perform similar services to those his bank provided to many landed families, for whom indebtedness was an accepted and common feature of life. He loaned thousands of pounds to Lord Moira (Francis Rawdon-Hastings, who later became the second governor general of India) in the form of a mortgage. He also sent regular sums to his aging, ailing mother in Exeter.[24]

Like many newly wealthy men, however, Jackson was reluctant to engage in excessive generosity, and he resented the numerous applications for financial aid from family and friends. Despite his willingness to fund aristocratic debt (if only on a business footing), Jackson's personal attitude toward money remained resolutely bourgeois. He was influenced far more by moral considerations than by his actual ability to pay. Debts, extravagance, expenditure on excessive luxuries, immorality, imprudence, or overindulgence of the senses in any form, he regarded as a personal failing that rendered the applicant less deserving. Slights, both real and imagined, were also inevitably dealt with by a tightening of the purse strings. In addition to his horror of profligacy of any kind, Jackson was still haunted by the financial fate of his own father—threatened with imprisonment for being unable to pay a bond (a legally binding promise of payment) of £1,500, he had been rescued only by the generosity of his son-in-law, who then pursued Jackson for at least five years to repay the debt. Initially, Jackson was willing to help other members of his family both financially and socially, but he felt they showed little gratitude for his generosity, and by 1806 he would write furiously of how

> fifteen hundred pounds were bestowed upon kin of my sisters, and every shilling of this sum has been lost by <u>treachery</u> and by folly. One of my Brothers, who had the aid of my best services at a moment of extreme peril to himself; who was placed by my efforts in the road to affluence; and who experienced my liberality in other respects, no sooner found that he could do without me than he repaid all the obligation by the bleakest ingratitude. He has taught me to be suspicious, and if my heart be growing callous to the importunities of distress those who suffer by it must attribute it solely to him. It is now my fixed determination to guard with caution what remains of my property.[25]

Jackson's determination to guard his property may have been based on a fear of losing the wealth he had acquired at such a high cost to his reputation, but it also betrayed the extent to which his wealth was inextricably entwined with disappointed emotional expectations. On his return to England, most of his aspirations for his family's future and his own well-being were fixed firmly on the small person of his son, William. Like most Georgian parents, Jackson hoped to live again through his child, who was expected to embody all the best family traits, achievements, and moral values without the faults and failed dreams.[26]

WILLIAM COLLINS BURKE JACKSON was a rather slight lad to bear the weight of such portentous names, freighted as they were with so many paternal hopes for his future. He had a well-cut head of dark brown hair and hazel eyes and, from a very young age, had learned the value of adorning his slim frame with elegant clothing. Soon after his father's return from India, when William was eight years old, the family moved to the fashionable town of Bath, which teemed with shops eager to sell high-quality goods to the many genteel visitors and residents who thronged its neatly paved streets.

The Jacksons' house stood on a corner of Catherine Place, overlooking a garden in the center of the square. It was handsome but less elegant than the creamy-gold stone homes that lined the Royal Crescent and enclosed the equally impressive Circus nearby. Behind the slightly plain façade were four bedrooms, two drawing rooms, a music room, and a stylish hallway, as well as accommodation for servants. Mr. Jackson had furnished the house with conspicuously stylish taste combined with comfort. Venetian and "best Brussels" carpets covered the floors and stairs; rich curtains festooned the windows; "beautifully finished," often ornately carved, or inlaid mahogany furniture graced most of the rooms; and "superior feather bolsters," soft pillows, and thick mattresses ensured the family slept in great comfort. Such a home demonstrated financial security to the world, and its elegant interiors were the perfect surroundings to boost the family's claims of high social status. William grew up well aware of his elite status and in the knowledge that his father was a very wealthy man. That wealth, combined with his own cultivation of good manners, usually assured William a warm welcome from shopkeepers and tradesmen around Bath who made it their business to know which families were worth extending credit to.[27]

As a young boy, William seemed to have everything going for him. He had long basked in the adoration of his mother, Jane, and his elder stepsister, with no competition from the distant father he hardly knew. When Mr. Jackson returned, he was a broken man, and the East India Company put him on extended sick leave while the Court of Directors in England investigated events in Ramnad, yet there is no evidence to suggest that William was anything other than the apple of his distressed parent's eye. He was equally popular with his influential uncles, Sir George Shee and John Evelyn, who referred fondly to his nephew as "my friend William." But he was prone to bouts of ill health that inevitably alarmed both parents, for whom he remained a precious only heir.[28]

That status became even more significant when his stepsister tragically died in the summer of 1803; her brief existence was so totally extinguished that no trace of her name remains in the family's records. The Jacksons had already witnessed the appalling grief of Anne and John Evelyn when their eldest son, John, had died in Bath at the tender age of five in 1793. The daughter's death, although "inevitable" caused Mrs. Jackson to grieve deeply but silently—a grief made more lasting, as her sister-in-law observed, because "she vents it not in words." Yet the family was certain that "dearest William . . . will afford comfort to his poor distressed mother" and that this "sweet boy" would "prove a blessing" to both parents. This family tragedy and the fear of losing his own son put Mr. Jackson in an intolerable position with regard to his career in the East India Company.[29]

In 1803 the Court of Directors finally acquitted Jackson of all the charges brought against him during the trial of Kattobomma Nayakar and announced that he could be permitted to return to Madras "without prejudice to his rank." The considerable time it had taken the directors to reach this conclusion was, they admitted, due to "the extreme length of the discussions" about Jackson's conduct, a debate "argued and re-argued with so much sophistry, acrimony and acuteness" that it was only with great difficulty that they could agree on a decision. It was also due to the difficulty of extricating what could be considered culpable behavior from the more morally ambiguous standards of practice prevalent in India at the time. The directors concluded that, although Jackson had "no corrupt motives," he was guilty of writing an "improper letter" in an insubordinate tone to his immediate superior at the Board of Revenue, an action that would have damaged all future correspondence with that body and made it impossible for him to continue in the post of collector. The most serious accusation, that Jackson had accepted a huge *nuzzer* of thousands of pagodas from the poligar of Shevigheny, was laid at the door of his unfortunate *dubash,* who had been kept in prison until he agreed to confess. It was noted that Jackson had very creditably refused several offers of large sums of money regarding preferential commercial agreements and that he had "put an end to the pernicious practice amongst the Poligars of borrowing money at an exorbitant interest." Less positively, the directors decided that Jackson had contravened company regulations in having cloth made up for sale in a different district and in using another person to conduct commercial transactions to avoid the company ban on collectors exercising any trade in their own districts. However, as this was not an uncommon practice among company officials and one that the directors admitted was "not absolutely prohibited," they were not prepared to condemn it officially. Jackson always professed delight at this verdict and chose to see only that it cleared him of all wrongdoing, but the directors' reservations about his actions left him vulnerable to criticism for many years to come.[30]

The opportunity to return to India with his rank and reputation restored was almost certainly the best outcome for Jackson. But when Jane's daughter died, he declared that to leave for India after such a terrible family disaster would be "an utter violation of every domestic feeling." He resolved to stay close to his remaining family, whatever the cost to his career. That cost was high indeed for a man whose whole identity rested on a deeply felt sense of honor and integrity, which his dismissal from the company's service had unjustly undermined and impugned. The following winter Jackson still felt unable to tear himself away despite a warning from the company that he must sail for India before February 18, 1805, or forfeit his reinstatement. He would not be moved, and in staying with his family, he chose to forfeit not only his Indian career with the company, but also the best chance of clearing his name.[31]

He turned instead to rebuilding his reputation: through the civil courts, through an account of his case that he published privately in England, and through his efforts to set his son on the road to greatness. Jackson's later actions show that his long-term aim was to rehabilitate his reputation to such an extent that he could stand as a candidate for the company's Court of Directors in England—a position that carried both prestige and hugely influential patronage, which could provide lucrative employment for his family and friends. Young William thus became the main focus of his father's thwarted ambitions, and the question of educating his son for a prominent role in respectable society suddenly took on a new importance. So, too, did the impact of William's future behavior on his father's prospects.[32]

AN IMPROPER EDUCATION

Home, School, and Sponging House, 1805–1807

> *That some boys are continually, and that all boys are*
> *occasionally, prone to mischief and vice, is a truth of*
> *which every schoolmaster daily receives irresistible and*
> *painful conviction.*
>
> —William Barrow, *An Essay on Education* (1802)

"What shall I do with my son?" was a question that exercised the minds of many wealthy Georgian fathers, whose duty it was to see that their heirs became honorable, independent gentlemen; prosperous pillars of the social order; and virtuous patriarchs. It was a question that had continued to court controversy ever since the philosopher John Locke first posed it in his hugely influential *Some Thoughts Concerning Education* in 1693. It was a question that was beginning to weigh heavily on the mind of Mr. Jackson in the winter of 1805. Then, as now, writers on education, like the cleric William Barrow in his *Essay on Education* of 1802, recognized that

to determine upon what system the rising generation may be instructed with the greatest convenience and effect; by what measures

in early youth his offspring may be most successfully trained to learning and virtue, is a point of the utmost importance to a parent and
hardly less difficult than important.[1]

There was certainly no lack of advice on the subject: numerous authors engaged, with "much zeal and acrimony," in a battle to establish
whether a private education at home with a tutor or a public education
at one of the great schools was the best way to properly educate a
young gentleman. In 1802 Barrow suggested that the key factors in
making such a choice were rank, health, ability, and future prospects.
Should a boy be destined for public life—in the law, Parliament, medicine, or the army—then a public school, one of the endowed grammar
schools or one of the ever-increasing number of large private academies (provided the discipline equaled that of the public schools), was
the wisest choice. Only boys displaying a significant weakness of body
or mind, or those destined for a retired life in the country, should be
privately educated. Boys intended for commercial trades should seek
out one of the newer academies where the curriculum focused on the
more useful subjects, such as mathematics, rather than classical Greek
and Latin, knowledge of which had become the essential emblem of
an educated gentleman.[2]

Whatever educational route he chose for his heir, Mr. Jackson was
certain that it should provide William with a solid grounding in the
classics. The object of all this paternal concern, however, while equally
desirous of becoming a young gentleman, was considerably less convinced of the value of learning Latin and Greek. William had enjoyed
the relative freedom of being tutored at home until he was thirteen years
old, partly because he tended to suffer from chest infections. There his
anxious parents could keep a close eye on his health and his morals. Mr.
Jackson almost certainly believed he had the best chance of inculcating
William with his own personal ethical and social values at home and
also of preserving his son's innocence. Yet home-schooled boys were
thought to be in danger of developing an unattractive precocity of manner and, without the competitive rivalry provided by other pupils, of failing to acquire a desire to learn. Moreover, to succeed in the world,
William would need good connections with other boys of similar and
higher rank who were increasingly sent to the great public schools.

The dangers of sending boys to public school, however, were legion. Parents feared that their sons would be exposed to all kinds of riotous and depraved behavior, that they would emulate the most morally corrupted boys, and that they would discover cunning new ways to indulge their passions. Of growing concern to many parents was the widespread use by such schools of brutal corporal discipline to "encourage" boys to learn as well as to punish bad behavior. As Sir George Shee discovered, keeping up with high-status friends could also be a very expensive business that most sons expected their fathers to fund. Young George wrote to his father from Cambridge University in 1803 asking for more money but explaining that the extra cost was

> abundantly compensated by the opportunities I have of forming valuable acquaintances . . . & some of them are now in progression from Acquaintance to Intimacy and from there to Friendship. My acquaintance is not very extensive I admit, but then my Intimacies are comparatively numerous, & of these a great majority are remarkable either for <u>Rank</u> or <u>Abilities</u>.[3]

A third option was an endowed grammar school, but many of these had lost much of their appeal because of their exclusive focus on the classics, strict discipline, and the increasingly broad social mix of students they accepted, which discouraged the elites and aspiring merchant classes from sending their own sons there. Yet some endowed schools—such as Harrow, which now rivaled Eton in size and reputation—had clearly joined the ranks of the great public schools, boasting aristocratic patrons and pupils and strong connections with the Whig Party, which was supported by the Jacksons, the Evelyns, and the Shees. In Georgian Britain, to be a Whig meant not only to follow a particular political party but also, more broadly, to belong to the most powerful, elite social group in the country. Both John Evelyn and Sir George Shee had sent their sons to Harrow, which boasted an impressive list of actual and prospective dukes, earls, viscounts, lords, and baronets.[4]

In 1805, with his own personal reputation still disputed and the need to advance his teenage son more pressing, Mr. Jackson decided that Harrow would provide the best path for William. His cousin

George Evelyn was then at the school, and there William could continue his education as a gentleman, forge useful social connections, and begin the journey toward university to study law. Mr. Jackson's chief reason for training William as a lawyer was to provide his son with a liberal, polite education conducted "more with the view to direct your mind to laudable pursuits, than that you should depend upon the profession of the law for your maintenance and support." Jackson wanted William to become "an ornament to society" rather than the model of prudent industry and commercial success that he considered himself to be. He hoped that training for such a profession would confer a "commitment to . . . usefulness and rationality" that was lacking in the leisured lifestyle of many young gentlemen. It was also considered useful preparation for a career in Parliament, which was precisely the route followed by young George Shee after his time at Harrow, in preparation for becoming a member of Parliament (MP) like his father. For William, like George Shee, his education was also meant to leave him culturally and socially equipped to move in the best circles.[5]

Harrow, despite its dramatic rise in popularity, its reputation for producing great orators, and the talented leadership of a headmaster who taught five of the seven Harrovian prime ministers, did not prove to be the ideal institution to educate William. The school day, although harshly disciplined and strictly regimented, was only five hours long, and just three on Thursday and Saturday. This allowed the boys plenty of opportunities to indulge in a wide variety of sports: cricket, tennis, football, racquets, boxing, swimming, fencing, and skating in the winter. Such activities were considered an essential bulwark against moral depravity because, as Vicesimus Knox, headmaster of Tonbridge School, had advised parents in 1781, "the propensities to vicious pleasures are often at that age impetuous; Nothing tends more to DIVERT THEIR COURSE, and lessen their influence than a keen love of innocent sports, and an ardent pursuit of them continued even to fatigue." Less edifying but equally popular activities included throwing stones and just roaming the countryside.[6]

More problematic were the bullying, fighting, flogging, fagging (a system that allowed older boys to order younger ones to perform menial tasks for them), and casual cruelty between older and younger boys that were rife throughout the school. Swearing, drinking, and seducing servants were commonplace, and relations with local villagers were strained to the breaking point by the thefts, assaults, and widespread poaching routinely practiced by schoolboys of all ages. The privilege of wealth and class conveyed an equivocal sense of morality that William and his schoolmates adopted with ease and alacrity.

It was not Mr. Jackson's fears of contagious moral degeneracy that caused him to remove William from the school in December 1805, however, but rather fears for his health. Fortunately for the Jacksons, William was boarding at the house of the school doctor, so he received good care, but his illness clearly alarmed his parents.[7]

Nevertheless, William's brief stay at Harrow had taught him a good deal about young gentlemen's attitudes toward their peers, the lower orders, and schoolmasters. The latter were tolerated, even respected according to social rank, individual ability, and respect for pupils' privileges and rights; but failure in any of these areas commonly legitimated revenge, riot, and rebellion among public school boys. Between 1770 and 1820, there were twenty-three rebellions at great public schools. William had arrived at Harrow soon after the poet Lord Byron had led a minor revolt against the appointment of a new headmaster, but in schoolboy legend the poet had tried to blow up the schoolhouse. More significantly, rebellions were seen as a broadly acceptable response to actions that schoolboys believed oppressive. Indeed, resistance to tyrannical power in any form was considered a laudable national trait in Georgian Britain. William took from Harrow the seeds of a sense of legitimate grievances and of resistance to whatever he viewed as unjust authority, both of which would spring forth frequently throughout his life.[8]

It was probably Harrow, too, that first ignited his desire to embark on a military, rather than a legal, career. The revolutionary and Napoleonic Wars with France had not only increased Harrow's reputation for producing strong politicians and military leaders; these wars had also inspired many pupils to opt for military glory rather than for more prosaic studies at university, providing a fertile environment for discussions of heroism, which filtered down through the school. Military manliness, not the ornamental civic leadership of his father's generation, was at a premium among William's public school peers.[9]

Their ardor was further fueled by the huge popularity of military volunteering during the French wars, when nearly half of all able-bodied men in the southern counties enrolled for armed service. The English victory at the Battle of Trafalgar in October 1805, and the apotheosis of the heroic Lord Nelson after his death, inspired dreams of military glory in many public school boys. Their masters imbued them with "patrician patriotism" and instructed them in ancient classical stories of self-sacrifice, bravery, war, and empire. The schools also promoted celebrations of British naval and military victories. Harrow was the training ground for the generation that would fight at Waterloo, which was where George Evelyn would eventually serve, with great distinction but near fatal consequences—he was badly injured in the defense of the Château d'Hougoumont, leaving him with a permanently useless arm.[10]

Mr. Jackson, ignoring or ignorant of warnings from writers like Barrow about the dangers of sending a boy who had previously attended public school to a private academy, began to look around for one of the higher-ranking schools of this kind that ran along classical lines. Administered by Anglican clergymen or nongraduate laymen, these progressive academies often boasted an elite clientele but also offered a much broader curriculum and more comfortable accommodation than the public and grammar schools, thus providing a more useful, modern, and increasingly popular form of education. Because the family was looking to live in a property in London, Mr. Jackson wanted a school close enough to the capital that he could visit William, but far enough from the metropolis to ensure that his son was not tempted by the bright lights and vices of the city. Loughborough House School, situated south of the River Thames, half a mile from the Kennington Turnpike, seemed the ideal choice. The proprietors, Thomas Willett and the Reverend William Edwards, promised:

> Young Noblemen and Gentlemen are educated and completely qualified in every branch of useful and ornamental learning requisite to form The Gentleman, Scholar, or Man of Business. . . . The greatest care is taken of Young Gentlemen's Health and Morals. They lie in large, neat, airy Rooms and separate beds.[11]

An added attraction for the financially prudent Jackson was that the school cost less than half as much as Harrow at 55 guineas a year. For William, the best thing about Loughborough was that it introduced him to Thomas Potter Macqueen, the son of a wealthy doctor and close neighbor of the Duke of Bedford. The pair quickly became friends and disliked being apart during the holidays. Yet again the school did not prove a success in William's case.

William left Loughborough in the summer of 1807, just eighteen months after starting at the school. There is no clear record of why, but Barrow described how the masters of such an academy often found an ex–public school boy "the most turbulent and refractory of pupils; he comes prepared to despise alike the persons, the instructions and the authority of his teachers." It seems, too, that William came to fiercely dislike a number of his fellow pupils and was guilty of writing at least one "unfeeling and illiberal letter" to a boy who had been deserted by his parents and friends and left solely in the care of Mr. Willett, the schoolmaster. Willett appeared to be entirely ignorant of whether William taunted the boy because of his reduced position in society or for his friendship with one of William and Macqueen's bitter enemies, John Richardson. Whatever the cause of William's sudden departure, he had no desire to return to the school, which he was certain "would be a source of infinite mortification," so his disappointed father began to search for some other educational route into the law.[12]

ON LEAVING LOUGHBOROUGH, William returned to his parents' new house at 30 Gloucester Place in London before spending the summer holidays in Brighton with them. A more elegant and impressive building than their previous home in Bath, this London residence was a large, pale-stone, terraced house with a suitably imposing front door opening on to the street that ran between Marylebone and Portman Square, at what was then the extreme western edge of London. Close to the capital's smartest shops, it was also an address that, William soon discovered, was sufficient to send tradesmen scuttling to the door with goods on credit, eager to do business with such a wealthy, well-connected family. His equally wealthy and even more influential uncles both had houses nearby. John Evelyn lived just down the road at number 80 with his wife, Jane Jackson's sister, Anne. Sir George Shee's London residence was a short walk away in Manchester Square—not that Jane felt it appropriate to visit her brother's family in anything other than her liveried coach. Indeed, the social niceties involved in visiting meant that she was "not overfond of Going to Sir George's in a Hackney Coach" either. William had exchanged the elegant streets and superior shops of Bath for the equally genteel and even more socially exclusive environs of London's West End.[13]

The prospect of a seaside holiday with his parents, even in fashionable Brighton, was less appealing than it might have been after he received several fervent requests from Macqueen for William to visit him:

> I hope I am not to suppose from your letter, that I am to be denied the pleasure of seeing you through the whole of the holydays [sic]. . . . My health has been very bad since my arrival, but home has agreed better with me than old Loughboro, & I only want your company to complete my recovery. . . . We are in great bustle amidst carpenters &c so that I can only offer you, a well aired bed & a bottle of good wine, [but] I know your good nature will not mind to put up with being treated in the plain family way.[14]

Thomas Macqueen's family was delighted with his friendship with William Jackson and hoped it would lead to greater sociability between the two families—invitations to shoot grouse and stay at their country home in the autumn were issued to Mr. and Mrs. Jackson, too. Sadly, William informed his friend that his father wished him to explain that he would not be able to avail himself of the autumn invitation either. "We may not, during our school days be again together," he regretfully reported to Macqueen, "but I trust a friendship has been established between us, that will outlive our juvenile years."[15]

Mr. Jackson had no intention of letting William visit his friend and probable partner in crime at Loughborough that summer or in the autumn, by which time he hoped to have placed William in an education suitable to prepare him for entrance to university. He feared for William's health and morals in almost equal measure and worried that he was falling behind in his studies. William had had a near-fatal riding accident at Blackheath in London earlier that year—badly in-juring himself and his horse—the seriousness of which Jackson had contrived to hide from his wife, so he had banned his son from riding again until he could take more lessons after Christmas. Keeping William away from horses and his hard-riding peers was an extremely unpopular decision, but the goings-on at Harrow and Loughborough had also made Jackson think that the need for good connections was less important than the avoidance of bad influence.

Mr. Jackson decided to advertise (anonymously, through a local bookseller) in the *Morning Herald* for a more private educational es-tablishment for his son. The advertisement was promptly, even eagerly, answered the following day by the Reverend William Helps of Wad-ham College Oxford and former rector of Hawton, who had opened a school at Hadley, a village just north of London. "I have myself been much in the habit of qualifying young people to become members of the university both of Oxford and Cambridge," he assured Mr. Jack-son, enclosing a "Plan of Education" proving that his establishment was most appropriate for preparing young men for "both these venera-ble seats of learning." The Plan of Education was addressed to "those parents who take more than an ordinary interest in the welfare and im-provement of a Child." It described to perfection the transferrable skills and moral advantages that Jackson firmly believed a study of the classics would convey to a young gentleman:

> The REFINED MORALITY displayed throughout their writings, will be proposed as the guide of future conduct—The noble examples which they exhibit of the PUBLIC VIRTUES, will be proposed to the emulation of the Youth, destined to move in the active spheres of Life—Whilst the purity, the correctness, and the elegance of their language, will be studied as the most perfect model of Stile, whether applied to COMPOSITION, to DISCOURSE, or to the several de-partments of ORATORY—namely to the SENATE—the BAR—or the PULPIT.[16]

Students would also study English grammar, arithmetic, geography, philosophy, and the arts of public speaking, which would be carefully balanced with suitable "Manly and Athletic exercises" to contribute to perfect mental and physical health. Hadley was ideally situated—on a hill "noted for its pure air and dry soil" as an aid to health—and at a convenient distance of eleven miles from the Metropolis, yet the school benefited from "the tranquillity of a Country Village [which] has always been deemed favourable to the Literary Progress of the Student, as its retirement is obviously conducive to the preservation of . . . morals." Also, Helps reassured the anxious father, "the young gentleman will be assigned a separate Bed" and "experience exactly the same sort of treatment and attention as my own boys."[17]

Mr. Jackson could not have been more delighted. "Your plan of education is so truly eligible . . . that I cannot hesitate a moment in making my choice, I shall indeed, feel peculiar pleasure in placing my son under your care," he assured Helps, and immediately set about making preparations for William to join him at the beginning of August. Any minor qualms he might have felt about why Helps did not pay the postage on his letters were quickly erased by the character references provided by respectable titled gentlemen and the fact that the school had been the home of, and previously run by, the late Reverend David Garrow, father of leading criminal and civil lawyer William Garrow. This eminent alumnus had even paid for the refurbishment of the very buildings in which William would now be taught.[18]

Mr. Jackson had a great deal of respect for Garrow, whose own education at his father's school in Hadley Priory had launched him on a legal career that earned him a reputation as a great advocate at the Old Bailey. Garrow had also led the way in establishing defendants' rights to full legal counsel in criminal trials in the 1780s and the right to be presumed innocent until proven guilty. Mr. Jackson, whose much-persecuted mind was always preoccupied with proving his own innocence and seeking justice from the East India Company, had sought Garrow's professional opinion in 1805. That great defender of the unjustly accused had replied, regretfully, that it was unlikely Jackson would win in a civil or criminal case against the company, but that he should pursue his case by writing a memorial (an account or justification of events) to the Court of Directors. The problem was not that he doubted Jackson had been most unfairly dealt with, but, as the perceptive lawyer noted, that although "Mr. Jackson writes with facility and great force, his pen is directed by a mind full of a sense of undeserved injury." Garrow advised Jackson to adopt a more measured approach using "language more suited to the occasion"—advice his client duly followed. Hence, Reverend Helps's school seemed the ideal choice at which to relaunch William's educational training for the law.[19]

Small private schools of the type established by Helps at Hadley promoted classical studies as an essential foundation of a modern education, aiming to impart the values of ancient civilization without the mechanical methods and harsh discipline practiced in grammar schools. Usually run as small private boarding schools by clergymen in their own homes, often primarily to educate their own children and to supplement their meager incomes, such institutions abounded, but their survival and success varied widely. These schools were popular with many parents who believed that "classical learning tends most directly to form the true gentleman" with a "liberal and embellished mind," rather than with the "fashionable dress" and "few decencies of behaviour" currently so highly valued by those Barrow dismissed as "men of the world."[20]

Yet some educationalists feared that the masters of these schools rarely gave their pupils more time than did those of much larger establishments, and if they did, it was seldom beneficial. Too often the boys were treated with "the freedoms and familiarities of equals and friends," and the very indulgences that attracted parents turned their sons into "men of pleasure, not of learning." Mr. Jackson was anxious to let Helps know that William must understand the "beauties and complexities" of the classics, but, with a view to a career at the bar, he also required skills in mathematics, logic, reasoning, and oratory. Yet, most importantly, William "should not be required so closely to attend to his studies as to endanger his health," and he should be allowed to correspond freely with his friends and family. What Mr. Jackson failed to foresee was that, apart from the Reverend Helps's own sons, William would be the sole pupil at Hadley. The handsome gothic rectory with its high arched windows and pointed doorways, set in nine acres of secluded parkland, provided little stimulation or excitement for a teenage boy whose interest in Latin was at best tenuous. Writing, particularly to Macqueen, was William's only contact with the social world his friends and peers continued to enjoy, providing a vicarious pleasure in the gossip, rivalries, dinners, parties, theater, and hunting trips he was missing. Writing to his father was a more arduous task: every letter was checked for correctness of grammar, spelling, and allusions to the classics or current affairs, as well as for evidence of assiduous study.[21]

For the first week at school all seemed to be going well—William's letter home gave his mother "every reason to hope that we shall have happiness of seeing you in the course of two years—<u>all</u> our hearts can wish of you," and it pleased his father greatly. Unknown to his parents, however, to make up for the lack of companions and organized sport, William invented new diversions to keep himself occupied in the hours he was not studying. He purchased a fishing rod and a cricket bat, ball, and stumps; but he also bought a donkey to ride. Then he hired a horse so that he could explore the surrounding area, despite his father's strict prohibition on riding. Whatever the practical reasons behind the issuing of this injunction, it was a harsh one for wealthy youth to observe. Skill at riding and hunting was highly prized by young gentlemen, and most fathers regarded these as essential manly pursuits.[22]

Reverend Helps was mildly concerned that these diversions might distract from his new pupil's studies, but, mindful that Jackson had insisted the lad not be worked too hard, he did not interfere in William's pleasures. After two weeks, in response to frequent requests from William for their company, the Jacksons prepared to visit their son. Dinner for four people at three o'clock in the Green Man at Barnet was arranged. Mr. Jackson declared that William must not order any poultry and that they would bring their own fish (so the landlord could charge only to dress it), but he allowed that as William was not fond of mutton, he could order a "small piece of good roast Beef . . . with vegetables and tarts." All four prospective diners were looking forward to a convivial summer afternoon meal to celebrate William's brightening prospects.[23]

But in his haste to arrange all to perfection before his parents' arrival, William had scrawled a hurried letter home. "It is better not to write at all, than to do it in a slovenly way," thundered Mr. Jackson, and "it is no excuse for a person to say that he is hurried . . . unless it be the fact, which it cannot be in your case." For his own good, Mr. Jackson explained, William should suffer "the mortification of this admonition," not least because there were frequent misspellings of compound words, which were entirely due to inattention. There followed a lecture on English grammar and spelling, with strict instructions "not to destroy this letter" but to keep it for future reference. William was clearly mortified and not in the mood to behave with proper filial duty at dinner the following day when his father discovered his equine activities. A loud scene ensued, embarrassing to all but excruciating for the fifteen-year-old, who dealt with the humiliation of being publicly disciplined by resorting to outright defiance.[24]

Perhaps Mr. Jackson should have heeded John Locke's warning to parents that "rebukes and chiding" should be conducted in private. For "when being expos'd to shame by publishing their miscarriages," young men quickly felt their reputations ruined so that check on their behavior was lost "and they [would] be the less careful to preserve others' good thoughts of them" in future. Mr. Jackson felt that, although he had expressed himself "with a warmth beyond what I really feel," it had been necessary to make a strong impression on William that he had acted wrongly and broken a promise to his father. Also, "something very like vanity in his language and demeanour compelled me to take the Gentleman from his stilts and to give him a lesson."[25]

It was a lesson that Helps felt bound to explain to William the following day when they discussed "the duty of submission to a father's opinion, even should that opinion prove to be erroneous." Mr. Jackson, like all fathers, conceived of his paternal authority as absolute, but tempered with true affection and friendship for his son. Expressions of love between Georgian parents and their children were understood by all to involve the enactment of reciprocal duties, which meant that filial affection was best demonstrated by unswerving obedience in return for protection, education, and financial maintenance. William's disobedience was therefore a sign of ingratitude and a denial of love as well as authority. Reverend Helps reassured Jackson that William's outward defiance was only a temporary show, brought on by the "embarrassment into which he was thrown." Indeed, William was at that moment writing a letter that would prove "that he retains all the sentiments of filial submission and deference, which a dutiful son ought to feel towards a kind, liberal, and intelligent father." Mr. Jackson approved of the clergyman's actions and deputed him to act *in loco parentis* in all matters regarding William's behavior, but insisted that he also wanted to receive copies of all his son's essays to ensure that he was making suitable progress.[26]

In his neatest handwriting William penned a carefully constructed apology to his father, a candid avowal of how wrongly he had acted and a promise never to pen another slovenly letter. He remained defensive of his actions, however, claiming that

> with respect to buying the Donkey, as Mr. Helps never said it was contrary to his wishes, I did not think I was doing wrong, but as you have signified your disapprobation of it I am very sorry I ever bought it, as well as for any thing else that offended you in my behaviour on Wednesday. I therefore take this opportunity of begging your pardon sincerely for what I have done. I shall be at all times happy to yield to your opinion in every thing that concerns me because I know it must be for my good and benefit.[27]

These suitably submissive sentiments persuaded his father to "consign the matter to oblivion" and declare himself once more to be William's "affectionate Father and Friend," with the hope that there would never again be any "possibility of difference between us." If William was reassured by his return to paternal favor, he was almost certainly filled with envy at Macqueen's next letter, in which he described how at harvest time he would "take one of the whips belonging to the waggoners & mounting one of the carts or horses, set off at full speed, you would laugh sometimes to see me licking the horses, & making them go as hard as they can pelt at the risk of my own neck."[28]

The thrill and dangers of riding at high speed were as sought after by William and his friends as fast cars are by youths today. Both boys also looked forward to the prospect of attending balls and private theatricals organized by the Duke of Bedford around Christmas. But as William struggled to concentrate on his lessons and wrote letters to pass the time, Macqueen penned his effusive but rushed missives only when he could spare a moment between social engagements.

There was one epistolary entertainment, however, that equally obsessed Macqueen and William—an ongoing battle with their old

Loughborough House rivals, John Richardson and his brother, Ben. Letters were sent using nicknames, so Hen, Smyrna, Mr. Touching, and Timothy Twigg exchanged accusations of bullying and threats of beatings in the street. When the rivalry reached more warlike proportions, another "capital fellow" thought it a "good lark" to send cats and other dead animals to the Richardson brothers. Mutual friends who remained at Loughborough kept Macqueen informed of the latest developments, but the battle between ex-schoolfellows took on a more serious cast when John Richardson sent copies of anonymous letters he alleged had been written by William to Mr. Jackson. One read:

Sir,

it is my firm opinion that as such West India bullies as I am informed from the best authority that you and your Brother are should be kicked out of this free kingdom and that as you walked along the streets you will be hooted at for Bullies and have tied on your back "Behold the Bullies."

With free compts to Mr. Jackson and the Miss Motts
I remain your country cousin

Timothy Twigg[29]

Underlying the boys' personal enmity was a clash between Whig and East India Company families, who had supported the Abolition of Slavery Bill in March 1807, and the sons of West Indian plantation owners, whose slave-based wealth had enabled them to attend elite schools in England. Mr. Jackson, however, was less concerned by the sentiments in the letter than the manner in which they had been conveyed. He immediately berated William for behaving like a "Blackguard" in sending such base threats anonymously, in a fashion that would undoubtedly ruin the character of a gentleman forever. How can "you answer to your parents & the world for so wide a departure from every honourable, manly and upright principle?" demanded the furious father. Such a flagrant breach of libel laws would surely result in transportation to Botany Bay (a penal colony in Australia) for seven or fourteen years, he warned.[30]

There was little doubt in Jackson's mind that William was indeed the author because the postmark was Barnet, a village very close to Hadley. Both William and Macqueen were outraged and convinced they had been set up by the Richardsons. Commanded by his father, William wrote a letter of apology to the Richardsons as instructed, but the one he drafted first, calling Richardson "a viper who never opens his mouth but to cast out poison" and utter "infamous falsehoods," is a more accurate representation of his feelings on the matter. Macqueen was more sanguine: "I am inclined to laugh rather than give way to anger & as we know we are perfectly innocent, let us despise them than adopt any other means," he advised William. Reverend Helps was strongly convinced of William's innocence in the matter and tried to persuade Mr. Jackson of that fact. He also continued to write regularly, praising William's academic "talents," his superior understanding, and his remarkably quick memory, even describing his pupil as being "extremely tractable and obedient."[31]

Despite this second upset in their relationship, and perhaps because of Reverend Helps's glowing reports, William and his parents resumed warmly affectionate relations. William impressed his father with a measured assessment of the morality of the British bombardment of Copenhagen in September 1807. The British feared Napoleon was about to force neutral countries like Denmark and Sweden to join the war against them and that the Danish navy would soon fall into French hands. Without even a formal declaration of war, the British navy bombed Copenhagen for days, destroying swathes of the city and killing thousands of citizens. The Danish fleet was impounded, but the victory divided opinion in parliamentary circles. "Had Bonaparte adopted precisely the same measures we have put in execution," William argued, "what appellation would the British Government have bestowed upon such an expedition" but to condemn it as an act of "plunder, treachery, and aggression which Bonaparte has uniformly pursued since his advancement to power." But, he concluded more cautiously, in an effort to satisfy his father's "superior judgement," the attack on Copenhagen was "justifiable only from the extreme necessity of the case [because] . . . Bonaparte is now making such rapid strides towards the universal dominance of the whole Civilized World."[32]

By contrast, nothing more serious than the sudden coldness of the November weather and the relative merits of donning woolen or flannel clothing occupied his correspondence with his mother. Jane Jackson fussed anxiously about sending extra waistcoats and begged William to wear worsted stockings because "many young people fall sacrifice to the folly of going lightly dressed in the winter, in this vile climate," while simultaneously teasing her husband for wearing "his flannel night cap." Still haunted by the death of her daughter, Jane also suffered from recurring dreams or premonitions that some unknown harm might befall her son.[33]

UNKNOWN TO EITHER PARENT, William's health and morals were in considerably more danger than could be remedied by the wearing of warm clothing. Mr. Helps's venture into education for young gentlemen was not proving as successful as his illustrious predecessor's at the priory. His financial situation was becoming increasingly dismal, letters from creditors were more frequent, and local suppliers were less willing to deliver. Alert to the ever-present threat of arrest for debt, Helps was listening to William translate his Latin copy of Virgil one evening in November when he heard a commotion at the garden gate. Sensing danger, he fled from the room to hide upstairs, leaving his somewhat bemused pupil to his own devices. Mrs. Helps rushed to the door but was pushed aside by two bailiffs demanding to see the husband she promptly claimed was not there. Helps was unlucky; the bailiffs—experienced men who knew their quarry to be a "sly cock"—had already crept up to a window and spied the teacher with William in the parlor before making their entry. In his haste to hide, Helps had also left his hat and slippers in plain view from the door, so the men insisted they would stay until the reluctant rector appeared. William was dispatched upstairs to fetch Helps, but it took some pleading to persuade the agitated schoolmaster to descend. On his appearance, Helps was presented with an arrest warrant and told he must immediately proceed to London. William was sent out to procure a chaise for the journey, but no sooner had he returned with the carriage and entered the kitchen to air his damp clothes when, with tears in his eyes, Reverend Helps pleaded with his pupil for help.

Perhaps William had been too anxious to assert his social status in the locality, or perhaps he genuinely wanted to help a man who had praised his academic efforts and taken his side against his father's wrath, but in either case he had assured Helps that Jackson had £40,000 in Coutts Bank, implying that his father would lend Helps money. Helps begged William to go with him to London and deliver a letter directly to his father, or to borrow money from the landlord of the Green Man Inn on the strength of his father's name. In retelling the tale to Jackson, William related a reluctance to agree for fear of offending his parents; the master described his pupil's distinct enthusiasm for the whole adventure.

In any event, neither plan came to fruition. In the gathering gloom, the coach rumbled on across London until, nearing the River Thames, it deposited both William and Helps at 5 Palsgrave Place, a nondescript building situated between the Strand and Temple Bar. Helps was rather less surprised than William to discover that they were in a sponging house, so named because it was designed to squeeze every last penny from debtors, forcing them to settle their debts before prison became inevitable. While the prospect of being kept behind barred windows in a private house at his own expense was hardly appealing, Helps did then have a few days to raise bail, or enough money to pay the debt, before being committed to prison.

Most inmates were too poor to afford postage, so runners were used to deliver desperate begging letters to friends and relatives. Usually, impoverished youngsters hung around the streets outside hoping for just such an opportunity, but Reverend Helps had William, whose obvious gentility was a distinct advantage. Having cordially introduced William to the sponging house keeper, Helps dispatched the boy across the now dark streets of London to Bow Lane near Garlick Hill, where his attorney lived. The attorney was not at home, but impatient for rescue before news of his arrest seeped out and damaged his reputation, Helps sent his unwilling pupil out twice more along the Strand, into Fleet Street, past St. Paul's, and up to Cheapside and then down Bow Lane. In doing so, William was almost exactly tracing the major "sexual highway" that crossed London from St. James's and Charring Cross, via the Strand, Fleet Street, St. Paul's, Cheapside, and Poultry, to the Royal Exchange. It was a busy thoroughfare that conveniently conveyed the business of trade alongside the business of sex, linking the leisured west and commercial east of the city. At night it was a route that would alarm any respectable parent.[34]

While lamplighters had been busy illuminating London's main thoroughfares with smoky pools of brightness, and the glow from the numerous well-lit shop windows marked the way along the Strand and Fleet Street, the surrounding lanes and alleys remained murky places lit only by the dim flickering of candles inside the poorer residences. Most respectable Georgians feared for their safety (from evil spirits, as well as thieves, vagrants, and prostitutes) in the elemental darkness that enveloped the capital at night. The Strand and Fleet Street were notoriously crowded with prostitutes looking for clients—although those in the Fleet were less luridly filthy and reputed to be more honest than their more desperate sisters in the Strand—using the dark courts and alleys for sex or theft and sometimes both.

Just two weeks later newspapers reported how "an abandoned woman" dragged another fifteen-year-old youth through a passage into a dark room, where she and another woman hit him and stripped him of his clothing and money. On the third attempt, and after two hours of tramping across London in the dark, William returned to the sponging house with the attorney, exhausted but unharmed. Helps's momentary relief at their arrival was dampened by the attorney's refusal to lend him more than £100 for his release. Protesting exhaustion, William was nevertheless sent out once more with the attorney, this time the short distance to Chancery Lane, to procure an additional guarantor, who finally effected the schoolmaster's release.

Such a narrow escape proved to be sufficient cause for consolation, if not celebration, so around midnight master and pupil headed for the Bell Inn at Holborn. In the comfortable confines of this establishment, they consumed large quantities of veal cutlets and scallops, washed down with two pints of porter and "two capacious bowls of punch" of prodigious strength, for which the Bell was famous. Later, the defensive schoolmaster would insist that all this was at William's suggestion. Thus comforted and sufficiently inebriated to prevent any anxieties from seeping into their sleep, they spent an undisturbed night at the inn. Apparently suffering no ill effects, both were awake and ready to start the return journey to Hadley at seven the following morning.

Setting off just before sunrise, they walked north across the slowly waking city as darkness gave way to an unpromising gray gloom. After skirting east of Regents Park, they left the metropolis through the growing village of Camden Town and walked on across the hills through a ribbon of houses that formed Kentish Town and on to the village of Highgate. As they entered the village, the threatening skies turned darker still, and while they ate some breakfast, heavy rain began to fall. As they set out once more, William spotted the Hadley and Barnet coach driving up behind them, which then stopped at a small public house to water the horses. Viewing this as a stroke of good luck, he suggested they take the coach for the rest of the journey to Hadley. Reverend Helps, however, was less concerned about their health than about his reputation. "No," he objected, "perhaps there are some Hadley people in the Coach, and I would not have them know me for twenty Guineas, particularly as it is Sunday morning." The thing to do, he insisted, was to walk backward and forward through the village, hoping no one would notice, until the coach drove on. William complied with this farcical plan in mute resentment while the rain seeped through his clothing. When the pair eventually straggled, hunch-backed, through Barnet, they were so completely drenched that boys in the street hooted as they passed.[35]

William mentioned not a word of his ordeal to his parents, but Reverend Helps wrote the very next day to Mr. Jackson asking for a loan of £100 to defray his expenses and "preserve my character and credit inviolate," but without any mention of his arrest or William's role in his release. William did write to his mother asking for a fresh supply of cash. It was not an unusual request from a schoolboy, but Mr. Jackson's response betrayed the anxiety that Helps's letter had caused. Declaring that "there should be no secrets of importance between Father and Son," he demanded to know whether there was anything "which makes Hadley seriously unpleasant"—lack of food perhaps? William, as instructed, sent a sealed letter by servant in which he alleged that Mr. and Mrs. Helps lived very well, but that they were often away in town and then the dinners were bad at school, so he had spent his money on food at the Green Man Inn. Jackson replied to William immediately with instructions to tell Helps that they desired their son home early because friends were visiting, then to take the morning coach to Tottenham Court Road, where their carriage would meet him and bring him and his luggage home to Gloucester Place.[36]

For some weeks Mr. Jackson and Reverend Helps pretended there was nothing unusual in William's sudden early departure. Jackson, having already loaned Helps the money he had requested, wrote very cordially at the end of December to explain that the continuing lack of other pupils at Hadley meant that he was obliged to find an alternative school for the ensuing term. William, struggling to keep both parties happy, had told his father he wished to leave the school, but had also assured Reverend Helps that he wanted to return. Both had good reason to keep the other quiet about their actions: Helps wanted to stop William from explaining what had really happened in London; William wanted to prevent Helps from telling his father that just two months after the donkey incident he had used his silver watch to buy another horse, which he kept in Helps's field. Once Jackson announced he was taking William away, however, the alliance dissolved, accusations flew, and another fierce epistolary battle was ignited, this time between the furious father and the indignant cleric.

At a stroke, the Reverend Helps became, in William's words, his "most bitter enemy," whose "shallow brain" had invented the "most malignant falsehoods." The schoolmaster informed Jackson that his son's bad behavior had been the chief cause of his school's failure to attract other pupils. He claimed that William's lack of candor and outright lying had "conferred upon him a character throughout the neighborhood, which most certainly will not be soon forgotten." Yet it was Mr. Jackson who had most injured the boy's chances by allowing him to indulge in "silly, trifling," sometimes "pernicious" correspondence with his mother and friends. A boy "whose attainments are so lamentably disproportionate to his age" should not have had his mind seduced from his studies by contemplation of a ball several months before it was due to take place—arranging a party was, to the schoolmaster, "a very injudicious accompaniment to Ovid and Virgil." Letting William roam freely was an equally foolish instruction, leading to the purchase of both the donkey and another horse. Helps shared the opinion of many schoolmasters who believed fond parents were only too keen to rush to the defense of their precious offspring on the flimsiest evidence of maltreatment. Vicesimus Knox had warned parents not to listen to their sons' complaints, for if they did, the boys would not hesitate

> to propagate the most shocking calumnies against their instructor. The love of novelty induces them to wish to be removed to another place of education; or revenge for some proper correction . . . urges them to spare no pains in injuring their master's interests. . . . I have seen the most flagrant acts of injustice . . . committed by parents at the instigation of their children. I have known many a tender mother attack a truly worthy, benevolent, and a generous instructor with the fury of an Amazon . . . because a humoured child has told a false story.

Reverend Helps berated Mr. Jackson for the "uniform removal of your son every half year from one place to another," which would prove very injurious to his education and showed the lack of "prudence of your yielding to those idle and frivolous representations." [37]

Such an attack on his wisdom, his wife, and his son was beyond anything Mr. Jackson could bear, and it struck at his deepest desire to fight injustice. He retaliated with a fierce written interrogation of Reverend Helps, demanding answers to thirteen questions about the events that had taken place in London and the dramatically different assessments of his son's character. Helps, comparing himself to an already unjustly "condemned culprit," stoutly defended his actions and demanded not to be judged before he had been heard. The anger of the avenging father, whose son's health, morals, reputation, and honor, had been placed in such dire jeopardy, did not abate one whit. Rather, the flames were fanned higher every day as he considered new risks and implied insults. He drew up a list of twenty detailed refutations, followed by a further ten indictments of the schoolmaster.

If Mr. Jackson's behavior appeared a little extreme given that William had not suffered any physical harm, it should be remembered that most writers on education urged parents to consider the dangers of introducing a boy to the world too young. "Virtue is harder to be got than a knowledge of the world; and if lost in a young man is seldom recover'd," warned Locke. "To introduce boys to scenes of immoral and indecent behaviour is to give the young mind a foul stain, which it will never lose," echoed Vicesimus Knox nearly a century later.[38]

For Reverend Helps, the same advice held true, but it was Jackson who risked exposing William to the city's temptations, for now he would have at least two months' holiday solely "for the parade & perambulation of Bond Street." Mr. Jackson thought parading along Bond Street in daylight was considerably less injurious to William's character than performing the "servile task" of running through the streets "in the darkness of the night, when every villain was abroad for plunder and every strumpet in search of prey!" William's safety was a demonstration of God's providence in the face of the schoolmaster's wicked abandonment of his duty. Indeed, Mr. Jackson, who prized rationality above all and claimed not to be "superstitious," even believed his wife had been warned of William's danger in one of her dreams. But "Alas! Alas! It was no foolish dream—for her darling son was at the very moment in a tavern, perhaps drunk, and . . . in the arms of a diseased prostitute!"[39]

Gaining no satisfaction from Reverend Helps's replies, Mr. Jackson determined to seek judicial redress. Driven by the "sense of undeserved injury" that William Garrow had so tellingly detected three years earlier, Jackson produced as evidence all the voluminous correspondence that he had meticulously recorded and his minutely detailed summaries and refutations of Helps's replies. He included the letter that Jane had written to William when she heard of his frightening nocturnal experience in London—detailing her own nightmare and her horror when she discovered that her dream had been fulfilled—as evidence of divine providence.

All this proof was delivered by a servant to the Reverend Charles Cotterell, a Middlesex justice of the peace (JP), begging that he "rescue the character of my son" from "dark and malevolent insinuations." The magistrate, himself the father of a large family, was greatly moved by Jackson's position as a father and, though a stranger, desired to be on better terms with him. But ultimately he had to abide by the law, and the law could take no action unless a specific charge of a breach of the peace could be brought. The JP also had no evidence of any lack of respect shown by Reverend Helps in his dealings with Jackson, so, regretfully, the matter could not be taken any further.[40]

Mr. Jackson's reaction to this disappointment can only be guessed at; for once, he remained utterly silent on the subject. Instead, he turned his energies to finding another private school for William, in which he might continue his classical studies for the bar without gaining any further "general knowledge" of the kind his former master had imparted about the less salubrious world around him. Yet it was not from schoolmasters but from his peers that William was about to learn a great many more lessons about love and life in London.

3

LESSONS IN LOVE AND LIFE IN LONDON

London and Reading School, 1808

The rake who is debauching innocence, squandering
away property and extending the influence of
licentiousness to the utmost of his power, would
(if fairly represented) excite spontaneous and universal
abhorrence. But this would be extremely inconvenient
since raking, seduction and prodigality make half the
business and almost all the reputation of men of
fashion.

    — Theophilus Christian, *The Fashionable World*
      Displayed (1804)

F or tutors like the Reverend Helps, "respectable" parents like
Mr. Jackson, and a growing number of increasingly vociferous
evangelicals and moralists, London was a dangerous nursery of
vice, teeming with temptation on every street. For an aspiring young
man of fashion like William, the capital was the perfect city for the
pursuit of pleasure and status. As Helps predicted, the "parade and
perambulation" of Bond Street, along with many other of London's famous fashionable areas, became one of William's favorite pastimes. It

required great attention to detail—from the mode of his dress to the way that he walked—to create a good impression in society on the streets of London. "That's the fashion father, that's the modern ease," explained one fictional son to his bemused parent; "a young fellow is nothing now, not without the Bond Street roll: a toothpick between his teeth, his knuckles crammed into his coat-pocket. Then away you go, lounging lazily along."[1]

Beginning at one o'clock in the afternoon, the West End began to fill with people of fashion intent on shopping, socializing, and admiring each other's attire. One foreign visitor described how Bond Street became crammed with carriages making frequent stops at shops "abounding in every article of taste and luxury"; how gentlemen "walked up and down the street, to see and be seen; and [how] the foot pavement [was] so perfectly covered with elegantly dressed people as to make it difficult to move." The street was most famous for its elite tailors, boot makers, shirt makers, hatters, glovers, hosiers, and manufacturers of a bewildering array of fashionable accoutrements, from snuff boxes to guns and walking sticks. These were the merchants patronized by Beau Brummell, the leading dandy of the day, who had personally set the standard for men of fashion to follow. Indeed, every sort of pleasurable activity could be indulged in Bond Street: from eating the best French food at the Clarendon Hotel to purchasing tickets to the opera or a boxing match, from bathing and shaving to perusing books in lending libraries.[2]

Beyond the parade of stylish streets, squares, and pleasure gardens, walking, or "rambling" as it was known, was considered an equally essential part of any young Regency buck's day. It was an opportunity to see the range of life in London—in the more notorious as well as the fashionable areas—and to be seen doing so by those who mattered in society. William began taking long walks around the West End with Henry Keighly, a young man he had met during the Christmas holidays. Henry's mother had visited the Jacksons at Christmas, and when Mr. and Mrs. Jackson heard her son was bedridden with a lengthy illness, they encouraged William to visit the lad to cheer him up. The two youths quickly became firm friends, and William soon persuaded Henry to join him in yet another of his schemes to acquire a horse that they could both use to arrive in style at selected venues—up to thirty handsome steeds belonging to army officers and gentlemen could be seen tethered outside the Clarendon Hotel on most days.[3]

Riding the horse was initially William's preoccupation, but on his recovery, Henry took the lead for their forays into London's streets and pleasurable venues. During the very first of these perambulations, the two elegantly dressed youths headed toward the Middlesex Hospital and turned down Suffolk Street, a residential backstreet that ran parallel to the hospital. The modest brick façades belied the immodest nature of the trade plied by many of their gaudily dressed inhabitants, who displayed themselves to advantage in the large windows. William stared in disbelief as women began beckoning to them from almost every window, and near the end of the road, one young woman opened the sash window of her parlor and called out, "I have not seen you for a long time—where have you been?" Henry cheerfully replied that he had been ill but was better now and walked on a few paces before casually observing to his friend, "There are some damned nice girls living in this street. I know most of them—look at that window where two of them are standing, the one in the yellow gown is very handsome, and I am well acquainted with her." William (probably for his father's benefit) later declared that he was shocked at the suggestion that they visit a prostitute, and he refused to accompany Henry down Suffolk Street the following day, insisting that they now restrict their rambles to the "principal streets."[4]

A few days later Henry confided his plans to acquire a copy of the infamous *Fanny Hill; Or, Memoirs of a Woman of Pleasure,* and he promised to pass it on to William after he had read it himself. Both boys were well aware that the book was considered obscene by all except a select group of connoisseurs of erotic literature, and anyone found publishing it was likely to be prosecuted. John Cleland's celebration of sexual pleasure in a story about the life of a prostitute and her return to respectability by marriage to her true love had become even more repugnant to the moral majority since it had been republished with graphic illustrations, which entirely erased the subtlety of the author's language.[5]

There had been an increase in attempts to suppress all "loose and licentious Prints, Books, and Publications, dispersing Poison to the minds of the Young and Unwary and to Punish the Publishers and

Vendors thereof" ever since George III had declared it an essential aim in his "Proclamation for the Encouragement of Piety and Virtue, and for the Preventing and Punishing of Vice, Profaneness and Immorality" of 1787. The campaign had been pursued with renewed vigor by the new Society for the Suppression of Vice, set up in 1802, whose aims included the destruction of an industry that threatened to "enflame the mind, and corrupt the morals of the rising generation." William and Henry's visit to a bookshop to inquire about obtaining a copy of *Fanny Hill* was therefore spiced with the danger of discovery as well as the delicious frisson of pleasurable anticipation.[6]

It was not the first occasion on which Henry had tried to persuade the bookseller to acquire a copy for him, but this time he indicated his well-dressed companion and in hushed tones assured the man that he would recommend the shop to all his friends. The promise of such advantageous patronage persuaded the bookseller to obtain a copy forthwith, but, he insisted, "I will not part with it unless you pledge your honour never to mention my name, for if it should be discovered, I shall be fined fifty pounds, and run the risk of standing in the pillory." Henry returned that evening and handed over a copy of *Wilkinson's Atlas* in exchange for *Fanny Hill*. It was a good deal for the bookseller, because he could sell the *Atlas* for more than the 14s. he had paid for *Fanny Hill*. After both boys had read the book, Henry returned it to the bookseller, who gave him half a guinea (10s. 6d.), thus making a tidy profit on the transaction. Notwithstanding Henry's fear that his parents would find out what he was reading—which necessitated removing certain books from his house as soon as possible—the boys found the purchase of books on credit and their exchange for others, followed by a quick resale or return, an excellent method of acquiring what they wanted to read without actually paying any money of their own. William, while strenuously denying his own involvement in such schemes, later claimed that Henry was constantly "in the habit of exchanging [books] for the most diabolical publications that ever issued from the press."[7]

Two of these diabolical publications proved particularly instructive for William's sexual education. In addition to *Fanny Hill*, which William claimed to have read straight through in one sitting, Henry also lent him a copy of *Aristotle's Masterpiece*. In wide circulation since the late seventeenth century, early-nineteenth-century editions of the

Masterpiece had become a kind of witty Regency *Readers Digest* of the joys and practicalities of married love, instructing numerous young men in the mysteries of procreation. It presented sex as an entirely natural and enjoyable occupation for both spouses; indeed, like many publications, it insisted that regular sexual emission was beneficial to health, provided that valuable fluid was not exhausted by overuse or wasted on nonprocreative activities. Fanny Hill, after her numerous sexual adventures and on the eve of her marriage, also extolled the virtues of connubial bliss: "If I have painted vice in all its gayest colours, if I have decked it with flowers," she explained, "it has been solely in order to make the worthier, the solemner sacrifice of it to virtue."[8]

Such disclaimers and moral injunctions were of little interest to the fevered imaginations of teenage boys, and they were certainly not the reason for the commercial success of either book. Nor did these platitudes mollify the moral crusaders against obscene publications. William confessed that reading *Fanny Hill* and studying the "variety of plates of the most infamous kind" quickly convinced him to accompany Henry on his visits to prostitutes. They soon met an "extremely well dressed" young woman in Berners Street and subsequently visited her several times, so that by the time she moved to Newman Street, William was quite smitten with the charming Miss Clifford. Indeed, William's conversion to the pleasures of the flesh was so complete, Henry claimed, that he frequently insisted that they also visit Cousin Tom's, a famous fashionable brothel in the privileged parish of St. James.[9]

William and Henry both knew that their parents would not approve of their behavior, but it was understandable and far from atypical for boys of their class and generation. They were bombarded by the public nature of sexual material available in London, be it pornographic books and journals, erotic and scatological prints, or the high visibility of common whores consorting with customers in public parks and street corners, as well as celebrated courtesans who graced the best boxes at the opera and theater. They were further confused by the mixed messages and varying moral standards adopted by different classes. The royal princes and significant numbers of the aristocracy and landed gentry supported mistresses, as did top-ranking politicians and generals—a popular toast among leading Whigs proposed, "May elegant vice prevail over dull virtue." Adultery, if discovered, was considered scandalously bad behavior, but most gentlemen of fashion considered a comely courtesan an essential status symbol. Because most couples did not marry until their late twenties, many upper-class parents actively encouraged their sons (but never their daughters) to sow their wild oats among prostitutes and servants—not least in the hope that it would prevent the much greater evils of masturbation and homosexuality.[10]

For respectable middle-class parents, however, promiscuous sexuality of any kind was abhorrent, immoral, and dangerous, a sign of an irrational and profligate nature. The professional, merchant, and trading classes had a much more tenuous hold on their wealth and status in society than did the landed dynasties and power brokers, who could afford to ignore public moral indignation. Whereas Henry had to bribe a maidservant who inadvertently discovered his copy of *Fanny Hill*, William seems to have had no problem hiding the real nature of his rambles from his parents. Mr. Jackson was at that time wholly preoccupied with finding a new school for his son. He selected another small private establishment, this one run by the fervently evangelical rector of Fulham, John Owen. It may have been by accident, but more probably by design, that Mr. Jackson's choice had lighted on this famous moralist, a man who considered London to be a snare for unwary youths and had penned a diatribe against fashionable society just a few years earlier. In *The Fashionable World Displayed*, Reverend Owen (writing under the pseudonym Theophilus Christian) condemned the code of behavior that allowed a gentleman to "debauch the daughter of his tenant, seduce the wife of his friend, and be faithless and even brutal to his own, and yet be esteemed a man of honour (which is the same as a man of Fashion)."[11]

Mr. Jackson had no doubts that William's morals and education were now safe in the hands of the estimable Reverend Owen, a man whose eminent connections included the Bishop of London and the evangelical antislavery campaigner William Wilberforce. Owen's chief claim to fame was founding the British and Foreign Bible Society, and he clearly believed his school in leafy Fulham was sufficiently distant from the city to keep his pupils safe from temptation. William

wrote encouraging letters about his academic progress and assured his
father that he had no time to socialize with his companions because
he was too busy with "the improvement and cultivation of my mind
which is only to be acquired by Books." The irony of this statement
was quite lost on Jackson, who was happy enough to allow his son to
acquire a new pair of dress breeches for a dance that Mrs. Owen was
throwing the following week. Soon afterward William announced he
would visit home that weekend to get his hair cut, but Jackson had no
idea that the visit was a cover invented by Henry Keighly to get his
friend to London. William, accompanied by a school friend and
Owen, who was visiting the Bishop of London, alighted from their
coach at the White Horse Cellar in Piccadilly, where the boys took
some refreshments before setting off to a bookseller, ostensibly to acquire copies of Cicero. William kept his promise to visit his parents in
Gloucester Place but left promptly at three o'clock, saying he needed
to get back to the White Horse to catch a coach for school.[12]

Unknown to the Jacksons, William and his friend had met Henry
earlier in Bond Street. It didn't take much for Henry to persuade both
boys that they could catch a later coach so that they could have dinner
with him. At the appointed hour, the two schoolboys entered the Wheat
Sheaf coffee house in the Strand, where they proceeded to consume two
pots of ale, a pint of sherry, and a quart of port wine with Henry—a
heady mixture that soon put them in the mood for more adventure.
Henry suggested that they visit Miss Clifford, the pretty girl he and
William had met in their earlier rambles, and that by claiming to have
stayed with friends, the schoolboys could remain in town overnight and
sneak back to Fulham on the early morning coach without anyone
knowing. William's friend, a shy boy of limited mental capacity, wanted
to go to Covent Garden theater instead, but they were wearing boots
and day clothes, which would have prevented their admission to the
fashionable boxes, so he finally agreed to visit the prostitute and go on to
a theater later. The unfortunate lad soon discovered that his presence
was chiefly required to finance the evening's entertainment, and he lost
his watch and boots to that purpose, which William pawned without
scruple for ready cash.

Miss Clifford was alone and not expecting company when the boys
arrived, but she quickly went to change into her full evening attire and,

as Jackson later described it, "returned to the room elegantly dressed, and armed for conquest, where she fastened upon her prey." But in truth, William and Henry needed little persuading. Miss Clifford proposed a brief visit to the theater to "see the afterpiece and then return for the night." Henry needed to borrow 4s. from William to achieve this and proposed to meet the couple at the theater later. William was happy to comply, for an appearance at the theater accompanied by a stunning Cyprian would raise his fashionable status considerably.[13]

In the theater the audience was as much a part of the entertainment as the actors: all high and low life was on display, and the activities of elite patrons in the boxes was the most enthralling—and for elite society the most important—performance of all. Very few theatergoers went to watch the play alone, and for a man of fashion, regular attendance in the company of important, beautiful, or infamous women was essential. Regular prostitutes and high-class courtesans always arrived late to take their seats—in the pit for the former or in the boxes for the latter. Both boxes and auditorium were as well lit as the stage, providing the perfect backdrop for the observance of political, financial, and sexual intrigue among the great and the notorious. The Reverend Owen scathingly depicted the theater as the preferred institution for the education of youth in the fashionable world. For "there must be schooling for the man of pleasure as well as the man of letters," he fumed, and

> certainly no school exists in which the elements of modish vice can be studied with greater promise of proficiency than the public theatres. . . . When to all this is added, how many painted strumpets are stuck about the theatre, in the boxes, the galleries, and the avenues; and how many challenges to prostitution are thrown out in every direction; it will, I think, be difficult to imagine places better adapted, than the theatres at this moment are, to teach the theory and practice of fashionable iniquity.

Suitably stimulated by the theatrical entertainment, William and his friends returned to Miss Clifford's house, where more wine was poured and another girl summoned to aid their indulgence in modish vice until nine o'clock on Sunday morning.[14]

The Jacksons remained blithely unaware of their son's activities until ten o'clock that Saturday night, when their preparations to retire for the night were interrupted by a loud knocking at their door. Owen entered in a state of great agitation, asking if they knew where William was because he had gone missing, along with another pupil of "great mental imbecility." The Jacksons sent out numerous anxious inquiries seeking the boys' whereabouts that night, but when there was still no news early the following morning, Mr. Jackson set out for Fulham in his coach. To his great relief he spotted his son on the top of a stage-coach en route to Fulham, but there was no sign of William's unfortunate companion. When called to answer for his actions, however, William could not be persuaded to break what he believed to be an honorable silence about who had accompanied him in his pursuit of pleasure the previous night.

The Reverend Owen's reaction was harsh but inevitable—he expelled his unrepentant pupil on the spot. Mr. Jackson was left to return to London to discover the truth of the matter. William was eventually persuaded by some powerful paternal pressure to write a "full confession," in which he detailed Henry's key role in the night's proceedings and expressed a deep contrition:

> I have deeply reflected upon my late conduct, and am firmly resolved to amend it. I have heard it said that every person has one unfortunate year in his life. If so I sincerely hope that mine is over, and that for the future my conduct will be ever such, as to merit your approbation. I have inclosed [*sic*], for your inspection, a statement of the entire case, which, I trust, cannot fail to convince you, that my late behaviour was not so bad as you were led to suppose.[15]

William's confession convinced Jackson and Owen that the newly repentant sixteen-year-old and his fellow pupil (who had been discovered unharmed but minus his watch and boots) "were young men 'more sinned against than sinning.'" William's subsequent cover-up could be explained as arising from a misguided sense of honor to protect Keighly's identity. For both father and clergyman, this was an instantly recognizable story—of innocent youth tempted to sin by a "vile wretch," an "artful, malignant, and disinherited profligate." The evangelical Owen declared that William's sin could be forgiven and even transformed into a moral lesson for life, but he also warned Jackson:

> Lies become necessary in order to cover disobedience, expedients for raising money, in order to supply the wants occasioned by expensive pleasures; Besides Guilt weakens the moral principle; and the mind that has yielded to temptation in one instance, becomes less disposed to resist in all succeeding ones. Such a debauch as that by which the master-villain initiated his disciples, prepared them to enter without further compunction, into all the mysteries of systematic licentiousness. God be thanked the Fowler has been detected, the snare broken, and I trust, both your son and my unhappy pupil, not only rescued from his destructive wiles, but fortified, by an experience dearly bought, against every attempt that may hereafter be made, to seduce them from their allegiance to Virtue and Truth.[16]

Henry Keighly was, understandably, deeply unhappy to discover that he had been betrayed by William and painted as the "master-villain." In truth, he was also desperate to rescue his reputation. Henry's father had disinherited him within days of discovering that night of debauchery, and Mr. Jackson threatened to make the whole affair public and to inform the assignees appointed to look after Henry's property until he came of age, thus depriving him of even "the small pittance" he had left to live on. Disinheriting a son was an extreme sanction resorted to only rarely and even more rarely upheld in a court of law—it was the ultimate expression of paternal disapproval and ruined the prospects of a young heir for the rest of his life. That the eldest son should inherit his father's property was a God-given, not a man-made, right, which could be revoked only to punish the worst breach of filial duty to a parent. The threat of disinheritance, therefore, was believed to be an extremely effective parenting measure and a powerful incentive to good behavior. As both moralists and jurists made clear, one of the best reasons to carry out that threat was to punish a son who was "extremely wicked and immoral, and give[s] no hopes of reformation and amendment."[17]

Henry had told William he had been disinherited the day before the latter penned his "confession," which is probably why William decided to name and shame his friend, confident that Henry's reputation was already ruined beyond redemption. William certainly used the fact that Henry's father had seen fit to demonstrate the "depravity" of his son's disposition by disinheriting him to gain credit with his own father. The boys' friendship quickly deteriorated into bitter enmity as both wrote increasingly impassioned accusations and produced detailed statements for Mr. Jackson to adjudicate.

Even though Mr. Jackson clung to the hope that Henry and Miss Clifford had conspired to ruin William's morals, he nevertheless conducted another forensic investigation to ascertain the truth of the matter. He rigorously questioned the terrified bookseller who had provided the boys with the copy of *Fanny Hill*, and he interviewed the horse dealer who had kept and sold William's latest steed. To William's acute mortification, Jackson also had him examined by an "eminent surgeon" to check whether Henry's allegations that he had contracted venereal disease were true. William was pronounced clear at the time, but the examination could not prove that he had not suffered previously or that he would not do so again because the symptoms only became visible at intervals. Venereal disease was an occupational hazard for many men of fashion—widely termed the "*à la mode* disease"—but it was also seen as a moral indictment of the sufferer. Henry had twisted the knife deeper by suggesting that William had no idea if he had contracted the illness from Miss Clifford or a whore in a St. James's brothel, and that this was the real reason the Reverend Owen had expelled William so swiftly from his school. It is unlikely that Owen could have known of any venereal illness at that time, but the headmaster may have already found a list of names and addresses of five prostitutes that William had scribbled on a page torn from a school notebook.[18]

The slurs, claims, and counterclaims between the former friends continued to escalate. William retaliated by accusing Henry of catching "the venereal" from one of his mother's servants, and for this reason the poor girl was subsequently dismissed from the Keighlys' service. Henry countered William's description of his collection of pornographic books by alleging that his former "dearest friend" regularly swindled tradesmen by buying a guinea's worth of books from a shop where he had credit and then taking them to a pawnbroker to raise cash, only to redeem the books later and return them to the bookseller. Yet although Mr. Jackson's inquiries threw up niggling doubts, he concluded that his investigations extenuated William's conduct to a "substantial degree" and established that his son had, "generally," acted with probity. The boys were prohibited from ever contacting each other again, and Jackson agreed not to publish Henry's crimes if he behaved well in the future. For all these efforts to ascertain the truth and correct William, Owen warmly commended Jackson for acting as both "an affectionate parent and [an] honourable man," which served as both consolation and confirmation that he was indeed a good, if deeply disappointed, father.[19]

EVEN BEFORE HIS investigations had been concluded, Mr. Jackson began to search yet again for a school where William could continue his education in safety. Given the failure of an elite public school, a private school, and two small academies run by clergymen, his options were narrowing. In a final effort to channel William's energies into intellectual and virtuous pursuits, Mr. Jackson now decided to put his faith in the old-style discipline of a grammar school. He chose Reading School, which was enjoying an excellent reputation under the long-standing headmastership of Dr. Richard Valpy, a highly respected man with a formidable reputation for scholarship and discipline, whose devotion to the school caused him to turn down two bishoprics. Valpy's success at Reading meant the school had largely departed from its charitable origins and now primarily educated the sons of country gentlemen and noblemen.

The town of Reading was well placed on the main highway from London to the west, but was also a considerable distance from the lures of London and prided itself on being "neither a haunt of fashion nor a seat of manufacture" while still possessing "an air of gentility." It was also close to a new country property in Langley that Mr. Jackson was in the process of purchasing as part of his quest for respectable landed gentry status for his family. His son's behavior was threatening to undermine this laudable aim, and in his eagerness to secure William a place at Reading, Mr. Jackson felt it necessary to circumvent the truth of the matter. Dr. Valpy insisted that he never accepted boys from other public schools and would take only those of "a tractable disposition and free from any improper habits and propensities." Mr. Jackson explained that, although he wanted William to be educated at some distance from "this licentious metropolis," it was chiefly because he needed to be removed from the "over fondness of a tender mother." Valpy agreed to offer William a place at a boarding house for older boys run by an assistant master provided that Jackson could guarantee that he was "free from immoral pursuits or tendencies." Such a direct request was harder to evade. So along with the promise of making "a very liberal arrangement" with the housemaster, Jackson sent Valpy a copy of Reverend Owen's letter of forgiveness to William as a young man who had been led astray. This was accompanied by a sincere promise from William to strictly observe all the regulations Dr. Valpy laid down, including keeping his past a secret from his school fellows and never leaving the school grounds. On the very day that Valpy consented to this agreement, William found himself riding in a coach to Reading accompanied by his relieved father.[20]

William soon found a familiar face at Reading. His old friend Thomas Macqueen had made a similar educational journey and was now a pupil in one of the lower forms. William also made links with other boys from backgrounds very similar to his own. Benjamin Hobhouse, the son of Wiltshire MP and Secretary of the India Board of Control Sir Benjamin Hobhouse, became a particularly close companion. Hobhouse's eldest brother, John Cam Hobhouse, was a close friend of the poet Byron. Francis Bickley, the son of Benjamin Bickley, a prominent merchant and future sheriff of Bristol, was another with a similar outlook to William.

Macqueen, Hobhouse, and William shared dreams of military glory, which left them unimpressed by the demands of a classical education and possessed of a sense of social superiority that made them unwilling to submit to the rigorous discipline of a grammar school. Ironically, it was the improvement of Reading's reputation and the resulting increase in the number of pupils who were gentlemen boarders rather than local town boys that had caused the school to focus less on the more modern subjects, such as arithmetic and geography. What grated most on William, however, was the "tyranny" of the headmaster. Known as a "mighty flogger," Valpy seems not to have noticed any contradiction between his liberal principles and the severe punishment of any failures of learning or behavior in his pupils. Shortage of funds for the school also meant that conditions for boarders were uncomfortable, and the food provided frequently consisted of little more than sour milk and dry bread. Within a few weeks of William's arrival, mutterings of muted discontent were coalescing into plans for demonstrable defiance.[21]

The sparks that ignited talk of outright rebellion were the headmaster's refusal to allow the boys to play on the green that had previously been designated their own space and their even closer confinement to the boarding house. William, who had been amusing himself by trying to seduce Dr. Valpy's pretty daughter, found this last regulation particularly irksome. He shared his frustrations with Bickley and Wells, a boy from a more modest trading family but described by Hobhouse as far "too wild to be shut up in such narrow bounds, and to be under our cursed tyrant of a master." Wells was already in serious trouble with Valpy and under threat of expulsion, so he had little to lose. William, whose resentment of authority now included both his father and his headmaster, had no intention of putting up with his current confinement or with the thwarting of his youthful affections, which had fastened with some strength upon the seductive Miss Clifford. Bickley was "a tough fellow" but of less worldly disposition than the other two. None of the boys explicitly referred to being flogged, but the widespread acceptance of this practice in grammar schools—where it was considered no more than a "ritualized inducement to learning"—and the culture of physical bravery may have prevented them from doing so. That does not, however, negate the psychological effects of being flogged or watching others suffer; flogging and cruelty were the most common causes of school rebellions. Such was the bitter resentment at such treatment that some pupils returned as adults for revenge; one former pupil from Merchant Taylors' school horsewhipped his old tutor in front of the whole school.[22]

The three boys came up with a radical plan to escape from the tyranny at Reading to pursue the pleasures of London, or, more precisely in William's case, the charms of Miss Clifford. Thus on a Friday evening in late April, William, Bickley, and Wells squeezed into a fast post chaise and set out on their great London adventure in high spirits. They were well clear of the outskirts of Reading before anyone noticed they were missing, and Dr. Valpy did not write to Mr. Jackson to inform of William's disappearance until Sunday. William had carefully calculated that his father would not hear of his flight until Monday, by which time he hoped to be well "out of his reach."[23]

The boys arrived in London early on Saturday morning, and even though William had led Hobhouse to believe that he would be staying at the Clarendon Hotel in Bond Street, they actually spent their nights in lower-grade hotels, chiefly at the George and Blue Boar, a large inn at Holborn. William's first port of call was Miss Clifford's house in Newman Street, where he tried earnestly to persuade her to come away with him to Richmond (probably the elegant town just southwest of London on the River Thames rather than the market town in North Yorkshire). To his chagrin, the experienced courtesan made it plain that she had no intention of eloping with a sixteen-year-old boy and that he should inform his parents of his whereabouts immediately. It was a harsh lesson for a boy who believed himself to be an independent young gentleman of means and status, but a prospective heir to a fortune was neither a viable nor a certain financial prospect for a woman who relied on her looks for her income, and she could not afford to upset a wealthy, influential father.

William's flagging spirits were revived a little by the arrival of a trunk full of their belongings and a cheerful letter from Hobhouse reassuring him that "you are a damned deal too good a fellow to stew in this nasty hole." "Continue to be in good spirits and you'll all do devilish well wherever you are," advised Hobhouse, for "I am heartily glad that you are out of the lion's paw; I do not know what the devil we shall do without three such spirited heroes." The trunk contained notes from other school friends, too, sent from "Prison House" and addressed to "The 3 Independent Gents of R_S_B," all of which served to reinforce the boys' sense of adventure and heroic achievement. Their flight also seems to have had an effect on Dr. Valpy, for Hobhouse described him as already beginning "to speak in a lower style" and having given up some of his unpopular practices.[24]

Dr. Valpy's letter to Mr. Jackson expressed astonishment at William's inexplicable disappearance: "I never gave him one cross look," and he was doing "well" in a class taught "by my brother," declared the headmaster. Neither adult regarded the boys' behavior as in any sense heroic. Jackson recorded how on "receipt of this heartrending intelligence," he immediately "set out in quest of his wretched son," despite having been out of town on that Monday. A letter from a shopkeeper in St. James's gave Jackson a clue where to start searching, and as news of the missing boys spread through the West End, other shopkeepers and hoteliers began sending notes regarding their whereabouts. Jackson went first to St. James's for information and then back to the George and Blue Boar in Holborn, only to find that the boys had left. In desperation he spent many hours walking along Holborn, Fleet Street, the Strand, and most of the West End, asking at every inn and coffee house he came across if they had been seen, but to no avail. As dusk fell, he resolved to conquer his aversion to houses of ill repute and knocked at the door of 30 Newman Street to see if Miss Clifford knew where William was. The courtesan was out at the theater, but the woman who kept the house was sympathetic to Jackson's distress and admitted that William had been there, but that Miss Clifford had sent him away. With no other leads to follow, Jackson returned to his distraught wife in Gloucester Place.

Jane Jackson's relationship with their son was much closer than Mr. Jackson's, but William's disappearance in London was a matter for paternal discipline, and she had not the contacts that her husband could draw upon to find him. By Tuesday morning, however, William's conscience was beginning to prick him, and he hastily penned a letter to his parents explaining that he had left Reading because a rebellion was brewing and he wanted to escape Valpy's "tyrannical manner." He was quite safe, he reassured his mother, and not alone but accompanied by friends. That same morning the Jacksons received a note from the headwaiter of the Globe Hotel in Fleet Street. The boys had spent the previous night there, and clearly hoping for some reward, the waiter had followed William down to Duke Street in St. James's that morning and waited outside a brothel until William emerged and began to make his way to the White Horse Cellar, where coaches bound for the West Country stopped. Jackson set off in haste once more, but again the trail had grown cold.[25]

That night another ray of hope appeared in the form of a note from the landlord of the George and Blue Boar, saying that two of the boys had visited his premises and one had booked a room for the night. The note was written at six o'clock but had taken some time to reach the family in Gloucester Place, and Mr. Jackson did not reach the inn at Holborn until much later, by which time there was no sign of the boys. He sat down to wait, and by midnight fear had given way to the anger many parents feel when their children have committed some danger-ous folly.

Sitting in the flickering candlelight, apart from the other patrons, Jackson eventually decided it was time to give up his quest, so he called for pen and paper and began to convey the depth of his anger and de-spair in a letter to the wretched boy, "whom I once called my son." To go missing for three days, he thundered, was an act of shocking brutal-ity and callousness for which both parents had been unprepared, and he feared that William was now beyond redemption. The fact that he was writing this letter in an inn famous for being the place where con-demned prisoners bought their last drink on their way to being hung at Tyburn was almost certainly not lost on Mr. Jackson. He was un-doubtedly uncomfortable in such surroundings, explaining that his only reason for being there was to "acquit myself to God and the World" as a good father. To which end, his offered this parting advice to William:

> *Pursue, Sir, your plans—run through the career of licentious*
> *pleasure—drink deep of dissipation and debauchery—and when you*
> *have accomplished all this—you will have time enough for*
> *reflection. Even in the arms of Miss Clifford, or any other Harlot,*
> *you may feel a pang; and, as <u>an outcast of society</u>, you will*
> *sometimes regret that the example and advice of your parents were*
> *lost upon you.*
>
> *I am, Sir, Your much injured Father*[26]

The "society" from which William would apparently be cast was that of gentlemen, merchants, and middle-class families to whom the appellation "respectable" was most often applied. It was not the society of the elite fashionable group (the beau monde) that his son aspired to join and to whom such behavior would have appeared quite acceptable. At two o'clock in the morning, Mr. Jackson gave up, his hopes of finding William having faded away along with most of the customers at the inn. He returned home to tell Jane the bad news, well aware that the death of her daughter meant that even the temporary loss of her only son was a torment she could hardly bear.

THE SOURCE OF Mr. Jackson's anxiety about William's descent into depravity could be traced to his middle-class trading roots. Even though Jackson strove hard for social advancement, he was not and did not aspire to be a member of fashionable society and could not understand his son's efforts to emulate it. Like many of his class, mingling within genteel society, shared leisure pursuits, a liberal education, and the codes of polite gentility that united professional, landed, and merchant gentlemen did not negate Jackson's disapproval of the morals and manners of the more fashionable elites. Torn between attraction and repulsion for his social superiors, Jackson's moral attitudes remained firmly rooted in his family's merchant origins, and William's "debauchery" therefore signified a lamentable loss of rational self-control as well as a lack of moral fiber. Seeking illicit sex similarly heralded an inability both to control luxury consumption—whether of food, pleasure, or fashion—and to defer immediate gratification for future profit.[27]

William's loose behavior was disturbingly similar to that of the famously indebted aesthete and voluptuary the Prince of Wales and, from Jackson's perspective, to that of the promising young poligar who had ended his dissolute life on the gallows. As the educationalist Vicesimus Knox had explained, "Irregular and intemperate passions; indulged at a boyish age . . . will cut off all hope of future eminence. The mind will sympathise with the body and both will be reduced to a wretched state of weakness." Middle-class families, for whom financial security and social reputation were closely linked, commonly feared their sons would be seduced into emulating their superiors' spending habits and sexual mores, resulting in ruinous expense and a risk to the health of both the rising and future generations. Whereas prospective heirs to landed estates could use titles and wide acreages to protect themselves from the claims of creditors, the majority of middle-ranking families relied on the inculcation of virtuous habits to avoid the threat of imprisonment for debt. Prostitutes posed a more sinister threat to precious sons. Despite increasing sympathy for fallen women and public efforts to "reclaim" them, many remained convinced that they were agents of destruction bent on beggaring and infecting respectable families. It was not surprising, therefore, that when Mr. Jackson finally got word that William had reappeared at eleven o'clock that morning, he thanked God for his son's safe return and set off for the inn, praying that "my presence [may] bring you back to reason."[28]

William was sitting in the dining room of the George and Blue Boar Inn, eating breakfast with Francis Bickley, when his father burst through the door full of righteous indignation. With studied nonchalance, William listened to his father recite a catalog of his sins and, no doubt for the benefit of his schoolmate, read with barely feigned indifference the passionate letter Jackson had written the previous night. To his father's complete incomprehension, William insisted that he had been fully justified in escaping Dr. Valpy's severity and that he had no plans to return home. Reduced to a speechless fury, Mr. Jackson resorted to writing out questions for his son to answer while they sat at the table. Equally angry at his father's lack of understanding, but still mindful of the manners required from a dutiful son, William wrote underneath the note that he intended to leave town tomorrow but would still obey any "orders" that his father laid down. Not satisfied with this thin veneer of deference, Mr. Jackson returned to verbally questioning William on just what he intended to do to survive on his own. The teenager mustered all his adolescent pride and declared that he was determined to make his career in the army; indeed, he "would rather carry a musket" than return to Dr. Valpy's school.[29]

But soon his resolve crumbled, and he conceded that if his father required it, he would go home with him now. Mr. Jackson firmly insisted that both boys accompany him to Gloucester Place at once, but before they left, he sat down to write to Dr. Valpy. After days of anxious searching and nights without sleep, this letter revealed the emotional cracks that he so carefully concealed from his son. "My head is so disordered with anxiety and want of rest that I am scarcely able to hold my pen," he confessed, perhaps hoping to gain the headmaster's sympathy. But even though Valpy, who possessed a formidable temper of his own, expressed deep compassion for the troubled father and even greater regret that such a liberal connection should be so abruptly terminated, he adamantly refused to let William set foot in Reading again, agreeing only to send the rest of his belongings home in a trunk.[30]

William spent the next few weeks in deep disgrace, consoled only by the continued correspondence with his friend Hobhouse. But the news from Reading was hardly gratifying for the hero of such a noble action against tyranny. The threatened rebellion had not occurred after all, and Mr. Jackson, convinced by Valpy that discontent had never been widespread, now doubted that the pupils had really planned any uprising. Francis Bickley, who had been collected by his brother with the declared intention of delivering him safely home to Bristol, was taken straight back to Reading. There, according to Hobhouse, Valpy "<u>rewarded</u>" him for departing without leave of absence, presumably with some ferocity. Bickley was allowed to return to the school because Mr. Jackson claimed that he had been the most reluctant escapee, and he had expressed a wish to be found quite soon after their arrival in London, despite pressure from his companions. The absolutely unrepentant Wells had fared even worse than William. He had been found by a relation, a butcher residing in the Minories who, according to Hobhouse, "thought he could not give a greater instance of his consanguinity and affection than by chaining his runaway relation to a bedpost." Returned to Reading by his tearful mother, who begged earnestly for her son to be given another chance, Wells was expelled from the school forthwith. Since Wells's family was less able to afford any other form of polite education, Hobhouse opined that "poor Wells is doomed to wear an apron behind some detestable counter," a drop in status that would exclude him from fashionable society.[31]

Hobhouse was considerably more optimistic about William's future, however, and he fully expected his friend to matriculate very soon so that they could meet again as students at Oxford. He seems to have been unaware that William harbored no such wishes, for even though he shared his friend's long-term military ambitions, William had no desire to return to academic study of any kind and sought a much faster route into service for his country. It was a sad irony that, although the ebullient Hobhouse fulfilled his filial duties and, with his family's blessing, became an officer in Sixty-ninth South Lincolnshire Foot Regiment, he would die, like so many of his generation, on the battlefield at Waterloo in 1815. It was Thomas Macqueen—who in later life would satisfy his own love of galloping horses and glorious uniforms by commanding the Bedfordshire Yeomanry—who remained William's closest friend and supporter.

As the atmosphere in Gloucester Place became increasingly strained, Macqueen's friendship was the only source of comfort for William. Neither of his parents wanted him to enter military service at the age of sixteen—Jane feared losing her precious only son so young, while Mr. Jackson still hoped William would follow the profession of the law. Jackson bluntly pointed out that William's health had never been strong, and that because he could only secure a commission in a regiment destined for the Indies, the inhospitable climate there would ensure that "[your] first illness would, probably, be your last." While Jane pleaded earnestly with William to reconsider his decision, his father reminded him that his inheritance depended entirely on his behaving in a way that earned his parents' approval. William stubbornly stuck to his guns, and Mr. Jackson, despairing of finding a solution, asked his close friend John Evelyn to mediate in the family standoff.[32]

Evelyn, whose affable disposition toward his nephew had ensured that he remained a favorite uncle, agreed to meet with William. Jackson gave his friend a letter for William in which he proposed that William continue his education for another two years, during which time Jackson would continue to pay for all his "proper wants," but the level of generosity would be determined by the extent to which he approved of William's behavior. If, after two more years of schooling, William still wanted to join the army, Jackson promised to buy him a commission to become an officer. William and Evelyn were closeted together for hours while an agitated Jackson paced outside. At last the door opened and Evelyn informed him that, in deference to his parents' wishes, William had agreed to give up his plans to enter the army immediately and would now endeavor to behave in a way that earned his family's approval. A delighted Mr. Jackson stepped forward, shook William's hand, and promised instant forgiveness for all his past sins; it was probably the closest he could get to a demonstration of affection and approval for his son. The following day William wrote to his father thanking him for his generous behavior and candidly confessing that "at this time I have a great inclination for the army. How long it may last I know not. The minds of young men are hourly changing." Nevertheless, he now "heartily concurred" with his father's plans to continue his education. The household at Gloucester Place thus settled back into peaceful coexistence for a day while Mr. Jackson considered his son's capitulation. Then, as usual, he had to put his thoughts on paper.[33]

In the interests of rebuilding their fragile relationship, it was a letter that would have been better left unwritten. Even though William's written confirmation had afforded Jackson some "solid satisfaction," he still complained that there was "not in it all the explicitness, suitable for an occasion of such serious import." He proceeded to list the inestimable benefits of a good education and point out every area where William had shown himself woefully deficient. Lack of decisiveness regarding his future career would not do at all. For William, who had been persuaded to soften his resolve only by his mother's tearful entreaties, this last accusation stung worst of all.[34]

As their verbal skirmishes were increasingly replaced by written letters, relations between father and son began a calamitous and destructive descent. Words uttered in haste could be withdrawn or rephrased, but once they were committed to paper, only endless refutation and rejoinder ensued. If forgiveness or agreement ever hove into view, it vanished just as quickly, broken on the rocks of a minor point that one or the other could not help restating. As gentlemen it was essential for each to justify his honor and to earn the good "opinion of the world," and thus relations between father and son became a duel of words every bit as serious as dueling with pistols (which served the same code of honor).

William believed himself perfectly proficient in spoken Latin—an essential demonstration of his gentlemanly status—but he could see little reason for a soldier to need moral philosophy, poetry, or oratory. His father cited many glorious examples of the classics, particularly that of Julius Caesar as a military genius who could not have succeeded without also being a skilled orator. Mr. Jackson was also convinced that Thomas Macqueen, not William, had started to compose the passionate and eloquent replies—an accusation that William indignantly denied. But the battle was in no small part determined by the generation gap and by wider debates about the benefits of modern, as opposed to classical, modes of education. The outcome of the dispute, however, was predictable. The more his father insisted on the need for William to improve his classical education, the more vehemently he refused. He lost his temper and declared that he would rather associate with the most contemptible men than pick up another book; he threatened to run away again if sent to another school like Reading.

Like so many long-running arguments, this one lost its course, then resurfaced. The battle over classical studies was replaced by a return to the bitterness stirred up by William's original disappearance from Reverend Owen's school, which prompted another outpouring of counter-accusations on both sides. Mr. Jackson began to doubt William's innocence in his dealings with Henry Keighly and regretted defending him so well in that case. William found life at home with his family increasingly "irksome," and even though he soon mended his relationship with his mother, matters with his father did not improve even when the family moved to the new country estate at Langley for the summer.

There Mr. Jackson spent a great deal of time planning improvements to the house and planting the gardens that would proclaim his newly landed status to the world. Under his watchful eye the pleasure gardens were landscaped with oak, copper beech, weeping birch, cedar, and cyprus trees interspersed with beds colored and scented with tulip trees, lilac, jasmine, red dogwood, pyracanthus, and pomegranate. The orchard was filled with every conceivable variety of apple tree, along with Moor Park apricots, May Duke and Morello cherries, plum, greengage, and pear trees. Mr. Jackson's social aspirations were further assuaged by a neighbor's recommendation that he be made a magistrate—a position that would command respect and the power to dispense justice in the locality. But none of this served to improve his temper with William. Once a child has badly hurt or disappointed a parent, it is all too easy to find fault again, until there are few actions he performs that cannot be construed as malicious or bad in some way.

William's relationship with his father was not dissimilar to that between the Prince of Wales and his father, George III. The king's affection for his heir was tempered by a fear that he would disappoint his father's aspirations for his future, and George's self-righteous, inflexible temperament was reflected in a complete intolerance of any form of filial disobedience. The king was equally given to expressing his anxieties about the development of the prince's character in letters to his son. Mr. Jackson viewed his heir's behavior as more than disappointing—it was dangerous. In his eyes, every minor sin that William committed was another significant step toward a life of crime. He believed in the view that "no man was ever perfectly vicious at once; but step by step graduates his height in villainy," which was presented in criminal biographies and discussions of juvenile crime by prison reformers and authors of advice literature aimed at the middle classes. Hence, hostilities resumed in July when Jackson accused William of forgery, probably for not signing a credit note correctly. William deeply resented this "harsh and undeserved" charge, but his every attempt to refute it was met by a stony silence, and family mealtimes became an ordeal. Indeed, he felt there was very little he could do that was right in his father's eyes that summer. Unable to speak, he explained to his father in writing that "I never sit down to your table that I do not feel I am a burthen to you, indeed I can have no doubt on my mind that such is the case when you do not think me worthy of holding any discourse with, and if I address you in conversation I meet with no reply."[35]

Jane Jackson then stepped in, as she so often did, to mediate between her son and her husband. Written correspondence between father and son ceased, which suggests that her efforts were at least temporarily successful, but they were unlikely to have reversed the damage done to her teenage son's sense of self-worth, which would increasingly require external bolstering. William, like the future Prince Regent, sought comfort in sexual assignations, fashionable shopping, and enthusiastic socializing.

Mr. Jackson, meanwhile, continued to collect evidence of his son's inevitable descent into crime. In the autumn he preserved (but did not copy) just one more letter from William that year, complaining about the cost of medical treatment he had received from a London doctor, which he could not afford to pay from his own allowance. There is none of Jackson's usual annotation against this letter, no outright condemnation of its author; it simply stands alone as proof that Mr. Jackson's former belief in his son's sexual continence and freedom from disease was finally crushed. William had visited Messrs. Currie and Co., Surgeons, at 107 Hatton Garden in October. Despite the respectable address, and claims to have been trained at the Royal College of Edinburgh, Currie and Co. advertised that they specialized in "certain complaints and diseases of debility," from which they could cure their patients in complete secrecy, whether in person or by post.

This polite reference to venereal disease and masturbation was less blunt than many of the medical quacks offering cures in the press, but it was symptomatic of the blurred line between them and professional surgeons. Currie and Co. promised to cure mild "infections" within two days, and, with perseverance, even more inveterate cases would respond. William had visited the surgeons, who charged "only one pound a time," on five occasions but had run up a bill of 10 guineas. He was outraged at this "<u>unfair</u> charge," but he had been assured that the medicine had "never yet failed," so any further treatment, in the unlikely event of a relapse, would be free. If his father could settle the account, it would be worth it because it was "a matter of great pleasure to be restored to perfect health, which I now think I am."[36]

A real return to health was unlikely, however, because the main advantage of these usually vegetable-based cures was that they provided a temporary cosmetic effect, whereas the more common treatment with mercury often caused worse symptoms than those of the gonorrhea or syphilis being treated. Indeed, the chief advantage of vegetable cures was secrecy: sufferers taking mercury would be struck with a fever, endure aching joints and swollen gums, produce excessive salivation, and exude a fetid smell that could hardly escape notice. It is most likely that William was suffering only from a recurrence of the clap, but for Mr. Jackson a physical cure was insufficient; the rot had clearly taken hold in his son's soul.[37]

4

AN OFFICER AND
A GENTLEMAN

London and Guernsey, 1809–1810

*Persons in a fashionable sphere cannot be entirely
agreeable to each other unless they are well dressed; nor
can that intercourse which they chiefly value be pleasantly
maintained, without splendid equipages, choice wines and
sumptuous entertainments. As, therefore, the necessity of
the case requires such accommodations . . . the law of
honour does not look very nicely into the means by which
they may have been procured.*

— Theophilus Christian, *The Fashionable World
Displayed* (1804)

William's "one unfortunate year" did not end with the passing of his seventeenth birthday in November 1808. In the
New Year, temperatures plummeted and the country was
beset with storms and heavy snow. Beggars died of cold on the streets
of London, and farther north birds were found frozen to death where
they perched. The atmosphere within 30 Gloucester Place remained
similarly glacial, punctuated with frequent stormy outbursts between
father and son. One of the worst of these storms was precipitated by

another of William's sexual adventures. On a cold night in mid-January, while the rest of the household was sleeping, William crept up the back stairs dressed only in his nightshirt. He opened the door to the female servants' room and walked over to where his mother's maid lay sleeping. The poor girl was startled from her sleep by this unwanted male apparition claiming to be Thomas the footman. William, with an arrogant lack of generosity, later protested that he had no intention of seducing the girl—had she "any pretensions to Beauty, she might then indeed have fallen a victim to all powerful love, but as she is more to be compared to one of the Devil's Nymphs than to a Venus, that [was] totally out of the question."[1]

This unflattering bravado was probably an aggressive form of self-defense because the seduction of servants was a popular pastime among young gentlemen and one that gentry fathers often condoned. Sexual conquests of any kind were proof of elite male virility among peers, and many fathers secretly applauded signs of precocious sexuality in their offspring. One father boasted that his boy was a "noble fellow" because he was "often found in bed with little Penelope's nurse." Another sagely advised his son, "Whenever you can, whomever you can with safety; let that be your maxim." For the moral middle-class parent, however, such attitudes were considered appallingly sinful.[2]

Mr. Jackson's fury at William's "abominable misconduct"—which included the whole black catalog of his earlier sins—produced one of his most bitter condemnations of his son:

> I am horror struck at the depravity of your mind, and from the bottom of my soul regret that I am the father of such a son. . . . You, who have destroyed all the flattering hopes I once had entertained of your passing through life with honour and credit—you, who have compelled me to swallow the very dregs of sorrow—you who have dared to fly in the face of parental authority, and to employ a mean and despicable threat to prevent me from the execution of a purpose directed, alas! how vainly directed, to save you from absolute ruin.[3]

The "mean and despicable threat" referred to William's declaration that he would leave his father's house and never see him again if Jackson still refused to give him a commission in the army after his eighteenth birthday. But now that "the seduction of innocence" had been added to the list of "many things . . . of which I never was guilty," William began to both hope and fear that Jackson would throw him out instead. To pre-empt this, he suggested that the best solution for all would be for him to enter his majesty's service immediately so that his father would no longer be burdened by such a villain within his house. But this plan also failed—Mr. Jackson only hardened his resolve to refuse his son a commission.[4]

The weather, too, conspired to keep William at home. Gales and heavy rain added to melting ice and snow caused the Thames to break its banks in London and at Windsor and Eton, close to the Jacksons' country house at Langley. The floodwater caused the main sewer in Portman Square to burst, leaving a gaping chasm at the bottom of Gloucester Place. In Sloane Street kitchens were flooded, but in Chelsea entire walls were washed away—people were forced to escape by boat from top-floor windows. In Deptford the water "rushed in tor-rents," sweeping great quantities of furniture down into the Thames. All over the country, floodwater caused havoc, destroying property and drowning people and animals.[5]

Even after the floods receded, the weather continued cold and unset-tled into the spring, while William nursed a growing sense of injustice. His father's accusations of lying and villainy touched William on the most sensitive point of a gentleman's honor. To accuse a gentleman of ly-ing was tantamount to calling him a coward, and had anyone outside his family accused him in that way, he would have felt instantly obliged to prove his courage by challenging that person to a duel. Dueling was also proof positive of superior social status. Only gentlemen were allowed to duel with each other because, as expert duelist Lieutenant Samuel Stan-ton explained, to duel with a man of lower rank would "entirely do away all distinction of person, and render the name, gentleman, a nothing, a nonentity. . . . It lowers him in the opinion of his equals."[6]

So when Henry Keighly circulated a pamphlet blaming William for their sexual escapades, William found a worthy opponent against whom he could prove his courage and status to himself, to the world, and, particularly, to his father. When Henry refused to retract, William wrote hastily to his father that they would duel at five the following morning, expressing the hope that "should I be victorious I trust I shall convince you that whatever my faults are, cowardice is not amongst them." Then he turned to the task of ensuring that each stage of the challenge and the duel was conducted according to the strict principles observed by all honorable gentlemen.[7]

William appointed his friend Edward Hollier to act as his second and present Henry with a written challenge to meet him at Chalk Farm, a famously popular place for settling "affairs of honour." Because dueling was strictly illegal, the distant location (Chalk Farm was on the northern outskirts of London), conveniently screened by trees and hedges, was supposed to protect the duelists from detection by officers of the law. Hollier's role as a second was crucial for the proper conduct of the whole process, for the aim of a duel was not to kill the opponent but to demonstrate courage under fire. If one of the protagonists died, the second was equally culpable in the eyes of the law, even though juries frequently refused to convict either party. Stanton advised all seconds that they should persuade their gentlemen to reconcile after the first shot had been fired. Indeed, any practice that increased the likelihood of death was to be frowned upon, and the number of fatalities had declined significantly since pistols had replaced swords as the weapon of choice. Combatants were also advised to adopt the fencing position to avoid exposing their full bodies. A gentleman should "look [his] adversary full in the face," but it was "highly improper for any person to put the pistol across his arm, or to be longer in taking aim than is necessary." By the early nineteenth century, it was equally acceptable for a second to effect a reconciliation between the protagonists before a single shot had been fired.[8]

Hollier solemnly presented the challenge to Henry Keighly, who, when faced with William's determination to pursue "desperate methods" to silence him, agreed to retract. Henry even offered to send a written apology to Mr. Jackson and John Evelyn, admitting that he had lied. By eight o'clock in the morning, the whole affair had been settled to William's satisfaction. He wrote triumphantly to his father from Cheapside, explaining how he had been vindicated but added that he would not be home until late that evening. Nevertheless, Jackson's disappointment, when he arrived home to discover that William had sufficiently recovered from his experience to attend a masquerade with his friends, was palpable.[9]

Mr. Jackson was almost certainly more upset that William had attended a voguish but scandalous masked ball at the celebrated Pantheon in Oxford Street—where young men and women were routinely assumed to be engaging in licentious behavior—than he was about his son's first duel. Even the most vociferous of the growing number of critics of dueling did not attack the notion of honor itself, and both father and son were proud to call themselves men of honor. Despite their many differences, William had inherited his father's pride, his deep sense of injustice, and his relentless determination to defend his public reputation at all costs. The code of honor that bound elite gentlemen was based on pride and on the belief that facing the possibility of physical death was infinitely preferable to undergoing social death. Even though a duelist might reasonably expect to escape the law—indeed, that proved that his social superiority placed him above the law—complete ostracism was the inevitable fate of both the man of fashion and the military man who was seen to refuse a challenge. William, as a man of fashion who desired to be a military officer, could not escape the social pressures of the circles in which he mixed.[10]

Evangelical campaigners like William Wilberforce, however, thundered against the sin of pride—for putting desire for the approval of man before that of God—while many others insisted that society would collapse if some groups were patently seen to be exempt from justice. In a moral and commercial age, it was argued that true honor was visible only in the internal virtue that should direct all a man's actions. This notion of moral and rational control was much closer to Mr. Jackson's understanding of honorable behavior than the impetuous passion that informed his son's, but he did not condemn William for his actions on this occasion because of their common understanding of what it meant to be a gentleman. Like an increasing number of men, however, Mr. Jackson conducted his public disputes with his pen rather than with a pistol—although the many passionate denunciations of injustices committed against him by the East India Company reveal that the ardor that inflamed his son burned close beneath the surface of his more "civilized" approach.[11]

MR. JACKSON'S SENSE of personal injustice was equally exercised by his son's filial ingratitude in continuing to disobey him. In the warmer month of May, William found at least two opportunities to escape from his father's authority, and on another occasion he stole from the house in the dead of night and vanished for five days. The result of these nights of pleasure was a recurrence of venereal disease that required more money and time to cure. During the day, William resorted to his favorite fashionable haunts. Unfortunately, Jane Jackson was driving along Bond Street in the family coach when she spotted William strolling modishly along with a Cyprian on his arm. To Jackson, William's behavior was even more shocking because he was accompanying a woman of known easy virtue "in the broad face of day, with the eyes of the world upon you, without any sense of shame, of common decency . . . or of anything honourable or virtuous."[12]

Unable to bear this constant clash of views, William left Gloucester Place, without permission, to stay with friends. "I have, Sir, unfortunately for myself, a spirit, which ill accords with your disposition and for that reason I left your house," he explained. Staying with his wealthy young friends, however, produced precisely the kind of undesirable behavior his father feared most. Moralists and middle-class parents were well aware of the ill effects of peer pressure, which was viewed as an inherent danger to the moral development of young men. As Isaac Taylor warned in *Advice to the Teens*, "The known effect of association is assimilation. We grow . . . like to those in whose company we are often found." The fear was, as Taylor put it in 1818, that "since youth has seldom courage enough to venture upon gross sin alone," bad company was all too frequently the cause of personal destruction, a point Jackson reiterated on many occasions.[13]

William's efforts to bolster his own battered self-esteem by boasting of more sexual conquests—particularly a rash claim made to his friends that he had seduced Miss Valpy, the Reading headmaster's daughter—produced salacious gossip that caused more bitter acrimony between father and son. William heatedly denied the gossip to his father, but Mr. Jackson stopped paying William an allowance and threatened for the first time to involve the law to control his behavior. If William would not stop his wicked ways, Jackson would deliver a petition to the Lord Chancellor describing his son's outrageous behavior. That he did not then do so at this point in time remained a matter of profound regret to Jackson for the rest of his life.

Once again it was Jane Jackson, at William's request, who managed to effect a reconciliation between father and son. William returned home and promised that he would never stay away from home again without his father's permission and that he would accompany his parents on their summer holiday to Upton. As a reward for this avowed submission to paternal authority, Jackson doubled William's allowance to £24 a year. The provision of a suitable allowance was of great social significance: in *An Enquiry into The Duties of Men*, Thomas Gisborne declared in 1811 that it was a father's responsibility to fix his son's "rank and annual expenditure" at the right level. This should be

> about the middle point of the scale established by custom for persons whose future prospects are similar to his own. . . . To fix them lower is to teach him to think himself treated with unkindness, and authorised to endeavour to maintain the station which he conceives to belong to him, without being very scrupulous as to the methods of accomplishing his purpose.[14]

Had William left with his parents on July 1 and remained under their roof, £24 would have represented a not ungenerous sum for a gentleman's son, but it was not nearly enough to support a gentleman living independently in London—for that he would need ten times as much. Because Mr. Jackson deeply resented William's attempts to achieve filial independence, he had no intention of allowing him to live separately at seventeen, and the allowance was clearly intended to maintain paternal control. Instead of joining his parents in the Windsor coach for the journey to Upton, however, William sent a note explaining that he was "transacting business" that would detain him until the following week; he then failed to appear again until the end of July, when the next installment of his allowance was due. On arrival, he successfully deflected his father's anger by announcing that he had taken a paid position with a lawyer. While this was at least a step in the direction that his father wished him to go, it also meant that William achieved his aim of living as an independent gentleman about town.[15]

MR. AND MRS. JACKSON remained in the country throughout the summer months, during which time William made only two brief visits: to collect his allowance and to join them for a day's racing at Epsom. Without his parents' presence to prevent his overindulgence, and with only a nominal amount of actual employment—his work with two solicitors was swiftly terminated in both cases—William was free to go shopping and enjoy all the pleasures of life in London with his friends. In *Advice to the Teens,* Taylor warned that keeping "on a par with . . . a connexion with whom you are obliged to associate" was a danger for youths fresh from school; but aiming "to be head of the set" was an even worse ambition, for "notions of what belongs to a young gentleman to do, or to have or to spend, are very apt to take a sudden and extraordinary swell." A young man, warned Taylor, should "never aim to dash [appear dashing]," but this was precisely what William aimed to do.[16]

The acquisition of all the essential accoutrements for a gentleman was William's top priority, and in the same manner as his fashionable friends, he was not overly concerned about how he manipulated the system of long-term credit to obtain them. In just a few short months, William wrote copious credit notes and signed numerous bills, spending prodigious amounts of money with a large number of tailors, hatters, boot makers, watchmakers, gunsmiths, wine merchants, and other tradesmen. The hire of suitably elegant horses and carriages added half as much again to the bills, and then there was the odd night in a hotel and his bookmaker to pay. In addition, he would have had to buy tickets to the theater, opera, assemblies, pleasure gardens, balls, and masquerades that made up the round of fashionable social life. And he almost certainly paid much more (in cash) for the unrecorded services of various high-class prostitutes to accompany him and entertain him through the night. Because his allowance would not even begin to cover such a lifestyle, he had to borrow from his friends so that he ran up debts totaling nearly £800—more than even most comfortably well-off gentlemen could hope to earn in a year. Yet as William knew only too well, nearly all of those from whom he bought goods or borrowed money assumed that his wealthy father would eventually foot the bill.[17]

By law, even the most parsimonious father was obliged to support his son financially until he reached the age of twenty-one. He was deemed liable for all his son's "necessary" purchases; but what goods could actually be deemed necessary was determined by the social status of the family. William and his father had completely different views about what fashionable items were essential for maintaining the honor and status of a young gentleman. Because most items were bought by signing written notes rather than using hard cash, it was not difficult for William to obtain what he wanted simply by signing his name—or a version of it that looked very similar to his father's.

Credit was as ubiquitous in Georgian England as it is now, but the line between the use and criminal misuse of it was dangerously blurred. Most tradesmen, eager to close a sale and knowing that Mr. Jackson was a very wealthy gentleman, were not overly concerned about supplying his son with anything he wanted; they assumed Jackson would eventually be obliged to pay for it. The extension of credit, in an age before it was possible to verify a customer's financial status through a phone call or an electronic card, relied on personal reputation and worked in a similar way to giving a gift—it created a reciprocal obligation in the purchaser to repay the favor. Mr. Jackson regarded his signature as sacrosanct: a man's personal reputation rested on the sanctity of his signature and the guarantee of payment that it conveyed. Any lack of clarity, therefore, was in his view immoral and both imperiled his own position and undermined the system of paper credit that supported this vibrant commercial society.[18]

But William's sense of honor was based entirely on an elite fashionable code that was at best amoral in the eyes of many contemporaries. As Theophilus Christian had lamented in *The Fashionable World Displayed* (1804), the code of honor followed by those who lived in that world did not require its practitioners to look too deeply into the means by which they acquired goods. Granting credit also required the retailer to enter into a relationship of trust with the customer. That so many were prepared to do so with William was a further mark of social distinction, which served only to confirm his own sense of his identity as an honorable gentleman.

These differences became starkly obvious in September when Mr. Jackson received a letter from Thomas Mortimer, a renowned London gun maker, claiming that William had purchased a pair of dueling pistols for 28 guineas that he had not paid for. In William's eyes, the purchase of a pair of exquisite pistols meant that he had acquired supremely fashionable accessories that also signified a willingness to fight a duel—the pistols were thus clear evidence of his favored social status and, in part, defined what it meant to be a gentleman. William had passed his first test of honor against Henry Keighly and meant it to be known about town that he was now of an age and rank to challenge anyone who questioned his veracity or his courage.[19]

Mr. Jackson, however, viewed the purchase as an unforgivable exercise in unnecessary extravagance and accused Mortimer of being far too careless in granting credit to a youth under eighteen years of age. The gun maker had agreed to give William six weeks' credit because the family grocer verified William's identity as Jackson's son, and he had seen him enter the house at Gloucester Place, which confirmed the family's wealthy status. But the grocer had not guaranteed William's reputation, and his father had not given permission for the purchase. "It is solely owing to the facility with which boys of the present age can obtain goods from men in business by fallacious statements that so many of them are brought to ruin," Jackson berated the grocer. Worse still, "it induces them to bid defiance to parental authority and leads them into dissipation and vice."[20]

Thomas Mortimer was an experienced tradesman—one of three brothers from a famous gun-making family who regularly supplied royalty—and once he realized Jackson had a good legal case for refusing payment, he switched tactics. He threatened to accuse William of swindling on the grounds that Jackson would surely pay rather than see his son publicly arrested and shamed in a criminal court case; or he would sue the poor grocer for misrepresenting William's character. John Evelyn joined Jackson in reviewing all the evidence and questioned William at length about his actions. William was adamant that he had done no wrong and should have his credit extended, but admitted that he was in serious debt and had already been threatened with civil action by other tradesmen. Evelyn once more supported his nephew and convinced Jackson to resist all Mortimer's threats. The gun maker withdrew in the face of such opposition.[21]

The combination of unpaid debts and his insistence on walking around town wearing dueling pistols, however, proved far more dangerous for William. He was almost certainly worried that he might be threatened by one of his many creditors, particularly those from whom he had borrowed large sums, but walking ready-armed meant that the strict code of conduct for dueling that called for a delay while a challenge was issued and seconds arranged could be ignored. William's fears were realized at eleven o'clock one night in late October when he was suddenly confronted by four men in a dark street. William recognized his friend Read, who had helped him escape from debtors' court on more than one occasion by lending him money, but Read was angry that the favor had not been repaid. One of the men shouted, "Mr. Read, rush on, you are right!" At this signal all four ran toward William, who immediately drew his pistols and aimed at Read, calling for him to stand off or he would fire. Read stopped in his tracks, but one of the others stepped forward to reason with William, insisting that Read only "desired honourable satisfaction" and suggested that they adjourn to a coffee house to discuss the matter.

William could not refuse without losing face, so he surrendered his pistols and accompanied the men to a coffee house. But he could not settle the debt either, and to apologize before facing fire was to risk being accused of cowardice. Read decided to test his young opponent's nerve to the limit and demanded immediate satisfaction. Pride prevented William from asking for a delay, so he sent for a friend to act as his second and accompanied Read and his second to a lonely field near Devonshire Place. Read's second measured out a distance of just seven paces—much shorter than the ten or twelve usually recommended—but still William held his nerve and took his place opposite Read. On the second's signal both duelists took aim and fired simultaneously. Whether by accident or design, they both missed, and with honor satisfied, the two seconds managed to reach a mutual agreement so that no further shots were required.

That four men had forced a youth of seventeen to duel on short notice in the middle of the night was a "shameful business," declared a shocked John Evelyn when his nephew came to him for help the following day. William, still determined to keep up a show of bravado, tried to play down the significance of his "pop gun dispute" with Read, but he couldn't help feeling a certain pride that the duel had been reported in several newspapers. The newspaper-reading public, however, was more engaged with weeks of reports discussing the duel between the foreign secretary, Lord Canning, and the secretary of state for war, Lord Castlereagh. With such eminent role models before him, William had no doubts that he had taken the only honorable action in accepting the challenge. Mr. Read was considerably less content with the outcome. Having gained no financial satisfaction, he issued another challenge to William, and this gave the teenager rather more cause for concern. He wrote to his uncle, unsure of how to behave in such circumstances: his friends had advised him that he need not accept "for having given him one satisfaction must prove to the world that it cannot be any want of courage that prevents my again meeting him." Yet the pressure on William not to decline was intense.[22]

Aware of William's huge debts and the difficult situation he had gotten himself into, Evelyn at last persuaded Jackson that the only way to prevent William falling into further dishonor was to enroll him as an officer in the army and send him out of the country. William was therefore about to become an ensign in the British army, but even as the lowest-ranking officer he could not afford to be seen by his regiment to have refused a challenge. Such behavior would have earned him immediate social ostracism by his fellow officers. More concerned for William's immediate safety than his future honor, Evelyn instructed him not to accept the challenge and to keep himself concealed. Despite all William's bad behavior, Evelyn retained a great affection for his nephew and remained convinced that he would yet put his youthful follies behind him. He was a much more worldly man than Jackson, and he viewed life in less morally black and white terms than his old friend. "I do not think so badly of him," Evelyn explained to Jackson, "To get into the army is an object he has much at Heart, and I am much mistaken, if, when removed from his present associates, & placed among men of Honour, he do not yet turn out very well." Clearly, in Evelyn's eyes, the military code of honor was considerably better than that observed by men of fashion.[23]

SO IT WAS LARGELY due to John Evelyn's efforts that in early November 1809 Ensign Jackson found himself vomiting over the rail of a ship bound for Guernsey. He was on his way to join the Second Battalion of the Sixty-seventh South Hampshire Regiment of Foot stationed on the island, which was a Crown dependency in the English Channel of strategic importance because it lay just thirty miles from the Normandy coast of France. If the churning in his stomach was largely produced by stormy seas, William was also suffering the uneasy aftereffects of another near escape from his creditors, some of whom had pursued him all the way to the Southampton docks. It had taken considerable "dexterity" on his part to avoid the bailiffs' clutches and stow himself safely on board ship.

Jane Jackson was also ill. The recent threats to the life of her precious only child, combined with her utter dismay at the damage to his reputation caused by the creditors who continued to hammer on the door of Gloucester Place, had sucked away the reserves of energy necessary to fight off infection. Mr. Jackson, while horrified at the ever-increasing demands for money from him, determined to follow John Evelyn's example and take a positive view of William's departure for the army. Perhaps now that he was free from the influence of his "pretended friends" and settled in the career he had for so long set his heart on, he would at last begin to fulfill the high hopes his family and friends had once entertained for him. To that end, but without William's knowledge, Jackson began to take practical steps to ensure that his son could make an entirely fresh start in Guernsey. He instructed his solicitors to write to the attorney general of the island, Thomas de Saumarez, to engage the services of a respectable, professional lawyer to be on hand to defend William if any of his creditors tried to have him arrested during his service there. The laws in Guernsey, as in England, meant that a minor could not be held liable for his debts, so the attorney general was happy to reassure Mr. Jackson that the Guernsey Royal Courts would set aside any suits brought against him.[24]

That none of these honorable gentlemen felt any unease at helping William to evade the debt laws was also partly due to the fact that leaving the country to escape creditors was a widely acknowledged practice, which Parliament tacitly condoned in its frequent passage of partial amnesty acts that allowed thousands to later return. Notwithstanding his parliamentary position, Sir George Shee was equally happy to assist his wayward nephew in his new career. Shee drew on his eminent Anglo-Irish connections and wrote personally to the commander in chief of the Sixty-seventh and lieutenant governor of Guernsey, Sir John Doyle, warmly recommending William to his notice and providing an invaluable personal introduction.[25]

As William recovered from his stormy crossing in the comfort of McDougald's Hotel in St. Peter Port, his future looked set fair to improve at last. Safe from his creditors and with the welcome support and approval of both uncles and his father, who agreed to pay him an allowance of £100 per annum on top of his military pay, plus an introduction to the lieutenant governor that would ease his passage into the regiment and open the doors to elite Guernsey society, he was both happy and grateful to his family. He could now embark on the military career he had so long desired, proudly sporting the scarlet officer's uniform that gave him instant status in the town and made him an object of desire among the wealthy (and less-well-off) young women there.

The arrival of large numbers of British officers since Guernsey had been fortified to prevent a French invasion had made both a significant social and an economic impact on the town. Combined with the increasing wealth brought in by the port, their presence had encouraged the island's inhabitants to value the display of taste and fashionable style as a means to signify social status. The medieval stone streets of St. Peter Port wound their way up to areas lined with fine Georgian buildings and public spaces designed for conspicuous display and sociability, so that the port now rivaled English spa towns like Weymouth in appearance. A fine promenade at the New Ground, where bands played to attract the public, was a popular evening destination, but as one visitor explained, "The Naval and Military officers . . . were the real magnets . . . that drew the gaily dressed Belles."[26]

Within days of his arrival, William cheerfully reported that "the army surpasses even my expectations. We have a most excellent society, and a rubber of whist almost every evening with a ball once a week." Balls and suppers in honor of the garrison were held regularly in the town's assembly rooms, but entrance to these was strictly controlled by the most elite families, which "caused great heart-burnings" among the young. During William's first month on the island, Sir John Doyle invited him to a dinner party, a rout (an evening supper party with cards and conversation), and a ball, which was more than he did for most new officers. "I had the honour of dancing with the Governor's daughter at the ball," William proudly told his mother, "which has brought me quite into fashion," and "I have already been introduced to all the Beauties of the place—most of them girls of fortune."[27]

In *Pride and Prejudice,* Jane Austen portrayed the dangerous attraction of military men to young women through Lydia Bennett's unwise passion for Mr. Wickham, but the appeal of a military uniform had long exercised those moralists who feared its consequences were to increase young men's profligacy. In the essay "Hints to Young Men who are Designed for a Military or Naval Life," Vicesimus Knox had railed against "the irresistible charms of a piece of scarlet broad cloth" that frequently encouraged puerile vanity and excessive expenditure in those who had been commissioned too early in life. Knox described how the new young soldier

> dresses, he drinks, he blusters, he spends his money, he ruins his constitution and his peace; but the compensation for all this is, that he is a favourite of the ladies; and really in this his ultimate object he often succeeds; for too many of them, who are as weak as himself, are ready to run wild at the sight of a red coat.[28]

Within a fortnight of William's arrival in Guernsey, Thomas de Saumarez reported sadly that William's "late escape in England has not made him more cautious . . . and that from the dashing way I am told he goes on, his expenses certainly must exceed any allowance, tho' ever so liberal, that can be made him by his father." The attorney general felt that William now stood in immediate need of "some serious advice." To that end, he wrote to Jackson's solicitors offering to stand *in loco parentis* and to solicit paternal advice from Guernsey's governor:

> Having a family myself, I feel as a father, and would willingly do for Mr. Jackson, what I do not doubt from the character you give this gentleman, he would do for me. . . . I am intimately acquainted with our worthy Commander in Chief, Sir John Doyle, who on all occasions, has proved the Father and Friend of the younger part of

the military; and, on the least hint, he will, I am sure, join me in pointing out to the young man, the ridicule of his wishing to soar over his Brother officers, and of his continuing a conduct, which they themselves must laugh at, and must ultimately, if persisted in, prove his ruin.[29]

Gentry fathers commonly resorted to utilizing friends, relatives, and professionals as surrogate fathers when their sons left home to take their first steps toward independence, and Mr. Jackson accepted de Saumarez's offer with alacrity. He wrote at length describing William's failure to fulfill his youthful promise and his fears for his child's future if he did not stop his extravagant behavior. "For every transaction will be scanned by men of honour; and to gain their esteem, or even to mix in their society, he must act" with "honour and honesty" and not excite the envy or ill will of his brother officers.[30]

The attorney general was a devout, compassionate man who delighted in parenting his huge brood of twenty-seven children (of whom at least nine died young). He reassured Jackson that he had long "considered young persons, deprived of the presence of their parents, to have some claim on my protection," and would do all he could to advise William. De Saumarez went further and enlisted the help of the commanding officer of the Sixty-seventh Regiment, Major Sullivan, a man who had "always taken great pains with the young men belonging to it." It was common for the head of a military corps to be considered "the father of the family, so to speak," and to oversee the behavior of the "brother officers within it." Hence, William remained entirely unaware of his own father's intervention when Major Sullivan called on him for a private talk about the necessity of "retrenching his expenses," and he solemnly guaranteed that his future expenditure would never exceed his allowance. Both the major and the attorney general were impressed with William's "good heart" and assured Mr. Jackson that he need not worry further about his son.[31]

News of William's disastrous debts in England, however, had seeped into St. Peter Port soon after his arrival. Locals whispered about the danger of trusting the dashing young officer who had brought a personal servant to accompany him into his regiment. The purchase of a fine horse meant that William could gallop the five miles from Doyle Barracks to St. Peter Port with ease to indulge in all his favorite social and retail pastimes, and initially, while he was armed with a full purse, this presented few problems. But inevitably the money dripped from his fingers with alarming speed and his debts on the island began to mount. Equally inevitably, he believed that this was not his fault: the regiment's paymaster was reluctant to advance him his allowance; he had to pay to furnish his room at the barracks with carpet and curtains; he had been robbed in a public house; the horse, he conceded, was a minor extravagance, but he retained his manservant despite his father's fierce opposition. Most importantly, he needed to dress like an officer and a gentleman to maintain his status and honor. "You <u>must</u> be aware," William challenged his father,

> of the expense attending an officer's dress, and I am bold to confess I did not conceive that you intended me to discharge these <u>necessary</u> expenses out of my allowance, which, acting even with the greatest economy, I must submit it to you, if one can dress like a gentleman much under that sum.[32]

The thorny question of William's status and condition in life was thus once more at the heart of the dispute between father and son. In fact, William could have supported his claim with the commonly cited legal decision of Lord Chief Justice Kenyon, who had declared it "necessary" for "the honour and credit of his station" that a young officer purchase livery for his manservant (although not cockades for his soldiers). But by May 1810, Mr. Jackson had suffered assaults from William's creditors for more than six months, and his house in Gloucester Place had been transformed into a "scene of uproar, confusion and tumult, by the daily ingress of persons" he had never met before demanding money for purchases his son had made. His patience was at an end, and so was his willingness to support his son on the road to ruin. "No consideration shall induce me (not even you, who was once the nearest and dearest to my heart) to surrender my property to the vilest and most unworthy of purposes" he declared in a letter to William, "much you have to answer for—but God, I hope will forgive you."[33]

When de Saumarez informed Mr. Jackson that William had been arrested for debt by a Guernsey tavern keeper a few days later, the father resolved to take drastic action. He wrote to the attorney general asking him to ensure that, notwithstanding his age, William was sent to prison. He hoped that imprisonment might put an end to the dangerous "ideas of independence" his teenage son had imbibed. Because lenience had singularly failed to have any effect, it was now necessary for William to "suffer, and severely too, in his person." Jackson explained to de Saumarez that "however painful such a proceeding may be to my feelings it is a sacred duty which I owe to him & myself, to stop him . . . by the exercise of severity, since measures of moderation are of no effect." Therefore, William must be confined "until he shall have had time to reflect upon the dangerous Errors and Follies of his Conduct, and until with contrition he shall express a determination to amend." Only then, and without William's knowledge, would Jackson authorize his release through the repayment of the debt and reimburse de Saumarez accordingly for the legal costs incurred for arresting and imprisoning a debtor.[34]

On the European Continent, paying for the private imprisonment of an immoral or a profligate relative to protect a family's wealth and reputation was a not uncommon occurrence. But imprisonment without trial was an assault on fabled English liberties and the fairness of the English justice system, so there were no such facilities available to desperate parents in the British Isles. It was not unknown, however, for sons to be confined to debtors' prison because a father wanted to teach them a harsh lesson. In *Tom & Jerry: Life in London* (1821), Pierce Egan penned a catchy verse about a debtors' prison where "There walks a youth, whose father, for reform, / Has shut him up where countless vices swarm." Egan thus clearly regarded confining profligate sons in prisons with hardened debtors as a hazardous undertaking.[35]

There is no record of how William reacted to his imprisonment or how long it lasted, but there is evidence to prove that it did little to curb his behavior, which continued much as before. Dining in the officers' mess was a generally convivial experience that William engaged in with some relish—his brother officers were mostly "Irish but very pleasant fellows." In addition to pride in their appearance and adherence to a strict code of honor that regulated disputes over everything from minor aspersions of character and imaginary slights, to quarrels over debts and women, there was a strong culture of heavy drinking among officers.

They tended to consume considerable quantities of wine and brandy rather than the rum and spirit downed by common soldiers, but whereas the latter were frequently harshly disciplined for drunkenness, the officer who could hold his liquor without showing any ill effects was lionized. Army medical officers were divided over whether alcohol was bad or beneficial—many thought wine was therapeutic and believed even strong beer to be nourishing. Hence, as one regimental surgeon explained, "In the army, where so much conviviality reigns . . . to avoid intoxification, and even frequent intoxification, is no easy task."[36]

For an eighteen-year-old anxious to prove his military manhood, this was an impossible task. Without a horse to convey him swiftly to St. Peter Port, and as his money and credit with local traders ran out, William increasingly turned to alcoholic amusements with his fellow officers. Life in an army barracks that was not situated in enemy territory was often dull and fairly tedious, with little to do but attend parade twice a day and occasionally mount a guard. Doyle Barracks were situated on L'Ancresse Common; its gray granite walls squatted on the top of a hill overlooking a broad expanse of flat open land that in poor weather provided a bleak prospect for the fourteen officers and three hundred men stationed there. Its distance from any habitation that young recruits would consider interesting only added to the sense of isolation, and without an immediate enemy to face, military discipline sometimes fell short of ideal.[37]

William was one of several British officers and men whose behavior caused problems for the Guernsey governor in the spring and summer of 1810, and at least two of the officers were his friends. The Sixty-seventh Regiment was involved in an unfortunate fracas with the Guernsey militia in April, during which a high-ranking militia officer was injured. It had proved "difficult to restrain the men" of the Sixty-seventh, one division of which had behaved with particularly "unsoldier like conduct," for which Sir John Doyle had an officer arrested. Later that summer Doyle complained that, although the Sixty-seventh maintained a "very good appearance in the field . . . the conduct of the soldiers in quarters was indifferent." The reputation of British forces on Guernsey was further undermined when one of William's friends, from whom he borrowed funds, was arrested for "unofficer like and unmilitary conduct and neglect of duty."[38]

Lieutenant George Leabon had been on duty in charge of the Pier Guard in St. Peter Port when six soldiers abducted and raped a local woman in the strong room of the guardhouse. Two of the guards were executed, and four others were banished under Guernsey law. The victim claimed that Leabon himself had taken her into his room and offered her a drink while pointing a sword at her breast, and that he had refused to heed her cries when the soldiers carried her down into the strong room. At his court-martial in July, Leabon declared that he thought his men had arrested a drunken prostitute and that he had been called away to deal with another disturbance caused by sailors in the town. He did admit he had made an error of judgment in leaving the guardhouse, but, as William so often did, he fought hard to defend his honor. He strenuously denied that he would ever refuse to "protect a helpless female," for to do so could result in social ostracism. In the same month that Leabon faced disgrace at his court-martial, William, too, found himself subject to military justice over a matter he considered an affront to his honor.[39]

Colonel Prevost, commanding officer of the Second Battalion of the Sixty-seventh, had ordered that William and another young officer, Lieutenant Greenwell, be arrested (and confined to barracks) for an "irregularity." On hearing of William's arrest, Doyle sent for William and, adopting a paternal stance, delivered a mild admonition while recommending that he write a letter of apology to Colonel Prevost. Skilled as he was by much practice in composing such letters, on his return William wrote contritely to the commander, whom both he and Doyle assumed would immediately order a release. Prevost did not at once comply, and William, feeling severely slighted, began drinking in the orderly room one evening to drown his sorrows. At this point, William would have done well to heed the advice given in the *Soldier's Monitor*, which was issued to most new recruits and warned, "Intemperance, wherever it prevails, destroys a Man's Reason, Honour, and Conscience at once, and opens a wide Gap for any Sin or Folly to make its Entrance. . . . A very child exceeds him in strength and an Idiot is his equal in Discretion."[40]

The wine soon fueled William's anger, humiliation, and frustration at being confined. He began pacing violently up and down the room, and by one o'clock in the morning the sleeping barracks were disturbed by the sound of shattering glass as William began breaking windows. The noise woke Colonel Prevost, who listened in disbelief that such a disturbance could occur in his barracks and, still in his nightdress, sent for Adjutant Moyle to deal with the situation. Moyle, an experienced noncommissioned officer, thought he could get William back to his quarters, but on opening the orderly room door and conveying the colonel's orders to William, he met with considerably more violent resistance than he expected. In a drunken rage, William shouted that he "did not care a damn" about the adjutant, the colonel, or "any man that would order him to such a dark dungeon as this."[41]

As William continued his intemperate rant, Moyle sent for assistance, but before the guard arrived, Lieutenant Greenwell appeared on the scene in a state of intoxication almost as great as William's. "Mr. Jackson should not go to his room until he knows for what," declared the young officer, who was as offended as William that a noncommissioned officer who had risen from the ranks should challenge a gentleman. Moyle stepped forward to take hold of William, but the two young officers pushed him back. Sober and stronger than the drunken young men, Moyle easily threw them both aside. Greenwell came up sparring, but Moyle grabbed his elbow and tripped him up. Incensed at this assault on his dignity as much as his person, Greenwell ran to his room and returned armed with a poker, shouting, "Where is the rascal!" But his fury dissipated somewhat after the guards arrived and removed the poker from his drunken grip, so he returned to his room without further resistance.

Heartened by his friend's spirited defense of his honor and fired by a fury born of drink, William's discretion deserted him and he launched himself at Moyle as soon as the guards were out of sight. The adjutant expertly deflected the attack and threw William onto his back. Undaunted, William got up and flew at Moyle again with the same results. After his third unsuccessful attempt to knock Moyle down, William ran off along the dark passages of the barracks, hotly pursued by the armed guards. With his blundering gait and drink-impaired sense of direction, it did not take long for the guards to catch up with William and carry him back to his room. Moyle banged the door shut and placed sentries outside his and Greenwell's rooms, but William had no intention of giving up. He broke the window and tried to climb out of it to escape. On failing to achieve this objective, he pissed defiantly through the shattered panes instead. Then he began hammering on the door with a pair of heavy bellows, hurling abusive names at Moyle and shouting about how he "was born a gentleman and not sprung from the ranks" like the lowly adjutant. Moyle forced the door open again and wrested the bellows from William's hands. Undaunted, William picked up a poker, then tongs, and even a fender (a fire guard) in his frantic efforts to hit Moyle, who merely threw the teenager down on his back after every attempt. The noise drew another officer to the scene, who offered to see his now-winded fellow officer to bed. Moyle withdrew as William consented to be helped up by his similar-ranking companion. With peace restored in William's room, Moyle went to check on Greenwell, only to discover that the door to his room had been "completely destroyed" by the equally indignant and inebriated officer.

The following morning, Colonel Prevost, incensed at this breakdown in military discipline, demanded that both William and Greenwell hand in their resignations. However commendable the ability to drink heavily without ill effect might be regarded in the officers' mess, behaving badly when drunk was a serious offense. Prevost had not, however, reckoned on the deep sense of offended honor felt by both young men at the treatment they had received from a subordinate officer the night before. They complained to Governor Doyle of their unfair handling and insisted on pressing charges against Adjutant Moyle for striking them without provocation. A regimental court of inquiry found the charges to be groundless, but Doyle discovered that there had been some irregularity in the proceedings, and insisting on scrupulously fair justice, he instructed a garrison court of inquiry to hear the matter again.

The verdict was again in Moyle's favor, and there the matter might have rested had not two other soldiers from the ranks of the Sixty-seventh spotted an opportunity to profit from the disarray among their officers and escape from their service in the British army. The two men claimed that William and Greenwell had offered them money and the opportunity to desert their posts in return for testifying that Adjutant Moyle had attempted to bribe them to testify in his favor at the court of inquiry. Doyle ordered an immediate judicial inquiry and called in de Saumarez to oversee the proceedings. The attorney general and

Major Heron, second in command of the regiment, sat for two days sifting through evidence and hearing witness testimony, at the conclusion of which de Saumarez was relieved to inform Mr. Jackson that William, Greenwell, and Moyle had all been cleared of suspicion of involvement in the matter. The two soldiers were immediately prosecuted, but de Saumarez and Doyle were rather more concerned about what to do with William, because they had both promised his father that they would protect his interests.[42]

De Saumarez had already warned Mr. Jackson that William appeared to lack "that subordination so necessary in the army; and to have ideas of independence, which ill suit the profession he has got into." Now both he and Doyle were convinced that Guernsey was "a most improper place to continue in," not least because William had run up debts of £260; yet this in itself was a major impediment to him leaving the island while his creditors were seeking reimbursement. Keen to prevent any further embarrassment to the British army in Guernsey, both Doyle and de Saumarez used their influence in the island to convince William's creditors to let him leave. To effect this agreement, both men had to personally guarantee that the money from the sale of his commission in London would be used to settle his debts in Guernsey. It was a mark of the high esteem in which Doyle and de Saumarez were held that William found himself free to return to London without having to involve his father in paying any more debts and despite his disgraceful dismissal.[43]

William's military career had been brief and inglorious, but the Sixty-seventh Regiment had also lost three officers in the course of a single month. In addition, four soldiers had been banished, two were hung, and two more were prosecuted for perjury. The regiment's reputation on the island was clearly in danger, and William claimed that as a result Doyle was obliged to arrange for the regiment to be transferred to Gibraltar within weeks of Lieutenant Leabon's disgrace. The Second Battalion of the Sixty-seventh went on to serve with honors at Barrossa during Wellington's Peninsular Campaign but was disbanded in 1817. The three disgraced officers—William, Greenwell, and Leabon—all made their way to London, where they tried to rebuild their lives and finances without abandoning the style they were used to living in.[44]

The difficulties of achieving this aim meant that Doyle and de Saumarez found their kindness to William had been misplaced, for three months later no money from the sale of the commission had reached them. A polite inquiry to Mr. Jackson's solicitors revealed that William had directed the money from the sale to be paid to himself. However, the lawyers assured the governor and the attorney general that Mr. Jackson was rectifying the situation at that very moment, and "from the tenor of Mr. Jackson's letter we fear his son, should he not comply with his father's wishes, will repent it to the end of his life."[45]

BOARDING THE FLEET

London Debtors' Prisons, 1810–1812

It might . . . be denominated a small map of London; or
a peep behind the curtain into the artifices, trick, fraud,
deception, ingenuity, and low cunning exercised by the
DEBTORS of the Metropolis, who have had the "best" of
their creditors out of doors, and who now assemble . . .
to make them have the "worst of it"; or, in other words,
ultimately saddling their creditors with the whole of the
law expenses.

— The Fleet Prison, as depicted in Pierce Egan,
  Tom & Jerry: Life in London (1821)

M r. Jackson's ultimatum was delivered to William as he lay languishing in a hotel bed burning with fever and contemplating repentance. The Garrick's Head Tavern in Bow Street was a more salubrious place to reside than many of the more notorious public houses in Covent Garden, but it lay close to the clamorous market and almost directly opposite the Theatre Royal, which noisily disgorged its wealthy patrons after every performance. This was the signal for a battery of carriages to jostle their way to the steps, the shouts of drivers competing with the cries of linkboys, whose flaming torches guided theatergoers to coaches for hire, and the shouts of Bow Street officers attempting to maintain order.

A few weeks earlier, the Garrick's Head had seemed the ideal location for a pleasure-seeking young gentleman desirous of frequenting the many brothels, taverns, coffee houses, and theaters in the area. But the wages of sin had caught up with William remarkably quickly. He was deeply mired in debt and had no way of paying the nightly fee of 1 guinea to stay there, or of procuring food or clothing. His liaisons with prostitutes had caused a recurrence of the venereal disease, and the onset of a feverish cold had further weakened his constitution. An eminent doctor who had previously attended him at Gloucester Place wrote to his father in early October stressing that William's urgent removal from the hotel and the provision of proper care in a more peaceful environment were essential for his recovery.[1]

In response, Jackson had demanded that William revoke the order directing payment for the sale of his military commission to himself so that the money could be used to pay his debts on Guernsey and free the governor and attorney general from their obligation to pay them for him. Failure to comply would signal the end of all paternal financial aid, when "nothing on earth shall induce me to . . . rescue you from the jaws of a prison." Because William had only just escaped from the notorious debtors' side of Newgate prison and was in dire danger of being returned there, immediate compliance and complete repentance seemed his only option.[2]

THE ROAD TO NEWGATE had been paved with poor judgment and even worse advice. When he left Guernsey in August 1810, William avoided facing his parents by going to stay with an army friend in Weymouth. From there he tried to negotiate the immediate purchase of another commission in a regiment serving abroad. He sent his drinking companion, the hapless Lieutenant Greenwell, to deliver a letter notifying his parents of that plan, hoping to deflect his father's anger at discovering that he had been forced to give up his commission in the Sixty-seventh. Self-preservation was clearly uppermost in his mind, for he was now in danger of being arrested by his old creditors in London and chased by those in Guernsey, who were only temporarily held at bay by de Saumarez and Sir John Doyle.

William's options were exhausted: like many a harassed debtor before him, he would have to leave the country, yet to do so, he still needed an income. The scale of his debts on both sides of the Channel meant that only one set of creditors could be appeased by the sale of his commission, and if he did that, he would have nothing left with which to purchase another commission. He reasoned, quite correctly as it turned out, that his father would refuse to purchase a second commission, having made him swear never to relinquish the first. But in his anxiety about his own position, he had not considered the disastrous consequences for the governor and attorney general in Guernsey if he defaulted on more than £250 debts there or the ensuing shame and dishonor it would bring upon his father and both his uncles.

Concealing his return from his parents also proved to be an unwise move. Mr. Jackson was deeply indignant—he expected a dutiful son to visit his family immediately upon arrival, not least to explain why he had left his military post so soon. Instead, the first that Jackson heard of William's return was from a Guernsey creditor who had made his way to Gloucester Place. When William wrote again, he provided only the barest explanation of the problems that had befallen the Sixty-seventh in Guernsey, and he did not reveal the reasons that he now needed to join a regiment "on <u>actuall</u> [*sic*] service." Worse, he lied about his whereabouts, pretending that he was still in Weymouth and causing Mr. Jackson to believe that his request for a transfer was another ruse to obtain more money.[3]

In fact, William was concealing his true situation because he and Greenwell were confined in a private debtors' lockup in the City.* They wrote letters to every friend and acquaintance they could think of in an attempt to raise the two bails necessary to secure their release, but of the fifty letters William sent, only one produced an offer to stand bail for him. Every hour he remained in the lockup dramatically

---

* The City was the area within the boundaries of medieval London that stretched for a square mile around St. Paul's Cathedral and contained the capital's major law courts and financial institutions.

increased the amount of money he would have to pay for the privilege of being detained there. At nineteen years of age, William now found himself caught in the labyrinthine system of debt law, a machine manipulated by myriad people who profited from the principle of proceeding against the body of the debtor before proceeding against his property.

Campaigners for changes to the debt law were vociferous in their condemnation of this "system of extortions," a process that began the moment a bailiff arrested the debtor and charged a fee for doing so. Those genteel or desperate enough tried to delay their entry to prison by using a lockup or sponging house to raise money to settle with their creditors or to find bail. Once debtors were inside a prison, the chances of arranging their affairs decreased dramatically and the terrifying possibility of perpetual imprisonment loomed into view. Yet it was well known that once debtors were inside a sponging house, "the expences [sic] increase daily, like an overwhelming torrent." While writing begging letters in a barred room, the miserable debtor was plied with food and prodigious quantities of alcohol to drown his sorrows, all of which had to be paid for. Meanwhile, the owner of the house checked the validity of each bail offered, which he rarely hurried to do since his profits increased the longer the unwilling debtor remained. In addition, the debtor had to fund the cost of two officers and men, an attorney, and a writ and other legal fees. If he could not raise bail, he had to save at least £10 just to cover the cost of being transferred to prison—preferably the more salubrious King's Bench Prison or Fleet Prison—or risk being rendered to the debtors' side of Newgate, where on average one thousand poor debtors without funds were sent each year. Not surprisingly, officers delivered many of the inmates of sponging houses to prison in a state of serious intoxication.[4]

The chief purpose of arresting a man for debt was to terrorize him into taking any action possible to settle with his creditors or to "torture the consciences" of his friends and family into doing so. When William had exhausted all efforts to seek help from friends, Greenwell suggested they contact an attorney named Poole, who had assisted William before. Poole operated on the fringes of his profession and was one of those associates Mr. Jackson demanded that William never contact again. Poole had acted for William many times during his

London spending spree the previous summer and, according to William, had advised him to stay away from his father. In an effort to escape prison himself, the wily attorney had secured his young client's loyalty by getting him drunk and persuading him to accept a bill for £180, thus leaving William at risk of being called upon to pay the sum at any time.[5]

Poole had also introduced William to the infamous "Jew King," an enormously wealthy and successful money broker who specialized in negotiating deals to lend money to impoverished young heirs and improvident aristocrats. Despite his impecunious Jewish origins, King threw lavish dinners attended by the highest echelons of society, which ensured he gained inside knowledge of their financial dealings. He was widely condemned as an unprincipled rogue and a swindler—much like loan sharks today—yet he frequently did business with respectable propertied men wanting to earn high interest by loaning money anonymously to avoid charges of usury. King also regularly rescued titled gentlemen, MPs, and even royalty from financial embarrassment.[6]

His amoral approach to money was largely informed by the contempt with which he viewed the morals of his elite clients, who defaulted on their loans whenever they could. He also complained at length about the number of public school boys who quickly learned "all the mysteries of borrowing at high interest" but even more quickly "the mode of cancelling the obligation afterwards." Despite his notorious reputation, King was never short of clients, and in 1811 the satirical magazine *The Scourge; or, Monthly Expositor of Imposture and Folly* congratulated him on the many "schemes of comprehensive fraud which he had conceived with so much ingenuity." To Mr. Jackson's horror, Poole had persuaded William to become one of those privileged but desperately gullible young men who borrowed from King.[7]

Mr. Poole, no doubt scenting another profitable arrangement, arrived at the lockup within half an hour of receiving William's note and paid the bail to secure the immediate release of both young men. Attorneys like Poole were often connected with equally unscrupulous men who hired themselves out to provide bail, a practice that was also widely condemned by those not desperate enough to need their services. In order to hire a man to supply bail, the debtor "has to pay most exorbitantly, and every sort of villany [*sic*] and iniquity is practiced upon him," warned attorney James Pearce, in his *Treatise on the Abuses of the Laws of Arrest* (1814), adding that a bail had the right to turn the debtor over to the law at any time.

> A man, therefore, when connected with this description of people, is never safe, for, after having paid them their own charges and what the defendant considers is for the job altogether, he is constantly visited by them, and unless he gives them money, they threaten to get rid of their responsibility by rendering him.[8]

IN ACCEPTING POOLE'S help to pay his bail, William found himself bound to the attorney once more and at risk of being returned to prison at any time. Any relief at having secured seasoned legal aid was also tempered by the fact that William was obliged to follow Poole's none-too-scrupulous advice and to pay handsomely for his services. That advice consisted of persuading William to deny the validity of all his Guernsey creditors' claims so that they could not apply to his army agents, Cox and Greenwood, for relief against the cost of his commission. It also included another prohibition against William contacting or visiting his father. It was not until the attorney had completed his task in the middle of August that William finally returned to Gloucester Place.[9]

Mr. Jackson, already insulted that William should have taken another's advice before his own, was immediately suspicious of which "well-versed" solicitor William had employed and warned him yet again against taking bad counsel. Jackson also reminded his son that, even though he was still legally under age, taking the king's commission (i.e., becoming an officer) meant that he would now be widely regarded as independent from his father's authority. The meeting ended when Jackson declared that he would not purchase another commission if he discovered that William had lost his first through vice or extravagance. Because Thomas de Saumarez had kept Jackson fully informed of William's disastrous career in Guernsey, William's plans to escape from his creditors were doomed from the start.[10]

Two weeks later Mr. Jackson's worst fears were realized when William's uncle, Sir George Shee, received a letter from Sir John Doyle, lamenting that he had ever become involved with William and explaining that he and de Saumarez now stood to lose a great deal of money to pay his debts. "We both did everything in our power to keep him right," wrote Doyle. "If he were my own son I could not have felt more anxiety about him, and certainly I have never had so much trouble with any person in my life."[11]

Because Shee had written William's letters of recommendation, it now fell to him to persuade Jackson to take immediate action to prevent both the commander in chief and the attorney general of Guernsey from suffering a financial disaster. Mr. Jackson was utterly mortified. He asked John Evelyn to try to prevent William's army agents from selling his commission and giving him the money. Cox and Greenwood, one of the largest military agents and successful bankers, regretfully informed Evelyn that there was nothing they could do to counteract William's orders, particularly as he had employed a solicitor. On discovering the identity of the unscrupulous solicitor, Evelyn replied to Jackson in a despairing rage:

> This _ _ _ _ _ _ _ has got possession of him again and will never quit him, until he has completely ruined him—happy for himself, for you, and his afflicted mother, if he was no more. I feel for you, Jackson, but have no comfort or consolation to offer—it is a lost cause—and you must exert all your fortitude to bear it. You must do more—you must support his afflicted mother, who now has no resource but in your kindness and affection.[12]

Jackson immediately contacted his own solicitors to see if they could arrange an agreement with the army agents, but they were prevented from doing so when Cox and Greenwood called on the commander in chief of British forces, Sir David Dundas, for advice. Dundas declined to interfere and declared that because Ensign Jackson had ordered the agents not to honor his bills and asserted that he had complete control over his commission, they could only do as he instructed. The name of Jackson, and by implication those of Shee and Evelyn, too, had now been dishonored at the highest levels of military and civil government. Jackson wrote disconsolately to Shee, saying there was nothing more he could do, because to make himself responsible for his son's torrent of debts would swallow up his assets and result in his own imprisonment for debt. Worse than that, William had now "connected himself to some of the vilest wretches that London produces." The whole affair and the way that William had "tricked Sir John Doyle" appalled and sickened Jackson so deeply, he confessed to Evelyn, "that the door to my Heart with reference to him is shut forever."[13]

Immoral though his behavior undoubtedly was in the eyes of his family and wider society (although never in his own), William's desperation to escape his creditors drove him ever more frequently over the hazy line from immorality to criminality. He believed that if he could evade capture until his father died, the prospect of gaining a massive inheritance meant that he could justify having done so because he would then be able to pay off his debts. It was all too easy to reason that this would be better both for him and, in the long run, for his creditors too. Once he had money and property of his own, particularly his father's estate at Langley, he could reasonably expect not to be troubled by tradesman's bills more than once a year. Any propertied gentleman would disdain to pay any but the most trifling sums before Christmas each year, and few tradesmen would dare to ask—even then, many would accept payment on account. The chronic shortage of circulating cash meant that almost everyone, even those in the lower classes, lived on the expectation of extended credit, and many habitually negotiated to defer or deny repayment. Loss of reputation and personal credit, however, could bring an entire network of interlinked credit relations tumbling down, setting off a chain of prosecutions for debt.[14]

William was also freed of any sense of guilt because he was underage—he believed he was not legally responsible and should not be held to account for his debts by greedy tradesmen. He was certainly only one of numerous upper-class young men who exploited the uncertainty of their legal liability to acquire goods and credit, many of whom subsequently found themselves enmeshed in endless litigation. William's path from desperate debtor to "finished swindler," as Mr. Jackson saw it, was, as usual, marked with misfortune, mistrust, and adolescent arrogance.[15]

TOWARD THE END of an exceptionally fine and mild September, Jane Jackson received a letter from Lieutenant Greenwell claiming that "the danger I have been brought into by your son is of so heinous a nature" that she must help him. Since leaving the Sixty-seventh, he told her, William had caused him to spend more than £300, but he added earnestly that he "would never be lead away again as I have been by your son." Taking the letter entirely at face value, Mr. Jackson declared Greenwell was not the first "unwary and imbecile youth" that William had led astray.

But Greenwell had another reason for wanting Jane to help prevent William from being arrested: he was named as a co-defendant in the same writ. Greenwell's explanation was that William had hired a horse and gig from Joseph Moore, which he had then left at a livery stable as a guarantee against borrowing £10. He failed to pay back the sum, so the stable keeper refused to return them to Moore until the debt was paid. Moore could thus choose to have William arrested for the debt or for stealing the horse and carriage, a felony charge. Moore, like so many others, first tried to persuade William's father to settle the debt, but because he met with the same refusal as all of William's other creditors, he announced that he would go to Bow Street Police Office to press for a criminal prosecution. Yet what actually constituted a criminal act was often uncertain and subject to different interpretations according to the context in which the act was committed, so potential prosecutors carefully weighed up the relative merits of pursuing a civil or a criminal action according to which might prove most profitable for themselves.[16]

Moore evidently changed his mind soon after talking to Jackson and sought an action for debt against both William and Greenwell instead. Indeed, William claimed that it was Greenwell who had hired the gig. The ex-lieutenant had then left town, leaving William with two bills to be drawn on a city merchant should Moore demand payment while he was out of town, both of which were returned unpaid due to lack of funds. Greenwell had left London in good time, but William had not. He was arrested and conveyed to the very sponging house in Palsgrave Place from which he had been forced to rescue his former tutor Reverend Helps.[17]

Once more faced with the problem of raising bail, William turned to his favorite uncle, John Evelyn, apparently unaware that Evelyn felt the pain and shame he had caused Jane and Mr. Jackson so deeply

that he now bitterly regretted helping his nephew acquire a commission at all. Convinced by Poole, his solicitor, that he possessed an excellent defense in pleading his nonage, William wrote confidently,
assuring Evelyn that his creditors' claims would soon be declared
void; he just needed his uncle to stand bail by twelve o'clock that day
to keep him out of Newgate until a certificate of his birth could be
provided.

Evelyn replied coldly that, if there was "the slightest chance of
saving you from disgrace and ruin," he would have used his influence,
but as that was not the case, William would do better to rely on his
solicitor's advice. Yet Evelyn had other good reasons for not wanting
to help. Many debtors' relatives were reluctant to stand bail even if
they could afford it. Respectable gentlemen particularly objected to
having to go to court and wait among the dozens of shabby, shady-
looking men ready to offer hired bail to anyone they could, then having to answer intrusive questions from counsel regarding the extent of
their property. Worse still, they could remain liable for many years to
come, so if the debtor fled, they were often unaware that they were
personally at risk until they, or their property, was taken to cover the
debt. Such mishaps were so common that it was claimed some unfortunate bail found himself thrown into a sponging house on an almost
daily basis. Given William's habitual tendency to default, Evelyn
would have been foolish to stand bail for his nephew. He was also reluctant to offer any aid without Jackson's express wish that he do so,
and Mr. Jackson was determined not to help because he believed
William had at length met with his just desserts. Indeed, Jackson told
Evelyn it was

unfortunate for society that he was not long since under personal restraint. He has made others suffer quite enough, and it is high time
that he should be compelled to feel through his own sufferings. Were
there a spark of honourable principle in his nature with what happiness would I fly to his rescue! But I know him to be utterly abandoned in his conduct—his morals the most depraved—and inured to
vices which would lead him without hesitation to the commission of
every crime. Such a wretch ought not to be let loose on the world, and
I most deeply lament that he was not long since in his grave.[18]

The harshness of Jackson's last comment to Evelyn betrayed the depth of pain and shame into which William's behavior had plunged him, even as he sought to do the right thing for society. In his father's eyes, William had long ago ceased to be an unfortunate debtor who was to be pitied and had become a fraudulent debtor who should be punished—these were the terms by which society measured the degree of sympathy that should be extended to imprisoned debtors. Mr. Jackson had no comprehension of, or sympathy for, the desperate debtor, for whom the end justified any means of acquiring money.[19]

Hence to his horror, William found himself being delivered to the infamous Newgate jail in September 1810. London's forbidding principal prison for serious crime also had a section for debtors, the Common Side, which inspired dread in most debtors. It was an experience for which William's privileged upbringing had left him entirely unprepared. He could not believe that he was confined in such a "dirty place," surrounded by squalor and filth that clung to the prison walls and the bodies of the ragged debtors—many of whom, including William, had only the clothes in which they stood up and slept. Perpetually overcrowded, the prison provided the penniless debtor with nothing more than a pair of rugs to sleep between on the floorboards. If he had arrived just after a food delivery, the debtor could stay hungry for days because the pitiful bread allowance was dispensed only every other day and meat just once a week. "Picture to yourself, Sir, my situation," he implored Evelyn, I "who have been accustomed to every indulgence." Surely he deserved pity for his foolish behavior.[20]

Mr. Jackson thought not; indeed Mr. Jackson thought that "[over]indulgence" was probably the cause of William's heinous immorality. But only a few hours after William's arrest, another friend of the family, Mr. Morris, on the mistaken presumption that it would have been Jackson's wish, rushed to post bail of more than £100 to secure William's release. Jackson hurriedly penned a letter to disabuse his friend of this notion, but it was too late—William had left the jail to take up residence in the Garrick's Head Tavern, hoping to drown his horrible experience in wine and women. Instead, his exhausted body succumbed to a prolonged illness, from which position he could not possibly refuse his father's ultimatum. Still he delayed, for some weeks, before complying with Jackson's order to revoke Poole's instructions

and allow the money from the sale of his commission to go first to settling his debts in Guernsey. This capitulation, combined with the entreaties of his mother, eventually persuaded Mr. Jackson to allow him
to come home. William finally returned to Gloucester Place, with
nothing but the clothes he was wearing, in the middle of November.

For a few short weeks, he gained a physical (if not mental) respite
from the demands of his creditors and the fear of imprisonment, supported and cared for by his mother and tolerated by his father within the
comfort of their elegant home. But William found that confinement
with his parents, however restful, could not be endured for long, and he
was soon lured back onto the streets of London. Not yet as adept at
evading the sheriff's men as more seasoned debtors were, William soon
found himself locked up once more, in a less salubrious room in a sponging house. The immediate cause of his arrest was a suit brought by
William Norfolk Johnson, another attorney whose services William had
used during his previous summer of overspending in London. To this
was added the action brought by the carriage proprietor, Joseph Moore,
and on December 7 a judge in the Court of Exchequer had him committed to the Fleet Prison. William hired another attorney and sent an
urgent message to his mother, begging her to send his birth certificate so
that he could contest the debts on the grounds of nonage before he was
delivered to the gates of the prison, but he was too late.[21]

THE ARCHED DOORWAY to the Fleet Prison was deceptively innocu-
ous. Bearing the number 9 above, the prison door was situated in the
plain walls that bordered the east side of Fleet Market between en-
trances to ordinary houses. Number 9 Fleet Market was a famously
fictitious address used by those debtors, including William, who
wished to obscure the fact of their residence in a prison. Many hundreds of people passed freely in and out of that famous portal every day
until late at night, but the illusion of liberty was tempered by the fact
that those windowless walls were forty feet high and topped with stone
spikes. To the right of the entrance was a grated archway that made the
purpose of the structure all too obvious. Above the grate was an inscription, "Pray remember the poor prisoners, having no allowance,"
designed to inspire public benevolence toward debtors.

On entering the Fleet, William was obliged to sit in the entrance lodge for half an hour while the turnkeys scrutinized his features, committing them to memory so that he would not be able to walk out along with the other visitors who passed through the gates bringing food and other comforts to their friends and relatives. Inside the jail was a long four-story building, containing many small, dingy rooms leading off wide galleries on each floor, plus a taproom—for purchasing wine and beer—a coffee room, and a chapel. Outside were a racquet ground for exercise and a public kitchen for prisoners to make their own meals with produce donated by relatives or purchased from the market outside—for no provision was made for these impoverished inmates beyond what they could obtain from friends or through charity.[22]

The warden of the Fleet was granted his position by a royal letter of patent that gave him an income from the prison and from rents on other properties in London plus a small salary, but the real value of the position came from the much greater profits that could be made from charging the prisoners themselves for as many services as possible. John Eyles was an elderly man and almost blind, so he kept only an annuity for himself and turned over the daily running of the prison to his deputy warden. The prison officers explained the rules and choice of lodgings available within the prison to each debtor on arrival according to their assessment of "his rank and condition" and how much they thought he was able to pay. Rooms could be had on the Common Side for poorer men or on the Master's Side for the (previously) wealthy, and there was a vibrant (unofficial) trade in accommodation among inmates and prison officials. Senior inmates of long residence usually rented their room directly from the warden, who then assigned suitable new prisoners to share that room as a "chum," until each room might have two or three additional occupants paying "chummage" to the warden. But wealthier inmates could pay their poorer roommates to move out. The very poorest had to quit their beds every morning and wander around all day with no space to call their own.[23]

William's accommodation tended to reflect the state of his finances during his stay. Mr. Jackson paid him 1 guinea a week, but his outgoings always exceeded that. Hence at times he lodged in a private room on the Master's Side, at others in a dingy room lacking even basic furniture that he shared with three others on the Common Side, and he slept on a tabletop in the taproom when his funds were particularly low. It was a fallacy that imprisonment for debt erased those social differences that distinguished different classes of men in society outside, and William was determined to keep up appearances. Gentlemen debtors worked hard to maintain their superior position through their choice of lodging, their clothing, their refusal to work (as many common tradesmen did to maintain themselves), and their choice of companions as well as whether they socialized in the taproom or in the more genteel coffee room. William's lack of funds was therefore no bar to his belief in his privileged social status, and his financial relationships with other prisoners could still be conducted along similar lines of debt and credit. As the *Debtor and Creditor's Assistant* put it, "In prison much depends upon appearances and sometimes those who have neither principle nor resources, find means to get more in debt, than those who have both."[24]

When Mr. Jackson entered the precincts of the prison a week after William's arrest, he was surprised to find his son not only devoid of contrition, but also openly optimistic that he would soon be freed because, along with the majority of Fleet inmates, he was convinced that his creditors were pursuing unjust actions. His old school friend Thomas Macqueen had bolstered his confidence by promising to use his influence to help, but such was his mounting sense of injustice that William was determined to contest the cases without help from Macqueen or his father. As one debtors' attorney explained, in a debtors' prison

> law and the hardship of each man's case are the constant subjects of conversation and complaint, and every man's case is a hard one, though the plaintiff's family may be half ruined by the defendant's conduct; . . . the latter broods with his fellow prisoner over the favourable part of it so long, that he at last does really think his case a hard one indeed.[25]

As William's sense of injustice was already highly developed, it did not require much input from his fellow inmates to fan those flames; but they could and did instruct him in the intricacies of English debt law, aided by the circulation and perusal of numerous texts printed to assist imprisoned debtors in contesting their cases in court. These books were written by lawyers keen to aid the unfortunate debtor and prevent his perpetual imprisonment. One such author, Robert Dorset Neale, declared it would be an insult to the liberty and "birth-right of every Briton" if a debtor remained incarcerated because he was ignorant of "every judicial determination in favour of debtors." The rhetoric of liberty and legitimation that these books and the inmates themselves brought to fighting the efforts of cruel creditors to deprive them of that liberty, created a strong ethos of resistance in prison that William readily imbibed. Another effect of this self-taught legal knowledge was that once inside prison,

> the defendant . . . turns the tables upon the plaintiff. . . . He puts the plaintiff to all the expences [*sic*] he can, and presses on to trial, though he never intends, either by attorney or counsel to make his appearance in court. He pleads the general issue, which is, that he does not owe the debt and thereby puts all the proof upon the plaintiff.[26]

Indeed, it was a well-known scandal that some inmates deliberately sought to get themselves imprisoned through "friendly actions" in order to prevent their property from being seized and to escape from their more persistent creditors. Within a year even William, who detested confinement of any kind, would decide that a prison was the best place to deal with his creditors.

That winter, however, incarceration soon eroded William's initial optimism. The workings of the law were slow, and it was his misfortune to have been arrested at the end of the Michaelmas term, the first of four terms into which the legal year was divided. William's creditors did not have to declare whether they would proceed to court against him until the end of the following term, which meant he could be left kicking his heels in idle impotence until the end of April. He was advised that he could not take any action at all until January 23, which meant a very long, lonely Christmas within "this depot of misery." On Christmas Eve, when the weather began to turn really cold and he was again in poor health, William wrote to his father in despair, begging for his help to gain the warden's permission to live in the Rules of the Fleet. The boundaries of this porous prison had been enlarged beyond its walls to encompass accommodation in the surrounding streets—thus the Rules provided a profitable (for the privilege of residing in the Rules, like everything else, had to be purchased) and elastic extension to contain the huge influx of debtors, which always exceeded the space available within the walls.

Residence within the Rules would at least provide William with the illusion of a degree of freedom. Because it was not possible for guards to patrol the whole area, and the invisible boundary lines often ran through the middle of a street or coffee house, escape or unintentional straying was a risk the Fleet warden minimized by extracting financial securities from the prisoner. William hoped his father would provide this security and use his influence to convince the warden to grant him the freedom of the Rules. Mr. Jackson was unmoved, however; he remained bitter about the Guernsey debacle and declared himself unwilling ever to trust his son again. Worse still, William had ceased to use his full signature of WCB Jackson and was merely going by the name of William C. Jackson (under which name he had officially been committed). Using that version of his name and claiming Gloucester Place as his home when not actually residing there were to Mr. Jackson clear evidence of swindling. Indeed, Jackson went further and argued that such usage was very close to forgery, which meant "death by law," so William should beware of the villains who were even now leading him toward "the drop at Newgate" (where felons convicted of capital crimes were hung).[27]

This was not the seasonal greeting of good cheer that William hoped to receive from his father on Christmas Day, so the only solace he could seek was in the copious consumption of alcohol, in the company of the many other miserable souls who were separated from their families and facing an equally bleak festive season. In the following weeks William acceded to all his father's demands for detailed written statements of how his debts had been contracted—Mr. Jackson considered a verbal account insufficient even had he been prepared to visit his son again, which he was not. On New Year's Eve, Jackson ignored William's request to be sent a bed because the letter had not been signed with the correct initials. After six weeks of confinement, William was broken. He penned a miserable letter expressing the deepest kind of regret and contrition "which a father has a right to expect from a son," describing how he had been deserted by all his "professed friends," and promising reformation if only his father would help him "quit this horrid and irksome confinement."[28]

Mr. Jackson was sufficiently moved by this letter to put William's sincerity to the test one more time. William must renounce all his former associates and endeavor by "firm and manly determination" to retrace his steps toward an honorable and honest life. Despite ending with a threat to utterly abandon him should he fail in this task, Mr. Jackson signed himself "your <u>really</u> affectionate father" for the first time in years. The letter produced an outpouring of deep emotion from the prodigal son, who confessed that its contents gave him "more real pleasure than I have words to express." William was convinced at last that his father had "feelingly portray[ed] your tender solicitude and paternal anxiety for my welfare and honour."[29]

In any novel a tender scene of reconciliation should now have taken place, but it did not, for Mr. Jackson's jealous affection demanded more proofs, and he set about constructing "an innocent stratagem" to gain them. He told William that when he was walking in St. James's Park, he found an extraordinary letter there. It contained a heartfelt confession from a son to a father of all the wrongs he had committed during his short life. Jackson had the letter, which he claimed to have "found" but had clearly penned himself, delivered to his son in the Fleet. William read the faked letter with a mounting sense of dismay and anger, which snapped the fragile thread of trust once more. He wrote to his mother about this "strange communication," but suppressed his desire to defend himself with any force in the hope that his father would at least pay to get him day release from the prison.[30]

Mr. Jackson had offered to pay the exorbitant sum of £5 to procure "Day Rules" for William so that he would be allowed out of the prison to join his parents for dinner at Gloucester Place. The intention behind allowing prisoners out on Day Rules was that they could conduct legal business with their attorney or sort out their financial affairs with creditors, but it was commonly referred to as offering to "show you my horse," which more accurately reflected the freedom and sociable activities made possible on such day trips. William's forbearance was duly rewarded, and he gained permission to leave the prison one evening in late January. The release and the prospect of good food and domestic comfort—however short-lived—were particularly welcome because he had spent the previous few nights sleeping on a table in the taproom, having been thrown out of his own room for rowdy behavior.[31]

Like many inmates, William passed his idle hours drinking, gambling, and whoring with prostitutes who slipped unnoticed through the prison's porous security alongside the numerous wives and daughters bringing food for inmates. Such activities had become more enjoyable since he had begun sharing the rent of an apartment on the Master's Side with Captain Joseph Bradley, a fellow inmate of similar rank and disposition with whom he had struck up a friendship. Unfortunately, William chose his first dinner at home to complain about what he regarded as poor treatment by a "brutal turnkey" for forcing him out of a comfortable room because he could not afford the 2 guineas a week rent, but he omitted to mention the damage that he and Bradley had done while in the room.

Such was Mr. Jackson's outrage at his son's treatment that he made some excuse to withdraw after dinner and proceeded straight to the prison to ascertain the truth of the matter. In addition to the allowance of 1 guinea a week he paid William, Jackson had also paid additional fees for a more suitable room for his son, and he now demanded to know from the warden why any prisoner should be compelled to sleep in the common taproom. The turnkey on duty that night was summoned and quickly apprised Jackson of the dissolute behavior that had culminated in his son's expulsion. William and Bradley's revels had frequently included bringing prostitutes into the prison, and their excesses had resulted in broken windows and chairs. The turnkey was even more upset because the furniture belonged to him and when he complained about the damage, they had merely laughed at him.

Mr. Jackson returned grimly to Gloucester Place and late that night, after the servants were abed, challenged William to explain the turnkey's version of events. Father and son again confronted each other across a chasm of different values as William half denied and half admitted what had happened. At the conclusion of this interview, William bade his father an icily polite good night and set out in darkness to make his way back to jail and the debtors' culture that was now more familiar than that of his family.

To penal reformers, the Fleet and other prisons were notoriously lacking in provision to ensure the morality and industry of their unfortunate inmates. "Your Lordships cannot possibly form an idea of the profligacy and licentious intercourse between the sexes, and want of morals, and defiance of every degree of decency in the King's Bench, the Fleet and Marshalsea," the reformer James Neild had warned the Committee on Imprisonment for Civil Debt in 1809. It was well known that prisoners were regularly visited by prostitutes and other "abandoned women" who mingled with crowds of other visitors each day. Indeed, the Fleet had gained a reputation for being the largest brothel in London. In 1812 one lawyer argued that indefinite confinement for debt had a deplorable and inevitable impact on the debtor's morals:

There is an incessant continuance, of riot and disorder, indecent language, reviling, blasphemy, gaming, and drunkenness and sexual debauchery, and almost every species of vice to which human nature is prone. And the only effectual remedy which can be found is the shortening of imprisonment, as the unfortunate debtor having the consolatory prospect of enlargement at a definite period, will be better reconciled to his fate, and less inclined to dissipation and folly.[32]

Even though such inflamed rhetoric was designed to promote reform of the debt law, it contained a considerable element of truth. In addition to widespread dissipation, attorney James Pearce explained, almost anything could be got for money or bottles of wine, provided it was done on the quiet, for neither prisoners nor turnkeys would accept open payment. Instead, a "bank note properly directed, or a dozen of wine sent" were never returned, and a few days later the prisoner got what he wanted. Such bribery was common in every type of prison, but in all except the debtors' jails it was done more openly. William's expulsion from his rooms could almost certainly have been prevented had he sought to ease the conscience of the enraged turnkey with a suitable gift. Prisoners who behaved "handsomely" tipped the staff to earn a "trump card" as future indemnity against being caught in illegal actions.[33]

Imprisoned debtors' vast appetite for alcohol was kept supplied in a similarly underhanded manner. Wine and beer could be purchased

openly in the taproom, whereas spirits and liquor were strictly prohibited; yet everyone knew that they could be bought in rooms "called
whistling shops, it being supposed that those who frequent them only
whistle for spirituous liquor, being afraid to ask for anything of the
kind." Thus the world that William now inhabited was largely hidden
from the view of his father, who believed that the prison's rules were
there to be obeyed and remained ignorant of the degree of collusion
between staff and inmates.[34]

AT LENGTH the freezing winter weather, which caused sheets of solid
ice to bridge large sections of the Thames, began to ease into a milder,
cloudy spring. William tried again to bring his case to court, only to discover that he could not plead to Joseph Moore's action until early May
and that William Norfolk Johnson's claim for unpaid attorney fees could
keep him imprisoned until the end of July. His father either turned a
deaf ear to his requests for help in securing residence in the Rules or actively blocked his efforts. In February William tried to secure a transfer
to spend the summer months in the more airy King's Bench Prison—a
common preference among debtors—but at the end of March a friend
came to his rescue and paid the fees for him to live in the Rules. He
could now wander through the Fleet Market and enjoy the comforts of
numerous well-known coffee houses and taverns on Ludgate Hill to
while away the lengthening days of spring and early summer.

His mood lifted, and he even congratulated his father on his
strict policy of nonpayment of all debts, for William's creditors were
beginning to realize that no matter how long they kept him in jail,
his father would never pay to secure his release. William now reasoned that such steadfast refusal to give in to tradesmen's demands
was in fact "convincing proof" of his father's friendship after all. Mr.
Jackson thawed sufficiently to send his son some necessaries and
some "plain and gentlemanly attire," and he redirected his ire with
renewed vigor toward all tradesmen who extended credit to young
men and had thus been complicit in William's downfall. In June, as
he was about to set off for his summer stay at Langley Lodge, he instructed his agent to reinstate weekly payments of William's £100
per annum allowance.

The following month William seized the earliest opportunity for freedom. Norfolk Johnson had failed to officially declare a suit against William in court within the time allowed, which meant William could apply to the court to be released by a writ of *supersedeas.** William also managed to reach an agreement with Joseph Moore, the owner of the missing horse and gig, by confessing a warrant of attorney: this meant that he agreed that he did owe the debt but would not need to settle it for another six months after his release. Seven months in jail had left William understandably impatient to taste freedom. Although the legal paperwork was well under way to secure this, he left the Fleet Rules for Langley Lodge some three weeks before it was finally completed, leaving the two "friends" who had provided the security for his residence there liable for his debts and costs. As soon as William was officially discharged, the liability for his debts disappeared, but the two men still demanded that Mr. Jackson settle their costs, thus souring the reception William received from his father despite the good news of his release.[35]

For William, as for many debtors, freedom was a relative term. Reformers were quick to point out that a felon who had served his sentence was considered to have paid his debt to society, but no matter how long a debtor remained in prison, or how badly he and his family suffered from it, his debt was never cleared. Only men and women in trade could become bankrupt and avail themselves of the means of wiping the financial slate clean; insolvent individuals remained mired in debts, no matter how ancient, until every penny was repaid. Prison temporarily protected a debtor against all other creditors because those who had him arrested had prior claim, but once the debtor was outside the prison's walls, it was merely a matter of time and inclination as to when other creditors would take action. As he rode out of London toward the lush fields of Langley, William was therefore well aware that he was still living on borrowed time. Even the settlement with Moore was temporary, for if he could not pay the money owed by the date recorded on the warrant of attorney, it provided for his immediate rearrest. William stayed just three days with his parents before the demands of his boot

---

* *Supersedeas* was a writ ordering a lower court to suspend proceedings in a case.

maker in Bond Street, the creditor most likely to arrest him, forced him to return reluctantly to London. In that short time, however, he had convinced his parents that he meant to reform his ways and to live at home under their supervision while he did so. Mr. Jackson briefly believed that matters might yet be put right, and father and son parted in the expectation of soon being reunited to begin the good work.[36]

William had underestimated the persistence of his creditors, however, and within hours of his return to London found himself being pursued through the streets by the sheriff's men. He escaped capture only because a sympathetic groom allowed him to hide out in a hayloft above some stables. There was widespread public sympathy for the plight of debtors, and many people were happy to help them escape from the detestable "bum-bailiffs," whether they were trying to seize the person or his goods. After emerging cautiously from the hayloft under cover of night when he could not be arrested, William flew to Langley once more, where his mother was anxious to shelter him. But there was little she could do to help. William was convinced he was no safer there than in London, and he caused her even greater alarm by rushing to a window at the slightest noise, until she fancied the bailiffs were about to enter her home at any moment.[37]

William declared that he must head for Portsmouth but needed money to be able to live there. Jane was only too eager to oblige her only son in any way she could and packed him off furnished with what money she could amass at the time. Convinced of "the deep depravity" of his son, Jackson thought the Portsmouth trip no more than a ruse to acquire more money for dishonest ends. William's request for further funds to enable him to leave the country and find work in the East or West Indies was refused. A stormy interview ensued—William hurt and angry that his good behavior since living at Langley counted for nothing, Mr. Jackson declaring that "he knew him too well to be his dupe again"—followed by another swift and bitter parting.[38]

MR. JACKSON SOON discovered that the expectation of undesirable behavior in a person often produces the very effect it was designed to avoid. William returned to Langley and began to put to good use all the "artifices, tricks, fraud, deception, ingenuity, and low cunning exercised by the DEBTORS of the Metropolis" described in Egan's *Tom & Jerry* that he had learned during his sojourn in the Fleet. Some authors insisted that any law student should be able to distinguish between an unfortunate debtor and a fraudulent one, and therefore it was unjust to stigmatize all imprisoned debtors as cheats or swindlers. Yet defining fraudulent conduct remained difficult. Many creditors believed it fraudulent to promise repayment without a "reasonable" expectation of being able to do so or prudent anticipation of "avoidable" difficulties; even living "extravagantly" after borrowing money could be construed as fraudulent behavior.[39]

Few of these value judgments corresponded closely with the beliefs of insolvents like William, whose consciences provided a wide range of justifications for their risky financial transactions. Mr. Jackson already believed that his son was a fraudulent debtor, but William's activities around Langley, Windsor, and London during the summer of 1811 soon saw him labeled a "swindler" by press and public. William's various deceits included the usual promises to buy a horse and tack, which were not returned after he had ridden the animal on trial. He ordered shirts for himself from a tailor in Windsor, claiming to be "the proprietor of Langley Lodge"; he had dresses and caps made up by a milliner for his wife, "Mrs. Jackson," signing a bill that was to be drawn from a bank in which he had no funds. The milliner, believing that upright citizens like the Jacksons would want the matter hushed up, wrote to Jane promising to keep silent if she settled the bill for William. Mr. Jackson took the surprised milliner to task for even suggesting that such dishonest acts should be concealed from the public—honest people like themselves would certainly never pay "hush money."[40]

In London William's fraudulent activities spiraled even faster. A large number of tradesmen and tradeswomen, mostly in the luxury goods and fashionable trades, discovered to their cost that William Jackson Junior was not to be trusted, and that his father would not pay for anything that the son ordered. Most also discovered that the goods they had sold him turned up in pawnshops soon afterward, where they could be had for half their value. William progressed from pawning goods he had acquired on credit to raise cash, to using the duplicate pawnbroker's tickets themselves as a method of payment, and from there he graduated to making duplicates of his own.

Mr. Oldfield, the proprietor of the Old Hummums in Covent Garden, a well-known Turkish baths and hotel with a reputation for prostitution, had accepted two such duplicates from William. He soon became suspicious of their authenticity, however, and accosted Mr. Jackson's startled housekeeper on the steps of Gloucester Place, claiming that William had given him forgeries and that the pawnbroker whose goods they purported to represent was also seeking young Mr. Jackson with the intention of taking him to Bow Street Magistrates' Court. Mr. Barwise, a watchmaker in St. Martin's, openly accused William of swindling him out of a gold watch. Barwise made it known that he was a member of the Society for the Protection of Trade Against Swindlers and Sharpers, to which he paid an annual fee in order to avail himself of the society's financial backing for prosecuting offenders like William. The watchmaker also threatened to publish William's name in the papers, again with the backing of the society, which would offer rewards of up to 10 guineas to anyone helping to successfully convict a swindler for fraud. William was well on his way to becoming a "finished swindler."[41]

Mr. Jackson realized that the last remnants of his paternal power over William had disappeared. He wrote to his solicitor, Richard Colley Smith, in despair, admitting that his son was "completely beyond my control." The only time they met was when William came to collect his weekly allowance, yet he was "still taking up money, wherever he can get it, under false pretences." Because William had set his "authority as a parent at complete defiance," Jackson asked Colley Smith to inquire whether the Lord Chancellor could help prevent William from defrauding the public. The solicitor was not optimistic about the success of appealing to the Court of Chancery, even though the Lord Chancellor was the constitutional guardian of minors, which gave the court jurisdiction over infants and idiots. Smith explained that Jackson could not get William made a ward of Chancery, because the court exercised that power through the appointment of a guardian to control the child's interests, but if a natural father was still living, he would have to act as that guardian. Frustratingly for Mr. Jackson, had he lived on the Continent, he could have got his profligate son made a ward of the city and held under its guardianship indefinitely.[42]

Even without this official sanction, Jackson believed that William's defiance effectively dissolved the reciprocal duties that bound parent and child. He now informed William's creditors that his son had "long since ceased to acknowledge my authority, and therefore I can be in no respect responsible for his conduct." William became aware of this fact only after the sheriff's men caught up with him once more and he was delivered back to the debtors' side of Newgate—"a place most fitting for a person who has committed so many scandalous outrages against society," in Mr. Jackson's view. William wrote to his mother asking for food, but instead he received a solemn declaration from his father that "I no longer view you in the light of a son, nor as a man deserving of the smallest portion of my affection or regard."[43]

With an emotional blindness and a lack of empathy common in youth, William declared himself entirely ignorant of the cause of his father's rage because he believed that "by involving myself in debt, I am the only person to suffer by confinement." That statement alone propelled Jackson into an apoplectic orgy of denunciation, but still seething from his father's rejection, William planned a trick he hoped would further "irritate his feelings." William had for some time been visiting tradesmen accompanied by an elegant prostitute, whom he introduced as his wife, to order clothes for her. Indeed, about a month before his arrest, he had arrived at Gloucester Place and shocked the housekeeper there yet again by introducing his "wife" as a woman who had brought him £10,000 on marriage, "every shilling of which he had touched." The indignant housekeeper, who was not fooled by such claims, candidly speculated where things might end if William did not desist in this folly. When Mr. Jackson eventually heard of this scene, he wrote to William in Newgate expressing his moral indignation in considerably stronger terms, to which William replied with studied dignity:

> The lady alluded to in your letter, who you are pleased to call a "<u>prostitute</u>," will shortly be my lawful wife. Her character, Sir, is unstained, and her <u>pedigree</u> and <u>rent-roll</u> entitles her to a connection <u>higher than mine</u>. . . . I now beg to say that the Lady who I hope shortly to be connected to is Miss Rowel of Leicester, and George Street, Hanover Square; and my union with so rich and respectable a family cannot disgrace my family or dishonour myself.[44]

Mr. Jackson was stunned, briefly, into silence. William had produced an ace—marriage to a respectable heiress could still redeem all their fortunes. Yet Jackson wondered what Miss Rowel's opinion of the moral conduct of her intended husband could possibly be. On later discovering the truth of William's ruse, Mr. Jackson was left puzzled as to what could have driven his son to play such a trick, but even more certain of the inevitable fate that would soon befall him.

The satisfaction that the deception provided William was short-lived. He discovered that his actions had so provoked the housekeeper that she had not only informed his father of the incident, but had also told the bailiffs of his whereabouts, thus practically guaranteeing his arrest and return to Newgate. He spent the next five months there, writing nearly identical letters to his creditors. He created a plausible story about how he had been away in Brighton and then was disappointed on his return not to have received funds he was expecting from Ireland. Alternatively, he would offer a bill for a larger amount accepted by another (probably fictitious) tradesman, suggesting that the creditor keep the change as recompense for his long wait.

Few seem to have believed any of his promises, and Mr. Jackson continued to be plagued with begging letters and accusations. More seriously for William, one of his creditors chose to press criminal charges, and he found himself transferred in irons to the criminal side of the jail. He escaped from this predicament only because the prosecutor unwisely wrote a letter offering to drop the criminal charges if he was paid the money he was owed. With such damning written proof of the man's motives, the magistrates swiftly agreed to release William. His irons were immediately struck off, and he left Bow Street vowing to heed the magistrate's warning to "avoid placing himself in a similar situation hereafter" at all costs; but he remained ill equipped with either the willpower or the means to do so.

TO THE BRINK
OF DESTRUCTION

London, 1812

Having regained your liberty, be doubly chary of it;
Escape like an affrighted bird from the trap, and
beware for the future of every bait. Only with a weak
mind can the temptation to begin a fresh account
become successful.

— Isaac Taylor, *Advice to the Teens* (1818)

M r. and Mrs. Jackson had retired to the relative peace of their country home at Langley, where gossip about William's activities was temporarily muted (if not extinguished) by distance from London. Most news was mediated by newspaper reports or creditors' letters rather than by knocks at the door, and for a few weeks in May and June, even these ceased to intrude on their rural retreat. Indeed. Mr. Jackson hoped that, like "anyone with any common sense," William's narrow escape from being committed for a felony would be warning enough to prevent him from repeating his misdeeds. Yet he also worried that his son was still on "the high road to certain destruction," and the deceptions that William was practicing would make anyone "turn [away] with horror from" him. Despite these fears and the belief that his behavior would eventually lead him to the gallows, at this point Jackson still viewed William's behavior as vicious or sinful and therefore redeemable, rather than as specifically criminal.[1]

But the most important judges of that distinction were the victims of William's "depredations." In the absence of a professional police force and state prosecution, it was largely up to individual traders to decide at what point and to what extent the criminal justice system should close in on him. Once a tradesman pressed criminal charges, he could then decide whether to negotiate with the defendant's relatives over withdrawing the charge, refuse to attend court, or even fail to provide sufficient evidence in court if he believed the initial shame and imprisonment were punishment enough. As a foreign observer explained in 1822, "The business of prosecution, instead of being performed on the behalf of the public by an officer appointed expressly for the purpose, is committed entirely to the hands of the injured party, who, by this means, becomes the arbiter of the culprit's fate."[2]

William, who was now living in rented lodgings in London, was aware of the danger he was in, but keeping up appearances had become a way of life from which he could not escape. At the age of twenty, he was, as author Isaac Taylor predicted for youths in his situation, "saddened over by the consciousness of being by no means at liberty. Instead of surveying life as a fair field, open to energy; the remembrance of debts, and boyish incumbrances now loading the man, . . . [were] preventing the free use of his faculties and means."[3]

While edging ever closer to the criminal (and impoverished) margins of society, William clung desperately to the delusion that he still occupied a central space as the son of a wealthy gentleman. His allowance was now only an insignificant drop in the swelling ocean of debts that threatened to engulf him, but as long as his father did not disinherit him, the prospect of becoming a very rich man remained a tantalizing cure for all his current problems. This happy vision continued to provide the justification for pursuing patently dishonest actions that would later appear little more than the youthful follies of a rich man. He was supported in this belief by both the uncertain status of elite debtors and a criminal justice system that was devised and largely administered by wealthy, landed gentlemen. As a parliamentary report put it in 1828, the law tended to regard offenses committed by "the children of the poor as crimes of magnitude," but similar offenses were more often "passed over as frolics in the sons of the rich."[4]

A major exception to this was forgery—a crime most often carried out by educated people at the higher end of the social scale. Some were well-known swindlers, but others were of genuinely genteel status who had succumbed to temptation under huge financial and social pressure. If convicted, forgers were almost always executed, but public distaste for such a harsh sentence had grown after the trial and execution of a highly respected clergyman who had forged a note in a moment of panic in 1777. Around one-fifth of those executed in England between 1805 and 1815 were for forgery; most of them were prosecuted by the Bank of England, but many prosecutors balked at pursuing charges with such fatal consequences all the way through the courts. Yet among the many traders whom William was now routinely defrauding, three men were prepared to risk the time, expense, and possible damage to their trade to bring a young gentleman to court on criminal charges—and one of them was willing to press for a conviction for forgery.[5]

Within days of his release from the confines of Newgate in May 1812, William (who had taken to styling himself Captain Jackson) convinced Thomas Colville, a tailor based in Store Street, to rent him some smart lodgings. William paid Colville a month's rent of £14 for the use of the first and second floors plus the kitchen of a furnished house at 77 John Street, which he proceeded to share with his current mistress, a Mrs. Parker. Appearances would be well served both by his fair companion—a woman of polite demeanor and better manners than many of her profession—and by such an address. John Street was only a fifteen-minute walk from the smart West End squares where his father and uncles resided, so the address would guarantee attention from tradesmen alert to the respectability and social status of potential customers with the names of Jackson, Shee, and Evelyn. Had Mr. Jackson remained in London, retailers would have had some chance of appraising to what extent his credit extended to his son, but his removal to Buckinghamshire meant such inquiries would take too long to risk losing the custom of a well-spoken young gentleman from a wealthy family.[6]

At its southern end, John Street (now subsumed by Great Portland Street) opened into the shoppers' paradise that was Oxford Street, with its wide pavements from which crowds of passers-by gazed into the brightly lit bow windows of myriad shops that stayed open until ten o'clock at night. It also marked the edge of the more exclusive West End shopping district, which was frequented by fastidious, wealthy male connoisseurs such as the Prince Regent, Lord Byron, and Beau Brummell, but also by Mr. Jackson, who, despite his fondness for prudent economy, patronized a tailor in Duke Street.

William had thus placed himself within easy reach of the fashionable world, but he had few means of actually engaging in it without resort to the sort of "robbery, swindling [and] forgery" that advice writers warned was the "lamentable issue of a silly youth running into debt." The easy slip from vice to crime was acknowledged to affect even those scions of the affluent but moral middle classes. Many a successful businessman had indulged in the kind of youthful "vices" long feared by middle-class parents like the Jacksons, but now they were loudly condemned by reformers who saw such practices as part of a progressive disease that should be nipped in the bud by prompt prosecution and severe retribution. The Society for the Suppression of Vice had a familiar-sounding agenda and argued in 1801 that "modern youth are destitute of that decency of deportment and propriety of manner, which we denominate Respect" because of a lack of obedience to schoolmasters, parents, and employers, which would ultimately undermine obedience to the law.[7]

The society's attempts to clean up the streets in the early years of the decade resulted in the criminalization of many minor misdemeanors, such as swearing, lewdness, drunkenness, idling in public houses, and lighting fireworks. Yet the public image of "criminal" juvenile delinquency was created by newspapers and parliamentary reports that expressed alarm at the recent increase of crime committed by hordes of "ill-featured," animalistic urchins. These were the type of bold, cunning lads that Dickens later fashioned into his portrayal of the Artful Dodger.[8]

At twenty William was still a minor in the eyes of the civil law on debt, but considered culpable under criminal law. Alarmists who portrayed juvenile depravity as a major crisis tended to include anyone under twenty-one, but most reports about the problem of young offenders referred only to youths of seventeen or under. Yet from their late teens to midtwenties, young men in the extensive no-man's-land of "youth" were of an age most likely to be prosecuted for more serious criminal offenses and least likely to be accorded the leniency often granted to younger juvenile offenders. William may have been shielded by his appearance as a young gentleman from those on the lookout for juvenile delinquents, but his age now made him uniquely vulnerable to arrest and less likely to inspire mercy if charged. To his father, William was a "misguided youth" desperately in need of parental (or legal) discipline while he navigated the difficult transition to full adult independence that most young men did not acquire until they married in their midtwenties.[9]

With that recklessness acknowledged to be characteristic of youth both then and now, William endeavored to maintain the station he believed he was born into through continued swindling, forgery, and theft from West End tradesmen on the northern side of Oxford Street. In doing so, he took advantage of both those who knew his father and those forced to accept a "dropping trade," or customers who were unknown to them, something the showy retailers of busy Oxford Street did far more frequently than the more exclusive shopkeepers of Bond Street or Jermyn Street to the south, who catered to the *beau monde*. The latter vendors happily extended huge lines of credit to well-known customers, but they would have been harder for Captain Jackson to deceive, even if he had dared risk his precious reputation in such company.[10]

For William, shopping was still a leisure pursuit, a social occasion that briefly offered him an escape from the reality of his straightened circumstances—purchasing luxury clothing both reaffirmed his social status and provided a heady frisson of pleasure. But it was also a serious business, and amid the bustling crowds of browsing shoppers gathered around opulent displays of goods, it presented him with a golden opportunity for swindling and forgery. William had developed an intimate knowledge of those consumer practices most calculated to convince retailers to part with their goods for credit; this had served him well when he believed his father would pay the bill and continued to do so now that the transaction was fraudulent. The appearance of gentility was crucial to the operation—a well-cut coat or military uniform coupled with a proud demeanor and polite speech was most effective. Elite customers and shopkeepers regularly enacted a pattern of behavior that allowed the former to assess the quality of the goods and the latter the quality (and potential credit risk) of the customer. Both engaged in a ritual of polite browsing, conversation, and negotiation that allowed enough time for a skilled assistant to assess the social and credit status of a customer who was not personally known to the shopkeeper.[11]

IN EARLY JUNE William's disreputable female companion, Mrs. Parker, left their lodgings in John Street and sallied forth onto Oxford Street. She turned left to join the tourists and shoppers heading east until she entered a linen drapers' shop at number 72. Seeming a model of genteel respectability, Mrs. Parker convinced Richard Robson, the proprietor, to send some of his goods to her home in John Street. Robson's servant duly arrived at the house, where William impressed the lad by asking for the most expensive muslins they carried, so the youth ran back to the shop to obtain more for his discerning client. Because most high-class retailers still did not have fixed prices on display, genteel negotiation was expected before purchase. On the servant's return, Captain Jackson proceeded to explain that he had just arrived from the country and leased the house, so he would pay by a draft on his army agents, Greenwood and Co., for £22 12s. This was 2s. less than the goods were worth, but for ready money the captain had expected a reduction, so the lad agreed, convinced that he was dealing with a cultured, trustworthy man of high status.

That Captain Jackson was anything but trustworthy became abundantly evident shortly after this transaction when William disappeared from his lodgings without settling his rent. A worried neighbor contacted Colville, who went to inspect his property in John Street on June 13 and found that William and all the furniture within—including carpets, curtains, mirrors, beds, and tables—had vanished. In total this amounted to £150, a considerable sum for a crime more usually committed by poor tenants who would commonly pawn the contents of their lodgings to raise money. Some poor lodgers even remained in situ, with no furniture, in the hope that they could redeem it in better times. Many believed that this would force a renegotiation of rent between landlord and tenant, but legally, appropriating furniture from a lodging house with intent to defraud the owner was a felony. The fact that Colville later found his table at another house in St. Martin's Lane suggests that William sold or pawned the furniture in another attempt to raise cash. Mrs. Parker brazenly remained at John Street in a smaller apartment, but Captain Jackson was forced to keep changing his address (if always within the confines of the fashionable West End) on an almost weekly basis in order to stay ahead of his creditors. Colville bided his time while seeking the best opportunity to apprehend his former tenant.[12]

William knew that his situation had become perilous and wrote to his father in July, asking for his allowance to be paid in a lump sum to enable him to leave the country. On the same day, Mr. Jackson also received a letter from his London bookseller, whose premises were just minutes from the family home in Gloucester Place, informing him that he had discovered a draft from William to be a forgery. Horrified at this new proof of his son's depravity, Jackson ignored both the letter and William's request for money. Instead of leaving London to avoid his creditors, William continued to be fatally drawn to seeking money and clothing from shops closest to his family home.

Hence, during a summer afternoon on August 3, he strolled along Wigmore Street, close to Sir George Shee's home in Manchester Square, heading for a linen drapers run by a father and son, both named Joseph Christian. In the usual fashion William asked to see some fine shirts and then objected to the price. On reaching an agreement with the Christians' shop man, he boldly ordered eighteen shirts and matching handkerchiefs to be sent to 38 Park Street, close to St. James's Park. The following evening, when the shop man called to deliver the shirts, William was waiting there with Stephen Harper, one of his known "associates." On being presented with the bill, William observed that he should be given a reduction for ready money, particularly as he planned to purchase from the Christians again another time. The shop man hesitated but, judging that William's appearance meant that he must be a gentleman, finally agreed to knock 7s. off the price, whereupon William drew out a pocket book and signed a draft for £23 8s. in Harper's name.

Obtaining goods from tradesmen by false pretenses or by a forged order in writing was a common scam, known in the flash language of the criminal fraternity as "the order-racket." The slick deceptions practiced on Christian and Robson strongly suggest William and Harper both knew their actions had, at the very least, put them in danger of arrest. William was unaware, however, of just how close that peril was: Joseph Christian had already gone to the Marlborough Street magistrates to seek William's arrest for forgery. Stephen Harper had left London, and William planned to do the same, yet he had delayed because he still hoped that his father might find him a suitable paid position somewhere abroad. William claimed he was prepared to utterly humble himself to his parent, because "prison and public disgrace" were almost certainly awaiting him in London and he could not go to another country "without friends, money or clothes." Indeed, the clothes he had on now were "almost in rags, and the money I receive from Mr. Day, will . . . only pay for my board lodging in the humblest sphere."[13]

Charles Day, Jackson's London agent, carried out business for him when he was in the country, but Day was also a useful means for Jackson to avoid contact with his disreputable son. Unless William had given the eighteen shirts to Harper or failed to sell them profitably, his claims of poverty were clearly nonsense; they were calculated to move his father to "charity . . . to alleviate my sufferings." Mr. Jackson learned that William had recently been in Langley with Mrs. Parker but had stayed at the White Hart in Colnbrook instead of visiting Langley Lodge, using another "swindling draft" to pay for his accommodation, an act that further debased the family name in the locality. Jackson was therefore almost incandescent with indignation at this last request from

> a Being that, from the age of 17 to 21 never for a single moment erred from a career of vice and infamy . . . a Being who made it his study to wound the hearts of his parents, to treat with contempt even the exterior of decency, and to link himself with associates the outcasts of the moral world: With these dreadful facts before my eyes and fixed indelibly in my heart, I distinctly call upon you to state the grounds on which I could, with any colour of justice or propriety, go in search of an honourable ap-

pointment for you. . . . Your promises to me would be of no avail since hitherto they have only been made but for the purpose of being broken; and the time has long since elapsed when further deceit could be successfully practised.

I feel that I have done my duty by you and can answer it to God and my conscience; However deep may be my regret at the unworthiness of my son, I have nothing wherewith to reproach myself on his account.[14]

Thus far the letter provided little comfort for William, but if the son still hoped that emotional ties would prove stronger than disapproval, the father found it equally hard to abandon his son completely. Hurt and angry Jackson may have been, but the prospect that sincere repentance before God "may do much" still lingered, and in the final lines he assured William that the door to his house, if not to his heart, remained open.

An open door was a tantalizing prospect for William, whose situation had now become so desperate that he was unable to move about freely in daylight for fear of being arrested. He had also been ostracized from the polite circles of wealthy, influential friends he had once mingled with in his father's house. Indeed, one London guidebook declared in 1802 that it was proof of the "general decency and purity" of the city's population that

no family of rank can admit a <u>detected prostitute</u> or <u>detected swindler of fashion</u> into their houses or parties. Such tainted characters may, as long as they can keep open tables, draw a crowd who have no reputation to lose, or a few persons of good character, but of inferior stations. . . . But they wander, conscious that no reputable door is open to them; conscious that silent scorn (at least) is their attendant, wherever they are . . . and conscious that no knock at their doors announces a visitor of integrity, and sensibility to honour.[15]

Former family friends expressed their sadness at William's situation but wanted to keep their distance and were not prepared to provide the practical help that the obligation of "friendship" would normally have persuaded them to offer. Seizing on the welcome offer of an open door, William, in a flood of self-pity and remorse, poured out all the fears that self-delusion had kept hidden:

> Would to Heaven Sir, I had followed the advice I have invariably received from you, and the best of Mothers. I might then be every thing you could wish and enjoy that peace of mind which, for the last two years has been a stranger to me. For my past conduct I do not attempt to make the smallest defence. My eyes are now open and I see with horror that I am on the brink of destruction; but I trust not so far gone, but there is yet a hope.[16]

Jackson wrote the following day, still holding out the possibility of reconciliation and redemption, but effectively bribing William to remove himself from decent society (and definitely from London) for three years before the law did so permanently. He had no intention of publicly receiving William at Langley, however. Wounded by the renewal of damaging local gossip, Mr. Jackson was determined, even at the risk of his son's life, to stick to those principles that supported his unshakable belief in the justice of English law. "If you should be demanded of me by those whom you have defrauded I could not in honor and principle secure you for a moment," he warned. "My house never shall be a sanctuary for the open violation of the Laws of this country."[17]

On Friday, August 28, William sent a fast rider to Langley to accept his father's offer (but no doubt also hoping to collect the travel expenses at the same time), with the assurance that he would leave the country the following day. Mr. Jackson, who could no longer "place the smallest reliance" on anything William told him, instead committed all future financial dealings into the hands of Charles Day, thus delaying his son's departure. Day accepted the commission but was visited soon afterward by an irate innkeeper who claimed he had lost a hired horse and gig to William. Although Day thought the innkeeper had a good case, Jackson believed that the man was mistaken—neither of the descriptions of the perpetrators matched his son's appearance—but it was enough to make him fear that William was planning yet another deception of some kind.

The disagreement delayed matters even further, and although Day paid William his weekly allowance, he refused to advance any more money for travel expenses. This last delay proved costly indeed. If he had left the country when he first planned to, William would have joined an illustrious list of previously well-heeled debtors who sought refuge on the Continent, including Beau Brummell and the author William Thackeray. Instead, William was arrested the following night and became enmeshed in a sanguinary legal system that placed him among the ranks of common criminals. He found himself once more before the Marlborough Street magistrates, but this time he faced a capital charge.

MARLBOROUGH STREET Police Office stood to the south of Oxford Street, almost diagonally opposite John Street where the unfortunate Colville had lost the contents of his house to William's deceptions. It had only been established in 1793, one of seven new public offices where three magistrates sat on a daily basis and employed six constables "for the more effectual prevention of felonies." These constables were not a police force in the modern sense—the establishment of a state-sponsored force at that time was anathema to most British citizens, who believed it would severely threaten their fabled liberties. Unlike the "tyrannical" French system of public prosecution and policing, the detection and pursuit of criminals in England still lay largely in the hands of the individual prosecutor, although, often for a fee, the constables were expected to make actual arrests.[18]

One guidebook for visitors boasted of the lack of official police in London but helpfully provided the addresses of the police offices for visitors in need of assistance. Given that "swindling" was one of the most commonly perceived threats to public safety, however, guidebooks also listed the addresses of organizations that had solicitors attached to them, such as the Society for the Detection of Swindlers, which was located in Essex Street just a few doors down from the Society for the Suppression of Vice. It was only three months since William's last appearance before the magistrates, so although at this point it was only Joseph Christian's accusation of forging a check that was before them, they clearly suspected William's guilt. Early-nineteenth-century magistrates could exercise a good deal of discretion in deciding whether to discharge, bail, or commit a prisoner to trial, but a felony charge almost always resulted in imprisonment without bail before trial. William was therefore committed to Clerkenwell New Prison, but in the belief that other criminal accusations against him were likely to be forthcoming, the magistrates ordered a further hearing to be held the following Monday.[19]

Once committed, the accused had very few rights compared with modern suspects, and most were treated in the same way as convicted prisoners. William was taken from the magistrates' court and forced to walk from the fashionable West End right across London to Clerkenwell Prison in the east. One prison reformer described how such prisoners were routinely

> handcuffed to a file of perhaps a dozen wretched persons in a similar situation, and marched through the streets, sometimes a considerable distance, followed by a crowd of impudent and insulting boys; exposed to the gaze and stare of every passenger: the moment he enters prison, irons are hammered on to him; then he is cast into the midst of compound of all that is disgusting and depraved. At night he is locked up in a narrow cell, with, perhaps, half a dozen of the worst thieves in London, or as many vagrants, whose rags are alive, and in actual motion with vermin: he may find himself in bed, and in bodily contact, between a robber and a murderer; or between a man with a foul disease on one side, and one with an infectious disorder on the other.[20]

The New Prison in Clerkenwell had, as its name suggested, been relatively recently constructed, in 1775. From the outer gate a passage to the right led down six stone steps to the Men's Court. This was a paved courtyard containing just two partly enclosed, windowless sheds to shelter prisoners during the day and a pump for water. Each shed was sparsely furnished with a table, shelves for provisions, and a bench to sit on. William was fortunate to arrive in the mild early autumn, for prisoners had to spend all day, every day, in this bleak yard with only a single fireplace in each shed for warmth. At night the accommodation was worse. Inmates were herded across the courtyard into the dark confines of the Night Ward, a space divided into two apartments of smaller wards. Small barred windows allowed for the circulation of air to prevent disease but were placed too high to offer inmates any view of the world outside. For those with sufficient means, it was possible to share a wooden bed with sheets and blankets, but for most felons the only option was a barrack bed with no covers, and the destitute could find themselves sleeping on bare floorboards.

By the generally low standards of the time, the prison was relatively clean, but the courtyards were hugely overcrowded with every class of offender. Those awaiting trial mingled with "young beginners" and "fines" serving short sentences for minor offenses; yet this crowd of human jetsam also contained "daring desperate criminals," veteran offenders, and lunatics. All had to survive on a diet of beer or porter and a meager pound of bread a day. Yet there was one way an inmate could ease his lot: as in the case of debtors, the experience of prison life, even for felons, could be much improved by the possession of plenty of money. Several years earlier the eighteen-year-old James Hardy Vaux had the means to lodge in the better area, known as "between gates," in the space between the outer gate and the gate leading to the Common Side. Vaux found himself among similarly well-endowed "chums . . . several degrees above the common class of thieves" and managed to pass his time in a "most agreeable manner" reading, smoking, drinking, and conversing. Nevertheless, he also encountered

> some of the first characters upon the town, leading men in the various branches of prigging [thieving] they professed; both toby-gills [high-waymen], buz-gloaks [pickpockets], cracksmen [housebreakers], &c., but from their good address and respectable appearance nobody would suspect their real vocation. . . . My knowledge of life, as it is termed by the knavish part of mankind, and my acquaintance with family people [those "living by fraud and depredation"], increased daily.[21]

If Vaux was satisfied with his lot, he nevertheless pitied the poor wretches confined in the Common Side. To William's horror, it was into this area of the "seminary of Vice" that he found himself tossed, shackled in the particularly heavy irons reserved for forgers and possessing only the clothes he stood up in. What little money he had went to paying the keeper and the customary garnish (a fee paid by new inmates) of two pots of beer to his fellow prisoners. Most prisoners relied on family and friends to bring them food and financial support, but no one from William's "respectable" family came to visit, even after they heard of his arrest. He spent the ensuing empty days praying "most heartily to God to release me from my miseries."[22]

It was common practice for magistrates to place an advertisement—particularly in London, where newspaper publication was so frequent—to inform the wider public that an offender was being held on suspicion of having committed other crimes in addition to the one he was charged with. William's case was of great interest to the London papers, which were quick to report in their regular columns the shocking arrest of a young gentleman. The *Morning Post* broke the story on Friday, September 4, with all the appearance of a case of society gossip, and the other papers copied the account. The report alerted not only many of the other traders whom William had defrauded, but also members of his family, who had remained ignorant of his plight. The paper, not entirely accurately, described how

> a genteel young man, the son of a gentleman of fortune in Portland Place, the mention of whose name would only tend to distress the feelings of his unfortunate family, was charged, on more than one case, with having offered forged bankers cheques with intention to defraud Prescott & Co, and others. It appears that the offender has become so incorrigible as to render it next to impossible to receive the countenance of his parents or relatives—but he received £2 per week to prevent him being reduced to want. Upon a cheque produced, the prisoner was proved to have written the forged name of Harper by a person who witnessed it, and he was detected offering it in the Banking House. The further hearing was postponed to a future day.[23]

It was Jackson's agent, Charles Day, who first read the report and hurried down to Marlborough Street to check whether it referred to William. On confirming this, he wrote immediately to inform Mr. Jackson. He also sent £1 of his own money to aid William in Clerkenwell, although the gesture was ill appreciated by that inmate, who noted caustically that Day's "usual liberality" meant that he still could not even afford to pay for lighter leg irons.

Richard Colley Smith, Mr. Jackson's solicitor, read of the arrest in the evening papers, and he too rushed to the police office before relaying the distressing news to the Jacksons. Mr. Jackson, already apprised of the situation by Day, received yet more confirmation from a more malicious source. An anonymous author declared in accusatory tones that

> Mr. Jackson is hereby informed that a stop is at length put to the swindling transactions of his son, who is committed for trial in a case of fraud and forgery—having obtained goods, under false pretences (from hundreds of credulous tradesmen) and drawn cheques on Prescott & Co in payment thereof, signing himself Stephen Harper. The writer of this is aware of the distress such a son must have occasioned to his parents, but he has understood that they are not ignorant of his late way of life.[24]

This letter stung Mr. Jackson most deeply, for it seriously undermined his stated belief that he had nothing to reproach himself for regarding William's behavior. He had always adopted the moral position that to settle William's debts or pay for his extravagant purchases would only further encourage his son's dishonest behavior. But he could not have been unaware that a portion of public opinion supported the belief that wealthy fathers should help pay off their son's debts. Indeed, during debates over the Prince of Wales's debts in 1795, playwright and MP Richard Brinsley Sheridan had suggested that both parents should pay to rescue their offspring. "Was it not natural," he asked, "that a father and mother should contribute something to disencumber their child from his debts, and show examples of something like feeling and sacrifice?" If Jackson had failed to display "something like feeling" toward his son, he had, in the eyes of the anonymous letter writer, equally failed in his duty to stop William's criminal career. Both letters arrived at Langley on Saturday, but at ten o'clock that night, the Jacksons were disturbed again by a message from a Fleet Market attorney claiming that he had a plan that could rescue their son from "an ignominious death."[25]

Thomas Mawley was anxious to reach Langley as quickly as possible. Opportunities to make significant sums of money were rare among practitioners in the lower branches of the legal profession, and the chance to defend the son of an eminent gentleman was not to be missed. Langley lay on the busy Bath Road, so at his own expense he had taken a fast coach down from London and alighted at the Montague Arms, from where he sent a letter to the Jacksons. In fact, Mawley was already acting as William's attorney. He was aware that his young client was due to be re-examined on Monday and might be tried at the next sessions of the Old Bailey, which left only a few weeks to prepare a defense. No matter what the urgency, Mr. Jackson was taken aback at being addressed by such a person, who was utterly unknown to him. He sent a messenger to the Montague Arms refusing to receive Mawley at such a late hour; but his actions were less unfeeling than they might at first appear.

Lawyers in general, but particularly attorneys, suffered from a poor public reputation: often drawn from lower social ranks and serving an apprenticeship rather than the university training of barristers and judges, they stood accused of pettifogging, chicanery, quibbling, and sharp practice. Such was the opprobrium attached to attorneys that by the early nineteenth century the more respectable practitioners preferred, as Colley Smith did, to be known as solicitors, but that term, too, could be appropriated by less honest characters. Most worryingly for Jackson, there was a breed of criminal attorney known as "Newgate solicitors" who had a reputation for going to any lengths to secure the release of their clients, with little regard for truth or legal procedure. These men were to be found talking their way into Newgate (some were former inmates) to secure the confidence of potential clients. Others scoured the newspapers for news of promising-looking arrests. More than a few were retained by "family people" in the criminal underworld on a regular basis, because of their flexible principles and long experience at the Old Bailey.[26]

Despite the increasing regulation of all branches of the legal profession, in the 1830s the *Westminster Review* still lamented that "a considerable portion of the gaol business" was "in the hands of some of the most disreputable individuals in the metropolis." Mr. Mawley, who admitted to being in a less "respectable line of the profession" than Colley Smith, claimed to have thirty years' experience of criminal trials, a fact that would prove useful to Jackson's solicitor, who was more used to dealing with civil cases. Given William's recent associations with London's *demimonde* and other disreputable practitioners of fraud, it is almost certain that Mawley was recommended to him because he had connections with the criminal fraternity. Jackson's suspicions were hardly allayed when he met Mawley the following morning at the more civilized hour of ten o'clock. Mawley was far too confident that he could secure William's release if only he "were furnished with the proper means." Mr. Jackson strongly suspected that what the attorney actually meant was that he wanted sufficient money to buy witnesses or bribe the prosecutor.[27]

By now Jackson was convinced that he no longer had the power to stop his son's swindling activities; for this reason, he must rely on the law to restrain William. Nevertheless, he was anxious not to dismiss any lifeline that might be thrown to William for his mother's sake. By noon on Sunday, he had written several letters for Mawley to carry back to town on the understanding that their safe delivery and a rec-ommendation from Colley Smith would secure his employment. Charles Day was asked to accompany Mawley to the solicitors and pay whatever "was necessary for the prisoner" to save his life. Shaken by the suggestion in the anonymous letter that he could have stopped William's criminal career sooner, and frustrated by his earlier failed at-tempts to invoke the law to reform William's behavior, Jackson in-structed Smith *not* to save William

> from any punishment <u>short of</u> death, . . . because I am morally certain that unless the law can and will restrain him, nothing else would avail. . . . If his life could be saved, I shall rejoice, not on his, but on the account of others. To this point only do my instructions go—for I would not be the means of letting him once more loose on the world for any consideration that the world could offer.[28]

Unaware that the unhappy father wanted only limited legal protec-tion for his son and believing that he had almost certainly won the job, Mawley lingered another day in Langley before he traveled back to London—just in time for William's second appearance before the magistrates on Monday. Once there, however, he took pains to ensure the good opinion of his young client by paying for his removal to the better side of Clerkenwell Prison.

On receipt of Jackson's letters that Monday morning, Day and Colley Smith acted with extraordinary speed to secure legal represen-tation for William's second examination at Marlborough Street. For many magistrates, such hearings were still largely private affairs, but the London police offices had led the transformation of pre-trial examinations into public hearings at which both counsel and solicitors were increasingly present. Their presence, however, made little difference to the limited rights of the accused. William was not allowed to know the exact nature of the charges against him because it was believed that members of a jury would more readily ascertain the truth of the case if they could witness his initial reaction. His solicitor was not entitled to a copy of the indictment either.

Colley Smith therefore took copious notes of all the evidence presented, which he could then pass on to Jackson and to William's defense counsel, who was also prohibited from seeing copies of the depositions sworn against his client. Hence, when William entered the magistrates' office that day, he should have had a significant advantage over poorer defendants. There was a surprisingly large crowd present, and if the faces of Day, Mawley, Colley Smith, and the well-known Old Bailey barrister John Adolphus provided some reassurance, the sight of the angry countenances of a number of his defrauded creditors did not. The Wigmore Street linen draper Joseph Christian had already successfully pressed charges without representation, but William's former landlord Colville was advised by another member of the Old Bailey bar, Mr. Barry Robson, the Oxford Street linen draper, was not represented, but he, too, convinced the magistrates of the strength of his case, and so William was committed for trial at the Old Bailey on three counts (but it could have been for many more).[29]

The other creditors present at that hearing were less keen to press formal charges. Colley Smith was so convinced that William would be convicted on the existing charges that he thought there was little point in their doing so, but many still hoped to benefit from William's arrest. As they watched the proceedings, a rumor began to ripple through the crowd—that the young gentleman's wealthy father would pay off all his debts if the injured parties did not press charges. The failure of the accused to show any evidence of contrition for his actions only served to fan the belief, which Mawley secretly planned to encourage despite Colley Smith's refusal to endorse it. It was far more common for victims to enter into negotiation with, or employ informal sanctions against, the accused than to press charges. Even after magistrates had become involved, a short spell in jail awaiting trial was satisfaction enough for many prosecutors or acted as a sufficient inducement for the accused or his family to offer reparations. It was technically illegal to compound a felony by paying off the prosecutor, but Parliament had repeatedly failed to enforce such legislation effectively.[30]

Although they could seek financial assistance from the court to finance a prosecution, at least three creditors believed they had more to gain by entering into negotiation with William's father. Two had young families to support and were being pressed for payment by other traders; another had lost a hired horse to William and wanted to prosecute him for swindling. The unscrupulous Mawley took it upon himself to visit these creditors and assure them that they would all be paid, but Colley Smith soon dashed all hopes of receiving any financial recompense from Jackson.[31]

Mr. Jackson would not pay any of William's creditors, even at the risk of further endangering his son's life, but he did not want the youth to walk free either. He clung desperately to the belief that he had done his duty as a good father and that "no man can say with truth that any sort of blame can attach to me for the disgrace and ruin of an unworthy son." He was equally convinced that William was "incorrigibly vitious [sic]" and that it was no longer "in the power of man to reclaim him." If William was discharged or helped by any member of his family, he would merely continue to prey upon the public in the belief that "the atrocious acts of which he has been guilty would be permitted to pass with impunity." His actions could no longer be forgiven as "the mere indiscretions of youth," for they bore the stamp of "determined vice" for which he felt no shame and upon which "the dictates of moral and religious duty have [not] the slightest effect."[32]

IT IS TEMPTING, from a modern perspective, to comment that Jackson had never tried to understand the frustrations of youth or to openly express his love for his son; nor had he provided positive incentives to change William's behavior, relying instead on constant censure and surveillance. Yet Jackson had acted in accordance with the moral beliefs of his class and much of the advice literature available for parents at the time. Jackson was not being unusually heartless when he directed Colley Smith to refuse to negotiate with William's creditors on the grounds that he would never "be responsible for any debt contracted in defiance of the laws under which I live, and by which I am myself protected." He wholeheartedly subscribed to the popular notion that the English "rule of law" was a shining example of good government. It was widely believed that every member of society, from the highest to the lowest, was equal before the law and that it operated entirely for the good of the public. If the actual application of the law was not infrequently challenged, this principle—which was often cited by those wishing to legitimate their actions—was not. This view also underpinned Jackson's moral certainty "that unless the law can and will restrain him, nothing else would avail" to protect the public interest.[33] Yet principles can serve personal aims too, and their articulation provided Jackson with a reason to abandon his parental duties that was difficult to challenge. They also protected Jackson from the consequences of his son's actions, behavior that threatened to destroy both his physical and mental health, and the wealth and position in society he had worked so hard to rebuild in the aftermath of his humiliation by the East India Company.[34]

Not everyone in William's family, however, shared Jackson's unbending belief that the criminal justice system should be allowed to take its course for the good of the public. Sir George Shee was more than willing to exercise a degree of discretion when it came to a member of his own family. He was very anxious about the distress caused to his sister and to Jackson and assumed that they would sanction any means to save their son's life. A friend of William's called at Shee's home in Manchester Square and left a letter informing him of William's imprisonment and begging that "humanity will induce you to intercede on his behalf with his family and friends." With fewer financial means and considerably less social standing than the baronet, the friend had been unable to persuade the linen draper to drop or lessen the severity of the charges.[35]

Shee immediately left his home and walked round to Christian's premises, where they engaged in a lengthy conversation about the nature of William's crime. The discussion left the MP little hope that his nephew could be saved by legal means. Convinced that the prosecutor had both a strong case and little desire to show leniency, Shee wrote urgently to Jackson, advising him that

> without some very prompt and active interference, the <u>result</u> will be <u>most unpleasant</u>. In short, there appears to be but one way in which the calamity can be avoided—namely—in plain English—by <u>buying</u> off the <u>prosecutor</u>, and I have doubts even whether that measure would succeed. At all events, it is clear that no time should be lost, and I have given you this intimation in consequence, without a moment's delay.[36]

The MP was aware of his brother-in-law's strict morality and, loath to interfere in a matter of paternal discipline, so he added tactfully, "How far you may feel disposed, or may think right, or may deem it of any use to interfere, it is not for me to say, and therefore [I] hazard no comment upon the case." Mr. Jackson was moved by Shee's concern but remained determined to do no more than rescue William from death, for his mother's sake, and only then if it could be achieved by strictly legal means. Because William's "monstrous" behavior had continued for several years, Jackson explained to Shee that his mind had

> long been prepared for the event which has taken place. . . . The sums which he has raised by fraud and plunder, and squandered among prostitutes and pickpockets are <u>immense;</u> and the truest description that was ever given of him . . . I have extracted from a newspaper . . . [:] "<u>No swindler since the days of Hatfield, who married the beauty of Buttermere, has committed more depradations on the Town than William Jackson</u>."[37]

With such a black picture painted by William's father, it was little wonder that Shee did not renew the offer to help his nephew. Jackson could have paid Christian and still seen William convicted on the lesser charges, a course of action that would have fulfilled his stated aim to preserve his son's life while ensuring his removal from society. Instead, he carefully omitted the illegal advice to buy off the prosecutor from his narrative of *Filial Ingratitude,* probably to preserve both his own and the MP's reputation. Yet despite the strength of his moral convictions, Jackson also provided Shee with a revealing glimpse of the true bitterness caused by paternal love when it is soured by years of disappointment and shame. Jackson's blind pursuit of principle masked an emotional pain that could be assuaged only by seeing his son endure the same. William had made "others suffer quite enough," he told Shee, "and it is now high time he should himself suffer." So while Jackson delivered his own unbending judgment, his son was condemned to contemplate his likely fate alone in Clerkenwell Prison. Apart from visits by Jackson's solicitor and the insidious Mawley, William waited in vain for any sign that his parents and former friends cared about whether he lived or died. Believing himself deserted, he had been plagued with insomnia ever since his counsel, "who seldom apprize their clients of danger," advised him that there was "faint hope" of escaping the hangman's noose.[38]

7

A MANSION OF MISERY

Newgate and the Old Bailey, 1812

Newgate itself is, both in its construction and constitution, of all places the most horrid. It is not, as every prison ought to be, an establishment to keep the prisoners with safety and oeconomy, and, at the same time, to preserve their health and insure some reformation in their morals. It is not an institution to promote good behaviour amongst prisoners within the walls, . . . It is a place for the safe custody of the body if it live and for nothing else. . . . There are always many hundred prisoners. . . . They herd together in large parties. Sensuality is their only enjoyment. They are at war with society. They hate all men; for, as they suppose, all men hate them.

— Basil Montagu, *An Inquiry into the Aspersions Upon the Late Ordinary of Newgate* (1815)

With the next sessions at the Old Bailey due to start in late September, William knew he would soon be disgorged into the dismal depths of the felons' side of Newgate jail— no longer with the rights and privileges of a debtor but confined with convicted criminals. The brooding "mansion of misery" stood at the junction of Holborn and Newgate streets, linked to the nearby Old

Bailey courthouse by a subterranean passage. The addition of a ventila-tion system and more rigorous efforts to clean its interior and super-vise the health of its inmates had led to a reduction in the noisome stench that used to overcome residents in Newgate Street. Yet the prison's massive, rough-hewn stone walls, designed to give off an air of grim impenetrability, did no more than disguise the chaos that still reigned within. Built to hold around five hundred prisoners, the prison might house nearly double that number, particularly when the other London jails, like Clerkenwell, delivered their contents prior to the start of each new session at the Old Bailey.

Constant overcrowding threatened the health and what sparse comfort there was available to prisoners. They had little to do but dis-tract themselves by gambling, drinking, smoking, and seeking sex with prostitutes—"wives" paid "bad money" to the turnkeys in order to stay overnight. Overfilling of the jail posed an even greater problem for the turnkeys, whose surveillance duties were already frustrated by the dark maze of passages, wards, cellars, and stairwells that undermined the otherwise orderly division of the prison into three quadrangles for debtors, male felons, and female felons. The prison population was daily swollen by the vast number of visitors—friends, family, and op-portunistic purveyors of food and drink, prostitutes, attorneys, gangs of thieves, and groups of curious tourists—who thronged the crowded yards. The turnkeys insisted that the wearing of leg irons was the only safe way to distinguish between felons and visitors. Children, whether the innocent offspring of an inmate or offenders as young as nine, weaved in and out of adult company, along with an assortment of pigs and poultry. Despite the use of shackles, the criminal side of the jail has been aptly described as an "inmate netherworld, ruling an institu-tion of the state with its own officers, its own customs and its own rit-uals." John Newman, the prison's humane but ineffective keeper, admitted to a parliamentary committee in 1811 that there was "no dis-cipline of any kind in Newgate."[1]

HAVING ALREADY BRIEFLY tasted the filth and the fear of being locked up with the "vilest of the vile" in Newgate, William wrote to his father from Clerkenwell, begging him to pay the necessary fees to place him in "the best side" of the prison, but to no avail. In early September 1812, he entered Newgate by the Felon's Gate, beneath a looming archway ominously festooned with stone-carved fetters that symbolized his new status. He was pushed into the Common Side of the male felons' yard, where his gentlemanly manners made no impression on his fellow inmates. That year there had been some attempt to separate untried prisoners from hardened offenders, which meant that William could spend his days in the chapel yard, but at night he slept with other prisoners charged with murder and violent theft.[2]

The wards were fitted with wooden boards placed on an inclined plane and a beam running across the top to serve as barrack beds along one side, but when the prison was overcrowded, the whole fifteen-foot width of the ward could be so covered, with only a small channel left down the middle. Each prisoner received two rugs in which to sleep, but because the keeper estimated each man needed only eighteen inches to be able to turn over, there was no escaping from the frequently malodorous felons on either side. The risk of fire meant that no straw could be allowed for bedding, so, like the debtors, prisoners slept and lived in the same set of clothes in which they entered the jail. Visitors were frequently menaced for money by inmates reduced to wearing little more than rags, who also stole clothing from better-dressed newcomers, as William soon discovered.

The wards themselves were relatively clean, with regularly white-washed walls, and an eerie light filtered through from the rows of green glass windows that overlooked the courtyards. There was a fire at one end, the smoke from which, combined with the vast quantities of tobacco smoke puffed by prisoners every day, stained the ceilings and stifled the air. William was obliged to pay garnish or risk being refused access to the fire and forced to swab the filthy, dark oak floors. Each morning at seven o'clock, he shuffled forward to be counted with his fellows before consuming whatever meager ration his friends had provided for breakfast. Apart from the onerous tasks of emptying his chamber pot and cleaning the rooms while hampered by four pounds of iron around his legs, he had nothing to do until midafternoon, when the main meal—often no more than bread, rice, or potatoes and water supplemented by tiny amounts of beef three times a week—was prepared. In the long hours before lunch, and between then and dinner at seven o'clock, William had every opportunity to spend his weekly allowance seeking oblivion in the consumption of wine and beer provided by the obliging Anne Sell, mistress of the prison taphouse. Spirits were strictly forbidden but often smuggled in by visitors, and drunkenness was endemic—fights between prisoners were not uncommon, and more than one turnkey lost his life as a result of a violent attack by an intoxicated inmate.

Because the other prisoners stole any cash they could from him, William's other means of gaining (or losing) more money while also entertaining himself was gambling. Games of chance such as bumble puppy, what's clock, dice, dominoes, and cards were played obsessively long into the night, and even those who would rather have abstained were put under heavy pressure by their fellows to join in. If William had any spare coins remaining to supplement his now rather shabby veneer of charm, then he almost certainly used them to procure sex. As one visitor remarked, "The depravity of the Metropolitan prison is proverbial. . . . Every man is visited by a woman . . . for the purposes of general prostitution."[3]

Despite access to such consolations, William found being confined with men charged with violent felonies to be a deeply distressing experience. Not only did he still fail to view his actions as truly criminal; it also was the first time that he had been completely bereft of the protection usually provided by his status and appearance. There was no escaping the fetters that marked him out as a possible felon (only those on misdemeanor charges had any chance of remaining unshackled). Respected legal opinion held that those awaiting trial should not be fettered because they should appear free from them in court. But in Newgate the practice of "loading" prisoners with heavier irons to force them to pay for "easement," or to pay for them to be removed before a court appearance, was particularly pernicious. Just days before William arrived, an anonymous "prisoner" had sent a lengthy diatribe against the practice to a London newspaper, denouncing the Newgate jailers as "frequently a merciless set of men" who by "being conversant in scenes of misery, [were] steeled against any tender sensations."[4]

Yet it was the administration organized by the prisoners themselves, rather than the jailers' insensitivities, which was the bigger threat to William's peace of mind. Daily government of the prison effectively lay in the hands of officers elected by the prisoners. These men—the gates-men and wardsmen, who received extra rations as payment—collected the garnish money used to buy collective supplies for the prisoners, chose who should receive any charity distributed, and set up discipli-nary tribunals. "Outsiders"—those of a higher class unfamiliar with the flash language and culture of the criminal underworld, those who re-fused to join the swearing, drinking, gaming, sex, and singing of ribald songs, or anyone who committed an offense against the community—were stripped, ostracized, or subject to a mock trial. As one unfortunate ex-attorney with respectable connections discovered, this involved an inversion of the trial procedure they would all soon face:

> Someone, generally the oldest and most dexterous thief, is appointed judge; a towel tied in knots is hung on each side of his head, in imita-tion of a wig. He takes his seat, if he can find one, with all form and decorum; and to call him any thing but "my lord," is a high misde-meanour. A jury is then appointed and regularly <u>sworn</u>, and the cul-prit is brought up. Unhappily justice is not administered with quite the same integrity within the prison as without it. The most trifling bribe to the judge will secure an acquittal, but the neglect of this for-mality is a sure prelude to condemnation. The punishments are vari-ous, standing in the pillory is the heaviest. The criminal's head is placed between the legs of a chair, and his arms stretched out are at-tached to it, he then carries about this machine; but any punishment, no matter how heinous the offence may be commuted into a fine, to be spent in gin, for the use of the Judge and Jury.[5]

William wrote to both Colley Smith and his father begging to be moved to the better side of the jail. The ever-diligent solicitor had swallowed his distaste and visited William in Newgate to compose a statement of his version of events—prisoners accused of felony could use a room where the turnkeys lodged to consult with their legal advi-sors in greater privacy—but no member of his family had crossed the shameful threshold or communicated with him in any way. William was unwilling to provide further details about what had happened, but despite finding his efforts to help largely frustrated, Colley Smith was not unsympathetic to his young client's plight in prison.

Smith subscribed to ideas made popular by prison reformers, like John Howard and Jeremy Bentham, that criminals were not incorrigible reprobates but could be rehabilitated through shame, discipline, and faith. Because reformers believed that criminals were rational creatures, possessed of consciences, and capable of choosing between good and evil, they argued that the aim of punishment should be to arouse a sense of guilt and regret for past sins. This aim would be achieved by separating criminals from the evil influences of their peers and forcing them to reflect alone without any opportunity for sensuous diversion. Appalled by the "lowest and vilest miscreants" William was mixing with, Colley Smith wrote to Jackson, using just such an argument to convince him to allow William to be moved, explaining that the other "miserable wretches" in the Common Side would not allow William "to reflect, if so disposed." Smith reassured Jackson that if William was not sentenced to death on the forgery charge, he thought it very "probable that the Court will see that he is taken proper care of and has no means of committing other enormities on society for some time to come, during which period it is to be devoutly wished that the Almighty will be graciously pleased to work a reformation in him."[6]

In fact, there was little chance of William undergoing any form of reformation while he remained in Newgate. Despite regular services held in the imposing and austere prison chapel, Dr. Forde, the prison chaplain (known as the Ordinary), admitted that he had no incentive to "make vain and imprudent attempts to reform eight hundred misguided fellow creatures." Indeed, any effort to reward a man for his piety would most likely lead to his being attacked by the other prisoners. Jackson, however, who had taken to wondering whether the only explanation for William's decision to squander all the advantages of rank and wealth was some form of insanity, became convinced by Colley Smith's argument. He authorized Smith to negotiate William's removal to the better side of the prison, but only on the condition that

> it should appear to him as your act than mine. The only possible chance of bringing him back to a sense of his proper duty, and to reclaim him from those fatal errors in which he has involved himself is,

by giving him clearly to understand that, while he persists in such a course he will in vain look for any protection or assistance from his family or relatives. Unhappily for him, he fancied otherwise. . . . It is, therefore, a point of great necessity that he should learn from experience that if he transgresses the law, there will be no interference to shield him from disgrace and punishment.[7]

Colley Smith negotiated a fee with keeper Newman to allow William to reside in the State Side of Newgate. He could have purchased lodging in the Master's Side of the jail, but apart from sharing a proper bed with only one other, usually "more decent and better behaved" prisoner, there was little difference in their treatment. The State Side was the very best section of the jail, reserved for those "whose manners and conduct evince a more liberal style of education." The twelve rooms housed thirty to forty men for a charge of 2 guineas for admittance and 10s. 6d. for a single bed or 7s. for a bed shared with another, but once there, prisoners no longer had to pay garnish, and food was plentiful. Such an arrangement usually excluded suspected or convicted felons, so Colley Smith had to pay an extra guinea to get William admitted. This was another practice that outraged the anonymous author who wrote to the *Examiner*. Jackson and Colley Smith had no such qualms; their sole aim was to separate William from the common convicts. William himself was less grateful than he might have been and complained bitterly to his mother about the "exorbitant rent" he had to pay for his "miserable apartment."[8]

WILLIAM'S COMPLAINT is perhaps more explicable in the light of his growing fear of the hangman's noose and his belief (fostered by his father's tactics) that his family would not try to save him from a shameful, agonizing death. During September the letters William wrote from the felons' side of Newgate affected a penitent resignation toward his possible fate in the hope that he would "meet with mercy in a better world than this." Jackson did not believe the sincerity of these expressions because they were linked to requests for removal to the State Side and for a new suit of clothes from his tailor. By October a note of desperation had crept into William's numerous but unanswered letters.

Separated as he now was from the bulk of felons and those awaiting execution in the condemned cells, William found the cultivation of brave insouciance practiced by those who aspired to make "a good end" on the gallows increasingly difficult to maintain. If he was not yet suffering the full "horror of mind" that drove many of the condemned to madness, he could not entirely escape the pall of fear and death that permeated the prison. Following a visit to Newgate in 1835, Charles Dickens described how

> contact with death even in its least terrible shape, is solemn and appalling. How much more awful is it to reflect on this near vicinity to the dying—to men in full health and vigour, in the flower of youth or the prime of life, with all their faculties and perceptions as acute and perfect as your own; but dying.[9]

That William was very close to facing his own death was forcibly brought home to him when he found himself arraigned before the Old Bailey court at the start of the September sessions without any defense counsel present. He had good reason to be anxious. Prisoners arraigned on a felony charge would normally be tried immediately after they entered a plea. Because the presumption of innocence had not yet been fully established and only around a third of defendants had any counsel, many had then stood trial unprepared, only to emerge hours, or more frequently minutes, later stunned to find themselves convicted of a capital crime. Still wearing what was left of the clothes he had been arrested in, William and the other prisoners were herded, still fettered, along the filthy subterranean passage that linked Newgate to the Old Bailey. They were left to wait in the basement and brought up to stand before the judge in batches, with little chance to say more than whether they wanted to plead "guilty" or "not guilty."[10]

William had more legal knowledge than most of the lower-class defendants with him, but even he would not have known the full details of the charges against him until they were read out to him in court that day. But with his usual presence of mind and enough knowledge of the law to understand the procedure (no doubt acquired from Mawley or fellow inmates), he successfully presented an affidavit to postpone his trial to the next sessions on the grounds that a vital witness was not present to give evidence. Nevertheless, the experience left him shaken to the core and uncertain whether anyone in his family or legal team could be trusted to provide a proper defense for him. Unknown to William, Mr. Jackson seems to have been once more assailed by doubts about helping his viciously immoral son escape just punishment, and he failed to arrange for the defense to be present at William's arraignment.

William's suspicions were further fueled by a belief that his shady attorney, Mawley, was misappropriating funds for his defense. Yet he was afraid of the attorney's knowledge and influential contacts and dared not terminate his services. Jackson, who had long believed the man was not to be trusted, particularly after Colley Smith had fired him from his legal team, refused all William's frantic requests to keep paying him. Panicked by this refusal, William used the prospect of his "ignominious" death to try to shame Jackson into doing

> the duty of a parent, and endeavour to save me from a fate that cannot but bring disgrace, and surely some portion of sorrow on you. I implore your's and my mother's forgiveness, and entreat to see you without delay since not one moment should be lost, before it is yet too late, to save me from death and ignominy.[11]

But this plea came too late to have any effect on Jackson. He felt that William had long ago broken all the bonds of reciprocal family duty, so by way of reply he sent William a parcel containing copies of his earlier incriminating letters and broken promises to reform. In order to justify this apparently hard-hearted tactic to readers of *Filial Ingratitude,* he drew their attention to exactly where the relevant deceitful passages of each letter could be found.

As October wore on and his full trial was scheduled for the sessions that started in just three weeks, William became increasingly desperate and willing to resort to any underhanded tactic of bribery or blackmail to ensure that he had a proper defense on the day. The criminal justice system ensured that Englishmen of every rank had the right to a fair, if brief, trial, but the increasingly adversarial nature of court practice meant that wealth conferred a significant advantage on defendants who could afford to pay for skilled defense counsel and solicitors to conduct factual investigations. This advantage was particularly marked at a time when the majority of defendants and prosecutors were still unable to do so. William knew that his father had the means to pay for top barristers but was terrified that his continued silence signaled a refusal to do so. On October 4 William wrote "a penitent letter to my father and expressed deep contrition." On October 9 he blamed Colley Smith for failing to attend his arraignment and to do his duty "as the friend and solicitor of my father"; William even threatened to make this letter public should he be convicted because he was convinced that his father's "money, as well as my life, is this present trifled with." On the same day he wrote a long and emotional plea to his mother in the hope that she at least might be moved to continue to act as his "friend" by performing her parental duty to protect him:

> *Mercy, my dear mother is a God-like attribute. Recollect I am your only Child, and in a few weeks may be torn from you forever.*
> *I conceive myself at this moment one of the most miserable beings in existence, and it adds to my sufferings when I reflect you who I know to be the only real and sincere friend I have left upon earth, do not think me even worthy of replying to my letters. You, who I am convinced was always the first to alleviate the fortunes of the oppressed. The miseries I have endured since my imprisonment in this Gaol, are more than I can describe. . . . For God's sake, my dearest Mother, do not renounce me entirely in the hour of danger. I have little hope of mercy, but my last prayers will be for the health and welfare of my best friend. I therefore trust my dear Mother you will not be biased by the assertions of <u>Hirelings</u>, but still perform that duty, which you invariably performed in my juvenile years both of parent and friend. Let me impress your mind that my trial comes on next Wednesday fortnight. My life depends entirely on the evidence of one man, and he positively refuses to attend unless I send him six pounds to defray the expense of his journey to London, as he resides at Willingborough, Northamptonshire. In the hope of a line from you in answer, I trust you will believe the sincere professions of contrition and amendment of your unfortunate son,*

> *Burke Jackson*[12]

Jane Jackson did not reply to William, but her resolve began to crack. Mr. Jackson remained convinced that he and his wife were both utterly absolved of the bonds of friendship and parenthood they had happily embraced during William's early childhood, "when he was innocent and good." But Jane Jackson found the thought of seeing her only son die on the gallows increasingly unbearable and begged her husband to take action. A week later Jane's pleas proved successful: Colley Smith at last informed William that he had been employed to manage his defense team. Indeed, he had already retained the services of John Adolphus (who had represented William before at his committal hearing) and Peter Alley, both of whom were highly regarded barristers.[13]

Despite this, and unaware of his mother's role in retaining defense counsel, William tried new tactics to force his father to support him openly. His letters were a mixture of threats, gratitude, and desperation. Mawley, he warned, had deemed it absolutely necessary that Jackson should be subpoenaed to appear in court during his trial—an action that would bring huge shame on his father and the rest of the family were William found guilty. Yet he would ignore Mawley's advice if only Jackson would reply in person and provide him with a new suit of clothes to wear in court. Such was his confusion and desperation that William then declared himself equally determined to follow different advice from everyone in the defense team and from some who had not even been hired.[14]

Still there was no reply, but Smith conveyed Mr. Jackson's objection to Mawley's presence in court. So William was forced to adopt a more conciliatory tone—promising not to subpoena his father and to dismiss Mawley, even though he still wanted the attorney present in court. William also agreed that the clothes he needed could be of any description as long as they arrived before the sessions commenced the following Wednesday. Jackson relented so far as to order his tailors to make William a new coat, waistcoat, and breeches, but he stipulated that they must be "neat and plain without any thing gay or gaudy. <u>It should be a suit of mourning</u>."[15]

A suit of clothes may not appear to be of much significance, but this battle over the mode of William's appearance in court symbolized in vivid terms the gulf that lay between father and son. For

William, a gentlemanly appearance was essential to produce a favorable impression in court, to draw sympathy from observers and jurors saddened to see one of such youth, wealth, and status at risk of losing his life for a crime many of middling and higher rank had been tempted to commit to keep their place in society. A gentleman's word was his honor; to be clothed as a gentleman provided a better chance of being understood as a gentleman—a man whose testimony should be believed above that of a tradesman. If he was condemned, William could appear to die bravely, dressed in his best, as a gentleman should. For Mr. Jackson, William's trial was a disgrace to his rank, fortune, and family, so he should appear soberly dressed, contrite, and ready to atone for his sins in prison or in exile. If his son was convicted of forgery, the suit was appropriate for a man about to make a good end on the gallows (by confessing his sins to God and for the edification of the watching crowd); it was a suit he could be buried in.

William's fears about the amount of effort Colley Smith was prepared to put into organizing his defense were somewhat unfair, but they were not, as Jackson declared, "a most scandalous and abominable falsehood." Colley Smith was determined to "pay proper attention to the youth and his defence," but he was also deeply ambivalent about the morality of the case because its "real merits are . . . unfortunately too obvious" and could badly affect his own reputation and his relationship with his other clients. To be associated with an unsavory character from the lower branches of the legal profession like Mawley was also a risky business, so Smith lost no time in persuading William to accept the services of Mr. Fletcher, a more reputable attorney with greater criminal law experience than himself.[16]

Hence, during his exhaustive and tactful preparations for the case, Smith carefully balanced his loyalties so as not to "disregard what is due to myself, to you, and to my other worthy connexions." Nevertheless, his services certainly provided William with an advantage that he had good reason to be grateful for. Most Newgate prisoners were left to write their own briefs or prepare them for their fellow inmates. Those who could afford no more than the 1 guinea fee either had to contact a barrister themselves or hope that the court might appoint one for them at trial. Both courses were likely to leave counsel poorly prepared, and most barristers still received their briefs only the night before a case came on.[17]

With Fletcher's assistance and advice, Colley Smith convinced William to retain John Adolphus, who had some prior knowledge of the case, and to hire Peter Alley as his principal counsel instead of John Gurney. All three were colorful characters and well-known practitioners at the Old Bailey bar, although Adolphus had less experience than the other two. William wanted to hire John Gurney, who had played a significant role in every forgery case tried at the Old Bailey that year. Then William eagerly proposed hiring all three barristers, but Colley Smith eventually convinced him that two counsel would be "quite sufficient" for the case and that Peter Alley was an excellent choice to lead his defense. One contemporary described how Alley

> knew the criminal and sessions law well, argued his points with force and clearness; but too roughly, on the assumption that his client was an unfortunate man against whom the constables, magistrates and grand jury had been prejudiced by the prosecutor. This style was sure to be popular within the gaol, the residents of which knew that, even were the cases against them too clear to leave a doubt, they would have a chance from Mr. Alley's great skill in discovering any defect in the indictment, and the certainty that their prosecutors would be roughly handled.

Colley Smith knew that William's innocence would be extremely difficult to prove, so finding a fault in the prosecution's indictment could well be the only way to get him acquitted.[18]

Peter Alley and John Adolphus were an imposing team for any prosecutor to contend with. Adolphus was a strong and eloquent speaker who had honed his oratory skills in debating clubs and in speaking for electioneering MPs. Both men were occasionally hot-tempered as well as impassioned and impetuous orators in court. Adolphus was particularly prone to losing his temper when provoked by rudeness—a not infrequent occurrence at the Old Bailey. It was also his common practice, as his son later described it, to ply "the jury with a sort of by-play, stares, shrugs, laughs (I have even heard of winks), while the adverse counsel was addressing them."[19]

Alley and Adolphus were among a small group of top lawyers who gained almost cult status among the lower orders, from where most Old Bailey defendants originated; but their aggressive tactics drew criticism from the press and from members of the bar anxious to present a more gentlemanly image of their profession. Vociferous barristers, it was claimed, were hiding their ignorance of the law and indulging in tricks to prevent the court from determining the truth—too many guilty men were set free by the skills of an immoral barrister. A wily prosecutor, however, might exploit the long-standing rivalry that existed between Alley and Adolphus. Indeed, the "warmth of feeling" between them generated by a later case in 1816 finally degenerated into personal insults that led to a duel in Calais, during which Alley was shot in the arm. Nevertheless, many contemporary observers believed that both men usually abandoned all show of professional rivalry on leaving court, and given the difficulties of William's case, they were now obliged to do so within it, too.[20]

On the night of October 23, just four days before the Old Bailey sessions were due to start, William's legal team met with Colley Smith to discuss his case. Both Alley and Adolphus were deeply apprehensive for his life because they believed the forgery charge would almost certainly be proved. Their only hope was to try to show that William had written the "forged" check in the presence of Stephen Harper and at his request, before giving it to the linen draper's shop man in payment for the shirts. The barristers thought that neither William's account of the transaction nor his witnesses were likely to convince the jury, but Colley Smith was more hopeful. He had spent over two hours interviewing William's "woman," the redoubtable Mrs. Parker. He told Jackson that she had stoutly maintained throughout that she "perfectly recollects" Harper had asked William to sign the check in the name of "Stephen Harper"—words that "struck her at the time as being very odd," as "well they might," Smith added cynically. Yet even if she were to be believed, Mrs. Parker would be considered at best an interested witness. Stephen Harper and his woman had vanished beyond the solicitor's reach, but because Smith did not believe William's version of events, he thought their disappearance was probably less disastrous than putting them on the stand would be.[21]

Filial Ingratitude &c.

Early in the year 1808, Mr. Jackson placed his only son under the tuition of the Reverend Mr. Owen, rector of Fulham, who had, for some years, been accustomed to the care of a select number of young men, preparatory to their going to the University. Soon after the young man had been so placed, he addressed the following letters to his Father.

My dear Father.　　　　　Fulham
　　　　　　　　　　　March 2d 1808.

I now take up my pen to acknowledge the receipt of your last kind letter. It will afford me great pleasure to accept of your edition of Pliny – He is, certainly, a most excellent author, and the perusal of him cannot fail to improve the mind, if read with attention. I find much pleasure in informing you, that I am not the least behind the rest of my companions. I have I assure you, very little to do with them, for I am determined, for the future, to spend my time to more advantage, namely. to the improvement and cultivation of my mind, which is only to be acquired by Books.

Mrs. Owen gives a dance on friday week, and as she has done me the honour of giving me an invitation, I shall esteem it a favor, if you have no objection, to my ordering a pair of dress breeches of Tautz for that occasion. I have now nothing more to say, but remain by subscribing myself, ever most affectionately yours
　　　　　　W. C. B. Jackson.

P.S. Remember me most kindly to my mother.

My dear Father,　　　　　　Fulham
　　　　　　　　　　　10th March 1808.*
　　Next Saturday being a whole holiday, I shall do myself the pleasure of calling upon you early, as I shall

* This letter was sent by the two penny post, and marked on the cover. "8 o'clock 12 march." It was at ten o'clock

FIGURE 1. The first page of *Filial Ingratitude* shows Mr. Jackson's typical style of combining brief narrative explanation with copies of letters, plus comments in the margins, to prove William's deceitful behavior.

FIGURE 2. This satirical print from *Life in London* represents the status and financial fortunes of men in London society. Beneath the monarch stand a noble of inherited wealth and a respectable merchant (like Mr. Jackson) who earned his elite status. His son wanted to be one of the fashionable "Ups" but joined the ranks of the "Ins and Outs," who were imprisoned for debt (or crime) but then released. The "Downs" have fallen too low to be noticed by society. The "Tag-Rag and Bobtail" man is selling a condemned criminal's "last dying speech"—the ignominious end of those who fell too far.

FIGURE 3 *(left)*. John Evelyn, William's favorite uncle, shown in later life after he had inherited the house and estate of Wotton in Surrey. FIGURE 4 *(right)*. Thomas Potter Macqueen (1791–1854), seen here in uniform as lieutenant colonel of the Bedfordshire yeomanry cavalry, was William's closest friend during their school days and became an MP. He set up a scheme to encourage free emigrants to settle in Australia, and went there to live in 1834 after losing his inheritance during a corrupt election campaign. He returned to England but suffered from chronic indebtedness for the rest of his life.

FIGURE 5. This satirical print from *The Scourge* showing paths to the Temple of Fortune includes an attack on moneylender John "Jew" King and his wife *(left)*, fleeing downhill to escape fire from the Sword of "Justice." The outcome of King's unscrupulous activities is suggested by the signpost "High Road to Newgate" pointing to the felons' side of the prison and the gallows.

FIGURE 6. Thought to be the first recorded example of a whistling shop—a room in debtors' prisons where illegal spirits were sold secretly—this shows the mix of social classes in Fleet Prison: an educated gentleman, two gamblers, a smuggler smoking a pipe, a haberdasher pouring drinks, a "tradesman" confronted by his desperate wife and children, and a poor author leaning against the fireplace; two racquet players take a break from the game used to pass the idle hours.

FIGURE 7. This picture of the interior of the first police office to be set up in London illustrates the public nature of a typical pretrial examination by magistrates, who are seated on the bench to the left facing the accused on the lighted stand.

FIGURE 8. This satirical print shows William's Old Bailey lawyers Peter Alley (*left*) and John Adolphus (*right*) arguing over an unflattering remark Adolphus made about Alley at the Old Bailey in 1816. They fought a duel in Calais to avoid the law; Alley was wounded, but the two later reconciled and remained close friends.

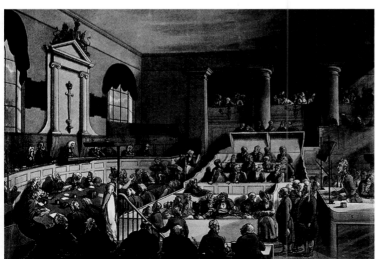

FIGURE 9 (*left*). In the Sessions House in Old Bailey, the judges sit on the left with legal counsel around the table below. A female witness gives evidence; the accused stands in the dock beneath a mirror that reflects light onto his face so the jury to his right can assess whether he is telling the truth.

FIGURE 10. In this view of Newgate Prison, the figures and horse-drawn vehicles in front of the walls give an idea of their massive size.

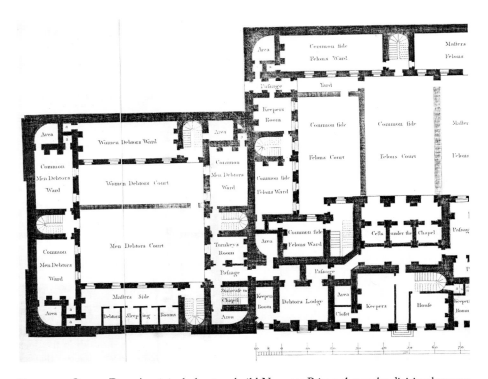

FIGURE 11. George Dance's original plan to rebuild Newgate Prison shows the division between debtors' and felons' sides. The wards were divided by gender and wealth of inmate. William was confined in the "Common" wards as a debtor and then a felon, but his family paid to move him to one of the exclusive "State" rooms.

FIGURE 12. The *Discovery*, a merchant ship converted for use as a prison hulk, is shown beached at low tide. The buildings added to the top deck are clearly visible, surmounted by laundry drying on the rigging.

THE FAIR ON THE THAMES, FEB? 4.1814.　　　LA FOIRE SUR LA TAMISE, FEVRIER 4.1814.

FIGURE 13. This view of the Frost Fair that took place while William was imprisoned in the hulk shows the variety of traders and amusements available for Londoners when the Thames froze over.

FIGURE 14. Originally drawn in 1817, three years after William arrived, this view of Sydney is from Observatory Hill looking out over Port Jackson. In the distance are the cliffs known as the Heads of Port Jackson through which all convict transport ships sailed to reach the harbor.

Colley Smith's letter describing this meeting only served to increase Jackson's despair as the appalling consequences of his son's profligate behavior, and the ensuing "scene of . . . complicated misery" for himself and his family, were laid out before him:

> Enough has been brought to light to convince me that if the jury be not mercifully inclined, there is scarcely the shadow of a hope that the prisoner's life can be saved. Unhappy wretch! Even taking it at the best, and supposing that the evidence of his "woman" would acquit him of the Capital part of the charge, what consolation remains for his unfortunate relations? His character is irretrievably ruined. Disgrace and infamy will ever attach to his name. Would to God that I was in the peaceful grave for he has made me drink of the cup of sorrow, until life is absolutely a burthen to me.[22]

Perhaps out of solicitude for his long-standing client and friend, the attorney had actually withheld some of the details about the "despicable characters" he had to deal with in order to procure any witnesses for the defense. Smith had spent two hours questioning a "navy agent" who, during the course of the interview, revised the description of his employment to "wine merchant" and later to "wine dealer on commission" before finally admitting that he was actually a brothel keeper. The man had produced a bill for goods received months earlier from Jackson and Harper that could have helped William's case, but just days later he returned and solemnly declared to Mr. Fletcher that his whole testimony had been "utterly false." That left just one other witness, whose whereabouts was proving difficult to find, giving rise to the suspicion that he had either provided a false address or fled.[23]

The people who were conspicuously missing from Colley Smith's list were character witnesses. For a youth of his social status, William's lack of character witnesses would look suspicious to any judge and jury looking to mitigate the seriousness of a charge. For many of Newgate's inmates, unable to afford the means to track down witnesses themselves, character witnesses were their only form of defense. The word of other men of property carried great weight and provided evidence of the accused's good standing in the community. It was not unusual for prisoners accused of capital crimes to call four or even a dozen character witnesses. Some defense counsel at the Old Bailey used many more—one even declared that he had eighty-four prepared to give evidence. In typical forgery trials, it was the very respectability of the defendant and the efforts of his or her well-connected friends to save a genteel life that drew the greatest sympathy from observers. William would appear strangely lacking on both counts.[24]

THE NIGHT BEFORE the October sessions at the Old Bailey began was a stormy one in London. "Dreadful gales" tore through the streets and ripped the roofs off houses. A ten-year-old boy from Newgate Street watched in horror as his father was blown from the streetlamp he was lighting and drowned in the turbulent Thames. The residents within Newgate were better protected from the elements by the jail's massive stone walls, but for most it was an equally dreadful night. Virtually all the inmates, except debtors and those already serving sentences or awaiting transportation, would find themselves before the bar at nine o'clock the following morning, and few would return in a less tormented state of mind. Many of them would be standing trial on capital charges. Yet despite the large number of crimes punishable by death, it was well known that juries, judges, and even prosecutors often did their best to find some reason to reduce the charges or mitigate the punishment.[25]

Unfortunately for William, forgery was the exception to this rule. It was regarded as extremely serious despite the fact that it was "not a crime of violence but of fraud," committed by those with a "depraved intellect" rather than hardened criminal intent. Such was the gravity of the threat of forgery to economic exchange, and to paper credit in particular, that no amount of public sympathy, or recent campaigns by penal reformers, could convince judges, MPs, or commercially minded conservatives that change was necessary on humanitarian grounds. At the previous sessions, when William had so narrowly avoided standing trial without counsel, two men were tried for forgery. One had been acquitted, but the other had been sentenced to death and spent his last days in Newgate—a fact William could hardly fail to have noticed even if he had avoided attending the "condemned sermon" preached on the

Sunday before an execution in the presence of an empty coffin. In fact, half of all those tried for forgery at the Old Bailey that year had been found guilty, and they had all been condemned to death. The fate of forgers was not helped by the fact that juries in Europe's largest commercial capital city were also much more likely to convict than their provincial counterparts. No longer young enough to expect clemency on account of his age, William was well on the way to becoming a character in one of the numerous pamphlets sold beneath the gallows that recounted the sorry tale of a talented but indebted son from a respectable middle-class family whose desperate attempts to maintain his position in society had led him to succumb to a fatal temptation.[26]

Early the next morning, when the storm had abated, William shuffled through the underground passage in his new suit and shackles to the basement of the Old Bailey. There he waited with other groups of dirty disconsolate prisoners for his case to be called, while the judges and the grand jury assembled in the magnificently appointed rooms above. Outside, coaches drew up beneath a covered colonnade and crowds began to gather in the courtyard. Excitement mounted as people queued to pay a shilling—or up to a guinea for "very interesting trials"—to gain entrance to the public gallery in the hope of witnessing a day of scandalous entertainment. Indeed, London guidebooks encouraged visitors to tour Newgate as well as attend the Old Bailey. Around the courthouse, public houses opened to serve refreshments to visitors, and to the prosecutors and witnesses, despite the provision of a separate room in which the latter were supposed to wait. Hence, later in the day many of the participants in this legal drama would be more than a little intoxicated.[27]

It was William's good fortune that his trial was called before the judges and court officers went up to the lord mayor's dining room (at three or five o'clock) to eat a sumptuous dinner, which was usually accompanied by generous amounts of fine wine. It was not unknown for judges to descend the stairs hanging on to the banisters—so drunk they could barely read the depositions or understand the witnesses' answers. The impressive ceremony of the court was also frequently undermined by spectators seated in the semicircular galleries above, whose noisy chatter, chewing, and throwing of nuts provided a boisterous contrast to the studied solemnity of the proceedings below.[28]

William stepped up to the bar of the Old Bailey courtroom once more to face charges on six counts of forgery. He was no doubt relieved to see that this time his black-gowned team of lawyers were seated at the mahogany table beneath the semicircular bench of scarlet-robed judges. Above him a large rectangular mirror reflected light onto his face from the two large windows on either side of the massive sword of justice. The mirror was designed to highlight his facial expressions as he answered his accuser in order to help the court assess the truthfulness of his testimony. A similar mirror was placed above the witness box for the same reason. The jurors sat in a tiered box to William's right. There were two juries at the Old Bailey—one drawn from the city of London and one from Middlesex—and they sat alternately to try the cases of batches of prisoners from each area, or switched if one jury needed to retire to consider its verdict, which had to be unanimous. In practice, they rarely left the box between cases, usually huddling together around the foreman and reaching a verdict within a few minutes. Because most jurors served more than once, experience, plus a reluctance to be confined to a room without food or drink until they had reached a decision, contributed to the speed at which verdicts were reached.

William was tried by the Middlesex jury, which on this occasion was drawn from among the ranks of well-to-do shopkeepers, traders, and craftsmen whom he had spent so long defrauding. It was considered an advantage for jurors to possess both knowledge of the local community in which the crime was committed and a degree of background knowledge to a case. Several of these jurors traded in the West End, so the chances of them having heard of William's fraudulent purchases were greatly increased. Mr. Jackson's hopes of saving William's life rested almost entirely on a merciful jury pleading that his sentence be mitigated; he could not see how the jury could possibly acquit his son. William needed to get the spectators on his side, for their sympathies often lay with the defendant in property crime trials. A sympathetic crowd could exert a significant influence on prosecutors and juries already inclined to mercy in capital cases: it could express noisy sympathy for the accused while the jurors discussed their verdict; murmuring, pointing and throwing missiles during witness testimonies were common tactics, and unpopular verdicts were greeted with loud hisses and boos.[29]

It was fortunate for William that his case was heard by Sir Alan Chambré, an experienced judge with a reputation for fairness. The French regarded English judges as masters of understatement who never displayed their feelings or personal opinions in court. French judge Charles Cottu described how they treated the defendant "throughout the trial as an unfortunate being, admirably seconded in his benevolent feelings by the whole auditory, people, counsel and jury." But this assessment underestimated the polite reserve and insistence on maintaining strict legal procedural rules that made a judicial code based on terror appear to be applied with absolute fairness and humanity to every English man and woman, no matter what their status.[30]

Sir Alan Chambré was a perfect example of this principle in action. He was highly respected for his knowledge of the law, his willingness to consult his brother judges on any matter of doubt during a trial, and his just decisions. But where the law demanded it, he was equally willing to apply its full severity. In 1803 he had had no qualms about convicting a woman of the capital crime of infanticide at Hereford Assizes (one of many assize courts periodically held to try serious cases in county towns), but when all the prisoners came to be sentenced at the end of the assizes, he omitted to state in court that her body should be dissected and anatomized after execution. Realizing his mistake, he consulted his fellow judges on the legal effects of this omission and accepted their decision that the failure of correct procedure meant the sentence could not stand. The woman was reprieved.[31]

After the clerk had read the indictment and instructed William to hold up his hand to identify himself to the jury, which was charged to inquire into his guilt, Joseph Christian Junior stepped up to the witness box and summarized the basis of his family's case against William for forging a check in payment for shirts he had ordered. Despite being relatively successful traders in a wealthy area of London, the Christians had chosen not to hire any defense counsel, convinced that the facts of their case were so clear that they could not fail to get William convicted. Initially, this was not as much of a disadvantage as it might appear. Compared to misdemeanor trials, the prosecuting counsel in a felony case had to limit his opening statement to a very restrained account of the facts—usually expressed in terms of regret for the serious consequences that would follow if the accused were convicted. As defense counsel in a felony case, Alley and Adolphus were equally restricted: they could not address the jury directly or state the accused's defense or posit any alternative scenario as modern barristers do today; nor could they interpret evidence in any way. Hence, Cottu commented,

> we do not hear the prosecutor's counsel paint the prisoner as a monster of whom the earth ought to be that instant rid, and compare him to all villains who have astonished the world by their enormities. Nor do we see the prisoner's counsel offering to the jury a thousand idle surmises on the manner in which it is possible the crime may have been committed nor see him belying his own conscience, inducing the jury to betray their's, and threatening them with divine judgement, should they dare to do their duty. No one has the right to pervert the light of the evidence by subjecting it to the prism of his own opinion or imagination: the jury receive it in all its purity.[32]

Alley and Adolphus's defense strategy therefore consisted of imaginative, aggressive, and damaging questioning of prosecution witnesses—something both men were highly skilled at. A successful prosecution for forgery required very exacting standards of evidence to prove the accused's identity and an accurate account of where the forged instrument was at all times between the moment of exchange and the start of the trial. If they could throw doubt on the validity of either of these essential strands of evidence, they stood every chance of convincing the judge to direct the jury to acquit William. Hence, when the Christians' shop man took the stand, he was closely questioned about every detail of why and how he accepted the check from a man he did not know and exactly what it looked like. Even though the man could accurately describe every detail of his exchange with William, he was forced to admit that he had never seen William before then. Joseph Christian Junior described how he had received the check and given it to his clerk to take to Prescott's bank, but he could not say what name William had used before he presented the check signed in the name of Stephen Harper. The cashier at Prescott's bank remembered receiving the check and discovering that nobody by the name of Harper or Jackson kept an account there, but he had never seen William before either.[33]

Alley scented a significant flaw in the evidence of William's identity, so he demanded to know if the Christians had "any witness that knows anything of the prisoner." This was enough to compel Sir Alan Chambré to direct the jury to acquit William on technical grounds because the prosecution had failed to provide sufficient evidence to prove that William was Jackson and not Harper. Mr. Jackson believed that the Christians *chose* not to provide sufficient evidence of William's identity because, like many prosecutors, they did not want to actually send him to the gallows for a nonviolent crime. Yet a growing aversion to capital punishment had also influenced the increasing number of acquittals on technicalities since the late eighteenth century, so the skills of William's defense counsel in raising them had also ensured that his life would be saved.[34]

The following morning a similar cast of characters assembled within the Old Bailey courtroom, but this time the judge was John Silvester, Recorder* of the City of London, otherwise known as Black Jack. Silvester, a former adversary of the redoubtable William Garrow, had made considerable sums of money during his practice as a barrister, but he had more often appeared for the prosecution, so it was said that his wealth had been "derived from the groans of the gallows." Described by one contemporary as "vulgar and ineloquent," Silvester had a reputation for sexual harassment and for severity as a judge who vigorously opposed any amelioration of the "bloody code" of capital punishment. One obituary declared that his character did not "inspire respect for the judicial office."[35]

Luckily for William, theft from a lodging house was not a capital crime, but he still risked being transported to Australia. Undaunted by Silvester's reputation, however, Peter Alley pursued similar tactics against another unrepresented prosecutor. Thomas Colville had barely finished his opening statement and proved that William had occupied his lodging house and vanished with more than £30 of furnishings (a smaller sum than he had originally alleged) when Peter Alley began

---

* The Recorder was a senior judge at the Old Bailey.

to question him about whether he had let William the whole of the house. He aimed to get the case dismissed on another technicality, because the law stated that a man could not be accused of stealing from himself if he leased the whole of a house. Colville's case disintegrated the moment he had to admit that the original contract showed William paid £14 a month for the whole house.[36]

Even the severest judge could not gainsay this point, and Silvester was, most reluctantly, forced to limit himself to delivering a severe reprimand to William before acquitting him of the charge. More surprisingly, Peter Alley concluded his case by "intimating" to the court that if William were acquitted of this felony, he would later plead guilty to the fraud brought by Robson, and by way of recompense to the unfortunate tailor, he recommended that the court should compensate Colville for his losses by paying his expenses. Whether this was to please Mr. Jackson, who wanted William to be convicted on at least one charge, or whether Alley was discomfited by a belief that he had just freed a guilty man, is not at all clear, but it suggests that few people believed that William was innocent.[37]

William waited another four days in Newgate before the grand jury declared the third charge of fraud, brought by the Oxford Street linen draper Robson, to be a true bill. Accompanied once more by Adolphus and Alley, William attended the arraignment, where, despite his counsel's earlier promise, he pleaded not guilty again. He was tried almost immediately, but his assiduous defense counsel objected to flaws in both the indictment and the evidence, which the court was again compelled to accept. After the trial there was little celebration—Alley and Adolphus had done their job well, but they remonstrated with William at length on the grossness of his behavior. Nevertheless, William was discharged from Newgate, much to the disgust of at least one turnkey, who described him as a "notorious swindler."[38]

Colley Smith and Mr. Jackson were also less than delighted by this outcome. Jackson's wealth and the employment of skilled counsel had effectively defeated his avowed intention to see that the court prevented William from committing further crimes. By contrast, increasing numbers of plebeian parents found that a combination of perceptions about plebeian juvenile criminality and the desire to prevent its spread resulted in positive action by magistrates and courts to discipline their delinquent offspring. In William's case, the criminal justice system had proven to be scrupulous in its application of the law but had failed to ascertain the truth or to punish a habitual offender. Yet to the French observer Cottu, it seemed that most English people would not have been unduly upset by such a result:

> They are indifferent whether, among the really guilty, such be convicted or acquitted: so much the worse for him against whom the proofs are too evident, so much the better the other in whose favour there may exist some faint doubts. They look upon the former as singled out by a sort of fatality, to serve as an example to the people, and inspire them with a wholesome terror of the vengeance of the law; the other, as a wretch whose chastisement heaven has reserved in the other world.

William was lucky this time, but one forger and ten other thieves and robbers were sentenced to hang as an example of the vengeance that the law could exact.[39]

WILLIAM WROTE immediately to thank his father effusively "for the manner in which my defence was conducted by your direction." But if he expected blessed relief and reconciliation with his parents following his acquittal, he was gravely mistaken. Both parents insisted that they would have nothing further to do with him until he reformed. Mr. Jackson demanded that William live at least one hundred miles from London and not contact any of his family again for at least three years. During that time he must disassociate himself entirely from all his disreputable "friends"—including Stephen Harper, Joseph Bradley, and all loose women—and endeavor to regain the "esteem of . . . Good and Virtuous" people. If he failed to comply with all these terms, he would find himself disinherited. "Not an atom of my property," Jackson warned, "during life, or at my death (mark what I say, or at my death) shall be at your disposal." Having witnessed the disinheritance of his former friend Henry Keighly, William knew that this would mean the end of all his hopes of regaining his former station in life and result in certain social ostracism.[40]

Jane Jackson also wrote in equally harsh terms—utterly dispelling William's belief that his father had secretly withheld his letters to her. She vowed that if William were disgraced again, she would never "through[out] my life, see you, or receive letter or message from you." Her "friendship," like his father's "protection," could be regained only by an abandonment of his vicious pursuits and depraved associates. Both parents reminded him that he would be twenty-one on November 26, which meant that he would no longer be an "infant" in the eyes of the (civil) law and they need make no further financial provision for him. But the warning William should have heeded most was that if he "ever again appear at the bar of public justice . . . no interest on the part of your family, no efforts of counsel, no consideration of youth, would guard you from the deepest vengeance of the law."[41]

8

CHELTENHAM AND GLOUCESTER UNMASKED

Town and Jail, 1812–1813

This county has become the example and model of the best system of criminal discipline in which provident regulation has banished the use of fetters and health has been substituted for contagion, thus happily reconciling humanity with punishment, and the prevention of crime with individual reform.

— Inscription on the tomb of Sir George Onesiphorus Paul,
prison reformer, buried in Gloucester Cathedral (1820)

The letters containing the "distasteful medicine" that the Jacksons desperately hoped would cure their delinquent son were faithfully delivered to William by Colley Smith, along with another quarterly installment of William's £100 allowance, in early November 1812. Smith recorded his meeting with William—the repentant youth's solemn promises to reform his behavior—and his written guarantee to quit the capital within twenty-four hours and not return to within one hundred miles of it for at least three years. As his father hoped, William did indeed quit the vicious metropolis and travel the prescribed one hundred miles to the elegant streets of Bath, where he had spent his childhood.[1]

Bath may not have been able to rival London in size, but it had grown spectacularly in the early 1800s to become Europe's premier spa resort and the eleventh largest town in England. It remained the supreme site for the fashionable consumption of health and entertainment and the perfect location for a dedicated consumer and stylish young gentleman in need of genteel sociability. From William's perspective, Bath society was not so very different from the crowds that frequented London's arenas of commercialized pleasure. It also served as an excellent marriage market, providing the pleasing prospect that he might yet persuade an heiress to marry him, thus solving his financial difficulties and regaining his family's approval in one stroke. His situation was not dissimilar to that of Jane Austen's charming fortune hunter Mr. Elliot, whose courtship of Anne in *Persuasion* was abruptly ended when she discovered the mercenary motives behind his first marriage and his subsequent search for a title to match.[2]

Bath, then as now, had a vast seasonal influx of visitors: most took short lets in the spring and autumn, but as permanent residents the Jacksons had sufficient status to be remembered by local tradesman more than a decade later. William may have intended to retrace his old childhood haunts and acquaintances in an effort to reform his behavior or even to raise the funds to leave the country. He wrote to Sir Robert Kennedy, an Irish family friend of the Shees who was then provost marshal of Bermuda, claiming that he had had a minor quarrel with his father and now hoped to secure a post for himself in the colony. Kennedy contacted Jackson, who informed the marshal of the exact cause of his "quarrel" with William, thus ending his chances of finding work abroad.[3]

Whatever his motives, William's efforts to mix in Bath society soon required more funds than he possessed, and within a week he had visited several tradesmen who had known his family and persuaded them to lend him money that he promised his father would soon repay. Upholsterers Bally and Bartram were pleased to discover that William wished to find a house to rent for his father to stay in Bath once more, but they stressed that they could advance him only £20 of the £100 he needed to tide him over until his father's arrival. Mr. Sigismond, a dentist, convinced that the young man he had known since boyhood was incapable of deceit, was equally pleased to carry out dental work for William and to give him £25, secure in the knowledge that his father would pay off the note.[4]

In London, Mr. Jackson, who had no intention of visiting the spa, was appalled at William's quick return to his deceitful ways. But he was equally angry with the gullible tradesmen who had hoped to increase their own profit. He wrote reminding them to warn other traders in Bath to be on their guard against William's fraud and demanded that they consider "whether it is not a duty which you owe to Society, to prevent him being at large while such atrocities continue to be his ruling passion." Early-nineteenth-century society, as Jeremy Bentham explained, depended heavily on believing the words of its citizens: "Were it otherwise, social business could not go on; every movement of society would be paralysed; we would not dare act." If Jackson felt that consumer society should be protected from his son's deceit, he was not blind to the exploitation of credit that same society condoned: this exhortation was both a means of calling for some form of self-regulation and a convenient way to transfer responsibility from himself.[5]

Knowing that word of his father's unwillingness to repay these debts would quickly spread among the shopkeepers of Bath, William was soon lured back to the anonymous streets of London in search of more fertile financial hunting grounds. Barely a fortnight later he was back in the Fleet Prison, from where, just one day before his twenty-first birthday, he assured his father that "a prison, Sir, is the best place to settle with one's creditors." The instigator of his rearrest was the furious linen draper Richard Robson, who had seen his criminal charges against William dismissed at the Old Bailey. By pressing a civil case for debt against William, he now had a (slim) chance of recouping some of his losses, but his prime motive was revenge. Robson's attorney wrote to William explaining that the linen draper would "with much pleasure pay every expense attending Jackson's arrest and imprisonment and that it is his will to keep him in prison as long as he exists." Mr. Jackson, unmoved by William's age or situation, and seeing their agreement broken, remained resolutely silent. Again he railed at tradesmen and blamed the system of consumer credit, which had "in a very great degree" been responsible for "the ruin in which [William was] involved." Yet because these tradesmen would now have resort to law, Jackson replied to their requests for payment by helpfully explaining exactly where they could find the dissolute "person" who had once been his son.[6]

Unknown to his father, however, William was also secretly writing to his mother once more. It is not clear how long she kept her resolution not to reply to her son if he was ever in trouble again, but she carefully preserved every one of his letters—tied in small bundles with his initials set out in fine lettering within a carefully etched border. By Christmas William was seriously unwell with another chest infection, and it was probably Jane's perennial fear for his life that made her succumb to his pleas for help once more. Mother and son found a way to communicate by using the cook at Gloucester Place to clandestinely convey letters and small sums of money to William in the Fleet. But even his mother's secret support could not sustain William through the prospect of spending the rest of his life in a debtors' prison. Robson was precisely the kind of malicious creditor that debtors feared most, for he had no reason to settle with William, who could no longer plead his infancy or procure money to pay the debt. He tried to circulate a petition so that the "public will see that I have been a <u>Persecuted Man</u>" and to raise funds for his release, but with no success.[7]

Having exhausted all other options, William took the most drastic action possible. He and his former Fleet cell mate and "disreputable associate," Joseph Bradley, escaped from the Rules of the prison and vanished from London altogether. The Bow Street magistrates tried in vain to return William to the Fleet and to capture Joseph, who had left a string of unhappy London jewelers looking in vain for payment on goods they believed they had "sold" to a wealthy young gentleman. Nobody knew where William had gone until Jane Jackson received a letter from him in early February 1813, and although she did not burn the letter as William instructed, she also did not reveal his whereabouts to her husband. It was a letter from a disgruntled Reading innkeeper some weeks later that provided Mr. Jackson with an all-too-clear idea of where both youths had got to. William and Joseph had, surprisingly, been searching for William's old adversary Dr. Valpy, the formidable headmaster of Reading School. But the two swindlers left the inn without paying and went in search of more fashionable society to prey upon in the up-and-coming Gloucestershire spa town of Cheltenham.[8]

SHELTERED FROM high winds by the fertile Cotswold Hills and claiming to possess a climate guaranteed to promote the longevity of its inhabitants, Cheltenham had grown in popularity since George III took the waters there in 1788. By 1813 it vied with Gloucester in size and openly competed with Bath to gain the patronage of gentry and aristocratic society. Cheltenham had no less than three spas, approached by broad gravel walks edged with elm trees, where the fashionable could be found conspicuously gathering soon after sunrise. The town had elegantly appointed assembly rooms where visitors could dance, listen to concerts, or play cards, billiards, and backgammon. It also possessed a popular theater that regularly attracted top London actors and actresses, with all their attendant glamour and scandal. To keep its visitors well informed, the town boasted four circulating libraries stocked with books and all the London and provincial newspapers, as well as a music library.[9]

As in all spa towns, traders in luxury goods and services flourished during the season, with the influx of genteel visitors, which began in late March or April. Charles James Fox and Lord Byron were regular visitors, and the Prince Regent, the Countess of Jersey (once his most influential mistress), the Duke of Gloucester, the Melbournes, the Hollands, and exiled French royals were among the company competing for social brilliance at the spa. As a health resort Cheltenham was also home to some eminent physicians. Chief of these was Dr. Edward Jenner, who had already become famous for inventing a vaccination against smallpox—despite the controversy over its use in 1812, he had been mobbed by nearly three hundred poorer inhabitants of Cheltenham eager to get vaccinated. Just a few doors from Jenner, at 5 St. George's Place, lived another keen experimental practitioner of the art of medicine, with a particular interest in promoting the health-giving properties of the spa water. Dr. Thomas Newell had gained the title of surgeon extraordinaire to the Prince Regent, a considerable public honor, and had become a long-standing and well-known resident of Cheltenham. He was also an acquaintance of Mr. Jackson's.[10]

As in London and Bath, the demands of polite sociability—dress, deportment, manners, sparkling conversation, and, most importantly, the elusive characteristics of "good breeding"—ensured that William and Joseph could mingle comfortably with both the elite visitors and the eager tradesmen of Cheltenham. William's unshakable belief that he was still a legitimate member of this society was bolstered by the fact that there were at least half a dozen families staying in Cheltenham at that time who were closely connected to the Jacksons, the Evelyns, or the Shees. These family acquaintances made it even easier for him to continue to abuse the system of mutual credit and obligation based on such connections.[11]

For several days William and Joseph were popular customers of the local traders and dealers. They pretended that they were taking a house in the town for two years and for payment used bills drawn on banks where they had no funds, or on Sir George Shee, whose name and station were well respected.* One of those from whom William sought funds was Dr. Newell. After calling on the surgeon, pretending to be merely a friend of his father's, William sent a draft for £30, apparently drawn on Shee and authorized by Jackson, on which he sought Newell's signature to obtain payment. Had William waited for the surgeon himself, he would have gained the signature without trouble (provided the surgeon had not checked with Jackson first), but in the manner of many swindlers, the aim was to acquire the maximum amount of money and goods in as short a time as possible and then leave town before arousing suspicion.

To that end, William and Joseph visited a goldsmith from whom they acquired two gold watches and a diamond ring, claiming that William was a patient of Dr. Newell's and that they were due to dine with him the next day. Walter Meyers agreed to deliver the goods, but when he arrived at William and Joseph's lodgings, instead of cash, they offered a draft drawn on a London bank. They assured the goldsmith that if he wanted cash, he need only take the draft to their good friend Dr. Newell, who would pay the equivalent sum in cash and present the draft to the bank himself. Despite its popularity, Cheltenham's trading life still chiefly revolved around its one main street, where gossip spread fast, so the pair would need to leave town before Meyer could contact Dr. Newell or present the draft to the bank, which would refuse it. William and Joseph quit their lodgings in the High Street without

---

* When a bill was drawn on someone's name, the named person acted as guarantor/personal banker to pay the amount on the bill.

notice or payment and hurriedly left town, heading toward Gloucester. Instead of getting far away from the scene of their crime, however, the pair stopped at the Cross Hands pub on the Gloucester road.

They badly underestimated the speed with which the local constables had been mobilized by the goldsmith with the assistance of the Cheltenham Association for the Prosecution of Felons. These associations had spread rapidly since the late-eighteenth-century panics about rising crime rates; they supported their members by assisting in the detection of crime and the recovery of stolen goods, and by paying the costs of prosecutions. Indeed, such was the speed with which they were pursued that William and Joseph were discovered settling into the pub that evening, along with the jewelry for which the bemused Dr. Newell had refused to pay.[12]

Cheltenham society reacted with shock and sadness that two such handsome, genteel, "fashionably dressed," and well-connected young men should find themselves before the local magistrates on criminal charges. "From the shock this affair has given me, what must be the feelings of a father and a Mother!" wrote Colonel Caulfield Lennon to Jackson, promising to act instantly to bail William. In his eyes, William "had not done anything more criminal than drawing on his Uncle Sir George Shee" for payment of the goods. Yet the drama of the situation also caused a frisson of excitement throughout the town as the local press took up the story. Ever proud of the judicial system, the Cheltenham newspaper declared it had "true pleasure in recording, that the magistrates . . . behaved in the most gentlemanly manner, extending every lenity compatible with their office" toward the prisoners.[13]

William and Joseph were confined in the Bell Inn, a local public house, for five days while they tried to raise bail and depositions were collected against them. The innkeeper was roundly condemned for his overzealous guarding of the pair in preventing both public and press having access to them. "A savage pursuance of justice makes humanity blush," lamented the press, until "the politeness of our *ci-devant* sheriff and magistrate Sir William Hicks" procured them access to the celebrity criminals. Colonel Lennon had already begun to call on the services of Lord Ashtown and other highly respected Cheltenham residents who knew the Jacksons, when a letter from Mr. Jackson arrived begging him to cease and leave William in prison to reflect upon his crimes. "From my soul I wish that he may not escape from thence, so long as he continues what he now is," explained Jackson, who was now physically and emotionally exhausted by William's continued "defiance to all parental authority and all moral principles."[14]

Without the active support of his family or their influential friends, William, despite his popular gentility, could no longer be shielded from the legal consequences of his deception. Walter Meyers's membership in the Cheltenham association ensured that he received advice from its solicitor, who pressed for the pair's committal to stand trial at the next Court of Assize. Also, despite their concern to treat fellow gentlemen politely, the Cheltenham magistrates were nevertheless assiduous in their duty and had notified London's Bow Street office immediately on hearing that William and Joseph might be guilty of other offenses. The Bow Street magistrates confirmed that both men were wanted in London, too, so the Cheltenham magistrates duly committed them for trial at the Gloucester assizes, and they were swiftly conveyed to the new prison at Gloucester.

CHELTENHAM and Gloucester were rivals as well as neighboring towns. "A very shouldering, unpleasant neighbour," commented Reverend Fosbrooke of Gloucestershire in 1819 of the increasingly popular spa resort that was beginning to eclipse its county town. Gloucester had but one minor spring and was falling behind in size of population. Although Gloucester lacked the glitter and society appeal of its neighbor, it was a busy, bustling market town on the banks of the River Severn, nestling at the center of an ever-improving web of transportation links by road, river, and canal, with its own dockyard for overseas trade. It also remained a popular haunt for the local gentry, who, though now deprived of a local horse-race meeting, still regularly gathered for markets, musical events, civic dinners, and the twice-yearly assizes, which were usually accompanied by a ball.[15]

In the early nineteenth century, Gloucester not only supported a new spirit of enterprise but also prided itself on the reforming zeal of its inhabitants, who embraced moral and humanitarian causes. A significant proportion of its population was evangelical—a movement strengthened by the formation of a branch of the British and Foreign

Bible Society there in 1812. Gloucester thus supported the push for a reformation of manners that had been gathering strength since the late 1780s. It was also the home of two of the most influential reformers of the day. Robert Raikes, editor of the *Gloucester Journal,* founder of the Sunday School movement, and philanthropic reformer, had died in 1811. But the indefatigable Sir George Onesiphorus Paul, famous philanthropist and prison reformer who had built and now oversaw the running of the new county jail, was still an active magistrate in the city. He and the criminal justice system he had worked hard to transform were about to play a crucial part in William's future.

Gloucester jail stood on open ground, apart from the main town and a short distance behind Booth Hall on Westgate Street, where the assizes would be held. Immediately behind the jail flowed the River Severn, which afforded inmates tantalizing glances of the tall masts of ships heading out to the freedom of the open seas, followed by the endless mournful cries of seagulls as they circled overhead. Less appealing was the smell from the open ground between the river and the jail, which had been used by the citizens to dump their night soil until Paul put a stop to the practice. Today, even with town buildings now pressing close upon them, the jail's massive brick walls give off an air of implacable efficiency rather than the dark menace of Newgate. Standing eighteen feet high, they enclosed three acres of land within which the prison was divided into three sections: the gatehouse, where new prisoners were admitted and physically examined, plus an infirmary; the jail, which housed prisoners awaiting trial, debtors, and the condemned, plus the chapel; and the penitentiary, which held those sentenced to transportation to Australia, or commuted sentences, and convicted felons. The two prison sections were surrounded by eleven separate courts with wooden palisades and bordered by open ground to prevent conversations between different classes of prisoner.[16]

Opened in 1792, the jail was a direct result of the Penitentiary Act of 1779, which embodied burgeoning beliefs about the importance of efforts to "correct" as well as to "punish" criminal offenders. To that end, new penal institutions were built and designed to enforce discipline, hard labor, religious instruction, and solitary confinement on their inmates. Paul was equally determined that the cruelty and abuses of power within old prisons like Newgate should be a thing of the past. At Gloucester, fetters and physical punishment were prohibited for those awaiting trial; inmates were to be fed well, kept clean and healthy, and separated according to their sex, seriousness of the crime, and whether or not they had been convicted. Prison officials were to be paid by the county (not self-employed), and the design of the prison meant that far fewer officials were needed. Approximately 135 prisoners were managed by the governor, Thomas Cunningham, two or three turnkeys, a porter, a matron for female prisoners, and an old woman who delivered food. Extra staff were hired for the assizes, and a salaried taskmaster oversaw the prisoners' work. All prison officials were carefully chosen for their ability to do the job well and instructed never to strike or lose their temper with prisoners, or swear in front of them; and on no account could they engage or interact with inmates beyond basic instructions. Prisoners were banned from consuming any form of alcohol, keeping animals, gambling, and charging "garnish" money. Gloucester was regarded across the country as the very model of a modern, humanitarian prison, designed to reform, rather than merely contain, criminals.[17]

The huge tomb of the jail's chief architect, Sir George Onesiphorus Paul, still stands in the magnificent town cathedral today, proudly carved with an inscription that bears testimony to his humanitarian reform efforts. But it would be a mistake to conceive that his vision of prison life was meant to be any less of a deterrent to criminals than the old system. "Prisons," he assured his fellow Gloucester magistrates, should not "be places of comfort—they should be places of real terror." The process of reform was to be achieved by isolation, spiritual examination, complete obedience, humiliation, and hard labor. Solitary confinement was the cornerstone upon which all Paul's reforms depended. Gloucester had fifty-two, eight-foot-square, arched stone night cells and the same number of identical day cells, each with a semicircular barred window, for prisoners to work alone in. The walls were eighteen inches thick and blocked up on the gallery side to prevent inmates from whispering to each other. The exercise yards for each class of prisoner had high walls to prevent any communication between them, and the chapel was similarly segregated. Kid Wake, a state prisoner in Gloucester from 1796 to 1801, observed bitterly that confinement in common gaols must surely be a very severe suffering; but if Judges and Juries would only reflect seriously on the horrors of solitary imprisonment, under penitentiary discipline. If they would allow their minds to dwell a little on what it is to be locked up, winter after winter, for sixteen hours out of the twenty-four, in a small brick cell—without company—without fire—without light.[18]

Isolation from the corrupting influence of "the world" outside, particularly from pernicious associates, was further ensured by severe restrictions on visitors—even family members could visit only every six months and were not permitted to bring any food or gifts. The word "Solitude" was deeply engraved above the entrance to the jail, through which William and Joseph were escorted on March 1, 1813. The two men were taken into the gatehouse, stripped, washed, and examined by the Gloucester surgeon's son, who pronounced them free from infectious disease and thereby spared them the humiliation of having their heads shaved. Rigorous hygiene and inspections were enforced daily during their confinement, because Paul believed that they promoted "a moral as well as a physical purpose": cleanliness was a sign of inner godliness and order. Such routines also improved the health of the prisoners. The young doctor noticed that William was suffering from a fever and coughing badly, so he prescribed a suitable medicine. The "two swindlers of genteel appearance" then had their clothes removed and replaced with the prison uniform of a coarse blue-and-yellow patchwork jacket, trousers, hat, and wooden-soled shoes. This meant that escapees were easily identifiable, and prisoners were clearly distinguished from staff and visitors, thus preventing much of the need for fetters. The uniform also removed most of the visual signals of status and was, as Paul put it, both "comfortable, yet humiliating." Thus, he explained,

secluded from the society of their friends, they are daily visited by gentlemen attentive to their spiritual and bodily welfare; food is prepared for them sufficient for all the purposes of life and health, whilst the use of money is denied and by this denial, every means of luxury or partial indulgence, and of corruption, is prevented.

Mr. Jackson approved wholeheartedly of this approach. "In the solitude of a prison, he will have time for reflection; and from my soul I wish he may not escape from thence, so long as he continues what he now is," he told Colonel Lennon on refusing his offers to help William.[19]

IF ISOLATION, humiliation, and obedience were designed to instill penitence, some prisoners still found ways to subvert the system, particularly in the period before trial when discipline was less demanding. While walking round the boundary wall one day, the chaplain noted disapprovingly that he heard some "very noisy & talkative" female prisoners, who had taken advantage of the absence of officers to "indulge in idle conversation." Determined to retain as much of his dignity and status as he could, William insisted on hiring gentleman's apartments in the gatehouse until his trial. Thus even within the reformed edifice of Gloucester jail, small pockets of elitism still stuck in the system. William also took steps to ensure that he had enough money to support himself well in jail and to provide defense counsel for his trial—none of which would have been condoned by Paul. In his defense, William was pushed to extreme measures to protect himself because his father was adamant that this time he would not "advance a shilling to aid his escape from justice." Mr. Jackson refused to reply to any of his son's letters, and William's to his mother also went unanswered, leaving him to suspect that they had been withheld from her (a tactic Jackson vehemently denied).[20]

As soon as his health had recovered sufficiently, William first tried to raise money by capitalizing on his notoriety; he inserted an advertisement in the very newspaper that had so eagerly sought to publicize his downfall at Cheltenham. It announced:

Shortly will be published

CHELTENHAM UNMASKED

By Burke Jackson Esqr

Late of the 67th regiment and now a prisoner in Gloucester Castle

Jackson viewed this as an act of pure insanity, but William had good reasons to go public. He planned to have his revenge on Cheltenham society, to defend his name, and to profit financially (like many infamous prisoners) from publishing in the ever-popular genre of true-crime stories. William, convinced of his innocence as usual, was very confident that "when Cheltenham Unmasked comes before the World I shall stand so high in their estimation as my enemies will low." Prisoners could even find themselves hot literary property, particularly between sentencing and execution, and some defendants used printed pamphlets to put their own side of the story, or to transfer blame, before their trial. This last was a tactic William had used since his youth, and perhaps equally significantly, it was also barely a year since Mr. Jackson had resorted to similar means of self-justification by publishing his *Memoirs* to absolve himself from charges of corruption in India.[21]

On the same day as the advertisement for *Cheltenham Unmasked* appeared, William tried to secure a loan from family connections unlikely to have been acquainted with his unsavory past. He wrote to a former family servant, Elizabeth Marshall, who had looked after them in Bath when William was a young child, informing her that he had "got into a scrape of a trifling nature" and needed her help as his parents were away. Elizabeth was now married to William Lewis, a poor tradesman, but both felt obligated to the family for "former kindness," so Mr. Lewis traveled to the jail and lent William £5. William could have used the money to supplement the county diet—of bread, boiled beef, and potatoes or pea soup—by paying the elderly woman responsible for buying fresh produce for inmates. Or he could have refused to work (as those who were awaiting trial could not be compelled to do so), but in that case he would not have received any money from the county. What he certainly could not have done, as he had so often in the past, was to purchase any alcohol to ease his confinement, because all inmates except debtors were restricted to drinking milk or water.[22]

Nevertheless, the success of his first letter prompted William to write to the Lewises again, this time asking for £10. Again the Lewises stretched their meager finances to provide what they saw as an essential service, all the time in the expectation that Mr. Jackson would honor the promissory notes William sent them to cover his borrowing.

William's last request was received by the Lewises on March 19; he explained that his father would return to London to pay them on May 15, but that in the meantime his trial was due to be held next week and he was still without defense counsel, which would cost £20. As proof, a letter purporting to be from John Adolphus (William's barrister at the Old Bailey) was enclosed. The Lewises could only manage to raise £15 this time, so William wrote to Mr. Ive, a neighbor at Langley, asking for the loan of another "trifle." All the letters were patently untrue because Jackson had not gone away and was living in London at the time, and the letter from Adolphus was either a forgery or the result of further deception.[23]

As March progressed, the jail became more crowded, filled with an increasing number of (mostly impoverished) inmates in preparation for the assizes. The chaplain, Reverend Edward Jones, canon of Gloucester Cathedral, was pleased to see that, despite this influx, the prison remained orderly, although he lamented that the calendar consisted of such "an extraordinary number of criminals for the ensuing assizes." Apart from his dismay at the increasing crime rate in the area, Jones knew the assizes signaled that he would soon be called upon to minister daily to the condemned, an often distressing task, and to prepare the sermon delivered at the service prior to execution (six years later he had become so sickened by executions that he asked his son to take over these services). The chaplain extended his advice and sympathy to both William and Joseph before the assizes began, even though he was first and foremost an establishment man. Nevertheless, he kept William apprised of his mother's health and gave him suitably instructive religious texts to read. "I have not as you may suppose read them," William confessed to Jane, "for my time has of late been so occupied in drawing up my Defence and submitting it for Counsel's opinion, a matter of much greater importance." He was also busy sending copies of his case to Lord Folkstone and Sir Francis Burdett, influential men he hoped would support him.[24]

By the end of the month, William's health had improved considerably and life in the jail was markedly better for him than it had been at Newgate, despite the imposition of rigorous discipline. The temperature in the jail was regulated and recorded every day so that it never fell below 39°F, he had enough reasonable quality food, and he was visited

every few days by the doctor, who kept an eye on his health and procured extra food or clothing when necessary. He remained remarkably
optimistic about the outcome of his trial, which may have been
bravado but was more characteristic of his inability to accept that he
had done anything criminally wrong. He had spent four years "swindling" traders, which he had convinced himself was no more than a
mildly reprehensible manipulation of the system of credit and debt of
which many wealthy young men availed themselves. Repeated residence in debtors' prisons and even criminal trials at the Old Bailey had
done little to change this attitude.

The long-term, negotiable credit offered by tradesmen and demanded by elite male consumers, coupled with the lack of clear legal responsibility for debt accorded to the sons of wealthy fathers, had clearly
contributed to William's belief in his own lack of culpability. William
was certain that his (usually unspecified) "enemies" were more to blame
for his misfortunes than he, so, at worst, he believed himself guilty of no
more than youthful folly. He assured his mother that he had "never been
in better spirits in my life, as I know I am an injured man but if there is
any justice in the country I will make those smart who have been the
means of sending me to this prison. I look forward every Day to my trial
with pleasure, as I am certain of gaining a Victory over my enemies."[25]

ON THE LAST DAY of March 1813, Gloucester readied itself to receive
the circuit judges and open its spring assizes. The newspapers had
been avidly following the progress of the assize judges since March 8,
when they reached Reading, the first town on their progress from
London around the western circuit of courts. Gloucester was crowded
with the cream of county society and considerable numbers of tradesmen and laborers, plus the prosecutors and numerous solicitors, barristers, and jurors. In addition to the assize ball and county meetings,
there would be private parties and a great deal of delightfully shocking
gossip about the trials and executions.

The full majesty of the force of law was on display as the high sheriff, accompanied by a richly dressed retinue of men bearing javelins
and playing trumpets, escorted the splendidly bewigged and scarlet-
robed Honorable Mr. Baron Graham and Honorable Mr. Justice

Bayley into the town. As the church bells rang and trumpets played, the procession made its way through the crowded streets to the doors of the picturesque medieval timber county hall, where the judges officially opened their commission to deal with all civil and criminal cases at these assizes. The following day the judges and a large crowd of "respectable" citizens packed into the cathedral to hear the sheriff's chaplain deliver his traditional assize sermon. This time he stressed the importance of educating the young in religious knowledge "as the most effectual means of stopping that increase of depravity, which if not timely prevented, must bring this nation to a speedy destruction." The chaplain then addressed the judges, jury, and witnesses in an "exceedingly appropriate" manner, which usually meant either a homily on the wisdom of the laws and correctness of punishment or a reminder of that great assizes before which every person would one day be called for judgment.[26]

The criminal court judge, Mr. Justice Bayley, was a particularly receptive member of the congregation. Bayley was an extremely devout man who had received a letter from the dean of Gloucester just two months earlier praising his production of an edition of the Book of Common Prayer and commending the way that "Law and Divinity thrive equally under your protection." Bayley was equally popular with his fellow judges, silks,* and barristers in King's Bench and was greatly respected for his mastery of the common law. Indeed, it was well known that Bailey enormously enjoyed his role as a judge, and he was considered to have perfected the solemn art of passing judgment in court.[27]

Immediately after the service, the judges set about their business— Baron Graham in the civil court of *nisi prius* (unless first)† and Bayley at the criminal bar. Bayley's first charge was to address the grand jury gathered in the ancient Booth Hall opposite the cathedral, where the assize would be held. Booth Hall was ill adapted to the solemn pur-

---

* King's Counsel (Queen's Counsel today), or silk, was a senior barrister distinguished from junior barristers by his silk robe.

† Civil cases were traditionally tried in the superior courts at Westminster "unless first" heard locally at the assizes, which became the more common practice.

pose of administering criminal justice, however. In addition to a complaint by the grand jury, Bayley himself declared that the hall's design
rendered the proper conduct of justice "impossible." The majestic theater of the law in operation required not only grander surroundings but
also more substantial ones. As Bayley soon discovered, the walls were
so thin that as he sat in his black cap pronouncing the awful sentence
of death upon some convicted felons, loud bursts of laughter were
heard issuing from the civil court next door. Before the grand jury
could begin its work of deciding which cases were suitable to be tried
in court, Bayley (like the prison chaplain earlier) expounded on the
shocking "length and enormity of the crimes with which the calendar
abounded." As the grand jury reached its decisions and the trials began, the Gloucester inmates became a little more restive—two were
put in the dark solitude cells for burning another's clothes—and the
high sheriff conducted an inspection of the jail.[28]

William and Joseph at last secured the services of a local barrister
to defend them both. But lack of funds meant that instead of the eminent Old Bailey barrister Adolphus, they had to rely on a Mr. Ludlow,
an eloquent and diligent man but almost certainly a trainee and last-
minute appointment by the court; he would have had little time to
prepare the case and lacked the supporting services of a solicitor. Their
opponents were considerably better organized. The Cheltenham
Crime Association paid for Walter Meyers, the injured goldsmith, and
all the necessary witnesses to travel to Gloucester to appear before the
grand jury. Two solicitors from the association had carefully prepared
the case and briefed three learned counsel to prosecute it—clearly they
intended to take no unnecessary chances.[29]

Despite the stately solemnity of the judge, assize courtrooms were
no more serious places than the Old Bailey had been. Charles Cottu
described (probably with some Gallic embellishment) how,

> according to an ancient custom, flowers are strewed upon [the judge's]
> desk, and upon the clerk's. The sheriff and officers of the court wear
> each a nosegay. By a condescension sufficiently extraordinary, the
> judge permits his bench to be invaded by a throng of spectators, and
> thus finds himself surrounded by the prettiest women of the county,
> the sisters, wives, or daughters of grand jurors, who have arrived for

the purpose of partaking in the festivities occasioned by the assizes, and who make it a duty or a pastime to be present at the trials. They are attired in the most elegant negligee; and it is a spectacle not a little curious to see the judge's venerable head loaded with a large wig, peering amongst the youthful female heads, adorned with all the graces of nature and set off with all the assistance of art.[30]

William and Joseph walked from the jail to the courtroom in a couple of minutes, unfettered as they were by the shackles that Sir George Paul detested. The great man himself was present on the bench as they were ushered into an unusually crowded court, full of people eager to follow the fate of two such handsome and respectable young men. They were largely disappointed, for there was very little drama during the trial. William and Joseph conducted themselves with all the decorum they could muster throughout the proceedings, taking notes constantly and passing them on to their counsel, Mr. Ludlow. A procession of witnesses, including Meyers the goldsmith; their Cheltenham landlady, Mrs. Calcott; a representative from the London bank of Selby and Wright; and the unhappy Dr. Newell proceeded to present increasingly clear and damning evidence for the prosecution.

At the end of this litany, Mr. Ludlow stood and delivered "an able speech" in an attempt to convince the jury that, despite the obvious imprudence of their actions, the prisoners had never intended to defraud the goldsmith. Such had been the publicity surrounding the case that Judge Bayley had to remind jurors not to take into account anything they had heard prior to the court proceedings. In summing up the evidence, Bayley charged the jury to decide whether it was the prisoners' "pretence" of knowing Mr. Newell and asserting that he would honor their draft that had persuaded Meyers to give them the jewelry. The jury barely took time to confer and pronounced the pair guilty at once. On being asked if they had anything to say before sentence was pronounced, first Joseph and then William assured the court that they had not intended to cheat the prosecutor. Their speeches made no impression on Judge Bayley.

Such was the importance of the manner of pronouncing sentence that advice books stressed, "a wise and conscientious judge will never neglect so favourable an occasion of inculcating the enormity of vice and the fatal consequences to which it leads." Yet judges were also expected to maintain an aura of pained compassion. Cottu described the typical judge as looking "like a father in the midst of his family occupied in trying one of his children." From Mr. Jackson's perspective, Bayley was acting *in loco parentis* as the state's representative with the power to punish and control William's feckless, immoral behavior. Judge Bayley did not disappoint on this occasion as he proceeded to address the prisoners "in a most feeling and impressive manner." He made it plain that they had been "convicted on evidence so clear as to leave no doubt in his mind, or in the mind of any person present, of their guilt"—a fact that Mr. Jackson would regularly repeat to concerned relatives in order to justify his abandonment of William. Having thus convinced the crowd of the rightfulness of the laws, Judge Bayley proceeded to deliver the obligatory homily to ensure that William and Joseph's conduct stood as a warning to all. Jackson, who copied out a report of the whole trial, recorded Bayley's speech, underlining phrases and adding comments (here in square brackets) of his own:

> It was most painful to him to see young men of apparent respectability, and whose education [Alas! One of them despised all education, and resisted every effort for the improvement of his mind] ought to have taught them better conduct in the situation they were, associated with felons of the worst description; and remarked, with much feeling, the distress and pain they had brought upon their friends by such abandoned conduct.[31]

In highlighting the pain caused to "friends," Judge Bayley was including families and thus implicitly supporting Jackson's own sentiments concerning William's disgraceful behavior. Indeed, Bayley had fulfilled the role of avenging patriarch to perfection. William and Joseph expected to be sentenced to a period of hard labor for a minor misdemeanor, but their calculations proved horribly wrong, and as the judge pronounced a sentence of seven years' transportation to Australia, they struggled to retain their composure. The local paper reported how the crowd muttered and sighed, full of "regret at seeing young men of respectable connexions in such a degraded situation."

But justice had been seen to be done, and the newspapers congratu-lated the Cheltenham association and local constables for bringing to "punishment two persons who have so long and so effectually de-frauded the Public."³²

There was also no doubt in the minds of William's parents that their son had been fairly sentenced, however harsh the penalty may seem today. Eager to display his mastery of legal technicalities and the justness of the sentence, Bayley had gone to some lengths to clarify why the pair had been convicted of obtaining goods under false pre-tenses. He explained that anyone who offered a draft on a bank in which he knew he had no money to cover a purchase, and who had clearly intended to cheat the vendor, was guilty of that crime. Seven years' transportation was the standard sentence for less serious felonies such as this. For Mr. Jackson, it was clear evidence that William was now a convicted felon, who, under the ancient English legal definition of felony as a crime deserving forfeiture of all personal lands and goods, could no longer claim any financial assistance from him.³³

William remained convinced that he had merely been convicted of a misdemeanor, and very unfairly at that, because large numbers of gentlemen paid for their goods knowing that they did not have *current* funds to pay for them, but could rationalize it as paying by "credit." Beau Brummell had famously declared after he had become bankrupt but continued to live in some style that "it is a truly aristocratic feeling, the gift of living happily on credit!" Indeed, fashionable society frequently regarded the indebted dandy or regency buck with pity, ex-pecting no more than an honorable withdrawal to France when credi-tors closed in. On hearing of Brummell's fate in 1816, the Duke of Devonshire, at whose magnificent estate William had once partied, observed, "Poor man. . . . We tolerate great swindlers in society." Per-haps the greatest of these was the Prince Regent; once described as "the first gentleman of England," his massive debts had provoked pub-lic and parliamentary debate about profligacy and eventually earned him almost universal condemnation.³⁴

Unfortunately for William, even though the line between credit and crime was a fine one in high society, the law surrounding fraud was tortuously complex. There was a subtle distinction between obtaining goods by false pretenses (a misdemeanor) and effectively stealing the goods, or "larceny by trick" (a felony). In the first case the owner must have parted with his goods voluntarily (even though he had been deceived); in the second, there must have been a clear *intention* to steal goods against the owner's will. Since Judge Bayley had stressed William and Joseph's intention to cheat the goldsmith because they had no means of paying for the jewelry, he clearly believed they had committed a felony, but official reports misleadingly recorded the offense as merely "obtaining goods by false pretences." This difference of opinion between William and his father continued to shape their relationship until death finally parted them.[35]

By the time Gloucester's Lent assizes drew to a close, Judge Bayley had also put on his black cap to condemn twelve men and two women to hang for grand larceny (theft of goods worth more than 1s.), stealing horses or sheep, burglary, highway robbery, and "maliciously cutting woollen cloth from a sack in a drying ground." The death penalty reflected the Georgian government's overwhelming concern to protect the private and commercial property that supported wealth, power, and trade. In a judicial system that sought bloody retribution for so many offenses, however, the exercise of mercy was also considered an essential demonstration of justice, and as Cottu pointed out, "Were these barbarous penalties rigorously inflicted, a place of execution in England would become a vast charnel-house." In fact, the standard 1s. value of stolen goods threshold for the death penalty had been set in the Anglo-Saxon period and never been changed. Hence, as one eminent jurist observed, "while every thing else was risen in its nominal value, and become dearer, the life of man had continually grown cheaper."[36]

To mitigate this, juries frequently contrived to convict prisoners of lesser offenses and judges strove to be merciful where they clearly saw good cause to be. Judge Bayley subsequently reduced the sentences of eight men and the two women to transportation. This meant that, along with William and Joseph, plus four others convicted of grand larceny, sixteen people returned to Gloucester jail after sentencing, knowing that they would soon be parted—probably forever—from their parents, children, partners, friends, and everything they called home. For most convicts, transportation was a distressing and traumatic severance. From the state's perspective, it was an efficient and humane alternative to the death penalty—it served to remove the diseased criminal from the healthy body of British society without loss of life, but with the possibility that the offender could still find redemption or reform in a new society.

William and Joseph displayed remarkably different reactions to their sentence. Joseph suffered agonies of remorse and fear at their prospective punishment and the pain it would cause his family. William believed himself the victim of a miscarriage of justice and claimed he had been convicted because he had had "no counsel" to represent him. He clearly did not view Mr. Ludlow as a skilled barrister. He also clung to the fact that he had been born a gentleman, and as such his position and (future, if not present) wealth set him apart from the vast majority of other inmates at Gloucester. He wrote to his mother immediately following his conviction, stoutly declaring that he would humble himself to no one but her, as he was "determined to uphold the dignity of a man!!" His father, deeply unimpressed with this misguided statement, scored through the paper in underlining his son's words and added exclamation marks of horrified disbelief. The gulf in understanding between father and son over what it meant to be a true gentleman had never been wider.[37]

RETRIBUTION

Woolwich Hulks, 1813

Here arts of fraud are taught; here leagues are made
Of blackest guilt, and plans of mischief laid . . .
Confine not youth in this abandon'd place,
To herd with everything most vile and base;
Let Justice rather strike her victim dead
Than send him here the path of sin to tread . . .
T'were better doom him to the lion's den,
Than to this curs'd abode of Wicked men.

—— The Convict's Complaint; Supposed to be written
on board the hulks in the beginning of 1815 (1815)

Immediately after William and Joseph were sentenced, life in Gloucester jail changed dramatically for them. From this moment on, William's ability to use his wealth or status to ameliorate his living conditions in the prison ceased. He and Joseph, along with all those serving more than six-month sentences, had their heads shaved and were issued the coarse uniform and badges denoting their status as convicted criminals before they were transferred to the penitentiary section of the jail. The chaplain visited both shortly after their return and noted the marked difference in their reactions. He found Joseph in tears, but he was shocked to see that William still showed "total insensibility either to his degraded situation or his offence."[1]

There was little opportunity for the two convicted men to talk to each other because they were now confined in solitude. Each occupied two separate but adjacent cells, one for sleeping and the other for working in. Both rooms were dark but warm enough and well ventilated; one was furnished with an iron bedstead, two mattresses, two blankets, and a flannel coverlet. Compared to the majority of early-nineteenth-century prisons, the accommodation was both clean and comfortable. Prisoners were also issued two sheets and a nightcap, which were washed every month by the female felons.

The daily routine—marked out by bells—never varied. The prisoners rose at six o'clock, made their beds, washed, and went to chapel. After the service the governor examined them for cleanliness and distributed bread and money to those who were clean and well behaved. They worked alone in their day cells making produce for sale in the prison shop. They were allowed to exercise for just one hour a day in a yard, but they were supervised by a guard charged with preventing them from talking with others—exercise was believed to be beneficial to body and soul, whereas "loitering" and conversation were not. The chaplain regularly praised the good dinners of beef and potatoes or pea soup fed to the prisoners, but if William and Joseph were less convinced of their quality, they chose to accept them rather than use the government allowance of 2s. 6d. to buy food and necessities from the prison sutler, who would purchase goods for inmates in the town.

William spent all his spare time writing more letters to procure money or support for his application for a pardon. He told the ever-generous Lewises of his "horror and surprise at so severe and unexpected sentence," but he assured them that he had petitioned the Prince Regent for a pardon, which he was sure would succeed as it had been signed by "a great number of personages of distinction." Attempts to borrow more money from them, however, proved unsuccessful. A day later he wrote to his father asking to be sent his usual allowance. Jackson's reply was uncompromising:

When that allowance was granted, you were under different circumstances. . . . By the conduct you have thought proper to pursue, my hands are completely tied; for the laws of the land not only prevent me from administering to your wants, but equally preclude me from continuing any allowance without the special sanction of his majesty's justices. It has not been my practice to infringe the law and there is nothing in the present case that could prompt me to it. Any application, therefore, from you for assistance must be supported by an acknowledged authority. Any other will receive no notice.[2]

Thus began the battle over William's status as a convicted felon. Strictly speaking, the prison rules stated that the county justices had to sanction any visits, and food from family and friends was prohibited, so the spirit, if not the letter, of the rules seemed to support Jackson's argument. Yet the situation also provided him with an excellent reason (or excuse) to sever paternal obligations and relinquish the support of his son to the prison authorities. This left William so short of money that he and Joseph asked to be taken off the penitentiary diet and receive their government allowance immediately.

LIFE FOR THE PRISONERS in Gloucester jail became more stressful as the time for the execution of the four remaining condemned prisoners drew near. Despite all the efforts to subdue, reform, and humiliate the inmates, acts of resistance were not extinguished. Prisoners still found ways of communicating through the walls and palisades or of engaging in outbreaks of angry, violent, or defiant behavior. The condemned horse thief and the three highwaymen were visited daily by the surgeon and the chaplain, who found "their behaviour is not altogether so penitent as it ought to have been." On April 24 the chaplain officiated in the usual way at the service prior to execution, noting with some satisfaction that the condemned were now more penitent. After the service all the other convicts were locked in their separate cells to be sure there was no trouble.[3]

Prior to 1792 condemned prisoners had been driven to the nearby village of Over while sitting on their own coffins in open carts. Their last journey was meant to impress upon the watching crowds the awful consequences of crime, but increasingly crowds at executions had either treated the occasion as a holiday or, worse from the authorities' perspective, openly supported the prisoners, who responded with acts of bravado in an effort to die "game." In keeping with its enlightened principles of punishment, Gloucester had consequently built a more humane "new drop" gallows on the flat roof above the prison gatehouse. It was to this lonely spot that the condemned men were led, still hoping for a last-minute reprieve—just two years earlier a convicted burglar had been hanged just minutes before an exhausted rider galloped in with his pardon. No stay of execution arrived, so the bell signifying that the "awful ceremony" was going ahead began to toll. An eerie silence fell over the whole jail while all four men plunged to their deaths.[4]

A few days later William fell ill, and the surgeon ordered both him and Joseph to be given an extra food and bread allowance. They had probably been saving their government allowance for use on the floating prison hulks (where felons were sent until their passage to Australia could be arranged) rather than spending it on food. After the executions and prior to the arrival of the wagon to convey convicts to the hulks, the sense of anger and desperation increased among both the remaining condemned prisoners and the transportees. Many viewed imprisonment aboard the infamous hulks as a worse prospect than hanging. Convict turned author James Hardy Vaux recalled how in 1810 a condemned cell mate in Newgate had said he was "happy" to hang, because he had "formerly been transported, but made his escape from the hulks; and the miseries he had witnessed and endured on board those horrid receptacles, he asserted to be such that he preferred death to a reprieve, which might subject him to years of similar suffering." So it was not surprising that when the Gloucester convicts were allowed to associate in the first-class felons' day room, their behavior rapidly became riotous and "improper." As a result, William, Joseph, and the other felons were all placed in solitary confinement in their cells until they were called to set out for London. During that lonely wait, they were visited only by the well-meaning chaplain, who gave them religious books to aid their journey to the next life—whether that was to be in "parts beyond the seas" or beyond this world altogether.[5]

Just over a week later, William and Joseph, along with five other men, were released from their cells to board the wagon waiting to carry them to the hulks at Woolwich in London. When convicts were being loaded onto the carts, it was usual for a crowd of families to gather outside the jails desperate for a last sight of a loved one in case they could not make the journey to the port when the prisoner set sail for Australia. Most were poor families for whom transportation of a wage earner spelled destitution as well as desolation, but there was no one to wave William off or send him their love—his family felt the shame too keenly to be present and still believed their absence was part of his punishment. Once the prisoners left the prison precincts, public scrutiny of them would be considerably less kind. Convict transportation was contracted out to private overseers, who rarely went to the expense of providing any cover to protect the convicts from the weather, and in winter it was not unknown for male and female convicts to arrive suffering from frostbite and exposure. Without cover, the transportees were equally exposed to the taunts and jeers of less-feeling members of the public they passed during their long journey.

The jail's governor, Thomas Cunningham, accompanied his prisoners to make sure they were safely handed over at the end of a ride that would cover more than a hundred miles. Some governors also took the opportunity to check up on the fate of their previous convicts, but this was probably because of attempts to record death rates, rather than out of compassion. The results of their inquiries were nevertheless frequently shocking. The infamous floating dungeons continued to spew out bodies at twice the rate of death in the wider population, and some mortality rates reached appalling levels. The length of time a convict was imprisoned on a hulk could vary enormously; for a lucky few it was just days, for many it was months, but others spent years, or even their entire sentences, on board. Convicts also greatly feared what would become of them after death. Their bodies were buried in Woolwich or Plumstead churchyards, on the marshes, or at Woolwich Arsenal itself, where the victims of cholera could be found still manacled in their graves.[6]

Convict corpses frequently became fair game for the resurrection men, or body snatchers, who supplied surgeons with human bodies for dissections. Nor was there any lack of informers keen to earn money for revealing the whereabouts of "fresh" subjects. Local legend had it that red dead-nettle, or "convicts flower," grew only on convict graves in the arsenal. Yet many ordinary people believed that the vengeful ghosts of those wrongly killed or prevented from resting in peace in the afterlife would return to haunt them. The state, and most citizens, felt that denial of a Christian burial and public mutilation were dreadful dishonors to the dead and their families. In 1752 the delivery of a hanged felon's corpse to the surgeons for dissection had been added to the punishment for murder to act as a further deterrent, but it led to riots beneath the scaffold between the condemned's friends and the surgeons' agents.

Selling his body to a surgeon meant that a convict's (and his family's) suffering did not end with his death on the hulks. If William died on the hulks, the Jacksons would suffer little less than if he had been executed. His likelihood of surviving was lower than they realized, for William's destination was the notorious *Retribution* hulk, which had recorded 170 deaths between 1804 and 1811. This was more than double that of its five sister ships and treble that on two other better-managed vessels, and the number of attempted escapes from the ship's detested decks was correspondingly high. Of all the hated hulks, *Retribution* was the most dreaded—one convict compared his arrival on board to "a descent to the infernal regions" of hell.[7]

Convicts for transportation were first taken to what was called the Woolwich Warren on the formerly marshy banks of the Thames. Originally named after the numerous rabbits that burrowed there, it was once the site of Henry VIII's royal dockyard, before being converted for the manufacture of ordnance in the reign of George I and then renamed the Royal Arsenal in 1805. Much of the site, in excess of one hundred acres, was filled with "immense store-houses, forming a grand national depôt of warlike stores, of every description, for the naval and military departments of the service." There were workshops, barracks, firing ranges, and huge stacks of timber and shot. The arsenal now also contained handsome houses for garrison and artillery officers; the grand buildings of the Military Academy; a fine-looking guardhouse with a portico supported by pillars of portland stone; and a lofty, stone-ornamented brass foundry built by John Vanburgh. The impressive elegance of the architecture on land contrasted starkly with the battered ugliness of the massive, decaying hulks moored just offshore.[8]

Retribution was itself a site of public interest—in spring and summer, boats carried curious tourists to view its awful bulk from close quarters. The once proud seventy-four-gun warship now sat squat in the murky water. Its masts had been removed, leaving the cumbersome deck surmounted only by low wooden excrescences: toolsheds, housing for the guards, and various makeshift modifications. Instead of billowing sails, chimneys belched black smoke onto lines of drying washing. Ladders hung haphazardly from the gunwales, and the lack of scheduled repairs meant that the hull was blemished from periodic patching up. Massive, rusty iron chains held *Retribution* immobile against the current or kept it upright when it baked on the mud at low tide. The bulging, thick wooden sides were punctuated with numerous empty canon ports, some of which were left open to provide light and air to prisoners on the gun deck, but were barred with cast iron grilles two inches thick to prevent escape. The lowest, or orlop, deck had narrow scuttles specially cut to frustrate convict breakouts and were similarly barred. Decommissioned and refitted as a prison ship to hold 450 men, *Retribution* had wallowed in Thames effluent since 1804. It was one of the largest and longest-serving hulks, but it was badly in need of a refit and was being considered for modernization when William arrived in the spring of 1813.

Like the other hulks, *Retribution* was a lasting symbol of the "temporary expedient" proposed in 1776 to deal with the numerous prisoners no longer able to be transported to America when Britain went to war over the colonies' independence. Permanently overcrowded jails and a failure to find a better solution left the hulks in service long after transportation to Australia had begun, despite several parliamentary reports about the serious problems on board. The hulks had been designed to embody some of the key ideas practiced in the new penitentiaries: religious instruction, penitence, and hard labor. The latter was intended to profit the state, as convicts could be set to work dredging river channels, strengthening shorelines, or working in dockyards and arsenals more cheaply than waged labor could. The first two ideals proved more difficult to instill in the prisoners, particularly among those on *Retribution*, where the inmates' animosity had even prevented the completion of a chapel. Indeed, it was acknowledged that reformation of any kind was almost impossible in the hulks. Sir George Holford, MP, chairman of a select committee assigned to investigate conditions on the hulks, acknowledged as much during a parliamentary speech in 1815:

> The Public believe that these vessels are scenes of disorder and schools of vice, where every spark of goodness that may yet remain in the breast of the offender, must be extinguished, and many a prisoner has been matured in vicious knowledge, and trained up to deeds of greater outrage, than those which originally brought him under the censure of the law.[9]

What both the public and politicians believed to be true of prison hulks in general, William and Joseph were about to discover for themselves on board *Retribution*. They crossed the short stretch of water to the hulk in longboats rowed by chained convicts. Once hauled up on deck, the prisoners were stripped and thrown into tubs of freezing lye water to be scrubbed clean. They were then issued with coarse jackets, breeches, shirts, stockings, shoes, hats, neckerchiefs, and a blanket each. The instructions to all hulk captains, issued by the inspector of hulks, were to use "the utmost economy" in giving convicts their yearly allowance and "to make [as] much less do as you can, without running any risk of endangering health." The clothing of escaped or dead convicts (unless killed by infectious disease) was washed and reissued. Not surprisingly, the clothes were often well worn and ill fitting. A blacksmith then encased each man with iron fetters, connected to each ankle by a chain, which was prevented from dragging on the ground by a strap fastened to a waist belt. These heavy metal bonds, which varied in weight but averaged around twelve pounds, had to be worn day and night, during hard labor and at rest, unless the convict was ill in the sick bay. Some prisoners got so used to wearing them that removal caused them to fall over or left them unable to walk normally for days.[10]

When someone lifted the hatch to descend, a nauseous stench emanated from the decks below, where five hundred men, youths, and boys as young as twelve were confined. Efforts had been made to improve hygiene on the hulks—hammocks, which could be washed, had been ordered to replace insect-infested wooden bunks, but William found that he was given nothing but straw to sleep on. Convict clothing was supposed to be changed at intervals, but the stench of stale sweat, excrement, vermin, and disease remained. In an attempt to contain the "foul air" to each deck—and to prevent the prisoners from preying on each other—the government ordered the decks on hulks to be separately sealed. Efforts to separate the three decks on *Retribution,* however, had been abandoned because whenever the builders finished their task and went home, "the convicts rose in the night and tore down the works."[11]

With a free run of the lower decks from evening lockdown until morning—which could last as long as sixteen hours in winter—the prisoners were poorly supervised and largely left to their own devices. Officers and guards rarely went below decks and never after dark because to do so would be to "risk personal injury." William had to sleep and live in one of the dimly lit, poorly ventilated lower three decks of *Retribution* with well over 150 other filthy, degraded, desperate men. It was not brutal guards that he feared, but, as he told his father, "the abominations prevalent among the convicts aboard this hulk, which . . . are too shocking to relate." Indeed, the only thing that made his stay on the hulk at all tolerable was the fair treatment he received from the officers. William even felt grateful to the first mate "for his kindness for he has rendered my suffering comparatively speaking, easy. But still my situation is horrible, truly horrible."[12]

Two inmates on each deck were nominally appointed to act as boatswain's mates—they kept the lights burning and would periodically shout out, "All is well" to the guards above—but they had no control over the other prisoners. Even if the captain spoke privately to individual prisoners, almost none would (dare to) admit to being harmed by their fellow inmates. Most hulk captains told the parliamentary select committee in 1813 that violence was relatively rare, but during his stay on *Retribution,* James Vaux witnessed one murder and one suicide. For many prisoners, the mere threat of violence was enough to cow them into allowing others to steal their belongings. William described how the scenes of "cursing and swearing, with robbing, and breaking open boxes of their fellow sufferers, . . . thereby robbing them of their little all, distracts my brain. I am not yet so hardened as not to shudder at such depravity."[13] Vaux, too, claimed that any offers of friendship were merely a cover for plans of robbery.

Yet the crime that both government and society feared most, but could never name, was homosexuality. The "abominations which make human nature shudder," or "unnatural crimes" as William and Vaux called them, probably referred to both rape and consensual sex. All penetrative sexual acts between men were still punishable by death, and homophobia was rife among all classes. Indeed, the select committee believed that the convicts themselves abhorred this most "atrocious vice" so much that any "person suspected of having been addicted to it has met with ill usage from the rest of the prisoners." Yet Parliament dismissed frequent references to predatory homosexuality in convicts' letters home as attempts to use the most effective method of persuading friends and relatives to obtain their release. Ministers were further convinced that the allegations were false because (not surprisingly) official investigators had failed to discover any proof of guilt.[14]

GIVEN WILLIAM'S MANY previous attempts to manipulate his father, it is tempting to view his letters from the hulk in the same light as those that one MP described as giving "exaggerated accounts . . . for the purpose of stimulating their friends and relations to procure their removal, by a pardon, from the scenes of vice and profligacy which they describe." William was aware that "it was common practice amongst the convicts to forge letters with this view" and, not wishing his father to be distracted by requests for help from other convicts, warned him "to pay no attention to such letters." Mr. Jackson should write only to an address in Downing Street, where a sympathetic friend would receive them. William was also anxious not to receive any letters by post because they would be opened and read before he received them. Letters sent to a "friend" could be brought unnoticed on board by a visitor and handed over in person.[15]

Nevertheless, William did describe how convicts nearing the end of their sentences were "busily occupied in preparing implements for house-breaking, and picking pockets, while others are employed in making base coin," and "coining counterfeit token and other silver, the detection of which must terminate their career." Captains of the hulks gave very similar statements to the select committee in 1812, in which it is clear that such activities were an accepted part of convict life on board. These practices were tolerated, if not condoned, by the guards, even though such crimes, if prosecuted on land, would earn the death sentence. Possibly because of the reluctance to go below decks at night, when guards heard noises "like rapping or hammering," they merely told the prisoners to "go to bed." Some convicts, however, were occupied in more honest pursuits making shoes, clothing, and trinkets or carving bone figures by candlelight (some of which were "obscene") to sell.[16]

If William's descriptions of criminal activities on board "this bastile of infamy" were meant to frighten his father, they signally failed to do so. In Jackson's eyes, none of William's fellow wretches aboard *Retribution* could possibly be "a worse or more dangerous member of society than himself." William's claims that "there is not one single instance upon record of any man serving his time on board . . . turning out an honourable character" may have echoed Parliament's concern, but it left his father utterly unmoved. William's ruin, Jackson stormed, had been sealed long before his contact with any of these debased convicts because it had been caused by his own depraved character, and Jackson had long ago given up any hope of his son's reformation.[17]

William's greatest hardship was lack of food, which inevitably contributed to his deteriorating health. Yet claims that he was starving were also framed as emotional pleas to excite his father's sense of duty and humanitarian sympathy. "I appeal, Sir, to your feelings as a Father," he begged "and I now tell you that I am in a state of starvation, and you, sir, who never knew what hunger was cannot feel its acuteness." "A lie!" exclaimed Mr. Jackson. "His Majesty's Government must find him in clothes and food." The government did indeed provide rations of barley, oatmeal, bread, and beer daily, supplemented by beef or cheese on alternate days, all of which were supposed to be of a similar standard to that issued to troops. Since the inspector of hulks insisted on captains measuring out all food deliveries and holding contracted suppliers to account for the amounts and quality of the food, this was believed to be sufficient. However, some convicts' letters and accounts suggest the provisions were "very scanty" and of the lowest, moldy grade.[18]

William was convinced that "having nothing but Barley and Putrid meat to eat will soon terminate a miserable existence." He suffered from frequent "bowel complaints" that left him thin and vulnerable to fever and rash, which are the main symptoms of "hulk fever," or typhus. James Vaux described how disgusting the food tasted—particularly the coarse boiled barley and oatmeal gruel served twice a day and boiled in the water of the beef on meat days to create a dish that convicts called "smiggins." By any account, the rations were small for men expected to labor hard every day and woefully lacking in fruit and vegetables. William claimed that "there is seldom a day three or four of the unhappy men do not die of the black scurvy," which was caused by chronic lack of vitamin C, particularly among those already physically weakened. Scurvy caused bleeding under the skin, which lead to the dark brown or black stains on the legs that gave black scurvy its name; if left untreated, it can result in death even today. William pined for simple "necessities" like tea and sugar, and he felt even more unfairly treated because Joseph Bradley's father sent money, ensuring that his friend could eat enough to remain relatively healthy. Equally problematic for William was the trade in food between convicts, which although strictly prohibited left those who were weak, vulnerable, or short of money at risk of losing what little they did receive.[19]

THE MOST OBVIOUS omission from William's letters home was any mention of the work he was expected to perform. Unless sick or skilled in making clothes or shoes, every convict was forced to work in the arsenal. Their labor provided part of the economic justification for balancing the costs of confinement against keeping the hulks running in harbors, which required much maintenance. Work began at seven and, after a midday meal back on board, continued until sunset. Accounts of the brutality of the overseers vary. According to Vaux, they were ignorant, tyrannical, and cruel men from the lowest levels of society who hit the convicts with a large stick on the slightest provocation. Official accounts of working conditions are considerably more favorable, and at least one casual observer in 1801 saw only moral, not physical, degradation:

> On our way to the boat, we had a melancholy proof of the profligacy of the times by a sight of the multitude of convicts in chains, labouring in removing earth; eight are employed in drawing each cart. They

were well clad, and by their appearance, seemed well fed; but in general the sense of shame is lost. If they had any at first, it soon is changed into hardened impudence by the depravity of their fellow prisoners. . . . There were about 300 busied on land.[20]

For someone like William, who was unused to physical work, the arsenal was a hard place to begin. Convicts not only struggled to draw bulky carts over the marshy ground, but also carried heavy loads of coal and timber for stacking; cleaned sewers, sheds, and drains; broke up huge stones; dredged mountains of mud and gravel from the riverbed; repaired butts and roads; and loaded and offloaded supplies to ships. Mr. Jackson was unlikely to be moved by or object to his dissolute and fraudulent son being made to work to earn money for himself. It was part of the reason he felt he need not pay more, for the English legislature made sure that no freeborn Englishman should be enslaved, whatever his crime. The state insisted that convict labor must be remunerated, albeit at lower rates than those of regular workers. That convicts should be "encouraged" to save their meager earnings for their future reform was another popular idea. Hence, the authorities undertook to retain part of each convict's earnings, which he could then claim back at the end of his sentence, but very few ever underwent the humiliation of making that claim.[21]

William's increasingly desperate letters failed to move either of his parents. After his conviction at Gloucester, Jane had ceased to answer him, and Mr. Jackson encouraged this silence and probably prohibited her from replying. Jane could also see the terrible toll that William's situation was taking on her husband—she watched, powerless to help, as the emotional hardening of Jackson's heart toward his son was matched by increasing physical weakness and loss of movement in his legs. Perhaps the most significant cause of Jackson's final severance from William was the receipt of a letter from the Lewises begging that he repay them the money they had lent to William during his imprisonment at Gloucester.

This was the first Jackson knew of the deception that William had played on the family's faithful old servant. Betty Lewis traveled all the way from Bath to put their case personally to her former employer at his London home. But Jackson was so ill when she arrived that the poor woman dared not bring the matter up for fear of making him worse. Jackson betrayed the emotional consequences of abandoning his son by admitting to his former servant that it had resulted in "a broken heart, for the conduct of the wretch is hurrying me to the grave." Jackson was appalled when he learned that William had deceived a family servant, and declared William to be a "mean, low-lived, dirty wretch, in attempting thus to take in a poor man." Servants who had provided loyal and long-term service were regarded as members of the household in which they worked. Despite not being blood relatives, they were often referred to as "family" and treated as "friends," albeit in an instrumental and unequal sense. Some employers would extend patronage to those who opened a business or offered help in times of sickness.[22]

Mr. Jackson felt it naïve and foolish of the Lewises not to have been more suspicious of William's pleas for help when he had so many other wealthier relatives to call on. Jackson made it equally clear that he felt it was also morally wrong to repay them when he had refused all other creditors. Nevertheless, he still felt that Lewis "had some claim upon me, on the score of the long and faithful services of your wife, independent of the satisfaction which you yourself always afforded in the little professional matters on which I was accustomed to employ you." On these grounds he declared that although he would not pay the debt, "I will make a present to your wife of fifteen pounds . . . solely in the recollection that something may be due to her, for the many years she formed a part of my family." Betty Lewis was the only creditor (of the hundreds who wrote) to whom Jackson offered to make any payment in "consideration for the losses . . . sustained with the reprobate on board the Retribution Hulk."[23]

Isolated and increasingly afraid for his survival for any length of time on board the hulk, William seems to have been unaware—or unwilling to accept—that both parents now considered him their "late son." He continued to believe that it was only the legal implications of his status as a convicted felon that prevented his father from assisting him, and these he believed to be unfounded:

Had I been tried and convicted of a felony, I should in that case be dead in point of law but even then the laws of the land could not prevent you from relieving my wants by way of *Douceur* [a gift]—but in

the present case, having been convicted of a misdemeanour, your solicitor, Mr. Smith, can inform you, that you can allow me what you
think proper, without the sanction of "His Majesty's Justices," who
have no more to do with me and my private resources, than they have
with the King of Rome's future domain.[24]

In a later letter William pointed out that, as a father, Jackson could
have stopped his son's allowance at any time "without making so irrel-
evant an excuse." William contacted an experienced solicitor to prove
that, even if he were a felon, Jackson could still provide "any pecuniary
assistance you thought proper by way of donation." In fact, offenders
convicted of a noncapital felony that carried a sentence of transportation were not subject to the same "legal death" as those convicted of
capital felonies. But Mr. Jackson refuted every point his son made,
scribbling more and more furious notes in the margins of *Filial Ingratitude* to "prove" that he was right to withhold support, sure that
William would use it only to make his escape and commit further
"abominations" against the public. His book was meant to stand as a
public record that he had acted as both a good father and a true citizen. In retaliation, William threatened to publish in the newspapers
the fact that Jackson refused to support his son. Sick, depressed, and
subject to mood swings frequently caused by typhus, William alter-
nated between despair and wild plans for his future release. He begged
his mother to forgive his "undutiful" sentiments, but

> struck with sorrow at being left abandoned to my unhappy fate which
> has now become worse than Death to me on account of the abomina-
> tions prevalent among the convicts, I have made up my mind to peti-
> tion government to let me enter the Army or Navy and forever bid
> farewell to a family which I regret calling my relatives.[25]

In early June William received a letter from his father explaining
that he had read all the correspondence between him and Lewis, and
that the thought of ever enabling William to practice "so foul a fraud"
ever again had driven all thoughts of providing any relief from his
mind. William's failure to fulfill his duty as a son and his conviction as
a felon enabled Jackson to deny that his son could make any further

claims upon him as a father. He ended his letter with the chilling declaration that "I have done with you forever; and all further letters will remain unanswered."²⁶

William's initial reaction was defensive, soon followed by desperate disbelief. He felt no remorse for asking the Lewises for money because, having been "deserted by my father and abandoned by my family," he had no other options. He wrote three more times, alternately begging for forgiveness or pretending that he had never received that last letter of June 7, 1813. Jackson read and commented on all these letters in *Filial Ingratitude,* more concerned to explain his motives to his imaginary readers than to his son. William begged him to "accept . . . my tears and sincerest contrition, and do not for God's sake abandon me to my present unhappy fate. Recollect, Sir that I am your Son, and that it is in your power to save me from utter ruin and certain disgrace." His father replied only in the margin of his own narrative: "Alas! It is not. These volumes prove that no effort could save him." There is no evidence that Mr. Jackson ever saw or communicated with his son again.²⁷

This final severance of all family ties was especially difficult for William to comprehend because Joseph Bradley's father had on "this heart-cutting and lamentable occasion, fulfilled the duty of both Parent and Friend." Mr. Bradley had written to Joseph in Gloucester jail, "However undutifully you may have acted towards me, yet it never shall be said that I *abandoned* my son to want, and by so doing led him to further acts of indiscretion." William had since discovered that Mr. Bradley not only sent money regularly, enabling his son to eat better, but he also had secured permission for Joseph to be transported to Sydney on the next available ship, a prospect, William believed, far preferable to remaining on the hulk. With his own fate sealed and with a departure for Botany Bay on board the *General Hewart* set for the end of August, Joseph promised, or was persuaded, to help his friend one more time. He signed a certificate claiming that he alone was to blame for events at Cheltenham, stating that he would be willing to sign an affidavit to the effect that William was "wholly innocent of any intention to defraud the jeweller."²⁸

This they sent to William's godfather, Mr. Huddlestone, at Old Windsor. Huddlestone, a long-standing friend of Jackson's who had served with him in India, immediately left his home to visit nearby Langley Lodge, where he read the certificate out loud in an effort to convince Jackson that William had "been unjustly used, both by judge and jury." As a consequence, Huddlestone declared that he would exert all the influence he had to convince the home secretary, Lord Sidmouth, to free his godson. Mr. Jackson roundly denied that there was a grain of truth in Bradley's statement, which he fervently believed William had persuaded his accomplice to write. The two men parted amicably enough, but still with widely differing opinions. The following day Jackson sent "proof" to Huddlestone in the form of letters from Mr. Newell, the eminent Cheltenham doctor who had been the key witness at William's trial. With these, Jackson wrote again to convince his friend that releasing William would be of no benefit to society or his family and could result only in his ignominious death on the gallows. Having read "the sad papers," Huddlestone modified his views but was not moved to abandon his godson completely, insisting that he could at least endeavor to effect William's wish to be transported immediately without upsetting his parents.[29]

OVER THE COURSE of the summer, William gradually came to realize that seeking help from his father was a useless task, but he was not foolish enough to concentrate all his hopes solely on paternal patronage. Even at this late stage, there was room for the discretionary nature of English justice to provide a way out of harsh punishment. Appealing to the monarch for pardon was a common and accepted practice for convicted men and women from all levels of society, and to demonstrate the exercise of merciful justice, a proportion of the most deserving cases would be rewarded with their freedom. A number of circumstances could influence judges, politicians, or the monarch to pardon offenders: youth, respectability, and reformability being among the most common. His father had made it clear that well-placed family members should not help William, but other friends, particularly those he had met through his military service, were keen to put pressure on politicians and William's parents.

Even though William did not fulfill the usual criteria for remission, elite influence played a significant role in the criminal justice system, and aristocratic support could still ultimately prove the most powerful. William had access to prominent politicians and titled landowners who had links to his mother's Irish family roots and/or knew her brother, Sir George Shee. Using these connections, however, was also another way to demonstrate how others had more faith or sympathy with him than his father did. William made an application for pardon to the Prince Regent soon after arriving on the hulk, pleading for mercy or permission to leave the country because self-exile was a possible alternative for wealthy convicts. "The misdemeanour I have been guilty of in drawing upon a banking house, having no effects there," William explained,

> is a crime half the nobility are daily guilty of. My friend Sir John Peshall Bart has exerted himself greatly on my behalf; and had I been guilty of theft, or any other crime that could disgrace you, I am sure so honorable [sic] a personage would not take me by the hand. He not only signed my petition but got Lord Warwick likewise to sign it, with a strong recommendation; and the Honorable Mr. Sheridan handed it to the secretary of state. Should it not succeed, Colonel Macmahon, through the interest of Colonel O'Kelly of Half Moon Street, who has strongly advocated my cause, has kindly promised to hand another petition for me personally to the Prince.[30]

William might well have expected a degree of sympathy from the Prince Regent, saddled as he had been with legendary debts and a frugal, unsympathetic father whose constant criticism was believed to have incited his son to yet further extravagance. Indeed, one anonymous pamphleteer had even suggested that George should remind the king of the link between paternal love and financial generosity in order to redeem his name from the "parsimonious stigma" it had acquired. By paying off his son's debts, the monarch would also earn the "most valuable species of compound interest . . . ample return of love, affection and veneration" from both his family and his grateful subjects.[31]

To gain the regent's signature on a pardon, however, required the services of a long chain of influential, eminent men. William certainly appeared to know such men. Yet most were not at the peak of their influence or careers, some had "colorful" backgrounds, and several had run into financial difficulties themselves—which lent a degree of support to William's claim that he was no different from half the nobility. Sir John Peshall was, like Shee, a relatively recent member of the titled classes. This son of an Oxford cleric had changed his name from Pearsall to Peshall in order to claim the baronetcy in 1770 after the title had been defunct for nearly sixty years. It was strongly rumored that Pearsall had erased and reinscribed the name on his grandfather's tomb to strengthen his claim. George Greville, Second Earl of Warwick, once a powerful man, a member of the Board of Trade, and a Recorder of Warwick, was now in his late sixties. He was still lord lieutenant of Warwickshire but was reduced to living in penury until his death in 1816.

The brilliant playwright and politician Richard Brinsley Sheridan should have been a powerful ally, but his reputation was often scandalous and his political position uncertain. Sheridan had lived precisely the fashionable, high-society life that William believed he was entitled to. The son of an Irish actor, Sheridan was even more concerned to consolidate his position as a gentleman than William was. He had fought two (near-fatal) duels to prove his honor and gain access to public life as a gentleman. He had lived in Bath and London, been welcomed in aristocratic circles, and lived well beyond his means to keep up with his new friends, who regularly ran up huge debts themselves. He loved the social whirl, drank heavily, entertained lavishly, and had numerous illicit sexual liaisons. He had been a close friend and political advisor of the Prince of Wales for many years, despite frequently being embarrassed for funds. Now Sheridan, too, was in the twilight of his career since his defeat at the election polls in 1812, and he was more often than not out of favor with the Whigs. By 1813 his finances were in a disastrous state, and his friendship with the regent, who since gaining power no longer needed Sheridan to whip up Whig support, was lukewarm. In the month that William asked for his help, Sheridan had "a violent quarrel in public" with the prince, who had paid more than £3,000 to buy the playwright a parliamentary seat in a rotten borough, which Sheridan then lost because his lawyer appropriated the money for himself, to pay outstanding debts instead of using it to pay election expenses. Sheridan was struggling to keep his creditors at bay, painfully aware that because he was no longer an

MP, he could himself soon be arrested for debt—a fate he finally succumbed to a year later.[32]

William's other chain of influence made use of his Anglo-Irish ancestry, based on contacts he had probably made while engaging with other young Regency bucks and aristocrats in the fashionable sexual indulgences of the *demi monde*. Colonel Andrew Dennis O'Kelly was a respectable landowner and member of the Jockey Club in his own right, but he was the nephew of the infamous Irish sharper, social climber, and racehorse owner "Count" Dennis O'Kelly, from whom he had inherited most of his wealth. One of his properties was an elegant house on Half Moon Street, overlooking Hyde Park, which had long been a favorite destination for members of the *beau monde* and *demi monde*. Until 1813 the house was still the residence of the count's long-term lover, "Mrs. Kelly," the very beautiful but infamous courtesan and brothel owner Charlotte Hayes. The pair had met in the Fleet Prison but built a fortune together through Charlotte's high-class brothels and the count's skill at cards and horse racing. His lowly background and dubious finances meant that he could never be admitted to the Jockey Club as a gentleman, but ownership of Eclipse, one of the most famous race horses of all time, gave him entry to racing and landed society. Charlotte had long been widowed, and now retired she was determined to end her days in the house at Half Moon Street, where Colonel O'Kelly could hardly have failed to join the glittering social gatherings she hosted there. One of William's military friends contacted Colonel O'Kelly, who corresponded with both the Prince Regent and his private secretary, Sir John MacMahon.

Unfortunately for O'Kelly, but more so for William, MacMahon's fortunes were also on the wane. Born the son of a butler, MacMahon had risen to become a lieutenant colonel, a member of the Whig Club, and a political go-between for the party's leaders and the Prince Regent, which had earned him a position on the prince's staff. But by 1812 MacMahon had lost his parliamentary seat and the Whigs were no longer in favor with the regent. MacMahon could neither effect a reconciliation with the party nor counter the rising public hostility to the prince's dissipated lifestyle and excessive debts. He was unwell, unsuccessful, and beginning to wish for retirement when O'Kelly contacted him about personally delivering the letter supporting William's petition for mercy to the prince. He was also the unfortunate messenger who had been sent to retrieve the prince's missing £3,000 from Sheridan's solicitor in May. In any event, neither O'Kelly nor McMahon succeeded in persuading the prince to offer William a pardon.

Sheridan's efforts initially met with slightly more success. He delivered William's petition to Lord Sidmouth, a highly principled, conservative man later renowned for his severe repression of riots and public disorder. Sheridan reported that the letter had been warmly received by the home secretary, who promised to discuss the matter with his "very particular friend, Sir George Shee." Lord Warwick, perhaps all too aware of his own financial embarrassment, had strongly recommended mercy but also advised William to write to his uncle. Knowing that Shee was unlikely to be harboring warm feelings toward his nephew at this point, William asked his mother to stand "my friend in that quarter," presumably hoping that her maternal instincts would induce her to persuade her brother to act on her son's behalf.[33]

Although there is no response from Jane, it seems almost certain that she did not talk to Shee—to have done so would have been to betray her husband and go back on her own promise to cut William off if he ever committed another criminal act. The interview between Shee and Sidmouth did not go well for William, and when Sheridan returned, it was to be informed that the petition had been rejected. Undaunted, Sheridan and Peshall tried again to gain some remission for William, but this time only to ensure that he could leave the hulks on board the first ship bound for Botany Bay. Lord Warwick also endeavored to gain the assistance of the recently appointed foreign secretary, Lord Castlereagh. A native Dubliner, Castlereagh had served the government in Ireland with Shee—both men had been congratulated on their combined efforts to repress the Irish Rebellion of 1798. In any event, Castlereagh consented to oblige Warwick by recommending William to Sidmouth (although ostensibly he did so to please Peshall). With so many connections in high places and such strenuous efforts being made on his behalf, William was confident that by mid-July he would be transferred from *Retribution* to a transport ship bound for Australia.[34]

In the belief that he would soon be leaving England, perhaps never to return, William wrote to his father on July 16 with a final plea for money, this time to help him survive in a foreign land far from friends and family. It was the final letter from his son that Jackson ever copied into *Filial Ingratitude*. But the very last letter Jackson copied into his narrative was from Betty Lewis, and in it she thanked him for sending her £18. By the autumn of 1813, Jackson seems to have felt more compassionate toward this faithful old servant; perhaps because he had disowned William, Betty Lewis was all he had left in the sense of immediate household family dependents for whom he still felt a paternal duty of care.

The reason for the abrupt ending to Mr. Jackson's account of his son's descent into depravity was that the weakness in his legs had become a paralysis that was creeping slowly up his body. The Jacksons had abandoned their elegant home in Gloucester Place and were now living entirely at Langley Lodge. By September Mr. Jackson was confined to sleeping on a bed on the floor because of the pains he suffered in his back and legs at night. The eminent London physician who was treating him was optimistic that the cause was local and at least in part due to Jackson's "practice of gulping fish, flesh and fowl, cooked in all ways and fashions with lots of bacon, butter and rich heavy sauces," an accusation the patient vehemently and repeatedly denied. Because blistering* and abstention from rich food failed to prevent Jackson's condition from deteriorating, he submitted to sitting in a daily bath of galvanic fluid while an electric current was passed through it in an effort to stimulate his wasting muscles.[35]

William's hopes of being transported that summer were dashed, but Joseph Bradley, his partner in crime and only companion on board the hulk, did succeed in getting a place on the next transport ship. He said his farewells to William on July 28 when the *General Hewart* began boarding its cargo of inmates at Woolwich. They did not breathe fresh air above deck again until the ship sailed, nearly a month later, from Portsmouth on August 26. At least fifteen of the convicts were already in a very poor state of health, although allegedly none were suffering from an infectious disease. Frequently during the journey,

---

* Blistering was the application of caustic substances to the skin to make it blister and thus draw out toxins that were thought to cause disease.

and particularly when the ship docked for nine days in Madeira, the convicts were kept closely confined below decks. Hot humid weather contributed to their misery, which worsened when tropical rainstorms saturated their clothing and bedding, which, as there was no opportunity to air or dry either, remained wet and stinking for days. On arrival in Sydney 165 days later on February 7, 1814, thirty-four of the three hundred men who had begun the journey were missing—having died of dysentery and been buried at sea—but Joseph was not among them. Unaware that he had had a lucky escape, William remained on board the diseased and slowly rotting *Retribution* without friendship or the comfort of family support. He also remained entirely unaware that his father was ill or that this sickness was, as Mr. Jackson feared, hurrying him to his grave faster than his son was.[36]

THE NATURE OF
A CONTAGIOUS DISTEMPER

Transportation, 1814

It may be here remarked that, unless the unfortunate Convicts in Prison Ships are frequently brought on Deck to enjoy the benefit of fresh air, and the Berths below thoroughly washed, cleaned and ventilated, Disease must be the consequence. . . .

[I] have only to express the hope that you will give this Report of the fatal Consequences, attending the rigid and unfeeling Conduct of the Captain and Surgeon, the Consideration due to the distressing circumstances detailed in it, and that you will give such instructions to the Masters and Surgeons of other Convict ships, as may tend to avert the recurrence of such Calamities in the future.

— Governor Lachlan Macquarie to the commissioners
of the Transport Board (October 1, 1814)

A s autumn passed and winter drew on, the weather remained favorably mild, but in the last week of December temperatures plummeted and thick fog enveloped the country. The Thames began to freeze, and by the end of January 1814, the ice from Blackfriars Bridge to Three Crane Stairs was thick enough to walk on. While the convicts on the hulk huddled in their meager blankets and thread-bare clothing, the citizens of London trooped out onto the ice in their thousands to enjoy themselves. Always quick to seize a commercial opportunity, tradesmen set up rows of drab tented stalls topped with bright flags, forming a road down the middle of the river. They sold warm drinks (often alcoholic) and hot pies or offered cheap amusements. A sheep was roasted on the ice and sold as "Lapland Mutton." Revelers could also enjoy donkey rides, games of skittles, musical interludes, and fairground attractions. The occasion was marked by hastily erected printing presses that created memorabilia of the great "Frost Fair 1814," and vendors sold souvenirs marked "Bought on the Thames." A week later the fair ended abruptly when a quick thaw set in accompanied by the inevitable tragedies—the successful rescue of three people was followed a day later by the loss of two more, swept away by the returning Thames tide as snow turned to sleet. Within twenty-four hours the ice had vanished. For the convicts, the end of the ice—and the last Frost Fair ever to be held in London—provided little relief. The bitterly cold weather persisted until late March, and the winter of 1814 proved to be one of the coldest on record.

At the end of December, in the midst of this freezing weather, William and 199 other severely weakened convicts were transported to Graves End, where they began boarding the transport ship *Surry*. Just months later *Retribution* was emptied of inmates, and its battered carcass was towed to Sheerness dockyard to be refitted with internal cells opening onto a central walkway. This plan—to remodel all the hulks by separating prisoners into different classes and ensuring they could be supervised efficiently at night—had first been submitted to the select committee in 1812, before William's imprisonment. It was designed to remedy the vicious practices he had endured for nearly a year on board the hulk. William was not alone in his desire to be transported as fast as possible to escape the hulks—convicts regularly tried to disguise any health problems in order to pass the medical inspection conducted before they were allowed to travel—but for those who succeeded in boarding the *Surry,* the improvement in conditions was minimal.[1]

Stripped of their filthy woolen garments, the convicts were washed and dressed in lightweight duck trousers, blue cloth jackets, waistcoats over coarse linen shirts, and woolen caps. For those leaving in the summer months, this was ideal clothing because the length of the voyage meant they would also arrive in Sydney in summer. For William and his fellow prisoners, however, it meant enduring two winters wearing only summer-weight clothing. Their voyage would initially take them down across the cold east Atlantic Ocean to stop in Rio de Janeiro, then they would head south round the Cape of Good Hope using the "Roaring Forties" winds to pick up speed, but once in the Southern Ocean they would be inside the ice zone, where the risk of encountering icebergs was significant. The length of the journey meant that what clothes they did have would wear away and rot, so transports were supposed to carry enough spare clothing for each convict. Even though this lack of warm clothing did not, as many surgeons believed, contribute to scurvy, it certainly weakened resistance to disease. The navy believed, not entirely erroneously given the lack of washing facilities on board, that the convicts' heavy woolen and flannel hulk uniforms fostered disease, but the sudden change of attire was a shock to the system, even of men hardened to deprivation and the rigors of English winter weather.

THE MEN CONFINED on the *Surry* that year, still ironed to ringbolts and shivering in their light linens, endured another month of freezing cold and heavy snowfalls before the ship finally sailed for Australia. During that time most of the convicts attempted to contact their families—to arrange to meet them for a final farewell, and to ask for money or supplies that they could take with them to help them survive in New South Wales. Government officials disapproved of such donations, which they believed merely encouraged the convicts to gamble away their possessions during the long voyage, causing tensions between crew and convicts and bitter disputes over ownership on arrival. William tried again and again to raise some kind of response from his family, particularly from his mother, for whom he continued to feel great affection. Despite his fears of leaving England with no means of support, he was in better spirits than he had been for some time. He told one friend that

> however unfavourable she may at present think of me I trust I shall yet turn an honourable member of society and return in a few years to my native country every thing she can desire, and having my interest

at heart which I still trust she has, I am sure she will be happy to hear of my being removed from the Hulks, as any situation would be favourable to my present one.[2]

On January 16 William's prayers were finally answered. Jane Jackson had received letters from friends of William who were passionately opposed to transportation on humanitarian as well as personal grounds, which seem to have persuaded her to break her silence at last. But as the time for the *Surry*'s departure drew near, she must also have realized that this might be the last chance she would have to communicate with her only son. William was overwhelmed with delight and gratitude and begged her to seek his father's forgiveness for him before he left. That was a hopeless task, but Jane was prepared to help William in more practical ways. She sent him money and then packed a trunk with clothes to send to him. William seems to have gained practical knowledge of what was needed in New South Wales from other convicts—probably from those repeat offenders who were being transported for the second time. He asked Jane to send money in 3s. or 18d. or old penny pieces as these fetched the best rates, whereas "Bank notes do not go current in the Country."[3]

William's requests for material supplies, however, were less demanding than usual, and he began to long for a more lasting emotional reunion with his parents, even as he realized that his father would never relent. His letters reveal that even as a small boy his relationship with his father had not been warm, and that it had always been his mother to whom he had turned for affection. He wrote bitterly to her that

> with respect to Mr. Jackson I cannot help observing that I conceive his conduct as it regards me <u>cruel</u>, to an <u>extreme</u>, had he made a <u>friend</u> of me, as you invariably did in my juvenile years, I might now be possessed of <u>Friends, Fortune,</u> and <u>Happiness</u>—but cruel fate ordained to the contrary.

Typically, William could still see no connection between his own behavior and his current unhappy situation, but Jackson's inability to empathize with his son as a child had significantly contributed to the tragedy that now enveloped the whole family.[4]

The box of money and clothing that Jane worked hard to send by mail coach in order to reach William before he left failed to arrive in time, but he scribbled a note to her saying that it did not matter—just knowing that she cared enough to try made him feel better. The *Surry* letters between mother and son reveal a warmth and an affection that rarely appear in William's other letters, in most of which he battles with authority figures and creditors, and are only briefly glimpsed in his correspondence with his boyhood friend Thomas Macqueen. At the time Jane seems to have inspired in him a genuine desire to turn his life around, something no amount of moral lecturing had ever achieved. It is equally true, however, that his situation would have heightened his emotions. For most convicts, the trauma of exile from parents, children, lovers, and friends was devastating. Some were able to say good-bye with tearful embraces on board ship; others left "leaden heart" tokens—coins engraved with heartfelt messages for loved ones. Some, like William, sent moving farewell letters. He promised to write to Jane from every port but warned that once he was in New South Wales, it would take a year for any mail to reply. At the end he said simply, "Farewell My Dear Mother, God Bless you with every wish for your health and welfare, I am your affectionately Burke Jackson."[5]

THE *SURRY*, like nearly all the convict transports, was not built to be a prison ship. Constructed from the finest materials at Harwich in 1811, it was a first-class merchant ship of some 443 tons and 117 feet 6 inches in length. At sea it was an impressive sight: fully square rigged, with quarter galleries, fourteen cannons, and a bust of Minerva for a figurehead, the ship's copper-sheathed bows sliced through the waves. Although it was one of the slower vessels, the *Surry* became one of the longest-serving transports and the only ship to complete eleven voyages carrying convicts and stores to Australia, the last of which ended in 1842. Despite an elegant appearance above decks, the *Surry* was far less attractive below. At this time it had just two decks, but the height between them was only 5 feet 8 inches, providing extremely cramped conditions by modern standards, but in the early nineteenth century the average height of a male convict was only around 5 feet 5 inches.

William, who stood 5 feet, 5¾ inches tall, had just over 2 inches of headroom to negotiate the dark, overcrowded, and poorly ventilated prison on the 'tween deck.[6]

In convict transports what little ventilation there was to dissipate the foul smells emanating from bilges, ballast contaminated with dead rodents, filthy bodies, and overflowing night-waste buckets came from air scuttles studded along the sides of the ship, but these were closed in bad weather, and in winter the need to do so was more frequent. The air scuttles should have been augmented by a windsail—a long, wide tube of sailcloth designed to bring air from the upper to the lower decks—but many seamen found these cumbersome and unreliable, requiring two men to operate the pump. The master of the *Surry* saw fit to remove the regulation windsails. The stove below decks, intended to warm but also to fumigate the prison, was also removed. Added to these physical deprivations were the usual problems of confining convicts in small spaces—intimidation, theft, gambling, and depression—which quickly reappeared in the transport ships' prisons. Access to fresh air and to space to move on deck was therefore high on every convict's wish list and, in theory, built into the recommended daily routine to be followed on all transport ships.

Even in his weakened physical state, William's chances of survival were better than those of convicts in the eighteenth century. Masters and surgeons were contracted under strict conditions that they would make every effort to deliver their human cargo to the colony in good health—a master would receive a £50 bonus for a successful delivery and be fined for losses and bad management. Regular routines to ensure that convicts received not only fresh air and exercise, but also sufficient food and even schooling in reading, writing, and math had been developed. Hygiene was considered a top priority, and both prisoners and prison were ordered to be washed frequently. Although far from salubrious, the early-nineteenth-century convict ships were faster and in theory better organized than their eighteenth-century predecessors, and the authorities believed that the system was now both efficient and safe.[7]

Rules and regulations that were so rigorously enforced on Royal Navy ships, however, were considered less binding by the merchant navy masters and officers contracted to take charge of the convict transports. Enforcement of navy rules at sea used to be overseen by a naval agent, whose powers had been, at best, ill defined, but even this rudimentary precaution had been dropped years before. So when the *Surry* set sail, there was no one to supervise the master and crew and almost no prospect of criminal prosecution should they not obey the terms of the contract. William's family may not have feared greatly for his life as he sailed for Australia, but then no one in England had yet heard what had happened on Joseph Bradley's ship, the *General Hewart,* which had limped into Sydney Cove just two weeks earlier. The many deaths and poor health of the survivors on board alarmed Governor Lachlan Macquarie and the assistant surgeon of New South Wales, Dr. William Redfern, but they were unaware that this was just the first of three disastrous transports to arrive in the colony in the first six months of 1814. The *Surry* would be the third.[8]

In England life on board the *Surry* ran fairly smoothly under the direction of its master, James Patterson, who commanded a crew of thirty men. Although some were mere boys, many had years of experience at sea on different types of vessels. It appears to have been Patterson's first command of a transport ship, but he was not, as soon became evident, the most enlightened of masters and had an eye to making a tidy personal profit for himself during the voyage from the sale of stores intended for the convicts. The military detachment of twenty-five men of the Forty-sixth Regiment detailed to guard the prisoners on board was commanded by Brevet Major James Stewart. Some years later, in 1821, Stewart was court-martialed for inflicting cruel and illegal punishment on two of his men while stationed in Van Diemen's Land (now known as Tasmania), another British penal colony, just off the south coast of Australia. The name of the *Surry's* surgeon was not recorded, and there was no mention of a surgeon's mate, so he almost certainly had to rely on the services of one of the more trustworthy convicts for medical assistance.[9]

The master and the brevet major were not ideal choices to command on board a convict ship, but the surgeon, as on many transport ships, proved an even less wise choice. Dr. Redfern declared that most transport surgeons were "either students from the lecture rooms, or men, who had failed in the respective lines of their profession. . . . They are but ill qualified to take charge of the health of two or three hundred men about to undertake a long Voyage, through various climates." Nor did the surgeon have any real authority over the master, even in health matters, and unlike Major Stewart, his position commanded little respect. There were no free settlers or other passengers aboard and no women, so there was little chance that the rough manners of soldiers, sailors, and seamen would be tempered. Masters in the merchant navy were not educated to the standard of Royal Navy officers, and although some were the sons of wealthy merchants, few of these took command of transport ships. In the crowded conditions and fraught atmosphere on board transport ships, the presence of three different sources of command and areas of expertise could, and usually did, lead to disagreements between naval and military officers and surgeons. After investigating events on the *Surry*, Redfern launched a tirade against masters of transports,

> who, with few exceptions, having little claim to education, refined feeling, or even common decency generally treat their Surgeons as they do their Apprentices and men with rudeness and brutality. Incapable of Appreciating the value of learning, and despising all knowledge beyond what they themselves possess, they avail themselves of every opportunity to insult and Mortify their Surgeons. Under this species of treatment, with no means of redress during a long Voyage, the Mind becomes paralysed, and they View their Situation with disgust, And, if they have the means . . . they soon become drunkards. Hence their duty is neglected, and the poor Convicts become the unhappy Victims of the Captain's brutality and the Surgeon's Weakness, want of Skill or drunkenness.[10]

During the first month, while the *Surry* was still in England, the prison on board was cleaned regularly, and the convicts were divided into groups of twenty-five and allowed up on deck in rotation fairly frequently. Divine service was held every Sunday, after which each prisoner received his weekly ration of half a pint of red wine, which was designed to raise spirits and combat scurvy, but in such quantities it is doubtful that many prisoners made the ration last the whole week. Any beneficial effect was thus likely to be limited to a weekly drinking session and ensuing oblivion. There were also plentiful supplies of food, vinegar, mustard, and soap to accompany each prisoner's daily sluicing with a bucket of water on deck each morning. On February 22 the *Surry* finally set sail, accompanied by the much larger 720-ton *Broxbornebury*, which was carrying 120 female convicts, 28 free families, a crew of 70, plus several wealthy private passengers.

Among the latter was Judge Jeffery Hart Bent, whom the Prince Regent had just appointed to take over the Supreme Civil Court in the colony. For Bent, the journey was a passage up the career ladder to take an important position, in which he would have a significant role in the lives of many of the transportees in both ships. The *Broxbornebury* also benefited from the presence of another important passenger, Sir John Jamison, physician to the fleet, who had been knighted for his services in the Baltic when he had cured a serious outbreak of scurvy. Jamison was on his way to take up possession of more than 1,000 acres of land he had inherited, but his skills were a valuable addition to those of the *Broxbornebury*'s official surgeon. As the *Surry* left the safety of the English shore and headed into the wide expanse and rough seas of the Atlantic Ocean, however, it lost sight of the accompanying *Broxbornebury* and proceeded on its journey alone.

FAR AWAY FROM official observation, conditions aboard the *Surry* began to deteriorate. The divisions of convicts allowed on deck were reduced to just twenty men for brief periods of time, except for fourteen convicts who were called upon to perform special duties on deck. William, who found that his social status could once more make a difference, was treated very "kindly" by Captain Patterson and the surgeon, so it is likely that he was one of these lucky few. Indeed, he found the fresh sea air invigorating compared to the squalid confinement on the hulk. The vast majority of convicts, however, were kept below for most of the day and all night, which meant that the prison could not be cleaned properly, nor could the bedding be aired and dried on deck daily as it should have been. It seems Patterson was wary of having too many prisoners on deck at any one time in case they caused trouble that the guards could not contain, but he had also cut the convicts' wine ration and withheld their soap allowance.[11]

It was common practice in the navy as a whole to purchase and withhold some types of ration, such as salt beef, and sell or exchange it for other foodstuffs in port, but this was rarely harmful and often beneficial in varying the seamen's diet. Masters of transport ships like Patterson, however, withheld stores from convicts to sell for their own profit. The effects were much more harmful because convict rations were smaller and no substitution was made to the men. The wine was also almost certainly being withheld for sale later. Of the 400 gallons stored in the *Surry* on sailing, less than 170 gallons were actually given to the convicts. That Patterson and his officers considered this withholding absolutely acceptable is evident because it was clearly recorded in the ship's log for all to see. Convicts were supposed to wash daily first thing in the morning, and wash days for clothes were usually held twice a week; by reducing the amount of soap issued, Patterson effectively nullified the benefits of such routines. Nothing was done to improve the ventilation, and the divisions of convicts allowed on deck were soon reduced again to just eight.[12]

Below decks the crowded convicts breathed damp, fetid air. They sweated, vomited, and defecated in the dark prison; their clothes grew filthier; and the stench became nauseous. In the rough March seas of the North Atlantic, the air scuttles were frequently closed, admitting neither light nor air. The presence of so many ill-clothed, weakened, filthy men in such squalid conditions provided an ideal breeding ground for lice and fleas and the rats that carried them. As the disease-laden insects fed, the men began to scratch—their heads, their bodies, and their pubic hair—breaking the skin and allowing bacteria to enter the open wounds. Just two weeks after the *Surry* had set sail, the surgeon recorded a case of typhus on the ship. He redoubled his efforts to get the prison cleaned and fumigated, but Patterson and his officers only hindered his attempts to improve conditions below deck.

Given the known prevalence of typhus, also called "ship fever," and its usually fatal outcome, their resistance was willful negligence. Headaches, nausea, coughs, chest pain, and vomiting began to spread to other convicts. These symptoms were followed by chills, fever, vomiting, delirium, and a rash of pale red that darkened and spread over pain-wracked trunks and limbs. At the fever stage the lice jumped to new hosts and the fever began to spread. The sick fought their illness for up to two weeks and either recovered or died. On March 12 the surgeon recorded the death of John Sansome as the first fatality from typhus. For lack of any other support, the surgeon appointed convict James Wright to help him tend to the sick. Patterson did not relent in his opposition to alleviating conditions for the prisoners, who were now forced to watch helplessly as their fellow inmates grew sicker and their chances of surviving the voyage slimmer.

In early April land was sighted and the *Surry* headed into port at Rio de Janeiro and the prospect of some relief. Supplies of fresh fruit and vegetables and beef were taken on board, and there was little record of the sickness other than mention that no boats were allowed alongside the stricken ship. Patterson had stocks of sugar, coffee, and tobacco sent aboard for prisoners who were willing and able to pay for them. William wrote to both his parents from Rio, but while one letter was warm and optimistic, the other was stiff and formal. The latter was a last attempt to gain some form of absolution from his father. He promised that he would never return to England even if he regained his liberty and that if "I have your forgiveness, although you may with-hold pecuniary assistance, it will releave [*sic*] my troubled mind." He made no mention of the sickness sweeping the ship—either because he did not want to worry his mother or because his better treatment by the ship's officers meant that he was less affected by the sufferings of his unfortunate companions. He had also witnessed, and probably ac-cepted, the inevitability of fever in any situation where prisoners were closely confined in unsavory surroundings. Given that he had almost certainly contracted the disease on board *Retribution* and survived, he would also have acquired a degree of immunity from the infection.[13]

His thoughts were instead directed toward the future and the pos-sibility of receiving a pardon on arrival in Australia. He believed that two years' imprisonment—on the hulk and then on the transport ship—ought to be regarded as punishment enough for a man of his rank. Before William left England, he had asked Jane to use her friendship with Lady Kennedy to persuade her husband, Sir Robert Kennedy, as commissary general in the army, to help get a pardon for him. Another military friend had written to the deputy governor of New South Wales, Colonel O'Connell, who also commanded the Seventy-third Regiment there. From convicts and crew on board the

Surry, he had discovered that he needed to make contact with Reverend Samuel Marsden, a "Magistrate and man of Consequence in New South Wales," whom he believed could be trusted with any supportive letters sent from England. William was therefore cautiously optimistic about his chances of achieving freedom on reaching Sydney. But soon after the *Surry* left Rio on April 21, there were signs that routines were beginning to break down as the sickness spread. No wine was issued after May 1, and Sunday service ceased after May 24. The surgeon recorded a single death on May 22, but as the epidemic took hold, the surgeon ceased to record subsequent deaths. Redfern noted in his report to Governor Macquarie, however, that, according to the ship's journal, deaths became "awfully frequent" from June 9.[14]

In mid-July the *Broxbornebury* spotted the *Surry* struggling round the coast of Van Diemen's Land but, mistaking the transport ship for a whaler, did not come any closer. Over the next few days, the typhus on board the *Surry* raged unabated and the death toll among convicts, crew, and soldiers rose to forty-one. The surgeon fell ill, so the untrained convict James Wright found himself nursing Captain Patterson; the first mate, Mr. Crawford; and the second mate, Mr. Raine. Although Crawford was seriously ill, he remained sensible enough to issue orders and to take observations in order to keep the ship on course. The practical management of the ship devolved to boatswain Alexander Ross, a seasoned sailor of twenty-five years' experience on many different vessels, who had served as a second mate and a gunner on board an East Indiaman.*

Nevertheless, Major Stewart became increasingly concerned—he feared a breakdown of discipline with so many of the officers ill and the crew forced to release prisoners to help sail the ship. It was not unknown for prisoners and crew to conspire to mutiny together on convict ships. Even more dangerous was the prospect of the ship losing its way or running aground now that it was sailing close to the rugged New South Wales shoreline looking for the entry to Port Jackson. The master was primarily responsible for navigating the ship, but by July 24 Patterson was delirious, as was the second mate, which left only Crawford

---

* A ship owned by the East India Company.

capable of setting a course, and he was too ill to do much more than stagger to a chart table in his cabin.[15]

There were now only three seamen capable of taking an observation on board the *Surry*, but none of them could work out a position from it, and it seems they were unable to use a chronometer. At this time not all ships were issued with chronometers, which were portable marine clocks accurate enough to enable the determination of longitude for navigation. Alternatively, observations could be taken using the lunar method, provided that the sky was not cloudy, but this required steadiness, patience, and a good deal of mathematical skill. The navigator had to stand still on a pitching deck to measure the distance between moon and sun or stars with a sextant. Then he had to calculate the distorting effects of light and lunar parallax and refer to complex tables of planetary positions at a particular hour of the day before he could even begin to estimate the time difference accurately enough to plot a position. Boatswain Alexander Ross; a thirty-seven-year-old German gunner, Andrew Johnson, who had been at sea since the age of fourteen; and purser Joseph Andrews, who had spent twelve years at sea and had sailed the Australian coast once before, all believed they could take an observation well enough to bring the ship into harbor. To work it accurately, however, would require Crawford's assistance, and his health was deteriorating daily.

The least precise method used to estimate a position without observations when out of sight of land was "dead reckoning." A log line (a piece of cord knotted at intervals with a piece of curved wood at the end) was dropped over the stern every half an hour and the speed measured by timing with a sandglass the number of knots run out. This was compared with the course steered by compass and corrected by making allowances for drift until a more accurate reading by sun or moon could be made. The inaccuracies of this method accumulated over time, so it was generally used only as a last resort. But as the *Surry* sailed closer to the shore and visibility decreased owing to poor weather, Crawford and Ross were forced to resort to dead reckoning, hoping that combining it with depth readings from the lead lines that scooped up sand and gravel from the seabed would guide them safely into the heads of Port Jackson.[16]

At half past two on the afternoon on July 25, the *Broxbornebury* was sailing some eight or nine miles off the coast of New South Wales when it spotted another ship passing close by on the opposite tack. On hailing the other vessel, the crew raised shouts of "great joy" when it turned out to be their former sailing companion the *Surry*. Captain Pitcher's voice, amplified by a speaking trumpet, carried clearly across the wind, but time was short as neither ship could stop in midtack and they would soon sail too far apart for any communication to be heard. Major Stewart seized his chance to seek help for the ailing *Surry* and ordered boatswain Ross to hail the *Broxbornebury*. Ross refused to do any such thing. As acting commander of the ship, he was reluctant to take orders from an army officer, and it was an affront to his pride and ability as a seaman to ask for help to bring the ship into port. As Ross left, Major Stewart seized the speaking trumpet and shouted that there was "raging fever on board" and requested to come aboard. Pitcher only had time to urge caution before the wind and waves drove the vessels too far apart.

It took considerable time for both ships to tack again and pass close enough to continue communicating. On the next sweep Stewart managed to convey more information about the disease: that the ship had no medical assistance and the boatswain was currently in command. Captain Pitcher informed his crew and passengers that he intended to stand by the *Surry* that night and shine a light to guide it. Throughout the night the *Surry* tried to keep up with the *Broxbornebury*, but the distance between the two ships gradually lengthened. Boatswain Ross began to suffer the early symptoms of typhus and at midnight was forced to hand over command of the deck to gunner Johnson. This arrangement did not go down well with the crew. In attempting to assert his authority, Johnson had struck one of the seamen while the ship was in midtack. Major Stewart arrived on deck to find the sails flapping out of control while a gaggle of angry sailors had gathered on the forecastle shouting loudly. Stewart, seeing the danger, ran up and forcefully persuaded them to return to their duty and trim the sails to enable the ship to complete its maneuver, but he was determined not to let such an incident occur again.

By seven the next morning, the watch on the *Surry* saw that the *Broxbornebury* was a considerable distance ahead and had to request that the ship slow its passage. Major Stewart signaled again that he wanted to come aboard. Once the two ships were close enough, he ordered the now partially recovered Ross to lower a boat and row him over. Initially, Ross refused, claiming that the boats were too "leaky." But on Crawford's orders, he finally agreed to lower a jolly boat with the gunner and four men to row the major over. When the little boat reached the stern of the huge transport vessel, Captain Pitcher refused to allow its occupants on board. Balancing precariously, Major Stewart shouted that there was no one left who could navigate and that nearly all the convicts and most of the guard were too ill to "do any work for their general preservation." He begged Pitcher to send one of his officers on board the *Surry* to plot a course for the stricken ship. Pitcher, torn between a desire to help and his duty to protect his own vessel, called for physician Sir John Jamison and the *Broxbornebury*'s own surgeon to talk to Stewart about the symptoms of the disease so that they could make up some medicines; but he was not prepared to risk the life of one of his own officers. The most he would promise at that time was to stay close throughout the night and burn blue lights to guide the *Surry*.[17]

The weather conditions continued to deteriorate, and Jamison reminded Pitcher that he had a "responsibility" (both morally and legally under maritime law) to the distressed ship should it get separated from the *Broxbornebury* during "a dark and squally night and be lost."[18] Captain Pitcher called for a volunteer to board the infected ship, but fearing the effects of disease on his officers, he turned down an offer from the second mate and accepted the *Broxbornebury* surgeon's claim that the infection was too dangerous to leave his position. Instead, Pitcher sent for able seaman Samuel Nash, a young man he believed competent to take charge of the *Surry*, who bravely agreed to go. Although the risks were high, there were also good incentives for Nash to volunteer. He would not only do his reputation and career a lot of good, but he would also be in a position to claim a financial reward as "salvage money" for rescuing a stricken ship. Captain Pitcher at last signaled the *Surry* that he would send someone over to help armed with medicines and instructions for their use.

When Ross heard the news, he retorted angrily that Major Stewart had wrongly taken the authority upon himself to bring an officer from another ship on board. But the affronted boatswain's declining health soon forced him to retreat below decks once more. It was not until midafternoon that Samuel Nash stepped on board the *Surry*, where he was met by Major Stewart, who immediately handed over the charge of the ship to him. The convicts viewed Nash "as a deliverer," but some of the crew were suspicious that the young seaman did not look very like an officer. There were murmurings of discontent below deck, not least because if Nash took salvage money, the ship's profit and their benefits would be reduced. Nevertheless, they were prepared to obey him on the grounds that they believed he was an officer. Stewart took Nash to Patterson's cabin, but the captain was at that moment "in the act of dying" and had lost the power of speech. The second mate was insensible, but Crawford was still able to instruct the purser that "an officer had come on board [and] to see that he was treated as an officer should be." Whether Crawford believed this to be true or acted for strategic reasons is not clear. Nash found only three or four sailors capable of duties, being helped by some of the less seriously ill convicts. His task was further hindered by Patterson's last order to the purser to issue additional liquor as a reward to both crew and convicts who had worked the ship the previous night.[19]

Throughout the night the weather worsened. The *Surry* alternately pitched and rolled in gusty winds or wallowed sullenly in the swell when they dropped abruptly, which made steering increasingly difficult. Nash ran up and down the decks shouting orders to trim the sails, and on at least one occasion he climbed out on a yardarm himself to help his beleaguered crew of exhausted sailors and convicts haul in sail. Such heroic action was welcomed by the men, but later the marginalized boatswain and gunner condemned it as both un-officer-like behavior and proof that Nash was merely a "foremast man." At the time, however, it was crucial that Nash combat the danger of the high winds snapping a mast or blowing the ship off course onto the shore, but he had only ten or eleven men to help him.

At some point during the night, Captain Patterson lost his battle with the illness he had been largely responsible for causing, but few on board had time to notice his passing. During one of the lulls, Nash went below decks, leaving Johnson in charge, but the ship was suddenly hit by a heavy squall that threatened to lay it on its beam ends. Below decks sick convicts and crew grabbed at anything to hand as they were thrown violently sideways and water poured through the hull, drenching their clothing. It took the gunner by surprise, and he had no time to call for

Nash before shouting for the topsails to be lowered. Seamen and convicts clung to the bucking masts as they hauled in sail while Johnson ran below to fetch Nash, then back up again to help haul in clue-lines and braces. As the wind howled through the rigging, gunner and "officer" argued fiercely over when the sails should have been shortened. For nearly two hours crew and convicts fought the elements for possession of the *Surry*. Then a signal fired from the *Broxbornebury* lit up the sky over the starboard bow. The larger ship had decided to give up the battle and heave to—by facing the waves at an angle of 45 degrees under fore topsail, main topsails, and mizzen staysail—for optimum stability in order to ride out the storm. The *Surry* followed suit and hove to close astern of the *Broxbornebury*. The tactic worked, the squall eventually blew itself out, and the weather calmed. That morning the body of captain James Patterson was consigned to the sea. After the ceremony was completed, Pitcher signaled Nash to bring the *Surry* alongside and gave him directions to follow the *Broxbornebury* in to land.

BETWEEN EIGHT AND nine o'clock in the morning, the steep cliffs of the heads of Port Jackson at last loomed into view and the small convoy sailed up the coast toward the entrance of Sydney harbor. At about two o'clock that afternoon, the ships paused to allow a small boat to draw alongside and set a pilot aboard each vessel to guide them between the heads and on down the long, wooded estuary toward their final destination. Nash welcomed Robert Watson, the principal pilot and harbormaster of Port Jackson, on board and took him straight to Crawford's cabin, where the first mate sat propped up in a chair in order to formally transfer charge of the ship to the pilot. He also made it clear that Nash had come from the *Broxbornebury* to take command only because of the sickness on board.

Pilot Watson was not a happy man: he was alarmed at the poor state of the ship, he had not slept for two nights, his vision was blurred, and he had sought respite from the rigors of his job in a glass of grog before boarding. He wanted nothing more than to crawl into a cuddy and sleep. He stayed on deck for just half an hour before ordering Nash to stand off for four hours and then headed for the tiny cabin clasping another bottle of remedial rum as the *Broxbornebury* sailed on out of sight, relieved of its duty of care. Nash and several other crew members and convicts were convinced that the pilot was drunk. Nash waited about an hour and a half before giving the order to go about without telling the pilot. When Watson eventually reappeared on deck that evening to discover the *Surry* was not where he believed it should be, he demanded to know why Nash had not woken him. The shock of discovering that the ship was sailing independently of his directions did little to shake Watson out of his drunken stupor, however. The pilot soon retired to the cuddy again, forcing Nash to stand the *Surry* on and off all night to avoid the rocks, until Crawford shook Watson awake the following morning.[20]

It was not entirely unusual for pilots to be intoxicated while guiding ships into harbor, and Watson remained deeply affronted by Nash's failure to carry out his orders to the letter. In his own defense, Watson candidly explained that

> I did not like to anchor the ship from the state she was in & did not
> like to work her that night, my eyesight was so bad. I did not consider
> it dangerous keeping the ship twelve hours longer at sea. I could do
> no otherwise than I did—I was not perfectly sober when I went on
> board . . . but I was not incapable of doing my duty.[21]

The *Broxbornebury* had been moored in Sydney harbor for well over twelve hours before the *Surry* hove into view on July 28, which gave Judge Bent time to go ashore and warn Governor Macquarie of the distressed and dangerous state of the incoming vessel. Alarmed at the prospect of such a "malignant fever" spreading through the colonial port, Macquarie immediately ordered that the *Surry* and everyone on board be placed in strict quarantine on the wooded North Shore opposite the town of Sydney. Nash, Stewart, and those soldiers and seamen who had recovered were therefore held under guard with the sick and all the other convicts, still unable to communicate with anyone in the colony after 156 days of confinement at sea. A temporary camp was set up, where William and the other surviving convicts disembarked. Most of the filthy, emaciated men had to be carried or helped ashore. Even the relatively healthy convicts could barely walk after their long incarceration in cramped conditions on rolling decks and hampered by heavy irons. Those fit enough to help sail the ship during the storm must have had their irons removed. But even after a relatively smooth passage on a well-run vessel where shackles were struck off once at sea, it could take days or even weeks before a convict ceased to stagger like a drunkard on land. The *Surry* and the state of its miserable occupants were common gossip in the streets, but the *Sydney Gazette* confidently reassured its readers that the colony's "salubrious climate" and access to fresh air and exercise would soon "put an end to the pestilential terrors." The only people empowered to break the quarantine restrictions were the principal surgeon and his medical officers, including William Redfern, who had already been alongside the vessel to confirm the contagious nature of the disease.[22]

Now just entering his forties, Dr. Redfern worked in the dilapidated old hospital at Dawes Point, but he also conducted a daily outpatient clinic for convicts working in the government gangs, and he had the most extensive private practice in the colony. He was popular with the elite of Sydney and was the governor's family doctor, possessing excellent skills in obstetrics. With Macquarie's support and admiration, he should have had a glittering career. That he did not lay in the fact that he was an emancipist—a freed convict who could never quite rid himself of the taint of his arrival on a transport ship in 1801. As a young man Redfern had taken a position as surgeon's mate on board HMS *Standard,* one of twenty-six ships to have taken part in a major mutiny at the Nore on the Thames in 1797. His role was merely supportive to the disaffected seamen, but he was condemned to death along with dozens of others, then reprieved on the grounds of youth and transported.[23]

With his natural sympathy for and expertise in convict health, Redfern was Macquarie's first choice to investigate and report on the heavy mortality suffered by the convicts transported in the *General Hewart,* the *Three Bees,* and the *Surry* that year. There had been fewer deaths on the *Three Bees*—just nine—but the Irish convicts on board arrived in a "dreadful state" and fifty-five required hospitalization. The residents of Sydney, however, were rather more alarmed by the huge fire that broke out on board just two weeks after arrival, while the ship was moored at

Government Wharf. With no hope of fighting the flames, the crew had abandoned ship and set it adrift in the cove. While other ships weighed anchor and fled, terrified onlookers watched the

> ship of nearly five hundred tons, set loose . . . in the middle of a town, unmanageable and pouring forth smoke and fire, threatening desolation all around her, with her guns all loaded, first pointed upon one object and then upon another, and every instant expected, by her explosion, to throw down or cover with the dreadful blast all the buildings around or near her.

The event remained seared into the memories of the inhabitants for a considerable time, but in fact the two hours of cannon fire and the final explosion of the *Three Bees'* magazine as the ship struck the rocks at Bennelong Point did little damage to the town's buildings and nobody was injured.[24]

Far more serious for the governments of both Britain and New South Wales was the loss of convict lives in 1814. Whereas the total death rate on board the *Broxbornebury* and three other ships that arrived in Sydney that year was less than one in ninety, for the *Three Bees*, the *General Hewart,* and the *Surry*, it was closer to one in nine. In just six months ninety-four convicts had effectively been killed by mismanagement and poor hygiene. The *Surry* lost thirty-six, or 18 percent, of the convicts it transported, plus eleven crewmen and four soldiers. By way of a rough comparison, mortality rates on late-eighteenth- and early-nineteenth-century British slave ships varied between 10 and 15 percent. One reason that slave mortality rates were generally lower was because in 1788 Parliament had legislated to restrict the number of slaves carried according to the size of ship and made provision for bonuses to be paid to captains and surgeons of ships with low mortality; these practices continued until 1808, when slavery was made illegal. Even though similar inducements were offered to masters of transport ships, it was Dr. Redfern's task to find out why convict death rates had climbed so high in 1814. Redfern concluded his investigation into these three disastrous voyages by questioning the crew of the *Surry*, pouring over the logs of the now-deceased master and surgeon, and checking through the ship's cargo before writing up his report.[25]

At first his inquiries were blocked: "There was none, it was all ex-pended" was the reply to his demand for soap to wash the filthy con-victs while they were in quarantine. A few days later a quantity of soap appeared on the published invoice of goods for sale. The threat of an additional general inquiry into the proper expenditure on goods and clothing provided for the convicts subsequently produced the desired effect. Five large boxes of soap were delivered to Redfern's hospital, described as "remains of unexpended stores." A little more digging un-earthed at least 240 gallons of unused wine—more than half the 400 that had been loaded for the convicts' use but kept back by the master and purser to profit from its sale. It seems the prospect of such profits had outweighed the government's financial inducements. Both Red-fern and Macquarie blamed the inhumanity, avarice, and poor man-agement of the master and, to a lesser extent, of the surgeon for the *Surry*'s disastrous voyage.[26]

As a result of his investigations, Redfern's report made several key recommendations that were considered a landmark contribution to both public health and good practice on board transport ships. He proposed that all convicts should have daily time on deck so that their bedding could be aired, and that the prison should be thoroughly cleaned and whitewashed with quicklime every two to three weeks. The number of convicts boarded on each transport should be restricted to the amount who could comfortably fit on deck at the same time for exercise. Convicts should also be issued more soap and fresh water to wash themselves daily and their clothes regularly. The wine ration should be increased and drunk on deck daily from a measured cup to which had been added lime juice and sugar to ward off scurvy and de-pression. Despite these undoubtedly beneficial health measures, Red-fern (and the medical profession worldwide) remained ignorant of the actual cause of typhus. He still believed that the disease took such a fatal hold on board ships because "the bodies of men when closely con-fined . . . possess a power of generating a most subtle poison" that quickly spread. He had, however, made the connection between mind and body so that throughout his report he sought to give the convicts both "some exertion of the body and . . . some amusement to the mind" to combat the debilitating despair so common among those ex-iled from their families and confined below decks for long periods.[27]

Yet in the fight against contagion, perhaps his most effective weapon was his insistence on better training and more power at sea for surgeons on transports. Redfern realized that their lack of practical training and experience of conditions at sea, plus employment by the ship's owners under the command of often ignorant and frequently brutal masters, was a recipe for disaster. Surgeons were also expected to care for up to two hundred men each with little or no support, except for the services of a willing convict, the combination of which would inevitably result in high levels of sickness and death. To redress this condition, Redfern proposed that transport surgeons be appointed by the government from among the ranks of qualified, experienced naval surgeons. Each surgeon superintendent should be assisted by another qualified surgeon on every ship, and he should be assigned the rank and power of a naval officer who could not be controlled by transport masters.[28]

William Redfern's proposals were not entirely new, and similar attempts had been made to improve conditions on board transport ships twenty years earlier, but in 1815, the year after Macquarie sent his strongly worded letter containing the report to the British Board of Transport, the first naval surgeon superintendent was appointed to sail on a convict ship and the system was immediately made permanent. Redfern's proposal certainly proved immensely beneficial to convict health. The issue of making masters and officers of the guard obey the surgeon superintendent in matters concerning convict welfare, however, was a step too far in the reversal of long-established hierarchies of power on board ship and remained a vexed question until the 1820s. In 1822, John Thomas Bigge, commissioner of a parliamentary inquiry into the transportation system, explained that "the two points in which such a collision of authority have most frequently occurred" were "the admission of the convicts to the deck, and the taking off of their irons, at an early period after leaving England"—both of which were important to the maintenance of health and discipline on board.[29]

Nevertheless, Bigge also noted the "very considerable improvement" in the system that had occurred since the fatalities in 1814, thanks to the "ample and accurate means of providing against similar calamities" set out in Redfern's report. For William and his friend

Joseph Bradley, these improvements had, like those on the hulks, come too late. Both young men were extremely lucky to have survived at all. Given William's frequently precarious health—and the fact that London prisoners were known to suffer far more from scurvy, lung diseases, and general debility than the more robust rural prisoners did—his endurance was extraordinary.

The traumatic experience of imprisonment on a hulk and transportation on one of the most disastrously mismanaged ships, however, was visible in the gray streaks that dulled William's once dark brown hair. The mental scars were deeper, if less immediately visible. Commissioner Bigge was adamant that "mental suffering forms but a small part of the punishment of the voyage," but he admitted that "where it is felt . . . weighs most heavily upon those feelings that are most respectable." Edward Eagar, an emancipist lawyer and campaigner who had been transported himself for forgery in 1811, had few doubts about the life-threatening "horrors of a sea prison" and the trauma of exile. He explained to Sir Robert Peel that

> it is banishment from family, home, friends, and all the endearing connections and social ties of life; a man is torn from the land of his fathers, the scenes of all his early associations and happiness, and doomed to be banished to a country at the other side of the globe, of which he has little or no knowledge, uncertain of the fate that awaits him, except in this—that it will be painful and penal in the highest degree. . . . If a man has not lost all his better feelings, banishment must be the greatest of all punishment short of death.[30]

William's "better feelings" had been seriously blunted by his own suffering and that of the many others he had witnessed. The comfort that reconciliation with his mother had brought had not been matched by that of his father or any other member of his family. The filthy, emaciated, traumatized convict who struggled onto the shore of New South Wales bore little resemblance to the proud, privileged son of a wealthy gentleman who had once mixed with England's elite. Yet the experience had failed to eradicate William's sense of superior entitlement, which fostered his belief that he had suffered a deep injustice and would continue to shape his future in the penal colony. Edward Eagar was also possessed of a contradictory character, which was increasingly hardened by an equally deep sense of injustice during his time in the colony. The two men's lives were about to become inextricably entwined in a struggle for freedom, property, and status.

OF GENTLEMEN
AND CONVICTS

Australia, 1814–1820

*Deeming the colony to have been founded as much with
a view to the reformation as punishment of offenders,
he justly concluded that the surest way of achieving the
former object was, by elevating the character of the
emancipated convict, in raising him to a suitable moral
station in society again. But, unfortunately, the mode
Governor Macquarie took of carrying out his . . . views
into execution, entirely frustrated the attempt.*

— Peter Cunningham, *Two Years in New South Wales* (1827)

From their camp on the North Shore, the surviving *Surry* convicts could make out the contours of the growing city of Sydney. Instead of a jail or ramshackle huts guarded by uniformed soldiers, however, they saw a neat replica of a minor English Georgian town emerge from the curved shoreline of Sydney Cove. Rows of pale square buildings were interspersed with wide spaces of green, and the skyline was dominated by two large windmills and the imposing walls of Fort Phillip. Yet no English town could boast the same "towering forests and projecting rocks, combined with the infinite diversity of hill and dale on each side of the harbour" or the numerous coves and islets studding the coastline. The cove itself was formed of two ridges, between which ran the Tank Stream, which supplied the town with water, and to the right of this George Street, the town's main road, which formed the center of a uniform grid that all other streets either intersected or ran parallel to. Many of these streets were wide but unpaved and lined with light airy brick or stone houses covered with weatherboard or pale plaster. But despite the construction of handsome public buildings and a program of road building, Sydney remained "rude and irregular" in appearance in many areas.

Sydney was a work in progress, and the newcomer was quite likely to step into "a street in anticipation," only partly lined with wooden huts and temporary housing or devoid of any buildings at all. The wealthier inhabitants' homes were detached white cottages with verandas and neat gardens bordered by geranium hedges and wooden palings. Perhaps the most impressive of these was the white house of the merchant Simeon Lord. An emancipated convict, Lord had risen to become a wealthy merchant and prominent citizen, a potent symbol of hope for newly arrived felons. The western ridge was nicknamed the "St. James" of Sydney after London's elite fashionable quarter. Here stood the governor's house: an elegant, if somewhat unstable structure, built in the Palladian style and surrounded by four acres of parkland, ornamented with fine trees and a broad promenade along which the more elite inhabitants of Sydney strolled. Rather less familiar to English eyes were the kangaroos and emus that wandered through Governor Macquarie's domain. The western ridge was also the location of government offices as well as the multistory commissariat stores, which issued supplies of food and clothing, purchased all the wheat and wool produced in the colony, and functioned as a major financial exchange for the currency-poor colony. Below it stretched Government Wharf, where official trading vessels loaded and discharged their cargoes.[1]

The eastern ridge of the town was less salubrious. It was referred to by educated wags as the "St. Giles" portion of Sydney, after the infamous, impoverished London rookery of that name where crime, prostitution, and disease were rife. Here, barracks for the military regiments that guarded colony and convicts overlooked a large parade ground, while the jail and the burial ground served as reminders of what could happen to refractory felons. The shore was lined with dockyards, storehouses, wharves, and the houses of more successful merchants. Above them rose the Rocks, a notorious area built on a ridge of bare white sandstone that climbed in successive steps to the summit. Most of the poorer inhabitants lived here, surrounded by disreputable public houses, prostitutes, grog shops, and drinking dens of every description that contributed substantially to the city's reputation for rampant alcoholism. One inhabitant described the area as a "chaos of building . . . [that] was for many years more like the abode of a horde of savages than the residence of a civilized community."

Yet the East Shore was not entirely devoid of the signs of social climbing so prevalent in Sydney. Some handsome houses connoted the presence of more respectable inhabitants who frequented St. Philip's, one of only two churches in a city that generally spared little thought for religion except to commemorate those essential ceremonies of birth, death, and marriage. The latter was considered a vital part of the route back to respectability for the increasing numbers of emancipated convicts. A married man was thought far more likely to persevere in honest toil to support his family than to fall victim to the demon drink, which provided welcome oblivion to so many. Nor was he so likely to engage in sinful sexual relations with prostitutes, female convicts who were abandoned when pregnant, or, most dreaded of all, other male convicts.

The Rocks was also the site of Sydney's dilapidated hospital, where Dr. William Redfern battled with disease among convicts and colonists alike. On his arrival in 1810, Governor Lachlan Macquarie, dismayed by this ramshackle collection of temporary portable buildings and tents, determined to build a new hospital as part of his ambitious program of public works to turn Sydney into an elegant, respectable city. Hence, when William arrived, the walls of a neoclassical Georgian hospital were clearly visible on the western edge of the governor's residence. But the new hospital, like so much of what was well intentioned and apparently stylish in Sydney, became a classic symbol of compromise that epitomized the problems faced by a penal colony in the process of transforming itself into a free commercial society.

Refused funding by the British government, Macquarie did a deal with two Sydney businessmen and the principal surgeon—a new magistrate and part-time businessman named D'Arcy Wentworth. A charming, handsome, wealthy man of elite Anglo-Irish stock, Wentworth had voluntarily transported himself as a ship's surgeon when facing capital charges of highway robbery at the Old Bailey for the fourth time. The technical fact that he had not been convicted meant that Wentworth did not suffer the degree of social ostracism that blighted the career of William Redfern, who was by all accounts the better doctor. Paying for the new hospital, however, was problematic and required the kind of pragmatic solution that the penal colony frequently had to adopt, but that outraged the mother country.

Because there was still no form of stable currency in the colony, many financial transactions had to be based on credit notes or exchange in kind—the dominant form of which was rum (a generic term covering all forms of spirits). Hence, Macquarie paid the three men the £4,200 needed to construct the hospital by giving them eighty oxen, the use of twenty convict laborers for three years, and permission to import 65,000 gallons of rum. The British government balked at the morality of this arrangement but was pacified by the promise of payment of import duty, so the "Rum Hospital," as it became known, was duly built. Like the governor's residence however, its imposing façade concealed serious structural defects that needed frequent repairs, and its size proved excessive for the colony's needs—part of it was eventually given to Judge Jeffery Hart Bent for his chambers and was used as a temporary site of the new Supreme Court. For political and economic life to thrive in early Sydney, concession and cooperation between colonists and convicts on many levels were essential, but both only obscured the deep social rifts between the two groups that Macquarie continually sought to paper over.[2]

AFTER WILLIAM AND his fellow *Surry* inmates were fit enough to be officially mustered for the documentation of their sentence, age, height, and physical appearance, they were ferried into Sydney Cove. On landing, William had his first taste of the porous nature of penal life in the colony, as the convicts were marched up to the jail by city constables who conspicuously failed to control them. The constables were themselves convicts or ex-convicts, poorly paid and mostly illiterate men who frequently succumbed to drink and corruption. The *Surry* men could call out to friends and connections, or pass letters and money into eager hands concealed by the crowd, with little fear of retribution. Some of the more desperate even managed to leave the ranks long enough to exchange their clothes for food.[3]

Thomas Bigge, the British government commissioner charged with investigating the running of the penal colony, described how new convicts proceeded to the jail "in the noisy and joyous recognition of their friends and acquaintance, in the tumult of hasty and unequal bargains, or in disappointment for the loss of their property and bedding." Once there, convicts were lined up before the governor and usually asked if they had any complaints about their treatment on the voyage over, before being assessed for their competence to work, which was based on their physical strength, craft skills, and disposition of character rather than the seriousness of their crimes or length of their sentences.[4]

It was William's good fortune to have arrived in New South Wales just four years after the liberal-minded, humanitarian governor Macquarie had taken up his post, replacing the disciplinarian William Bligh, whose rule here had ended, like his captaincy of the *Bounty*, in rebellion. Macquarie's ambitious plans to reconstruct Sydney were matched by his fervent belief in promoting the reformation and reinstatement of ex-convicts to respectable society. As Macquarie had explained to the British colonial secretary, Lord Castlereagh, emancipation was "the greatest Inducement that Can be held out to the Reformation of the Manners of the inhabitants," which would "lead a man back to that Rank in Society which he had forfeited and, do away . . . with all Retrospect of former Bad Conduct."[5]

Macquarie had since made it a tradition to give a speech to each newly arrived batch of transportees, inspiring the hope that good behavior and industry would be well rewarded. So it was that William stood in front of the governor and listened to him explain the conditions of punishment while offering the potent hope that the slate *could* still be wiped clean for him in this "new Britannia." What Macquarie did not mention was that even if William regained his legal status as a free "gentleman," elite Sydney society would close its doors to him every bit as firmly as London society had.

Two years earlier the newly evangelized Edward Eagar had listened to that same speech. Of a not dissimilar appearance to William—they shared similar dark hair and hazel eyes—Eagar came from a well-connected family in Killarney and had successfully studied law at Trinity College, Dublin, before becoming a registered attorney in 1805 at the age of eighteen. Taller and paler than William, he, too, had led a life of "depravity," the funding of which had similarly tempted him to utter a forged bill of exchange. He was just twenty-two when he was convicted and sentenced to death for forgery. While awaiting sentence in jail, Eagar underwent a sudden and dramatic conversion to Methodism that so impressed the prison chaplain and the bishop of Cork that they pleaded for clemency. Eagar almost certainly genuinely believed in his personal redemption by faith, but it was in his nature to fervently believe any idea or action that also contributed significantly to his own benefit.

He was a complex character whom contemporaries found humble, pious, law-abiding, trustworthy, and responsive at one moment, and, like William, worldly, proud, vindictive, unreliable, and rebellious in the next. His striking conversion, however, combined with the pleas of a wealthy family to a judge who knew him personally, saved his life. Eagar's sentence was commuted to transportation, and he arrived in New South Wales with glowing letters of introduction to the Reverend Samuel Marsden, the senior chaplain there, whom, William had told his mother, he hoped would soon perform a similar service for him.[6]

Marsden was a fervent believer in dramatic conversions and an equally committed materialist. He got Eagar assigned to teach the children of a fellow clergyman's family in the pretty rural settlement of Windsor. This was a soft option granted only to educated men of genteel status, but within three days the redeemed attorney had been granted a ticket of leave by Governor Macquarie, which allowed him the freedom to work for himself in the colony for the rest of his sentence. Eagar's fellow Methodists were delighted that such a promising and pious young man had been so quickly set back on the path to redemption and useful citizenship. Eagar fulfilled their expectations by proceeding to help set up the first Methodist church in Australia.

On being granted a conditional pardon by Macquarie, which gave him free citizenship within the colony (but not in Britain), Eagar took up a post as manager of a government school in Windsor until 1813.

Then, in a manner Macquarie's humanitarian system was designed to support, Eagar sought to restore his former status as an attorney. By the time William arrived in 1814, Eagar had built up a sizable practice as a solicitor and an attorney in the civil court that Judge Jeffery Hart Bent had traveled on the *Broxbornebury* to take over. He had also acquired a smart house in O'Connell Street and was, to all intents and purposes, a respected citizen of Sydney. Indeed, his restored status gave Eagar an unattractively lofty perspective on those whose origins were less fortunate than his own. Following a dispute with his former benefactor Samuel Marsden, Eagar condemned the reverend as "a man descended from the lowest ranks in life, brought up to the trade of Blacksmith, of a narrow Inferior education, of coarse vulgar habits and manners, accustomed to no better Society than the original confined unimproved Society of New South Wales." Were it not for Marsden's appointment as chaplain to the colony, he "would to this day have remained in that obscurity, out of which neither his birth, education, talents or manners gave him any right to emerge."[7]

Eagar's astonishingly fast reward for industry and good behavior was symbolic of Macquarie's ideal route to emancipation and an example of the power of good connections. But it was precisely the kind of social ascent that deeply offended those more righteous settlers whose families had sailed to New South Wales as free immigrants. Commissioner Bigge shared the free colonists' concerns and was shocked that those guilty of capital crimes received so little punishment in the colony. He declared that transported forgers caused "the greatest embarrassment to the colonial government," not least because their lack of ability to perform hard labor meant they had to be employed in lighter duties in towns where they could "indulge their vanity" and "outrage public feeling by their ostentatious appearance." Worse, their literary skills meant that they frequently became clerks and schoolmasters, which thereby provided ample opportunity for corruption of their own and other's morals.[8]

IF THE LETTERS recommending mercy from his mother, Colonel Kennedy, and his military friend had arrived, then William, like Eagar, would also have had good reason to believe that he might find himself in a better position in the penal colony. Indeed, distinctions of wealth and rank affected the way that convicts were treated there every bit as much as they had in Newgate and other unreformed English prisons. Most poorer convicts found themselves assigned to hard labor in the government gangs engaged in rebuilding Sydney and the colony's roads, or stationed on farms miles from civilization tending sheep or tilling the hard-baked soil. Men from the higher ranks of society, however, arrived with money and letters of introduction that could procure them a significantly better assignment as teachers or clerks.

Information about the situation, character, and means of convicts seeped into Sydney soon after the arrival of each transport ship. Gossip was rife: ship's surgeons wrote reports on a convict's behavior on board that could aid or harm his prospects in the colony, and they could have a word with the governor at the jail muster. Settlers competed for the best-behaved and physically strongest or most skilled men and petitioned the governor for their services. Convicts tried to contact friends to secure a good position for themselves from the moment they arrived. Hastily written messages could be passed to those on board the numerous small ships that swarmed around each transport as it sat at anchor in Sydney Cove. Letters of recommendation could be conveyed to settlers who were related or connected to a convict's family, resulting in beneficial applications for his labor. Settlers who heard of the arrival of a convict with significant financial means were not above striking a deal: in exchange for the convict's money, they would nominally take on the role of master and supply his keep, but expect no work from him.

William's situation however, was more complicated. The *Surry's* surgeon had died, and William had left England carrying no money or letters of recommendation from his family to present on his arrival. The letters he believed would earn him a pardon had either not arrived or, in the case of the one addressed to a deputy governor, missed the man for whom it was intended because he had been posted elsewhere. William had no craft skills, and there is no evidence that he had any friends or contacts in the colony, at least none of a respectable or influential nature. It is possible that he could have met up with his former partner in crime, Joseph Bradley, but no trace of any contact remains. Bradley—almost certainly through letters from his more supportive family—had managed to get himself a comfortable clerkship with the magistrates in Parramatta. William, by contrast, was summarily assigned with twenty-two others to labor for a settler in Windsor, whose previous convict laborers had been sent to work in the mountains to build a road into the Australian interior that cost Governor Macquarie 400 gallons of rum.[9]

The tiny "town" of Windsor nestled on the banks of the Hawkesbury River at the base of the verdant forests of the Blue Mountains, about twenty miles northwest of Sydney. There was just one proper street, but it was lined with well-built and "tastefully laid out" houses, and there were shops and two good inns as well as the usual government buildings. The town's picturesque situation did little to soften the shock of hard labor in the unforgiving outback for Englishmen unused to such conditions. Here the local magistrate assigned each convict to a master in the area. Convicts were paid for their labor, but lack of currency meant that most received at least part of those wages as food and drink—on average about seven pounds of meat and eight pounds of wheat each week that they ground for their own use in small steel hand mills.

Macquarie had tried to insist on monetary payment, but this arrangement had led to an even greater rise in alcohol consumption because, in the absence of most other forms of entertainment, convicts spent all they had on spirituous liquor in an effort to obliterate the emotional pain and dislocation caused by separation from their families. As in Sydney, heavy drinking was endemic, and Windsor had been (in)famous for an illegal distillery set up by a local emancipist in a salt manufactory that he had built at the mouth of the Hawkesbury. This enterprising entrepreneur had risen to become superintendent of government convict labor at Windsor, and his local philanthropy had then earned him the appointment of magistrate, much to the horror of Macquarie's friends and enemies. Yet numerous campaigns against illegal distilleries had failed, and drunkenness had become so difficult to control that the Windsor chief constable wanted to stop the weekly Sunday inspection muster. He believed it merely offered a better opportunity for convicts to meet, drink, gamble, and plan crimes than as a method to improve their manners and morals by sending them to church.[10]

The absence of records frustrates any attempt to find what kind of labor William was assigned to, and whether he worked for a liberal or a tyrannical master. The common wisdom among settlers, however, was that kindness and firmness encouraged greater productivity from the laborers, even though some settlers persistently resorted to harsher methods. Moreover, convict servants were not slaves, and in common parlance they were referred to as "government men" or "servants"—"convict" was considered a term of abuse verging on libel. Convict workers also had set hours of work, from dawn until three in the afternoon, Monday to Friday and just until ten in the morning on Saturday, which left a considerable amount of time that they could use to earn money for themselves or, less profitably, to seek their own amusement. Convicts referred to these hours as their "own time," and all efforts to regulate longer work hours were fiercely resisted.[11]

Unlike the slave societies to which the colony was later unfavorably compared by campaigners, masters had no power to flog refractory workers; only magistrates could inflict secondary punishment. Nevertheless, opportunities for abuse abounded, and even liberal masters did not understand why some convicts loathed work even when well treated and rewarded for it: they failed to realize that, for some, "subordination itself could be hateful." For William, subordination was and always had been a complete anathema. Even when his status as a gentleman had been unquestioned, he had refused to submit to the authority of his father, his family, his schoolmasters, or his commanding officers in the army. To willingly obey the orders of a poor immigrant or ex-convict settler would have forced a complete denial of his identity.

The author of a later government report in 1838 noted that those who had been born into slavery knew no other life, but those who had known better times in Britain and acknowledged no man as master hated their masters in the colony. Such hatred found expression in idle, insolent, and drunken behavior that tested the limits of the most tolerant master. William had long had a weakness for alcohol—since his earliest imprisonment it had provided solace for what he considered the monstrous injustice of his sentence—and in New South Wales he found himself in a society that, almost literally, ran on liquor. Even had he been possessed of formidable willpower and supportive friends, he could not have avoided alcohol; without either, he began to sink into a sea of alcoholism. William, like many other convicts, had neither the disposition nor the emotional strength to endure colonial penal servitude passively.[12]

JUST WEEKS AFTER his son began life as a propertyless convict servant, William Collins Jackson senior died, on September 14, 1814. He was only fifty-three years old at the time, but the mental and emotional stress of the previous five years had undoubtedly contributed to the paralysis that slowly immobilized his limbs and finally stilled his heart. William's transportation to Australia may have removed the cause of that stress, but the stain of his shame on his family's reputation could never be erased. Despite their desire to remove William from society, for both parents William's "civil death" caused as much grief as bereavement by natural causes would have done. Yet Mr. Jackson did not disinherit his profligate son. The most likely reason for this can be found in a single torn scrap from a letter kept by Jane Jackson, which records a statement that could only have come from this most disappointed of parents: "I, forgive you, all the <u>anguish</u> you have caused me to feel, may God, forgive you."[13]

William never saw this longed-for phrase, but it suggests that Mr. Jackson did not wish to punish his son further—that he left in God's hands. His will also provided for the possibility of a grandchild inheriting the Jackson fortune, indicating that his hopes lay in future generations. Jane Jackson proved* her deceased husband's will in October and almost immediately made arrangements for her son to receive the annuity of £500 sterling per annum bequeathed by his father. It would take a minimum of six months, however, for the news to reach William that he had at last inherited the fortune he had been hoping would solve all his problems. In currency-poor New South Wales, his annuity alone represented a vast sum of the most highly prized kind, a sum that could set him up as an emancipist gentleman in Sydney society as soon as he gained a ticket of leave. But, tragically, William

---

*An executor had to prove legal ownership of and authority to manage a deceased's estate via a grant of probate from the high court.

remained wholly ignorant of his new wealth, and he continued to rebel against the system until in June 1815 he was brought back before the Windsor magistrates. Either this was not his first offense or his crime was of a serious nature, because he was sentenced to the harshest penalty short of death in the colony: secondary transportation to the penal settlement at Newcastle. Commissioner Bigge noted of Newcastle that in "the opinion of most of the magistrates . . . transportation . . . to the Coal River, is felt and sometimes dreaded as a punishment; and that it succeeds in breaking dangerous and bad connections, but it does not operate in reforming them."[14]

Newcastle was situated at the mouth of the Hunter River. The settlement had originally been called Coal River because its primary purpose had been to supply coal and timber to the colony, but it was later renamed after England's chief coal port. It was about fifty miles north of Sydney and took a day's sea voyage to reach. The *Estramina* set sail from Sydney on June 10, 1815, carrying William plus two other male and two female convicts, to deliver them to the penal settlement and collect government supplies of coal and cedar for the return journey. The unfortunate heir to a fortune he had been expecting to save him since his early teens, had been sentenced to one year's hard labor in a penal settlement containing five hundred of the most "incorrigible offenders" in the British Empire. Newcastle convicts were forced to work in chains from dawn until dusk; they felled trees, cut lumber, mined coal from a shallow seam beneath the sandstone coast, or collected oyster shells and burned them to make lime.[15]

The oysters were burned on the shore six miles from Newcastle itself, and the convicts had to carry the resulting lime in baskets on their shoulders some distance to boats moored offshore. Frequently, the lime seeped out of the baskets onto their already sunburnt, seasprayed skin, burning and blistering their shoulders. The smoke from the burning oysters stung their eyes, but for some the risk of damaging their sight was worth it because they hoped then to be removed from the camp on medical grounds. Many more attempted to escape from Newcastle by fleeing into the wilderness of the bush. Bigge described how few lasted longer than three weeks "living upon snakes and grubs, or roots and shrubs" that reduced them to a "miserable and emaciated state."

Groups of Aborigines soon caught up with the weakened escapees, whom they beat or speared, stripped naked, and marched back to Newcastle. The Aborigines were rewarded with maize and blankets; the convicts—when they were strong enough to stand it—were severely flogged and sent to work on a chain gang. Nevertheless, those who were well behaved could find lodgings with ordinary settlers in the town, and some got better employment as clerks or constables. During William's internment, the storekeeper's clerk was none other than James Hardy Vaux, who later wrote of his confinement in the prisons of Clerkenwell and Newgate, as well as on the hulk *Retribution*, through which William had followed him just a few years later.[16]

Despite a harsh regime, discipline at the settlement could also be lax at this time, and the enforcement of sentences was at best haphazard. Delay or failure to send proper documentation with the convicts—Windsor magistrates were particularly poor at producing paperwork—meant that the commandant at Newcastle often had to rely solely on the convict's own memory to determine how long he should remain. Because no man could be forced to serve a term beyond his original sentence, his stay could be briefer than the magistrates had intended. William's imprisonment at Newcastle proved mercifully short, for three months after his banishment a letter arrived announcing that his sentence had been remitted and he was to be brought back to Sydney. This was very probably because either one of the letters requesting a pardon had arrived and been approved, or because news of his sudden enrichment had at last reached Sydney. Governor Macquarie granted William a ticket of leave—the first step toward a full pardon—which gave him a limited form of freedom, including the right to seek employment within a specified area, but he had to report regularly to the authorities and to attend religious services.[17]

THE SPRING AND summer of 1815 had proved an almost equally trying time for Edward Eagar. His right to practice as an emancipist lawyer in the civil court depended on a lack of properly qualified lawyers in the colony, and on Macquarie's desire to give emancipists positions of public repute. The arrival of Jeffery Hart Bent as judge of the new Supreme Court the previous year, however, signaled trouble for Eagar. Bent was a conservative with a high opinion of both himself and the independent status of the law; he also believed that only true gentlemen should be admitted to the legal profession. Eagar and two other emancipist lawyers, Bent opined, "have never been admitted into the company of Gentlemen here, or at all considered as respectable members of society." He refused to open the Supreme Court until properly qualified lawyers arrived from England, and he also impugned (quite wrongly) Eagar's qualification to practice.[18]

Eagar turned to Macquarie to support his petition to continue practicing in the courts—a privilege initially granted by Bent's brother and fellow judge for "practical" reasons. Macquarie supported his "convict attorneys": he pressed Bent in the strongest terms to accept them but was firmly rebuked by the judge for his improper "tone" in assuming that he "had a jurisdiction where he had none." Incensed but impotent, Macquarie could do nothing more to help Eagar but complain to the Colonial Office and threaten to resign unless Bent was removed. The court remained closed until October 1816 when two properly qualified lawyers arrived in the colony. The Colonial Office eventually sacked both Bent brothers.[19]

Eagar had tried to put the seal on his respectability by marrying Jemima McDuel, a freeborn but illegitimate daughter of an emancipist couple, in July, but he now found himself out of a job with a new wife to support. This was a severe blow to his personal prospects and ambition, but Judge Bent's ruling also seriously challenged the extent to which emancipists could ever be granted full legal civil status and what powers the governor could actually assume in granting them. It was to have serious consequences for Eagar, William, and the futures of all freed convicts. In the short term, Eagar turned to the more commonly successful path for redeemed ex-convicts and set up in trade while continuing to play a leading role in consolidating Methodism in the colony. In this religious endeavor he earned fulsome praise for his pious works and financial generosity, and he maintained his position as steward of the Wesleyan congregation.

As a new merchant trader, Eagar's profile was rather less pious. He set up an office in his home and began to buy up or exchange large quantities of promissory notes—the most common form of credit accepted in lieu of currency. That Eagar thrived in trade was partly

owing to his own energy and sharp practice, but also owing to his notorious success at suing anyone who dared default on payment. His legal skills may not have been officially recognized, but he remained a
prodigious litigator through the civil courts. As his financial and social
status improved, Eagar became friends with other eminent emancipists, including Dr. Redfern (who was interested in commercial invest-
ment) and William Hutchinson, principal superintendent of convicts,
who was also in charge of investing convicts' property on their arrival
(sometimes for his own benefit). In 1816 the three men joined a group
of others keen to support Macquarie's plan to set up the first proper
colonial bank and suppress the circulation of promissory notes. Eagar
became the largest shareholder and a committee member but, in another blow to his self-esteem, was prevented from becoming a director
because he had not yet received a full pardon.[20]

While Edward Eagar was rebuilding his personal and financial status, William, too, was attempting to reinvent himself as a gentleman in
Sydney society. William began to receive his annuity from his mother
in the autumn of 1815. This influx of money would have provided
proof positive of his former status as a gentleman and given him the
means to engage in financial transactions with other pardoned convicts
(emancipists) but also with free settlers and government officials
(known as exclusives). News of his newfound wealth, and of its source,
would have spread quickly.[21]

News and gossip were circulated with surprising ease throughout
the British Empire by the movement of an elite group of governing individuals, plus a steady stream of merchants, missionaries, and settlers.
The practice of reprinting the same news items across provincial, national, and colonial papers was an equally proficient means of spreading information, gossip, and scandal. Sydney, like London and most
colonial ports, conducted its social, economic, and political business on
a largely face-to-face basis within its streets, and by personal letter
without. In the early nineteenth century, fortunes and reputations
could be built or destroyed on a local (and international) scale long before the advent of telephones and internet speeded up this process.
Once William knew he could draw upon funds held by the illustrious
bankers Messers Coutts and Co. in London, his new life in Sydney almost certainly became the subject of widespread local gossip.[22]

A man with the ability to draw on sterling in a London bank was always going to get a good credit rating with people desperate to acquire pounds sterling rather than the debased local currency or the ubiquitous and unreliable credit notes. That was why colonial-born children were commonly referred to as "currency," while those born in the mother country were called "sterling." Within a year Macquarie himself was willing to endorse a set of bills William had drawn on Coutts to pay D'Arcy Wentworth, so confident was he that the demand would be met. Whether William's change in circumstance influenced Macquarie to grant him a ticket of leave is less easily ascertained, but much to the disapproval of the British government, the governor commonly exercised his extensive powers and personal choice in giving tickets of leave to gentlemen before even their minimum term had expired, as he had done for Eagar. In addition to relative freedom and a good reputation, William needed three other things to reinvent, or to his mind reinstate, himself as a gentleman in Sydney: stylish clothes, a good address, and a respectable wife.[23]

FASHIONABLE STYLE is not usually connected with the lower and criminal orders of any society, but in colonial Sydney the exclusives did not have a monopoly on smart dress. To English visitors, the streets were a strange mixture of the exotic, the stylish, and the criminal. Elite men and women clothed in tailored London fashions rubbed shoulders with some of the most smartly dressed ex-foot-pads, pickpockets, highwaymen, burglars, swindlers, and forgers, all now "retired from their wonted vocations" and following more industrious pursuits, but almost indistinguishable from the permanently respectable in their attire. Indeed, the difference between the sober and the inebriate might have been an easier distinction to make: drunken sots stained with vomit could be seen staggering to their next drinking hole or passed out oblivious by the roadside. For, as one observer commented, while "neatness of dress and personal cleanliness . . . form a very marked feature among a great proportion of Sydney inhabitants even when moving in a rather humble sphere," sobriety did not rank "among the conspicuous virtues of our general population."[24]

Of course, passers-by could equally meet with government gangs of chained convicts dressed in the black-and-white parti-colored suits (adapted from the uniform William had had to wear in Gloucester jail) recently imposed by the government in one of many attempts to distinguish convicts from citizens. Assigned convict servants did not have to wear any distinguishing marks, but the socially informed discerning eye could easily spot the short ill-fitting jackets and side-buttoned trousers fashioned from cheap cloth that such men usually wore. Yet such signs were not reliable. Gentlemen convicts frequently escaped this stigma by wearing well-cut clothes and long jackets that they had brought with them. Even the ordinary worker, particularly if he was industrious during his "own time," could afford to buy good-quality clothing to wear on his day off. People of all ranks spent large amounts in the rapidly expanding numbers of haberdashery shops, hatters, tailors, and dressmakers, but only the very wealthy could afford to import their clothing from London.[25]

For William, this was a fashionable society that closely mirrored the one he had left, the "convict dandy" was a role he was perfectly fitted for, and the significant status signals conveyed by color and cut were ones he was well practiced in deploying. The difficulty for Sydney society, when so many from such disreputable backgrounds could dress as gentlemen, was in judging just who was really eligible to join their ranks, and this gave rise to increasingly elaborate codes of etiquette to ensure that class boundaries were preserved. Potentially, William possessed the wealth, education, manners, and charm to assuage such doubts among all but the highest echelons. Thus suitably attired, he could go in search of a wife.

William sought the hand of a freeborn daughter of an emancipist—a woman of slightly higher but not "exclusive" status—just as Edward Eagar had done. The "Currency," as one contemporary explained, were held in good "esteem with all the well-informed and right-feeling portion" of the population, save for a few snobbish "Sterling Madonnas" for whom they remained ill bred. The colonial elite, however, generally preferred returning to England to find suitable spouses untainted by doubtful parentage and endowed with a reliable dowry. Yet despite the stain of their parentage, the majority of emancipist children turned out to be healthy, honest, and hardworking citizens, as well as useful living proof that the system had worked to reform their parents' character, much to the colony's pride.[26]

Mary Jones was the perfect example. Just sixteen years old, Mary was the daughter of Sydney's assistant superintendent of police, Robert Jones, and his "wife," Elizabeth. The couple had met on Norfolk Island, to which Jones had been transported in 1790 for the theft of a shawl worth 7s. Jones would have sympathized with William's experience on the *Surry,* for he had survived even worse conditions. He had been kept chained below deck, often waist deep in water, aboard the *Scarborough,* which was one of three ships that formed the infamous Second Fleet. A total of 267 men and women died on that voyage, and of the 692 who made it to shore, at least 486 were sick. When Jones arrived, the colony was just two years old and on the verge of starvation, yet he had not only survived but also risen rapidly to become a prosperous farmer, jailer, and superintendent of police on Norfolk Island.

Mary's mother, Elizabeth Goldsmith, was an equally robust woman in every sense. Condemned to death in 1788 for robbing a woman in the street of clothing and money worth 2s. 14d., Elizabeth was described by her victim as a "stout, sturdy body" that she dared not resist, despite the fact that the pair had been out drinking gin together just before the alleged highway robbery took place. Elizabeth's sentence, along with those of twenty-one other women, was commuted, but such was their fear of transportation at that time that many were reluctant to accept the king's mercy, preferring to risk hanging rather than be "eaten by savages" or torn from their families. The remaining were transported aboard the infamous *Lady Julian,* which became known as a "floating brothel," the following year. All the seamen and soldiers chose a "wife" from among the prisoners, and more were entertained with sex and drink at various ports of call, resulting in a great many pregnancies. When she met Jones, Elizabeth had been freed and married to a Quaker man by whom she had two sons, but the relationship was breaking down. She bore Jones a daughter, Elizabeth, in 1798, and another, Mary, in 1799, but her boys returned to their father. In 1809 the Joneses had moved to Sydney as man and wife with the two girls, and Robert was appointed assistant superintendent the following year. He was now a clearly respected public man and a good ally for a yet-to-be-pardoned ex-convict like William.[27]

Young Mary Jones was almost certainly impressed by the educated conversation, impeccable manners, and stylish appearance that marked William out from the majority of emancipated convicts she would socialize with or could expect to marry. No doubt William's tales of wrongful conviction, inherited wealth, and a country estate in faraway England made a significant impression on the mind of a girl raised in the social confines of Sydney, where, according to one former resident, "agreeable amusements [were] still much wanted to relieve the dull monotony of a town cut off . . . from . . . other parts of the civilised world." Presumably, her father was equally impressed with his prospective son-in-law's future assets, for within three months he was signing the register at William and Mary's marriage in St. Philip's Church.[28]

The newlyweds took up residence in Castlereagh Street, one of those unfinished roads running north-south through the city with large areas still occupied by temporary cottages and timber huts. The following year Mary gave birth to a daughter they named Mary Ann Jane Collins Jackson. A year after that, in December 1817, a son they named William Collins Jackson was born, but he became known to all as George. Despite the break with his own parents, William ensured that both children's names continued the family tradition and that they conformed to the terms of his father's will in case there was any dispute over their parentage. In his will Mr. Jackson had made a virtue of the fact that his wealth was the result of "a Life of Industry and Economy," but his rise into the higher echelons of society made him equally determined that if a female inherited that property, she must continue his lineage by giving her children the Collins Jackson name and adopting the Jackson arms.[29] This lineage was hardly ancient—Jackson's parents had merely given him both their surnames to distinguish their eldest son—but William was taking no chances.

For a few brief years the lives of William Jackson and Edward Eagar appeared to enter a period of relative calm and good fortune, and both families had begun to socialize together shortly after William's wedding. William slipped seamlessly back into his former extravagant spending, secured a smarter address, and moved his family to George Street. He also began, as many emancipists and exclusive gentlemen did, to invest in business on the side. That way he could continue to style himself a gentleman and earn money without actually getting his hands dirty by working.

Edward Eagar, too, found his commercial concerns continuing to grow, but his social status remained questionable, and he became increasingly politicized. Governor Macquarie partly rectified the situation by granting Eagar a full pardon in January 1818. But this consolation mollified Eagar only slightly; he was still smarting about the British government's insistence on his removal from the post of provost marshal to which Macquarie had appointed him the previous year. Nevertheless, the ever-resourceful Eagar continued to increase his commercial interests to include the first paper factory in Sydney. Then in 1819 he went into partnership with Francis Ewen Forbes as a full-scale merchant trader importing and exporting goods to and from the colony. Eagar combined his commercial and religious interests by supplying missionaries in the South Pacific with goods for the London Missionary Society and by involving the prominent Methodist schoolmaster and merchant John Hosking in his business; Hosking returned to England that year to become a London agent for the company. Redfern and Hutchinson were also useful supporters of the increasingly successful merchant house of Eagar and Forbes. Meanwhile, Eagar used his standing in the community to become secretary to a committee of emancipists who met, with Macquarie's blessing, to draw up a petition calling for recognition of their civil and political rights, including the right to trial by a jury of their peers rather than by a panel of military men.

Meanwhile, William's lack of practical business experience and financial self-control meant that his economic and domestic harmony were soon under threat. The Sydney trading markets were extremely volatile, and the days of a business monopoly by gentlemen and officers were over. Success in the markets required considerable skill and a merchant's full attention to gauge the sudden swings between glut and scarcity, to import the right amount and type of goods, and to ride out the slumps successfully. As a ticket-of-leave man, William was officially banned from issuing promissory notes—not that many people heeded Macquarie's repeated attempts to stop their use even among the free population. Indeed, William began to discover just how difficult it could be to become a creditor, reliant on promissory notes issued by "wretches . . . [who] either become actually insolvent, or declare themselves so, in order to defraud their unwary creditors."[30]

The sudden possession of wealth had also made William too willing to make risky business speculations—a field he had little experience of—and inevitably his debts began to mount. William petitioned Macquarie for a conditional pardon because his business ventures had been "unsuccessful" in that he had given others "credit to a considerable amount." As an emancipist, William argued, he would be able to manage his concerns "with more confidence and efficiency." Macquarie granted him a conditional pardon in January 1818, which gave him freedom within the colony and carried the additional benefit of entitling him to a land grant, but not the right to return to England.[31]

By the autumn William had acquired a farm in Parramatta, a rural settlement surrounded by rich agricultural land about fourteen miles west of central Sydney. Macquarie was one of several early governors who also kept a country residence there, which added a degree of social cachet to the area. In his own mind at least, William had at last acquired the status of a landed gentleman, and the wheel of fortune appeared to have returned him to a social position close to what he might have expected to hold in England.

Yet there were signs that all was still not well within the Jackson household. Just eight weeks after the birth of their son, on Valentine's Day, 1818, Mrs. Jackson announced in the *Sydney Gazette* that she and the family would be leaving the colony, so creditors should immediately present their claims to William at the George Street house. It is impossible to say whether this was an attempt to find some kind of resolution for financial problems or a sign that Mary Jackson had become deeply disillusioned with her profligate (and almost certainly heavily drinking) husband. But in either event, William remained in Sydney, and a letter from his daughter suggests the family was still together in 1820. But that year proved a pivotal one for William. It marked the point when all his attempts at self-reinvention and reform began to be blown off course by events in England largely beyond his control, which sent him into a spiral of self-destruction. It was the beginning of a period during which he would see his new family, friends, and fortune vanish from his life.[32]

RUINED SUITORS

Australia and England, 1820–1828

This is the Court of Chancery; which has its decaying
houses and its blighted lands in every shire; and its
dead in every churchyard; which has its ruined suitor,
with his slipshod heels and threadbare dress, borrowing
and begging through the round of every man's
acquaintance.

—Charles Dickens, *Bleak House* (1853)

William's downfall in Australia was initially precipitated by a happy event in England. After three years of widowhood Jane Jackson met and then married Irish lawyer Edmund Molony at Dunmore, Sir George Shee's Irish estate, in 1817. Molony seems to have been deeply taken by his new bride's ardent nature and artistic talents, memorably erecting an epitaph to her as "hot, passionate and tender, a highly accomplished lady, and a superb drawer." But that same tombstone shows that her wealth and, particularly, her family connections were equally attractive propositions for an ambitious lawyer with social aspirations.[1]

On marriage, a woman's property came under her husband's control, and Molony gained some £5,000 of his new wife's personal property as soon as their nuptials were completed. At fifty-four, however, Jane was no blushing bride, so she had persuaded her new husband to sign a premarital agreement to guarantee that the property she had gained from Jackson, particularly her annuity of £800, should remain separate from his and under her own control. She also continued to manage Jackson's estate and ensure that William received his annuity in Australia from the proceeds. Yet neither Jane's charms nor her financial foresight proved enough to make her new marriage a success: within three years the couple's relationship began to founder.[2]

The Molonys moved to London in 1819, but in the following summer business drew Edmund back to Ireland and Jane refused to accompany him there. Jackson's death, loss of contact with her only son, and emotional distance from her new husband almost undoubtedly resulted in physical as well as psychological manifestations. Her health began to fail, her eyes to lose their sight, and she increasingly refused to leave the house. In London she sought medical help for cataracts in her eyes. A year after the couple had separated, Jane was evicted from their home in Crawford Street by an angry landlord who seized the house and everything she owned except her clothes, claiming that it was to settle unpaid arrears of rent. Whether this was because Edmund would not or could not pay the rent is less clear.

Jane moved nearer Sir George Shee's house—to George Street, Manchester Square, where, as her world grew darker, she increasingly kept to her bedroom. She did not inform Molony of her whereabouts, and it was not until 1823 that he returned to London to look for her. Perhaps inevitably for a lawyer, Edmund Molony turned to the courts to find a way to mend his broken marriage. He sued Jane for restitution of conjugal rights so that she "might be compelled by the sentence of the court to live and co-habit with [him] . . . to treat him with matrimonial affection; and to render him conjugal rights." In fact, the court could only direct that Jane return to cohabit with her husband, not to share his bed, but if she refused, Edmund gained the right to seize her by force. Many restitution of conjugal rights cases were brought by spouses hoping to force their partners to come to a financial settlement, usually to pay maintenance after a separation. Edmund Molony, however, almost certainly hoped that a return to marital felicity or cohabitation would encourage his wife to direct more substantial sums from the Jackson estate toward him. He had already begun a separate suit in the Court of Chancery against Jane for improper management of those funds.[3]

AT THE END OF 1821 that venerable but ponderous judicial institution ground slowly into action and impounded all the property and proceeds of the Jackson estate while it conducted a minutely detailed investigation into the facts of the case. One of the most inconvenient of those facts was, as *The Times* explained, that the heir at law to the whole estate, "who was very respectably connected," had nevertheless "made his transit . . . to New South Wales in a manner by no means voluntary, [and] suddenly become entitled to a life interest in the sum of £21,000 vested in the 3 per Cents, and to other property amounting in the whole to nearly £50,000."[4]

Even with the £800 annuity that Jane Jackson received from the estate, the prospect of acquiring such a large sum evidently fueled both William's inability to rein back his prodigious spending and Molony's determination to funnel at least some of the Jackson estate toward his own household. Complicating matters further was the fact that nobody knew exactly what had become of William in Australia; Jane herself believed that he had married and produced male children, but she claimed to know no more. The immediate crisis for William was that his steady and not inconsiderable stream of income suddenly dried up while his prodigious expenditure continued unabated.[5]

Edward Eagar, who by now considered himself to be an "intimate friend" of the Jacksons, offered to help William through his financial difficulties by loaning him sums of money from company funds that soon totaled £5,000. This proved to be an unwise move for the pioneering emancipist, whose ideals and position in society were now threatened by the presence of Commissioner Bigge in the colony. He had been sent by the British government in 1819 to investigate the state of the colony because the MPs were concerned that it was no longer the fearsome and effective deterrent for felons that it was intended to be. Bigge's instructions for conducting his inquiry included determining ways to make transportation "an object of real terror" once more, and to report on the extent to which Governor Macquarie's "ill considered compassion for convicts" was undermining this objective.[6]

Bigge, an aristocrat, academic, and professional lawyer, found himself warmly welcomed by elitist free settlers, military officers, and civil servants, but was almost immediately at odds with the practical, humane governor from more humble origins who supported the emancipists. In his report Bigge singled out Eagar and Redfern as examples of Macquarie's bad practice. They submitted evidence to the commissioner, and Eagar sent him the emancipists' petition, but both men's fortunes took a downward turn. Redfern was removed from his position as a magistrate, and Eagar found that his legal status in court was suddenly denied on the basis of a technicality. The Supreme Court judge declared that Eagar could no longer sue his debtors because the pardons granted by Macquarie had not been ratified under the Great Seal in England on account of a procedural error. If the decision were more universally upheld, Eagar—and, by implication, most other emancipists—could not have their full rights as British subjects restored to them. It would wipe away the foundations of their status and position in the colony, because they could no longer legally hold property, make or enforce contracts, or give evidence in court, despite comprising the most economically and numerically dominant section of society. Another public meeting was hastily convened, and it was resolved to send a new petition to England explaining the adverse effects that could follow such a decision and asking for confirmation of their existing legal status. Macquarie again endorsed the emancipists' plan, and Eagar and Redfern were nominated to take the petition to England personally.[7]

Eagar became increasingly immersed in political campaigns, but he found his ability to sue for money undermined and some of his trading deals proved unsuccessful. A decision in a major court dispute over trade with the king of Tahiti went against him, causing the company significant losses, and Francis Forbes's declining health forced him to take a protracted break in Tasmania. Despite financial assistance from Dr. Redfern, the superintendent of convicts William Hutchinson, and John Hosking in London, the firm of Eagar and Forbes needed its money back from William rather sooner than either party had anticipated.

Eagar repeatedly asked William for his money until financial pressure and self-interest finally forced the emancipist lawyer to sue his former friend in 1821. William hired an attorney, but he had no defense against the claim, for he had signed a bond promising to pay Eagar the money. The court found against the profligate heir and ordered that his goods be seized to pay off the debt, but William and what was left of his property promptly vanished. Eagar was not so easily shaken off. The two men came to an uneasy financial agreement, which ultimately would benefit neither: William granted Eagar power of attorney to oversee the prosecution of his case in Chancery to win back his inheritance, from which funds he hoped to settle all his debts. So when Eagar set sail for England leaving his wife and children behind, he believed that his reward for a successful prosecution of William's case would include full payment of his debts from the dividends of the Jackson estate. But what else the campaigning lawyer expected to acquire for himself was never made clear and remained a source of private and press speculation in both countries.[8]

MARY JACKSON could no longer take the pressure from her drunken, dissipated husband, who had begun to socialize more with publicans and Sydney low life than with wealthy emancipists (the doors of those in the higher echelons of society had remained resolutely closed to him). Mary had no family support of her own to help her deal with the situation. She had lost her father in September 1819, and her mother and sister had made use of money given by the Police Fund in recognition of Robert's excellent service, plus a land grant in Tasmania, to move back to Hobart. After her husband's departure, Mrs. Eagar, too, began to discover just how bad her family's debts had become, so she could offer little help to Mary, and word of William's defaulting on debts would quickly have spread through the respectable emancipist community. With scant resources Mary took both children and sailed for Hobart, presumably to be nearer her mother and sister, where she accepted a job as a housekeeper to support her family.[9]

William had lost his family for the second time, but like most drunks in the later stages of alcoholism, he is unlikely to have realized that, yet again, his own actions had made it impossible for those who loved him to live with him. It is not clear whether William and Mary ever communicated again, but when William sued his case in Chancery through Edward Eagar in 1822, he did so also in the name of his son.

In fact, he kept the interests of both his children close to his heart, for when he made his will in 1824, he bequeathed all his property (and that of his father, which he should have inherited) equally to George and Mary Ann. This was a very unusual step, for land in England descended through the male line, and Mr. Jackson had expressly stated in his will that his property should also do so unless there were no living male heirs. Certainly Mary Jackson appeared to vest all her hopes and efforts in helping her son, George, rather than her daughter, to claim the inheritance. Like Mary and George, everyone linked to William's will saw it as a possible means to personal riches. Eagar was made a co-executor, which gave him an added incentive to prosecute William's case successfully. The other co-executor was another former forger, an emancipist silversmith named Jacob Josephson, but at the time he agreed to be an executor to the will, he was more than £12,000 in debt and clearly expected to benefit from his role.[10]

William's hopes for redemption rested solely on Edward Eagar in England and the exercise of justice by England's mighty court of conscience. The Court of Chancery had long been able to provide "fair" remedies for civil suitors, and its powers greatly exceeded those of the common-law courts. But the ever-growing numbers of litigants, coupled with the infamously slow and intricately technical procedural rules for filing bills of complaint, answers, crossbills, replications, and rejoinders; for issuing injunctions; and for instigating master's reports, meant that a case could be tied up for many years at a ruinous cost. In his withering portrayal of Chancery in *Bleak House* (1853), Dickens described how in pursuit of equitable justice the court instead gave

> to monied might the means abundantly of wearying out the right; which so exhausts finances, patience, courage, hope; so overthrows the brain and breaks the heart; that there is not an honourable man among its practitioners who would not give . . . the warning, "Suffer any wrong that can be done you, rather than come here!"[11]

One of the most honorable and long-serving members of the court was Lord Chancellor Eldon, a man of prodigious learning and scrupulous fairness. After his retirement in 1827, Eldon was honored for having settled nearly all the rules of equity law, and his decisions were referred to in 90 percent of Chancery cases. Unfortunately for William, Eldon exercised extreme caution when coming to any decision—he took an age to consider every angle and weigh up every fact in a case— which earned him the nickname Lord Endless and contributed in no small part to delays experienced by litigants.[12]

Eagar launched his first bill of complaint in Chancery for William and George in 1822, but it took a year for the court to order a report into the assets under dispute, and then another year before it declared that William was legally allowed to pursue the answers to his questions about what was owed to him and ascertain the full extent of his father's remaining property. As the case in England ground slowly on, William's circumstances in Sydney worsened. He acquired increasing notoriety as an eccentric character—an impoverished heir to a vast fortune that never seemed to materialize. The one positive sign for William was an injunction granted to prevent both Molony and his mother from any further "intermeddling" in the estate; he seems to have suspected that Edmund and Jane might have been pursuing a collusive suit for their mutual benefit. This was probably why William felt confident enough to include the Jackson estate in the provisions of his own will, although it may also have been to encourage more support from his executors by making the will demonstrably more beneficial for them. Much more surprisingly, despite being prosecuted for debt again in the Australian civil court, William began making arrangements to buy two very large and expensive estates in England, as his father had directed under the terms of his will, as if the matter were already settled.[13]

In England, Edward Eagar was beginning to struggle financially. As his finances dwindled in London, his debts in the colony mounted alarmingly, leaving his wife and children impoverished and in need of charitable donations. The extent to which their plight affected Eagar's infinitely malleable conscience, however, is debatable. He had set up house with a sixteen-year-old London girl called Ellen Gorman, who, in 1823, gave birth to the first of their ten children. Indeed, it was becoming abundantly clear to many in both countries that he had no intention of returning either to his family or to Sydney, where hostile creditors plus unspecified allegations of mismanagement of Methodist funds, and even a charge of forgery, awaited him.

Yet it also is clear that Eagar's patriotic campaigning zeal for the rights of emancipists did not diminish. He had delivered the emancipists' petition and continued to lobby the government hard; he also wrote a lengthy and vigorous attack on the three reports that Commissioner Bigge published on the state of the colony and its judicial system. These reports were used to provide information for the government to reassess British policy toward the colony. Eagar achieved visible, if partial, success in the passing of the 1823 New South Wales Act, which validated all convict pardons not yet confirmed under the Great Seal and granted a limited form of trial by jury in civil courts. Still Eagar did not rest; he wrote jubilantly of how he pressed Prime Minister Robert Peel to agree to restore "emancipists to all substantial rights and privileges" in *all* British dominions—a concession that was duly formalized by the Transportation Act the following year.

Eagar's joy at this success proved to be short-lived. Within a year he found himself in a startlingly similar position to that in which William had so often been—he was arrested for debt while waiting for large sums of money he expected to receive. Eagar found that his efforts for his fellow emancipists had garnered much written praise but little actual remuneration, and the steady stream of money from the Jackson estate suddenly ceased when the court deemed it necessary to obtain another warrant of attorney from William. Convinced that William still owed him several thousand pounds, Eagar demanded and got a second warrant of attorney from William to act on his behalf and to continue to draw money from the estate for the repayment of debts to his company.[14]

In 1826 the announcement that William had waited to hear for most of his short life was finally delivered. The Court of Chancery declared him to be legally entitled to all the rents and profits from Langley Lodge and other estates; it confirmed him to be the purchaser of the two new estates, from which he could now also claim an income; and it clarified that his only financial responsibility was to continue to pay his mother's annuity. Mary Jackson heard the news in Tasmania and clearly believed the case to be all but settled. Suppressing any maternal pain and anxiety, she entrusted her precious nine-year-old son to the care of his godfather, William Walkinshaw, and waved them both off on a ship bound for England. There George could appeal to one of the court's main equitable functions—the care and education of children who had no rights under common law—to claim a share of the estate in order to provide for his maintenance and education. There is no evidence that William knew his son had left the colony for this reason, but he almost certainly would have approved. The provision of a gentlemanly education was something William regarded as essential, even if he had not made the most of his own time at school. Chancery guaranteed payment of George's school fees and later appointed Colonel Charles Shee, a son of his father's illustrious uncle, Sir George, as the boy's guardian in England. So the young "currency" lad set out to learn how to become a member of the "sterling" English classes in a small Surrey school run by clergymen, not very different from the one his father had attended. It seemed that both father and son were about to be restored to a very comfortable, if not quite so respectable, rank of society on both sides of the world.[15]

IT IS NOT UNCOMMON for family tragedies to end in redemption, reconciliation, and restitutional justice, and this case appeared to be on the verge of just such a conclusion. But too often the intervention of the Court of Chancery resulted in endless delays, suits, and countersuits that could tie up property and ruin generations of the same family—the fate of the unfortunate Jarndyce family in *Bleak House*. By all accounts, instead of enjoying his newfound wealth, William was reduced to extreme poverty and could be seen walking the Sydney streets with no shoes or stockings on his feet. Instead of the respect and status he had always craved, he gained only notoriety as an "eccentric character" commonly referred to as Buck Jackson, who staggered about in a state of drunken stupor for days on end.[16]

The estate at Langley Lodge had long remained untenanted and was now so uncared for that its shabbiness threatened to put off any future tenants. There still remained lands, stocks, and shares to be liquidated and assessed before money could be sent to Australia, and William's erstwhile "friend" and attorney Edward Eagar delayed matters further by trying to establish his prior claim to the money under the second power of attorney that William had sent him. But some people were becoming increasingly suspicious of Eagar: his former business partner and London agent for Eagar and Forbes, John Hosking, accused him of forging this second power of attorney, claiming that he had already received all the money owed by William, but had kept it for himself instead of paying back the company. Hosking described Eagar as an unreformed forger who had "committed several acts of deceit" in England as well as having been arrested for debt. Unaware of William's facility with switching both his handwriting style and his signature among Burke Jackson, Captain Jackson, and William Collins Burke Jackson, the court also found that the signatures on the two powers of attorney did not match. Meanwhile, William's mother, Jane, who had by now been made painfully aware of her son's distress, started another action in the case of *Molony v. Molony* to prevent Eagar from gaining access to William's power of attorney and to save her son from "utter destruction." "Nothing" declared the *Times* report of her lawyer's emotive speech, "could be more deplorable than the state of this individual heir to [£]50,0000, able to will it away, and yet wandering in want and penury, because his property had got into the hands of Mr. Egar [*sic*]."[17]

Thus, despite all his successful campaigns to change the status of emancipists, Edward Eagar found himself facing accusations in a British court based on a discussion of whether an ex-convict could ever become a fully reformed character and be allowed to regain his former station in life. Surprisingly, such questions were not directed at William's behavior beyond some expressions of regret about his "old habits of profligacy and extravagance," which had caused him to borrow from Eagar and Forbes in the first place. Notwithstanding the tendency of legal battles to be presented (particularly by newspapers) as a contest between right and wrong, or good and evil, there is more often a murky marsh of misunderstanding and distrust to be navigated, in which any more solid legal evidence is gratefully grasped as if it signifies some greater truth. In this case that evidence was the eventual proof that William himself had indeed signed both power of attorney documents.

Whether he had done so under duress or in a drunken stupor, or whether Eagar had any further right to claim money from the Jackson estate, was not an issue that could be settled by a simple motion. The judge took the view that Eagar's good character had been more than vindicated by the trial and that Hosking had been, at best, unwise to share his private reservations with the public. Hosking did indeed have good reason to wish Eagar ill, for the company of Eagar and Forbes had suffered severe internal strife and financial losses, and many others continued to doubt Eagar's honesty for similarly personal reasons. The Reverend Samuel Marsden, still angry at his former protégé's insulting betrayal, felt more disposed to believe a later report that Eagar gained possession of the property of "drunken Burke Jackson" through a forged will purporting to show that he had been appointed guardian of "the young son."[18]

Whatever the truth of the matter, the curiously tangled, sometimes mutually supportive, but ultimately destructive relationship between William and Edward Eagar resulted in an ironic reversal of roles. Edward Eagar took up residence in William's former home of Langley Lodge, but the Jackson estate and the trappings and accoutrements of gentlemanly status could no more disguise his real financial position or quell the rumors about his immoral past than they had done for William. In February 1828 Eagar was again arrested for debt and, like William, locked within the walls of the Fleet Prison. He was released two months later, only to face a bankruptcy commission, but he was soon to be found living back at Langley Lodge. Eagar continued to dice with debt but survived; William, disastrously, did not. Neither did his previous partner in crime, Joseph Bradley, who despite his comfortable job was tempted back onto the path of fraud and forgery to augment his fortunes.[19]

The knowledge that Eagar had usurped his rightful place in England may have proved the fatal blow to William's slim hold on life. By 1828 his drinking had reached catastrophic levels—days would pass without him knowing a sober moment. His plight and his shabby streetwalking do not seem to have aroused sympathy among any citizens of Sydney, hardened by what was a common sight in the city. One surgeon superintendent described how many men drank continuously from year to year; he had seen at least one "who had been for some weeks in a state of oblivion." In William's case, it may have been his, at best, disingenuous and, at worst, criminal efforts to raise money that had left him no friends. One paper later scurrilously described him as "a man who from love of sport, preferred to trick a friend out of a sum of money, than to have it presented to him as a gift, and who was as generous as he was sportive."[20]

Even if some kind soul had taken pity on him, William was almost certainly beyond help now. In the final stages of alcoholism the sufferer no longer has a choice—he has to drink from dawn to dusk merely to function. He is assailed by moments of inexplicable fear and panic and often suffers from hallucinations and periods of extreme aggression or passivity as he comes to realize that he no longer has any control over his life or body. Mentally oblivious and physically malnourished, he finds his limbs frequently overtaken by a creeping numbness as his internal organs begin to fail. In March 1828 William staggered drunkenly through the streets for several days as he had done many times before, but this time when he fell, he could not get up. He died alone on the street where he lay, a pathetic figure with no friends or family to comfort him or to mourn his passing. Seven months later Joseph Bradley was publicly executed for forging a deed of gift for a property and thereby defrauding the rightful heirs. He was one of nine men that the state of New South Wales felt compelled to hang that day as "a salutary warning to others, and [to] be the means of checking the frightful spread of crime in our community," which the *Sydney Gazette* feared had "increased in more than a double ratio . . . beyond the past year." For William and Joseph (and many others like them), neither transportation nor emancipation had wrought reformation.[21]

William's death would have remained merely another unremarked drunken fatality were it not for his relationship with Edward Eagar and the vast property that he could never actually possess—a story that continued to fascinate the press. Indeed, the fate of that property filled more column inches in Australia, Tasmania, and Britain for years after his death than the relish with which his pitiful demise was recalled. Edward Eagar could not escape his association with William or his property. His residence at Langley and the belief that he had "a claim" on the property, which was variously reported as costing £3,000–8,000 per annum, caused frequent speculation about the estate's real value and its tenant's legitimacy. At least one paper threw doubt on Eagar's claim by asserting that Langley was actually "the property of the children" of the late Burke

Jackson. William's tragic fate and Eagar's relationship with him later haunted the emancipist's campaigns on behalf of the rights of the colonists and, in the opinion of several newspapers, had a direct impact on colonial politics. In February 1829 the *Sydney Monitor* insinuated that the relationship had set back the emancipists' fight for trial by jury:

> The Mother Country is well aware, that some of our freed Colonists are among the most valuable, patriotic and wealthy members of our state. . . . But the publication of Hardy Vaux's infamous book, Mr. Bigge's private pique and malice in characterising certain individuals here, the indefatigable exertions of Mr. Eagar in exposing the Commissioner and his proceedings; coupled with the unhappy and disreputable connexion of the last Gentleman with the unfortunate and miserable Burke Jackson, has it is said (though we do not ourselves give credit to the report), caused H.M. Home Government to put off Trial by Jury until the present generation of adult emancipists has died off.[22]

Eagar, who had spent the years 1827–1829 writing letters, lobbying ministers, and publishing at his own expense a nine-page pamphlet objecting to a bill to govern Australia, could not have been happy about this report, particularly as the paper's editor was a fellow reformer and supporter of his efforts. Nine years later, when the British government was considering the election of an official parliamentary representative for the colony, William's memory was again disinterred to discredit Eagar. The *Sydney Gazette* published a heavily ironic paragraph suggesting that the "Botany Bay Patriots" (a term of abuse for the liberal/emancipist party) should "appoint Mr. Eagar at once. Every person who remembers poor Burke Jackson must agree with us in thinking that they cannot find a more fitting representative." Eagar found himself sitting in on parliamentary discussions of a report on transportation when, as *The Colonist* reported, the passionate moralist Reverend R. D. Lang provided evidence on the endemic corruption within New South Wales society that was caused by the system of transportation. Unaware that Eagar was behind him, Lang detailed how this convicted forger had tutored the children of a respectable family, then abandoned his own family to live in sin, and never returned to New South Wales because he had acquired possession of the "very dissipated but wealthy . . . Burke Jackson's" property. This, the newspaper argued, helped prove that Eagar was a prime example of the type of now-emancipated gentleman convict who gave the whole transportation system a bad name—it could not be seen to work as either a deterrent or a reformative measure.[23]

Eagar's constant campaigning had cost him dear financially because he funded much of his activities himself. This clearly motivated his attempts to gain more money from the Jackson estate, but to what extent those efforts were immoral or illegal has remained obscure and contentious to both modern and contemporary commentators. Eagar was undoubtedly a committed campaigner, but the colony's primary parliamentary advocate remained, as one colonial diplomat put it, an emancipist of "very equivocal virtue." A similar epitaph could equally have been applied to the late and largely unlamented Burke Jackson.[24]

It is a final irony, perhaps, that whereas in Australia William's memory was periodically revived for political or other purposes, in England his family made every effort to erase it. Edmund Molony ensured that Jane's tomb commemorated all her marriages and eulogized her personal character but omitted any mention of her only son. Despite becoming a comfortably wealthy gentleman in his own right, William's own son, George, rewrote his origins to obliterate any stain of his convict father. Only Mr. Jackson left anything to remember the son he disowned, in a will that he was either unwilling or unable to change, and in his detailed account *Filial Ingratitude, or; The Profligate Son,* which was never published. In those volumes Mr. Jackson presented his son's life as a deplorable descent into depravity and a classic rake's progress. Today we might note the moral judgments of the past and recognize the destructive behavior of a deeply flawed individual, but retain a greater degree of sympathy for William. His character and his fate were equally shaped by his troubled relationship with his father, his family's sudden acquisition of wealth, and the economic, social, and judicial conditions in which he grew up.

EPILOGUE

I heard a small sad sound,
And stood awhile among the tombs around:
"Wherefore, old friends," said I, "are you distrest,
Now, screened from life's unrest?"
 . . .

But what has been will be—
First memory, then oblivion's swallowing sea;
Like men foregone, shall we merge into those
Whose story no one knows.

— Thomas Hardy, "The To-Be-Forgotten"

The demise of a ruined heir in Australia made very little impact in the dusty bills of Chancery. William's attorney and his widow had difficulty proving that his death had even occurred. For fifteen years afterward the case ground inexorably on as costs rose and profits from the decaying estate declined. The original litigants from the Jackson, Evelyn, and Shee families died, to be replaced by a new generation of interested parties, as did those of the Coutts family, whose bank was still holding a significant proportion of Jackson's money. But if nobody directly acquired the immense fortune under dispute, the court did make provision for those it was intended to protect, namely, women and children. Jane Jackson's annual income was guaranteed to her for life and kept safe from her third husband, Edmund Molony. Chancery also provided respectable guardians and an elite education for her now fatherless grandson, despite his convict ancestry. From the cold and impersonal depositions surviving in the court's records, it is possible to piece together what happened to the lonely boy who would eventually inherit the Jackson estate.

In 1830 after William's death, Mary Jackson visited George in England to support her son's claim in Chancery. She soon returned to Hobart, however, where she remarried and set herself up in business—her descendants and those of her daughter, Mary Ann, are still living in Tasmania today. In England George continued at school under the guardianship of Sir George Shee's son, Colonel Charles Shee, who made provision for the boy's education and clothing to be paid for under the terms of Mr. Jackson's will. In so doing, the court at last fulfilled its role as a surrogate "parent" and guardian of minors as Jackson had hoped it would do for William so many years earlier. George flourished at school, but his contact with his real family seems to have been limited. There is little surviving evidence, but it seems he rarely saw his elderly grandmother, and when George was nineteen, Charles Shee resigned as his guardian, leaving the solitary scholar under the care of another schoolmaster in Essex. As a young man George did not seem to have inherited his father's rakish genes or his inveterate dislike of school; he justified his grandfather's faith in the power of education by going on to do a degree at Oxford.[1]

Despite her poor health, William's mother, Jane, survived until 1838, although her brother, Sir George Shee, had died in 1825 and their friend John Evelyn, in 1827. Jane remained married to Edmund Molony and continued to receive her annuity from the Jackson estate until her death. It is not clear whether, or even to what extent, the two were reconciled, but the restitution of conjugal rights case seems to have been quietly dropped after 1826. On Jane's famous tombstone Edmund professed himself to have been deeply afflicted by the loss of a wife who possessed "great virtues and talents" and who was "beloved and deeply regretted by all who knew her."[2]

Despite such fulsome tributes, he omitted to mention the virtues of tender motherhood that Mr. Jackson had so often praised her for. Indeed, there was no mention that she had ever born or lost a son. Instead, the grieving widower celebrated his deceased wife's illustrious lineage and even the virtues of her previous husbands. Molony had the stone engraved with information about Jane's marriages to Mr. Stuart in India and to Mr. Jackson as military secretary to the East India Company. Molony also recorded Jane's parentage and thus her relation to "the sublime" Edmund Burke, whose name she and Mr. Jackson had so expectantly added to William's at his birth.[3]

Perhaps believing that George would soon inherit his grandfather's estate, Jane left nothing to her grandson in her will. The following year, 1839, with Charles Shee's help, George enlisted as a cornet in the First Dragoon Guards, where he proved considerably more suited to the discipline of military life than his father had. He eventually rose to the rank of major in the Seventh Hussars. From 1839 George received his annuity from the Jackson estate in person, but it was not until 1842 that he finally took full control of what remained. Soon afterward he married Catherine Lewis, a wealthy woman in her own right, and the couple moved to Roath Castle in Wales. There they raised ten children, eight girls and two boys: the eldest daughter was named Mary Shee Jackson after George's mother and guardian, but none of his father's family names were passed on. The largely fatherless George seems to have become the very model of a Victorian *pater familias*, a respected military man, and an esteemed cricketer (he played for the Gentlemen of Kent and once for England). This was the sort of eminent respectability that his grandfather had so desperately desired for his own son and of which he would wholeheartedly have approved. George retired from the army in 1856 and, after several moves, eventually settled into life as a country gentleman in a manor house with his wife and daughters in Dawlish, less than ten miles from the Devon town of Topsham, where Mr. Jackson had been born and lived as a child.[4]

I have found no evidence of whether George ever made contact with any other living Jackson relatives remaining in the area. Maintaining his respectability, however, required burying his convict father's past, so no matter where he lived, he always recorded his birthplace as India, not Australia. That respectability was not, however, supported by his inheritance. At his death in 1893, George left a mere £83 4s 10d, whereas his wealthy wife, who died just five years later, left more than £100,000. This suggests that it was her money that had continued to support the family's gentry lifestyle, not the long-contested, much-sought-after Jackson estate that George's grandfather had so painstakingly acquired and protected against profligacy.[5]

Edmund Molony's mention of Mr. Jackson on Jane's tombstone is evidence that his reputation at that point in time was still illustrious enough to warrant an elegant memorial. Modern history has been considerably less kind. It is not, as he might have hoped, his behavior as a "good" father to a profligate son that has been passed down, but rather the legacy of his actions in India. Popular Indian history has accorded Jackson's nemesis, the poligar prince Kattobomma Nayakar, the status of hero. He is now remembered as a "fearless chieftain" who refused to bow down to British imperial demands, a brave warrior and freedom fighter who allegedly inspired the first Sepoy Mutiny in 1857, and a man who "played a pivotal role in the freedom movement" of southern India. Kattobomma's life has been commemorated in Indian folk songs, a memorial has been erected near the spot where he was hanged, and his exploits were depicted in an early Technicolor Bollywood film. In the movie it is Jackson Thurai who is left standing uncomfortably while being harangued by the righteous poligar over the injustice of British taxes. In 1974 the Tamil Nadu government built a memorial fort in which stands a statue of Kattobomma, and the walls of the hall are covered with beautiful paintings celebrating his heroic deeds. In film, on Tamil nationalist websites, and in some academic histories, collector Jackson has been reduced to the minor role of archetypal arrogant British official, a symbolic focus for national anger against British imperial rule. The irony of this public judgment of his father would not have been lost on William. This book has, I hope, provided a more balanced picture of both father and son. Equally importantly perhaps, the story of a profligate son has been revised and retold for modern audiences.[6]

UNTIL VERY RECENTLY, "profligacy" was not a word much used in modern times. The financial crisis in Europe and America, however, has triggered debate about the profligacy of governments and the prodigious spending of parents that will leave a whole generation of children to pay off the resulting debts. Links between national and individual family profligacy have thus been raised once more. Concerns about the ease of obtaining credit, the impact of debt on families, and the purchase of luxury goods are now frequently discussed in the media. Shops entice customers to buy their goods using bank or store credit cards, enabling many of us to acquire goods we could not otherwise afford. Indeed, today the purchase of goods on credit is more common than purchase with cash, and the prospect of a largely "cashless" economy is beginning to resemble eighteenth-century credit-driven commerce caused by a shortage of circulating coin. Similar questions of financial responsibility are thus arising. When our spending on cards exceeds our ability to meet repayments, who is most at fault—the debtors who fail to control their desire to acquire fashionable goods, the credit companies that keep increasing card limits, or the storekeepers who encourage us to buy in this way? We tend to see such debt as the result of imprudent, rather than immoral or illegal, behavior, and efforts to regulate lending are more common than outcries against a form of consumer behavior that is seen as beneficial to the economy.[7]

In today's consumer-driven society, young people are again particularly vulnerable and becoming more so. In Britain, the Citizens Advice Bureau has identified debt as one of just four major issues facing young people under twenty-five, and most of this relates to personal loans, credit- and store-card debts, and bank overdrafts. The recent introduction of university tuition fees in England has suddenly forced more teenagers and young adults to take on, and learn to live with, even larger, long-term debt. Hence, there are now calls to educate children about the basic principles of borrowing and managing money. The Personal Finance Education Group charity has been set up to help build "a society in which all children and young people have the skills, knowledge and confidence to manage their money well." Like William Jackson, many teenagers and young men also face pressure from their peers to gain status in a group through the acquisition of fashionable clothing and stylish goods.[8]

Today, websites offer legal advice on the extent to which parents are responsible for their children's debts. On one such site, Mr. Jackson's attitude toward William's debts is almost exactly replicated in a warning to modern parents that they should not rush to bail out their children, because doing so will not teach them how to solve the problem. Unlike William, however, insolvent youths today will not be imprisoned; yet the mental and social consequences of indebtedness and the temptation to resort to crime can still affect boys and their families well into adulthood. Parents still seek ways to curb the consumption of, and help with the social pressures faced by, their profligate offspring.[9]

ACKNOWLEDGMENTS

This book is the result of a long and difficult but immensely enjoyable process of research, during which I was lucky enough to receive help and support from a large number of people, only some of whom I have space to thank here. To begin with, I must acknowledge a great debt of gratitude to Margaret Hunt, who first told me about a good primary source that might help my research on intergenerational conflict. She had discovered the three volumes of *Filial Ingratitude; Or, The Profligate Son* but had only a paragraph in which to discuss it in her own book. It was while reading these volumes that I was so ably assisted by Amanda Bevan and, particularly, Liz Hore at the National Archives, who alerted me to vast amounts of additional relevant material that had either been cataloged under a different name or remained stubbornly difficult to find because much of the vast Chancery Archive still remains to be fully cataloged. I will forever be grateful to them for all their help over several years; without them, large sections of this book could not have been written. I must also thank staff and archivists in the British Library, particularly those in African and Asian Studies, where the India Office records are read, and in the Map Reading Room and Manuscripts Reading Room. I would like to thank Frances Harris, then senior curator of manuscripts, for helping me track down records concerning the Shee and, particularly, the Evelyn families. In my travels around the country, I also had occasion to be grateful to the staff at Gloucester Record Office. In Guernsey, Darryl Ogier, the States Island archivist, provided enthusiastic help and invaluable advice, as did Keith Ribilliard, senior clerk to the strong room at the Greffe Royal Court. The owner of Sausmarez Manor, Peter de Sausmarez, opened his house and family records to me privately, with great good grace but without any prior warning, when I stumbled across the house on the island.

For the Australian section of the book, I could not have done without the assiduous and accurate services of Laurence Turtle, who transcribed, copied, or sent over reams of material and searched diligently for more evidence of William Jackson's Australian relations. The only living descendants of William's that I know of contacted me entirely out of the blue, from Tasmania—such is the power of the Internet. Jennie Amos enthusiastically provided details of her husband's descent from William's daughter, Mary Ann, along with letters from her as a child and a picture of her brother, George. I hope this book will in some way contribute to and complete their family story.

Numerous academic colleagues generously shared their knowledge and offered insights or comments on drafts. Among those to whom I owe a considerable degree of gratitude are Joanne Bailey for her research on the family and the discussions we had about models of fatherhood; Karen Harvey, also an expert on men and the family, for comments on a draft of an earlier article;

Michele Cohen for advice on education and masculinity; Brycchan Carey for his insights into East and West India Company rivalry and slavery; Penelope Corfield for her research on regency towns and the legal profession as well as advice about eighteenth-century monetary values; Pat Crimmin for her encyclopedic knowledge of shipping and transportation records; Gregory Durston and Michael Lobban for patient guidance through the more tortuous technicalities of early-nineteenth-century law; Tim Hitchcock and Peter King for their excellent advice on crime and punishment and comments on early drafts of legal sections; Amanda Goodrich for assistance with Edmund Burke; and Zeta Moore for help with military matters. Tony Stockwell, Sarah Ansari, and, particularly, Francis Robinson provided invaluable research guidance and comments on the Indian chapter. And last but not least, Zoe Laidlaw set me off on the right tracks for Australian colonial history.

No book gets written well, however, without professional support and comments, and for that I would like to thank my agent, Peter Robinson, but principally my editor, Lara Heimart, whose advice has proved invaluable. I am very grateful for a grant from the late Miss Isobel Thornsley's bequest to the University of London for assistance with the publication of this book. Finally, and particularly because this is a book about family, I would like to say my biggest thank-you to my own very patient and supportive family. My father, Roger Moore, read every draft chapter as soon as the last word was typed to ensure I kept up the pace of production, and he provided useful comments on how they read to a "layman." My father-in-law, Jeffrey Phillips, commented on a chapter and helped my research into nineteenth-century attorneys and lawyers. Penelope Speake in Cheltenham helped search for local history and newspaper coverage of the Gloucester Assizes. My eldest son, Sam, although he didn't realize it at the time, provided much of the initial inspiration for this book and thought-provoking proof of the difficulties facing male teenagers today. He is also probably unaware that writing it, I think, made me a more understanding mother. Finally, I could never have finished the book without the constant support, encouragement, and sterling editorial services of my husband, Jonathan—no one could have given more.

NOTES

ABBREVIATIONS

BL   British Library

CUP   Cambridge University Press

FI   *Filial Ingratitude; Or, The Profligate Son* by William Collins Jackson

GA   Gloucestershire Archives

HRA   *Historical Records of Australia*

LMA   London Metropolitan Archives

MUP   Manchester University Press

NSW   New South Wales

OBP   Old Bailey Proceedings Online

OUP   Oxford University Press

PP   House of Commons Parliamentary Papers Online

SRNSW   State Records of New South Wales (Government Archives)

TNA   The National Archives (UK)

INTRODUCTION

1. Margaret Hunt, *The Middling Sort: Commerce, Gender, and the Family in England, 1680–1780* (London: University of California Press, 1996), 49, 72. For examples, see "Infection of Profligacy," *Britannic Magazine* 5, 67 (1794): 336–338; "Singular Conversation of the Widow's Profligate Son," *Evangelical Magazine* (1796): 246–247; George Watson, *The Profligate: A Comedy* (1820), a play penned for private publication in 1808; and the poem "The Consolations of Universal Restoration," *Lancaster Gazette and General Advertiser,* December 26, 1812, depicting a widow's grief at the grave of her profligate son. Samuel Johnson, *A Dictionary of the English Language,* 4th ed. (1777), 1580. *Disobedient son and cruel husband, being a full and true account of one Mr. John Jones, a gentleman's son in Wiltshire, whose father left him an estate . . . and married a lady of great fortune . . . but . . . killed his wife and children, and afterwards hanged his mother on a tree in the orchatd* [sic]. *With the last dying words of this wretch, who was tried and executed this assizes before his mother's door* (ca. 1790). See also the ordinary (chaplain) of Newgate's accounts— criminal biographies and confessions of the convicted just prior to their execution as told to and published by the Newgate chaplain, http://www.oldbaileyonline.org/static/Ordinarys -accounts.jsp.

2. Anne Stott, *Hannah More: The First Victorian* (Oxford: OUP, 2003), 169; Sarah More, *The Cheapside Apprentice: or, The History of Mr. Francis H* (1796). The *Cheap Repository tracts* continued to be reprinted and sold until the 1840s.

3. Marilyn Morris, "Princely Debt, Public Credit, and Commercial Values in Late Georgian Britain," *Journal of British Studies* 43, 3 (July 2004): 340, also notes that these portrayals of the royal family relied on stereotypes of divisions between social classes that did not reflect a clear-cut reality. William Joliffe, *The Times*, May 16, 1795, cited at 346.

4. The Hon. Shute Barrington, Prince Bishop of Durham, *Parliamentary History*, 34:1307, cited in Ben Wilson, *Decency and Disorder: The Age of Cant, 1789–1837* (London: Faber and Faber, 2007), 16. Wilson examines in depth the clash of moral values at the time.

5. Wilson, *Decency and Disorder*, xxxiii. Pierce Egan, *Tom & Jerry: Life in London*, 72, 102 (London: John Camden, 1869 ed.; originally published in 1821).

6. Quoted in John Camden Hotten, "Introduction," to Egan, *Tom & Jerry*, 3.

7. John Moore, MD, *Zeluco: Various Views of Human Nature Taken from Life and Manners Foreign and Domestic*, 2nd ed. (London, 1789; originally published in 1786), 1:4. Pam Perkins, "Zeluco," in *The Literary Encyclopedia*, October 8, 2003, http://www.litencyc.com/php/sworks .php?rec=true&UID=13718, accessed August 13, 2007. William Shakespeare, *King Lear*, act 3, scene 4.

8. Kate Retford, *The Art of Domestic Life: Family Portraiture in Eighteenth-Century England* (London: Yale University Press, 2006), 114; Matthew McCormack, "Married Men and the Fathers of Families: Fatherhood and Franchise Reform in Britain," in *Gender and Fatherhood in the Nineteenth Century*, ed. by Trev Lynn Broughton and Helen Rogers (Basingstoke, UK: Palgrave, 2007), 47–48. On parenthood, the formation of personal and public identity, and patriotism, see Joanne Bailey, *Parenting in England, 1760–1830: Emotion, Identity, and Generation* (Oxford: OUP, 2012), 97–124.

9. William Collins Jackson, *Memoir of the Public Conduct and Services of William Collins Jackson Esq., Late Senior Merchant of the Company*, 2nd ed. (London, 1812).

10. I wish to reiterate my gratitude to Amanda Bevan and, particularly, to Liz Hore of the National Archives for their help with this material.

11. On the eighteenth-century culture of letter writing, styles, and conventions, see, for example, Susan Whyman, *The Pen and the People: English Letter Writers, 1660–1800* (Oxford: OUP, 2009), 19–45; and Sarah M. Pearsall, *Atlantic Families: Lives and Letters in the Later Eighteenth Century* (Oxford: OUP, 2008), 1–3.

CHAPTER 1: THE SINS OF THE FATHERS

1. There are many variant spellings of Kattobomma Nayakar's name. He is also known as Vira Pandya Kattobomman, and the eighteenth-century British referred to him as "Catobama Naig" or just the "poligar of Pandalumcourchy."

2. William Collins Jackson, *Memoir of the Public Conduct and Services of William Collins Jackson Esq., Late Senior Merchant of the Company*, 2nd ed. (1812), 46, presents a summary of a report from the East India Company commercial resident at Tinnevelly (Tirunelveli). For a contextualized, modern account taken from Madras Board of Revenue papers, see Raman N. Seylon, "Study of Poligar Violence in Late 18th Century Tamil Country in South India," *African and Asian Studies* 3, 3–4 (2004): 255–257.

3. William Hickey, *Memoirs of William Hickey*, ed. by Peter Quennell (London: Routledge and Kegan Paul, 1975), 106–108, gives a vivid description of his landing at Madras. Quoted in Tillman W. Nechtman, "Nabobs Revisited: A Cultural History of British Imperialism and the Indian Question in Late-Eighteenth-Century Britain," *History Compass* 4, 4 (July 2006): 645–667.

4. The history of the East India Company and its role in establishing British rule in India is complex. For a useful overview, see Philip Lawson, *The East India Company: A*

History (London: Longman, 1993). On the relationships among the company, city of London financial institutions, the state, and the empire, see H. V. Bowen, *The Business of Empire: The East India Company and Imperial Britain, 1756–1833* (Cambridge: CUP, 2006), esp. 29–52.

5. James Prior, *A visit to Madras: being a sketch of the local and characteristic peculiarities of that presidency in the year 1811* (London, 1821), 8; William Dalrymple, *White Mughals: Love and Betrayal in Eighteenth-Century India* (London: HarperCollins, 2004), 448. Alexander Dalrymple, *A letter to the Court of Directors for the Affairs of the United Company of Merchants of England Trading in the East Indies* (1769), 10–11. Bowen, *The Business of Empire*, 157–159.

6. Jackson, *Memoir*, 5.

7. Warren Hastings, cited in Nicholas B. Dirks, *The Scandal of Empire: India and the Creation of Imperial Britain* (London: Belknap Press, 2006), 55, 6–7.

8. George Shee, Calcutta, to Jackson, November 14, 1789, TNA, C/106/64/1. Edmund Burke, *Correspondence of Edmund Burke*, ed. by Alfred Cobban and Roberta A. Smith (Cambridge: CUP, 1967), 6:11; Edmund Burke, "Speech in Opening the Impeachment of Warren Hastings," February 16, 1788, in *The Writings and Speeches of Edmund Burke*, ed. by P. J. Marshall (Oxford: Clarendon Press, 1991), 6:346.

9. Hickey, *Memoirs*, 242–243. For more on Shee and for a detailed analysis of the case of company official Philip Francis and writer George Francis Grand, see Linda Colley, *The Ordeal of Elizabeth Marsh: A Woman in World History* (London: HarperCollins, 2007), 275–285; and Dirks, *Scandal of Empire*, 96–97.

10. Sir George Shee to Elizabeth Crisp (née Marsh), March 1783, BL, Add Mss. 60338, B2 fols. 54–55. For an excellent account of Elizabeth Marsh's life and travels, see Colley, *Ordeal of Elizabeth Marsh*; for Shee's courtship of her daughter Elizabeth Maria Crisp, see 284–285.

11. Dirks, *Scandal of Empire*, 9, 81, 88. Colley, *Ordeal of Elizabeth Marsh*, 285–286, argues that Shee's role in collecting and transmitting evidence against Hastings to Burke and Philip Francis was a form of revenge for the scandal he himself had suffered. On the trial of Warren Hastings (1788–1795), see Dirks, *Scandal of Empire*, 87–131. For an analysis of why Burke failed to secure a conviction, see Paul Langford, "Burke, Edmund (1729/30–1797)," in *Oxford Dictionary of National Biography* (Oxford: OUP, 2004), http://www.oxforddnb.com/view/article/4019, accessed February 14, 2011.

12. The East India Company List of Civil Servants (1771) shows both Shee and Evelyn joined as writers in 1770. Dalrymple, *White Mughals*, 34.

13. Helen Evelyn, *The History of the Evelyn Family* (London: Eveleigh Nash, 1915), http://archive.org/details/historyofevelynfooeveluoft, accessed May 3, 2012.

14. The Carnatic was a region of southern India that stretched from the Eastern Ghats to the Coromandel coast. Jackson, *Memoir*, 14–20.

15. James Balfour's testimony to the Ramnad Committee, Proceedings and Correspondence of the Ramnad Committee, BL, IOR/H/440; emphasis added.

16. Jackson, *Memoir*, 44–45; Proceedings and Correspondence of the Ramnad Committee, 352. Seylon, "Study of Poligar Violence," 252–253.

17. Seylon, "Study of Poligar Violence," 253–254.

18. Ibid., 263–270. My analysis of the protracted encounters between Jackson and Kattobomma Nayakar is based on Raman Seylon's use of the game metaphor to explain poligar politics in late-eighteenth-century Tamil country. The Ramalingavisam Palace was

the official office or court where administrative and judicial business was conducted. Seylon, "Study of Poligar Violence," 92.

19. Jackson, *Memoir*, 42–43.

20. Jackson, *Memoir*, 43. T. G. P. Spear, *The Nabobs: A Study of the English in Eighteenth-Century India* (Oxford: OUP, 1932), 138, notes that Lord Wellesley used to address the nawab of Arcot in "the tone of a hectoring schoolmaster." Jackson, *Memoir*, 37.

21. My account of events at Ramnad in September 1798 has been reconstructed using Jackson's *Memoir*, 39–46; Proceedings and Correspondence of the Ramnad Committee, BL, IOR/H/440, 327–382; Seylon, "Study of Poligar Violence," 255–258; Kunjukrishnan Nadar Rajayyan, *The Rise and Fall of the Poligars of Tamilnadu* (Madras: University of Madras, 1974), 92–93; and Robert Caldwell, *A political and general history of the District of Tinnevelly, in the Presidency of Madras, from the earliest period to its cession to the English Government in A.D. 1801* (London, 1881), 173–174, http://www.ebooksread.com/authors-eng/robert-cald well/a-political-and-general-history-of-the-district-of-tinnevelly-in-the-presidency -hci/1-a-political-and-general-history-of-the-district-of-tinnevelly-in-the-presidency-hci .shtml, accessed March 16, 2011. Jackson estimated that four thousand armed men appeared outside Ramnad, but Caldwell suggests that he may have exaggerated.

22. Correspondence of the Board of Revenue and Lord Clive, cited in Caldwell, *A political and general history of the District of Tinnevelly*, 168–170; Rajayyan, *The Rise and Fall of the Poligars*, 93.

23. Jackson, *Memoir*, 39.

24. See, for example, receipt from Coutts & Co for a deposit of £10,091 5s., June 5, 1809, TNA, C/106/70; correspondence regarding a mortgage Jackson gave to Lord Moira for more than £10,000, TNA, C/106/67; and letters from Thomas Coutts to Jackson, including offers of help and expressions of friendship, such as on August 12, 1800, TNA, C/106/67. In 1807 William claimed that his father had £40,000 deposited with Coutts. On banks and early-nineteenth-century aristocratic indebtedness, see David Cannadine, *Aspects of Aristocracy: Grandeur and Decline in Modern Britain* (New Haven, CT: Yale University Press, 1994), 37–45, 53.

25. See, for example, Jackson's refusal to help his deserted, impoverished sister-in-law: correspondence between George Shee in Dublin and Jackson, Bath, November 7, 1799, and reply, January 13, 1800; Jackson to Lt. Col. John Shee, February 16, 1800; letters from Selina Shee to George Shee, April 10, May 6, and September 27–December 5, 1800; and Jane Jackson replies, October 4–December 15, 1800, TNA, C/106/64/1. Letter from Mr. Bingley declaring it a "damned scandal" that Jackson had failed to honor his father's bond, September 17, 1807; and letter of March 25, 1812, regretting his former rage, TNA, C/106/66/1. Jackson to Mrs. Pyke, September 4, 1806, TNA, C/106/64/1.

26. On transferring family hopes and values to the next generation, see Joanne Bailey, *Parenting in England, 1760–1830: Emotion, Identity, and Generation* (Oxford: OUP, 2012), 174–176.

27. See Amanda Vickery, *Behind Closed Doors: At Home in Georgian England* (London: Yale University Press, 2009), 82, 87, on the home as "a cradle for personal happiness and a platform for social success" for married men.

28. George Evelyn to Jackson, August 24, 1805, TNA, C/106/69.

29. Evelyn, *History of the Evelyn Family*, 244. Mrs. M. Bingley to Jackson, August 18, 1803; and to Jane Jackson, August 30, 1803, TNA, C/106/68.

30. East India Company Court of Directors, London, to Fort St. George, Madras, May 4, 1803, TNA, C/106/64/1.

31. Jackson's description of his circumstances at the time recorded at a General Meeting of the Subscribers to the Civil Fund in Madras, May 1809, TNA, C/106/66.

32. Bowen, *Business of Empire*, 119–123. The salary was not huge, but at that time patronage was seen as a legitimate perquisite of the job.

CHAPTER 2: AN IMPROPER EDUCATION

1. John Locke, *Some Thoughts Concerning Education* (New York: P. F. Collier and Son, [1693] 1909–1914), vol. 37, pt. 1, para. 70, www.bartleby.com/37/1/, accessed May 28, 2012. William Barrow, *An Essay on Education* (London, 1804; originally published 1802), 87.

2. Barrow, *Essay on Education*, 89–90, 115. For the debate on public versus private education, see Michele Cohen, "Gender and the Private/Public Debate on Education in the Long Eighteenth Century," in *Public or Private Education? Lessons from History*, ed. by Richard Aldrich (London: Woburn Press, 2004), 2–24; and F. Musgrove, "Middle-Class Families and Schools, 1780–1880: Interaction and Exchange of Function Between Institutions," in *Sociology, History, and Education*, ed. by P. W. Musgrave (London: Methuen, 1970), 117–125.

3. George Shee to Sir George Shee, September 1803, BL, Add. Ms 60338/ B25.

4. John Lawson and Harold Silver, *A Social History of Education in England* (London: Methuen, 1973), 200–201. Christopher Tyerman, *A History of Harrow School, 1324–1991* (Oxford: OUP, 2000), 145, notes that in 1803 the headmaster claimed that among the present or future titled pupils at the school were three dukes, seven earls and viscounts, one marquess, four lords, twenty-one honorables, and four baronets.

5. Jackson to William, April 28, 1808, *FI*, 1:29, TNA, C/106/65. Margaret Hunt, *The Middling Sort: Commerce, Gender, and the Family in England, 1680–1780* (London: University of California Press, 1996), 65; Nicholas Rogers, "Money, Land, and Lineage: The Big Bourgeoisie of Hanoverian London," *Social History* 4, 3 (1979): 438; Penelope J. Corfield, "The Rivals: Landed and Other Gentlemen," in *Land and Society in Britain, 1700–1914*, ed. by Negley Harte and Roland Quinault (Manchester, UK: MUP, 1996), 13–15.

6. Vicesimus Knox, *Liberal Education: or, a practical treatise on the methods of acquiring a useful and polite education*, 7th ed. (London, 1785), 2:342. Winchester School, "The History of the School of Harrow," in *The History of the Colleges of Winchester, Eton and Westminster with the Charterhouse, the Schools of St. Pauls, Merchant Taylors, Harrow and Rugby and the Free School of Christ's Hospital* (London, 1816) 14; Tyerman, *History of Harrow School*, 140–166.

7. Bill and note from Mr. Bowen, Harrow School, December 9, 1812, TNA, C/106/70.

8. Catherine Dille, "Lessons in Liberty: Schoolboy Rebellions in the English Great Public Schools, 1770–1820," paper presented at the Institute for Historical Research, London, May 5, 2012. On Byron's revolt at Harrow in 1805, see Tyerman, *History of Harrow School*, 164–165, who downplays the poet's involvement.

9. Tyerman, *History of Harrow School*, 145, 155–156. Historians have noted that the impact of the French wars—when as many as one in ten men experienced some form of military service—meant that military manliness was highly valued, at least until 1815, particularly among the sons of those educated at elite schools. See, for example, Linda Colley, *Britons: Forging the Nation, 1707–1837* (London: Pimlico, 1992), 167–172, 178; and Vic Gattrell, *City of Laughter: Sex and Satire in Eighteenth-Century London* (London: Atlantic

Books, 2006), 110–115. Nicola Phillips, "Parenting the Profligate Son: Masculinity, Gentility, and Juvenile Delinquency in England, 1791–1814," *Gender & History* 22, 1 (April 2010): 92–108.

10. Boyd Hilton, *A Mad, Bad, & Dangerous People? England, 1783–1846* (Oxford: OUP, 2006), 100–101; J. E. Cookson, "The English Volunteer Movement of the French Wars, 1793–1815: Some Contexts," *Historical Journal* 32 (1989): 867–189, doi:10.1017/S0018246X00015740, accessed November 12, 2012. Colley, *Britons*, 167–169. Helen Evelyn, *The History of the Evelyn Family* (London: Eveleigh Nash, 1915), 247, 25, http://archive.org/details/historyofevelynfooeveluoft, accessed May 3, 2012.

11. Barrow, *Essay on Education*, 114–115. Lawson and Silver, *Social History of Education*, 204. Advertisement for Loughborough House School, TNA, C/106/67.

12. Bills from Loughborough House School from Xmas 1805 to midsummer 1807, TNA, C/106/70. Barrow, *Essay on Education,* 115. Thomas Willett to Jackson, May 31, 1807, TNA, C/106/70. William to Macqueen, June 22, 1807, TNA, C/106/65.

13. Jane Jackson to Letitia Shee, April 21, 1809, explaining that they had been unable to visit because they had only just moved to their London home and were "without a carriage to visit our friends," TNA, C/106/64.

14. Macqueen to William, June 19, 1807, TNA, C/106/65.

15. William to Macqueen, June 22, 1807, TNA, C/106/65.

16. Clergy of the Church of England database, http://www.theclergydatabase.org.uk/jsp/persons/index.jsp, accessed November 30, 2010. "Plan of Education," enclosed in letter from Reverend Helps to Jackson, July 8, 1807, TNA, C/106/65/1.

17. Reverend Helps to Jackson, July 8 and 19, 1807, TNA, C/106/65/1.

18. Jackson to Helps, July 18, 1807, TNA, C/106/65/1.

19. *Law Review* 1 (1844): 318–320, cited in J. M. Beattie, "Garrow, Sir William (1760–1840)," in *Oxford Dictionary of National Biography* (Oxford: OUP, 2004), http://www.oxforddnb.com/view/article/10410, accessed December 2, 2010; John H. Langbein, *The Origins of Adversary Criminal Trial* (Oxford: OUP, 2005), 254–255, 291–307; Allyson N. May, *The Bar & the Old Bailey, 1750–1850* (London: University of North Carolina Press, 2003), 106–117. A copy of William Garrow's opinion in a bundle of documents from Randle Jackson (Mr. Jackson's legal advisor, the East India Company's parliamentary counsel, and a contemporary of Garrow's at the Old Bailey in the 1790s), TNA, C/106/66/1. See also May, *The Bar & the Old Bailey*, 44, 251, 252–253. Garrow had become very successful in civil as well as criminal law, and since 1805 he had been a Whig MP.

20. Nicholas Hans, *New Trends in Education in the Eighteenth Century* (London: Routledge, 1951), 117–119. Barrow, *Essay on Education*, 106, declares "such seminaries" to be "the favourite of the day."

21. Barrow, *Essay on Education,* 107–108. Jackson to Helps, August 8, 1807, TNA, C/106/65. For a picture and description of the priory at Monken Hadley, see John Hostettler and Richard Braby, *Sir William Garrow: His Life, Times, and Fight for Justice* (Hook, UK: Waterside Press, 2010), 22–24.

22. Jane Jackson to William, August 6, 1807, TNA, C/106/65.

23. Ibid., enclosed note from Jackson.

24. Jackson to William, August 12, 1807, TNA, C/106/65.

25. Locke, *Some Thoughts Concerning Education*, para. 108. Jackson to Helps, August 13, 1807, TNA, C/106/65.

26. Helps to Jackson, August 14, 1807, TNA, C/106/65. The connection between love and family duty can be found in advice literature throughout the eighteenth and early nineteenth centuries. See, for example, William Fleetwood, *The Relative Duties of Parents and Children, Husbands and Wives, Masters and Servants, Considered in Sixteen Sermons: with three more upon the case of self-murther,* 16th ed. (London, 1811); Ann Taylor, *Reciprocal Duties of Parents and Children* (London: Taylor and Hessey, 1818); and Philip Carter, *Men and the Emergence of Polite Society, 1660–1800* (New York: Pearson Education, 2000), 99. Helps to Jackson, August 14, 1807, TNA, C/106/65.

27. William to Jackson, August 17, 1807, TNA, C/106/65.

28. Jackson to William, August 18, 1807, TNA, C/106/65. Macqueen to William, August 25, 1807, TNA, C/106/65.

29. Anonymous note enclosed in letter from Richardson to Jackson, August 26, 1807, TNA, C/106/65.

30. I wish to thank Brycchan Carey for information about the hostility at public schools toward the sons of West Indian plantation owners. The Abolition of Slavery Bill, which only prevented the carriage of slaves on British ships, was passed on March 25, 1807. Jackson to William, August 28, 1807, TNA, C/106/65.

31. Richardson to Jackson, August 26, 1807; Jackson to William, August 27, 1807; William to Richardson, August 29 and 30, 1807; Macqueen to William, September, 9, 12, 22, 29, and 30, 1807, October 1807, TNA, C/106/65. Jackson to Helps, January 12, 1808, reminding Helps of his former assessment of William's character, TNA, C/106/65.

32. William to Jackson, October 2, 1807, TNA, C/106/65.

33. Jane Jackson to William, November 22, 1807, TNA, C/106/65.

34. Dan Cruickshank, *The Secret History of Georgian London: How the Wages of Sin Shaped the Capital* (London: Random House, 2009), xvi–xvii, 164–165, 172–173.

35. William to Jackson, January 2, 1808, TNA, C/106/65, relates the whole of the events of Saturday and Sunday, November 21–22, 1807. On Georgian fears of the darkness, see Amanda Vickery, *Behind Closed Doors: At Home in Georgian England* (London: Yale University Press, 1998), 31–33.

36. Jackson to William, July 24 and 25, 1807; William to Jackson, July 24, 1807, TNA, C/106/65.

37. Draft copy of a letter from William to Jackson, January 1808, TNA, C/106/65. Helps to Jackson, January 1, 1808, TNA C/106/65. Knox, *Liberal Education,* 356–357. Helps to Jackson, January 1, 1808.

38. Locke, *Some Thoughts Concerning Education,* para. 110; Knox, *Liberal Education,* 73.

39. Helps to Jackson, January 1, 1808; Jackson to Helps, January 12 and 13, 1808, TNA, C/106/65.

40. Jackson to Cotterell, January 25, 1808, TNA, C/106/65.

CHAPTER 3: LESSONS IN LOVE AND LIFE IN LONDON

1. Roy Porter, *London: A Social History* (London: Penguin, 1994), 160–165. On the reformation of manners and religious revival, see Ben Wilson, *Decency and Disorder: The Age of Cant, 1789–1837* (London: Faber and Faber, 2007), esp. 106–130. George Coleman, *The Heir at Law: A Comedy in Five Acts* (London, 1797), Act 2, scene 3, 46.

2. C. A. G. Goede, *A Stranger in England; or Travels in Great Britain* (London, 1807), 76–78. For descriptions of Bond Street, see Ian Kelly, *Beau Brummell: The Ultimate Dandy* (London: Hodder and Stoughton, 2005), 188–190.

3. Jane Rendell, *The Pursuit of Pleasure: Gender, Space, and Architecture in Regency London* (London: Athlone Press, 2002), 31. Different modes of pleasurable walking around town, such as "a ramble," "a stroll," "a promenade," "a grand strut," "a turn," or just "a look in," are constantly depicted in Pierce Egan, *Tom & Jerry: Life in London* (1821). Rees Howell Gronow, *Reminiscences of Captain Gronow: Being anecdotes of the Camp, Court, Clubs and Society, 1810–1860*, abridged and with an introduction by John Raymond (London: Bodley Head, 1964), 58.

4. Jackson, "History of a Profligate founded on facts," his comparative notes of events that spring, quoting from William's statement about his relationship with Henry, TNA, C/106/65.

5. Peter Wagner, "Introduction," to John Cleland, *Fanny Hill; Or, Memoirs of a Woman of Pleasure* (London: Penguin Classics, 1985), 13–16. On *Fanny Hill* and censorship in the erotic book trade, see Julie Peakman, *Mighty Lewd Books: The Development of Pornography in Eighteenth-Century England* (Basingstoke, UK: Palgrave Macmillan, 2003), 6, 21, 39–44, 161–163.

6. See a copy of "A Proclamation for the Encouragement of Piety and Virtue, and for the Preventing and Punishing of Vice, Profaneness and Immorality; George R," *Gentleman's Magazine and Historical Chronicle* 57, 1 (1787): 534–535. M. J. D. Roberts, "The Society for the Suppression of Vice and Its Early Critics, 1802–1812," *Historical Journal* 26, 1 (1983): 160–161; Wilson, *Decency and Disorder*, 120, 119–123.

7. Jackson, "History of a Profligate." William to Jackson, March 22, 1808, TNA, C/106/65.

8. Roy Porter and Lesley Hall, *The Facts of Life: The Creation of Sexual Knowledge in Britain, 1650–1950* (London: Yale University Press, 1995), 35–44; Cleland, *Fanny Hill*, 224.

9. William cited in Jackson's account of events he labeled, "History of a Profligate," Henry Keighly to Jackson, March 21, 1808, TNA, C/106/65.

10. Porter and Hall, *Facts of Life*, 22–24; Leslie Mitchell, *The Whig World* (London: Hambledon, 2005), 42; Venetia Murray, *High Society in the Regency Period* (London: Penguin, 1999), 134–156; Anthony Fletcher, *Gender, Sex, & Subordination in England, 1500–1800* (London: Yale University Press, 1995), 342–343.

11. Margaret Hunt, *The Middling Sort: Commerce, Gender, and the Family in England, 1680–1780* (London: University of California Press, 1996), 71, 113, 162–163. Theophilus Christian, *The Fashionable World Displayed* (London, 1804), 18, http://www.archive.org/stream/fashionableworlooowengoog#page/no/mode/2up, accessed May 5, 2011.

12. William to Jackson, March 2, 1808, TNA, C/106/65.

13. Jackson's copy of William's "confession" and his comments on it, *FI*, 1:4–5, TNA, C/106/65.

14. Kelly, *Beau Brummell*, 262–269; Wilson, *Decency and Disorder*, 196–201; Murray, *High Society*, 220–221. Christian, *Fashionable World*, 46–47.

15. William to Jackson, March 22, 1808, TNA, C/106/65.

16. Jackson to Owen, March 18, 1808; Owen to Jackson, March 21, 1808, TNA, C/106/65.

17. William Fleetwood, *The Relative Duties of Parents and Children, Husbands and Wives, Masters and Servants, Considered in Sixteen Sermons: with three more upon the case of self-murther*, 16th ed. (London, 1811), 140–157; William Blackstone, *Commentaries on the Laws of England*, 16th ed. (London, 1811), 447–448.

18. Roy Porter, *Quacks: Fakers and Charlatans in Medicine* (Stroud, UK: Tempus, 2003), 212, 216. There was no distinction between gonorrhea (the clap) and syphilis (the pox), the former being seen as a mild form of the latter. Keighly to Jackson, March 21, 1808, TNA, C/106/65.

19. Owen to Jackson, March 21, 1808, TNA, C/106/65.

20. W. M. Childs, *The Town of Reading During the Early Part of the Nineteenth Century* (Reading, UK: University College, 1910), 13, 69–72, http://www.archive.org /stream/townofreadingduroochiluoft#page/12/mode/2up, accessed May 11, 2011. Jackson to Valpy, March 14, 19, 24, and 30, 1808; Valpy to Jackson, March 21 and 27, 1808; William to Valpy, March 30, 1808, *FI*, 1:12–18, TNA, C/106/65.

21. T. A. B. Corley, "Valpy, Richard (1754–1836)," in *Oxford Dictionary of National Biography* (Oxford: OUP, 2004), www.oxforddnb.com/view/article/28057, accessed August 8, 2007.

22. Hobhouse to William, Bickley, and Wells, April 23, 1808, TNA C106/65; Lawson and Silver, *A Social History*, 254–255.

23. Jackson's account of meeting Miss Clifford's housekeeper, TNA, C/106/65.

24. Hobhouse to William, Bickley, and Wells, April 23, 1808; Neville to William, Bickley, and Wells, April 23, 1808, TNA, C106/65.

25. William to Jackson, April 26, 1808, *FI*, 1:21–22, TNA, C/106/65.

26. Jackson to William, April 26, 1808, *FI*, 1:23, TNA, C/106/65.

27. On the mixing and the differences between landed and merchant society, see Amanda Vickery, *The Gentleman's Daughter: Women's Lives in Georgian England* (London: Yale University Press, 1998), 13–37; Penelope J. Corfield, "The Rivals: Landed and Other Gentlemen," in *Land and Society in Britain, 1700–1914*, ed. by Negley Harte and Roland Quinault (Manchester, UK: MUP, 1996), 1–33; and Nicholas Rogers, "Money, Land, and Lineage: The Big Bourgeoisie of Hanoverian London," *Social History* 4, 3 (1979): 437–454.

28. Vicesimus Knox, *Liberal Education: or, a practical treatise on the methods of acquiring a useful and polite education*, 7th ed. (London, 1785), 379. Hunt, *Middling Sort*, 67, 69, 71, 112–113, 162–163; Tony Henderson, *Disorderly Women in Eighteenth-Century London: Prostitution and Control in the Metropolis, 1730–1830* (London: Longman, 1999), 166–177. *FI*, 1:24, TNA, C/106/65.

29. *FI*, 1:24–25, TNA, C/106/65.

30. Jackson to Valpy, April 27, 1808, *FI*, 1: 27, TNA, C/106/65.

31. Hobhouse to William, May 29, 1808, TNA, C/106/65.

32. Jackson to William, April 30, 1808, *FI*, 1:28, TNA, C/106/65.

33. William to Jackson, May 1, 1808, *FI*, 1:30, TNA, C/106/65.

34. Jackson to William, May 2, 1808, *FI*, 1:31, TNA, C/106/65.

35. E. A. Smith, *George IV* (London: Yale University Press, 1999), 277–284. J. A. Sharpe, *Crime in Early Modern England, 1550–1750*, 2nd ed. (London: Longman, 1999), 7–10; quotation from James Neild, *State of the Prisons in England, Scotland, and Wales* (London, 1812), lvii; Isaac Taylor, *Advice to the Teens, or, Practical Helps Towards the Formation of One's Own Character*, 2nd ed. (Boston: Wells and Lilley, 1820), 173. William to Jackson, Langley Lodge, July 11, 1808, TNA, C/106/65.

36. William to Jackson, Gloucester Place, September 10, 1808; bill from Messrs. Currie and Co., Hatton Garden, TNA C/106/65; Currie and Co., surgeons, advertisement, *The Times*, August 23, 1825, cited in *British Medical Journal*, December 25, 1926, 1232, http://www.ncbi.nlm.nih.gov/pmc/articles/PMC2524210/pdf/brmedjo8358–0028b.pdf,

accessed May 23, 2011. On the blurred lines between professional physicians, surgeons, apothecaries, and commercial practitioners, see Penelope J. Corfield, *Power and the Professions in Britain, 1700–1800* (London: Routledge, 1995), 149–155. And see Porter, *Quacks,* 211–221, for common features of "Quack" cures for venereal disease.

37. Porter, *Quacks,* 217.

CHAPTER 4: AN OFFICER AND A GENTLEMAN

1. William to Jackson, January 18, 1809, *FI,* 1:43, TNA, C/106/65.

2. Thomas Parry, squire of Llidiadom, ca. 1800, and Henry Fox, 1750, cited in Anthony Fletcher, *Gender, Sex, & Subordination in England, 1500–1800* (London: Yale University Press, 1995), 343.

3. Jackson to William, January 20, 1809, *FI,* 1:46, TNA, C/106/65.

4. William to Jackson, January 18, 1809, *FI,* 1:43, TNA, C/106/65.

5. *The Times,* January 27, 1809, The Times Digital Archive, 1785–1985; *Morning Post,* January 27, 1809, 19th Century British Library Newspapers Online: Part II.

6. Joseph Addison, *The Spectator* 11, 99 (1794), explains that "the great violation of the Point of Honour from Man to Man, is giving the Lie . . . because no other Vice implies a Want of Courage so much as the making of a Lie" cited in Donna T. Andrew, "The Code of Honour and Its Critics: The Opposition to Duelling in England, 1700–1850," *Social History* 5, 3 (1980): 411. Lt. Samuel Stanton, *The Principles of Duelling; with Rules to be Observed in every Particular Respecting It* (London, 1790), 35–36.

7. William (note from Holborn) to Jackson, April 12, 1809, TNA, C/106/65.

8. Stanton, *Principles of Duelling,* 59–60, 77–78; Robert Shoemaker, "The Taming of the Duel: Masculinity, Honour, and Ritual Violence in London, 1660–1800," *Historical Journal* 45, 3 (2002): 525–545.

9. William (Cheapside) to Jackson, and later note with Jackson's comment, April 13, 1809, TNA, C/106/65.

10. See Amanda Vickery, *The Gentleman's Daughter: Women's Lives in Georgian England* (London: Yale University Press, 1998), 242–244. Public London masquerades were considered far worse than provincial or private ones.

11. Andrew, "Code of Honour," 409–434; Steve Banks, "Dangerous Friends: The Second and the Later English Duel," *Journal for the Society of Eighteenth-Century Studies* 32, 1 (2009): 104; Arthur N. Gilbert, "Law and Honour Among Eighteenth-Century British Army Officers," *Historical Journal* 19, 1 (1976): 775–787. Shoemaker, "Taming of the Duel," 542, 544–545, notes that, despite more "civilised" attitudes and middle-class opposition, dueling remained common in London, but was conducted almost exclusively between members of the nobility, gentry, and military.

12. Jackson to William, May 3, 1809, *FI,* 1:48, TNA, C/106/65.

13. William to Jane Jackson, May 2, 1809, *FI,* 1:46, TNA, C/106/65. Isaac Taylor, *Advice to the Teens, or, Practical Helps Towards the Formation of One's Own Character* (Boston: Wells and Lilley, 1820), 85, 87.

14. William to Jackson, May 2 and 4, 1809; Jackson to William, May 3 and 8, 1809; William to Jane, May 22, 1809, *FI,* 1:47–53, TNA, C/106/65. Thomas Gisborne, *An Enquiry into the Duties of Men In the Higher and Middle Classes of Society in Great Britain,* 6th ed. (London, 1811), 2:486.

15. Roy Porter, *English Society in the Eighteenth Century,* rev. ed. (London: Penguin, 1990), xv. Boyd Hilton, *A Mad, Bad, & Dangerous People? England, 1783–1846* (Oxford:

OUP, 2006), 127–128, suggests *"upper*-middle-class gentility" required an income of £200–300 (italics added). William to Jane Jackson, July 2, 1809, *FI*, 1:53, TNA, C/106/65.

16. Taylor, *Advice to the Teens*, 166–167.

17. These figures are abstracted from a later letter to William from Jackson of May 14, 1810, in which he included a "List of *some* of the debts" William incurred in 1809, *FI*, 1:83, TNA, C/106/65.

18. On the nature of credit relations and adolescent male legal agency, see Margot C. Finn, *The Character of Credit: Personal Debt in English Culture, 1740–1914* (Cambridge: CUP, 2003), 7–9, 14, 239, 273–275. On the importance of signatures, see Randall Mc-Gowan, "Forgery Discovered, or the Perils of Circulation in Eighteenth-Century England," *Angelaki* 1 (1994): 113–129.

19. Andrew, "Code of Honour," 415.

20. Jackson to Mr. Lee, September 24, 1809, *FI*, 1:62, TNA, C/106/65.

21. *FI*, 1:54–65, TNA, C/106/65.

22. William to Evelyn, October 21, enclosed in a letter from Evelyn to Jackson, October 21, 1809, both copied by Jackson, *FI*, 1:75, TNA, C/106/65. The duel between Castlereagh and Canning at Putney Heath on September 21 was first discussed in *The Times*, September 22, 1809, and then intermittently into October. William to Evelyn, October 21, 1809.

23. Gilbert, "Law and Honour," 80–83; Shoemaker, "Taming of the Duel," 540. *FI*, 1:66, TNA, C/106/65.

24. Aldridge and Colley Smith to Thomas de Saumarez, November 13, 1809, The Greffe Royal Court, de Saumarez Collection, X1/87; de Saumarez to Aldridge and Colley Smith, November 22, 1809, *FI*, 1:77, TNA, C/106/65.

25. Paul Haagen, "Eighteenth-Century English Society and the Debt Law," in *Social Control and the State: Historical and Comparative Essays*, ed. by Stanley Cohen and Andrew Scull (Oxford: Robertson, 1983), 224. Marginalia, *FI*, 1:80, TNA, C/106/65.

26. See Gregory Stevens Cox, *St. Peter Port, 1680–1830* (Woodbridge, UK: Boydell Press, 1999), 119, and 117–120, for a description of social life in the town.

27. William to Jackson, November 8, 1809, *FI*, 1:76, TNA, C/106/65. William to Jane Jackson, December 5, 1809, *FI*, 1:79–80, TNA, C/106/65.

28. Vicesimus Knox, "Hints to Young Men who are Designed for a Military or Naval Life," in *Essays, Moral and Literary*, 11th ed. (London, 1800), 1:135–136.

29. Thomas de Saumarez to Messrs. Aldridge and Colley Smith, November 22, 1809; de Saumarez to Jackson, December 20, 1809, *FI*, 1:76–78, 81–82, TNA, C/106/65.

30. Henry French and Mark Rothery, "Upon Your Entry into the World: Masculine Values and the Threshold of Adulthood Among Landed Elites in England, 1600–1800," *Social History* 33, 4 (2008): 402–422; Nicola Phillips, "Parenting the Profligate Son: Masculinity, Gentility and Juvenile Delinquency in England, 1791–1814," *Gender & History* 22, 1 (2010): 92–108. Jackson to de Saumarez, December 1, 1809, *FI*, 1:78, TNA, C/106/65.

31. De Saumarez to Jackson, December 20, 1809, *FI*, 1:81, TNA, C/106/65. See, for example, Robert Hamilton, *The Duties of a Regimental Surgeon Considered: with observations on his general qualifications*, 2nd ed. (London, 1794), 1:137. De Saumarez to Jackson, December 20, 1809.

32. William to Jackson, May 17, 1810, *FI*, 1:85, TNA, C/106/65.

33. Finn, *Character of Credit*, 274. Jackson to William, May 14, 1810, *FI*, 1:82–84, TNA, C/106/65.

34. Aldridge and Colley Smith to de Saumarez, May 29, 1810, The Greffe Royal Court, de Saumarez Collection, X1/88.

35. Pieter Spierenburg, *The Prison Experience: Disciplinary Institutions and Their Inmates in Early Modern Europe* (Amsterdam: Amsterdam University Press, 2007), 223–250; Catharina Lis and Hugo Soly, *Disordered Lives: Eighteenth-Century Families and Their Unruly Relatives,* trans. by Alexander Brown (Cambridge: Polity Press, 1996), 52–58; Benjamin Roberts, "On Not Becoming Delinquent: Raising Adolescent Boys in the Dutch Republic, 1600–1750," in *Becoming Delinquent: British and European Youth, 1650–1950,* ed. by Pamela Cox and Heather Shore (Aldershot, UK: Ashgate, 2002), 41–58. Pierce Egan, *Tom & Jerry: Life in London* (1821), 61. See also Margaret Hunt, *The Middling Sort: Commerce, Gender, and the Family in England, 1680–1780* (London: University of California Press, 1996), 66.

36. William to Jackson, November 8, 1809. Hamilton, *Duties of a Regimental Surgeon,* 1:125. On military attitudes to alcohol, see Paul E. Kopperman, "The Cheapest Pay: Alcohol Abuse in the Eighteenth-Century British Army," *Journal of Military History* 60, 3 (1996): 445–470.

37. My thanks to Rosemary Henry, a long-term resident of L'Ancresse, for supplying information about the barracks, and see her book *The History of L'Ancresse Common* (Guernsey, Channel Islands: R. Henry, 2008).

38. Letter Book of Lieutenant General Sir John Doyle, December 1807–April 1812, 320; Doyle to Major Prevost, April 30, 1810, The Greffe Royal Court. Proceedings of the Court Martial of Lieutenant George Leabon, July 16, 1810, The Greffe Royal Court, de Saumarez Collection, Box 112/25.

39. Letter Book of John Doyle, 341; Doyle to Adjutant General, July 16, 1810, The Greffe Royal Court. Proceedings of the Court Martial of George Leabon.

40. Josiah Woodward, *The Soldier's Monitor: Being Serious Advice to Soldiers to Behave themselves with a Just Regard for Religion and True Manhood* (London, 1776), 20, was a book of religious advice and prayers that was continually republished until the 1830s.

41. This whole account is reconstructed from *Proceedings of a Regimental Court of Enquiry held by order of Lieutenant Colonel Prevost, Commander 2nd Battalion, 67th Regiment,* Amhurst Barracks, July 9, 1810, The Greffe Royal Court, de Saumarez Collection, VII/2/4.

42. De Saumarez to Aldridge and Colley Smith for Jackson, July 15, 1810, *FI,* 1:85–87, TNA, C/106/65.

43. Ibid.

44. William to Jackson, August 2, 1810, *FI,* 1:88–89, TNA, C/106/65.

45. Aldridge and Colley Smith to de Saumarez, October 19, 1810, The Greffe Royal Court, de Saumarez Collection, X1/88.

CHAPTER 5: BOARDING THE FLEET

1. Edward Hollier to Jackson, October 8, 1810, *FI,* 1:101, TNA, C/106/65, states that the location of the theater was problematic. For a description of the noise, see Pierce Egan, *Tom & Jerry: Life in London* (London: John Camden, 1869 ed.), 363–364.

2. Jackson to William, October 16, 1810, *FI,* 1:104, TNA, C/106/65.

3. William to Jackson, August 1, 1810, and Jackson's marginalia, *FI,* 1: 84, TNA, C/106/65.

4. James Pearce, *A Treatise on the Abuses of the Laws, Particularly in Actions by Arrest; Pointing out the numerous hardships and abuses, in the different courts, from the commencement*

of an action to its conclusion. (London, 1814), 36; Margot C. Finn, *The Character of Credit: Personal Debt in English Culture, 1740–1914* (Cambridge: CUP, 2003), 117.

5. Paul H. Haagen, "Eighteenth-Century English Society and the Debt Law," in *Social Control and the State: Historical and Comparative Essays,* ed. by Stanley Cohen and Andrew Scull (Oxford: Robertson, 1983), 225.

6. *FI*, 1:80, 107, TNA, C/106/65. John "Jew" King had a son of the same name, and although Jackson does not state which he is referring to, both shared the same business methods.

7. John King, *Thoughts on the Difficulties and Distresses in which the Peace of 1783 has involved the People of England,* 5th ed. (1783), cited in Todd M. Endelman, "The Checkered Career of 'Jew' King: A Study in Anglo-Jewish Social History," *Association of Jewish Studies Review* 7–8 (1982–1983): 77. John King was born Jacob Rey but referred to by Jackson and commonly known as Jew King. Although there was considerable antipathy to Jewish moneylenders in general, it was King's unscrupulous dealings, not his Jewishness, that drew public condemnation. *The Scourge; or, Monthly Expositor of Imposture and Folly* 1 (1811): 3, ran a lengthy satirical exposé of King's long and scandalous life.

8. Pearce, *Treatise of the Abuses of the Laws,* 118.

9. Cox and Greenwood, whose offices were at Craigs Court, Whitehall, were military agents who organized the provision of clothing and payment for officers and men in regiments stationed around the world and acted as intermediaries in the buying and selling of officers' commissions. Cox and Greenwood also functioned as bankers, offering loans and accounts to London's elite.

10. *FI*, 1:89–90, TNA, C/106/65.

11. Shee to Jackson quoting Sir John Doyle, September 3, 1810, *FI*, 1:90, TNA, C/106/65.

12. Evelyn to Jackson, September 10, 1810, *FI*, 1:94, TNA, C/106/65. The dotted lines are Jackson's; their number suggests the missing word may have been "bastard."

13. Jackson to Shee, September 26, 1810, *FI*, 1:95, TNA, C/106/65. Jackson to Evelyn, September 29, 1810, *FI*, 1:96, TNA, C/106/65.

14. Finn, *Character of Credit,* 76–77, 95–97. See also Craig Muldrew, *The Economy of Obligation: The Culture of Credit and Social Relations in Early Modern England* (Basingstoke, UK: Palgrave, 1998).

15. On male adolescents exploiting their social and legal status to gain credit, see Finn, *Character of Credit,* 273.

16. See Peter King, *Crime, Justice, and Discretion in England, 1740–1820* (Oxford: OUP, 2000), 7.

17. Greenwell to Mrs. Jackson, September 26, 1810; William to Jackson, December 28, 1810, *FI*, 1:96, TNA, C/106/65.

18. Pearce, *Treatise on the Abuses of the Laws,* 111–114; *New Monthly Magazine* 14, pt. 2 (1820): 84–85. Jackson to Evelyn, September 29, 1810, *FI*, 1:100, TNA, C/106/65.

19. On hardening attitudes toward unfortunate versus fraudulent debtors, see Finn, *Character of Credit,* 152–154.

20. William to Evelyn, September 28, 1810, *FI*, 1:97, TNA, C/106/65.

21. TNA, PRIS 2/104, no. 14, 295; *FI*, 1:110–111, TNA, C/106/65. William was committed on "mesne process," the first step in an action for debt to await trial to prove whether the debt was valid or to settle with creditors, both of which could take many months to occur. If at trial the suit was decided in the creditor's favor, the creditor could

decide to proceed against the debtor's property (which could be seized and sold) or against his body and imprison him indefinitely until the creditor agreed to discharge him, known as "imprisonment on final process." For a clear explanation and diagrams of this process, see Joanna Innes, "The King's Bench Prison in the Later Eighteenth Century: Law, Authority, and Order in a London Debtors' Prison," in *An Ungovernable People: The English and Their Law in the Seventeenth and Eighteenth Centuries,* ed. by John Brewer and John Styles (London: Hutchinson, 1980), 251–254, 258–259.

22. *The Debtor and Creditor's Assistant* (1793), 6–7; Roger Lee Brown, *A History of the Fleet Prison, London: The Anatomy of the Fleet* (Lampeter, Wales: Edwin Mellen Press, 1996), 179–181.

23. "Report from the commissioners appointed to inquire into the state, conduct, and management of the prison and gaol of the fleet" (1819), 109, Parliamentary Papers Online, http://gateway.proquest.com/openurl?url_ver=Z39.88–2004&res_dat=xri:hcpp&rft_dat=xri:hcpp:fulltext:1819–005988, accessed November 28, 2012. On the numerous ways prison wardens and staff could make money, see Finn, *Character of Credit,* 134–137.

24. *Debtor and Creditor's Assistant,* 39–41, 48. On class distinctions and the economy of a debtors' prison, see Innes, "King's Bench Prison," 276–286.

25. FI, 1:114, TNA, C/106/65; Pearce, *Treatise on the Abuses of the Laws,* 93–94.

26. Robert Dorset Neale, *The Prisoner's Guide; Or, Every Debtor his own Lawyer,* 3rd ed. (London, 1813), iv–v; Pearce, *Treatise on the Abuses of the Laws,* 92–93. On the use of these and the existence of a "debtor ethos" in prisons, see Innes, "King's Bench Prison," 256–257.

27. William to Jackson, December 24, 1810; Jackson to William, December 25, 1810, *FI,* 1:114–116, TNA, C/106/65. On the Rules of the Fleet, see Brown, *History of the Fleet,* 268–269.

28. William to Jackson, December 31, 1810, *FI,* 1:118, TNA, C/106/65.

29. Jackson to William, January 13, 1811; William to Jackson, January 12 and 14, 1811, *FI,* 1:119–120, TNA, C/106/65.

30. *FI,* 1:121–125, TNA, C/106/65.

31. Egan, *Tom & Jerry,* 389–390; Brown, *History of the Fleet,* 260–264.

32. James Neild, cited in W. R. Minchin, *The Present State of the Debtor and Creditor Law, Being an essay on the effects of imprisonment: or, a consideration of creditors rights and debtors' wrongs* (London, 1812), 59, 70.

33. Pearce, *Treatise on the Abuses of the Laws,* 102.

34. *Debtor and Creditor's Assistant,* 50. See also Egan, *Tom & Jerry,* 383–391, on "the Humours of a Whistling Shop" and Cruikshank's illustration "A Whistling Shop. Tom and Jerry visiting Logic on board the Fleet," 382.

35. TNA, PRIS 1/25 Fleet Commitment Book, 271; PRIS 3/12 Writ of Supersedeas, July 29, 1811. Robert Webb to Jackson, August 27, 1811, *FI,* 2:25, TNA, C/106/65.

36. See, for example, *Debtor and Creditor's Assistant,* 83–85.

37. Finn, *Character of Credit,* 100–101.

38. FI, 2:7–8, TNA, C/106/65.

39. Jerry Hawthorn describing his fellow Fleet inmates in Egan, *Tom & Jerry,* 384. See, for example, *Debtor and Creditor's Assistant,* 87; and Haagen, "Eighteenth-Century English Society," 230–231.

40. "Note of Swindling Acts in the neighbourhood of Langley during the summer of 1811," FI, 2:22–25, TNA, C/106/65.

41. Barwise to Jackson, August 16, 1811, *FI*, 2: 15–16, TNA, C/106/65; *A List of Members of the Society of Guardians for the Protection of Trade against Swindlers and Sharpers* (London, 1812); *Rules and Order of The Guardians: or, Society for the Protection of Trade against Swindlers and Sharpers* (London, 1816).

42. Jackson to Colley Smith, August 12, 1811, *FI*, 2:12–14, TNA, C/106/65. Colley Smith to Jackson, August 15, 1811, *FI*, 2:19–20, TNA, C/106/65. Legally, as Smith explained, the court had jurisdiction over minors because it had received the king's power as *pater patriae*—in which the monarch was viewed as being the father of the nation and as therefore exercising patriarchal power over his family. On Continental customs, see Catharina Lis and Hugo Soly, *Disordered Lives: Eighteenth-Century Families and Their Unruly Relatives*, trans. by Alexander Brown (Cambridge: Polity Press, 1996), 52.

43. Jackson to Mr. Beaumant, August 17, 1811, *FI*, 2:21–22, TNA, C/106/65. Jackson to William, September 18, 1811, *FI*, 2:28–29, TNA, C/106/65.

44. William to Jackson, September 23, 1811, *FI*, 2:30, TNA, C/106/65. *FI*, 2:42, TNA, C/106/65. William to Jackson, September 23, 1811.

45. FI, 2:44–45, TNA, C/106/65.

CHAPTER 6: TO THE BRINK OF DESTRUCTION

1. Jackson to William, August 13, 1812, *FI*, 2:47–49, TNA, C/106/65.

2. The state only rarely brought prosecutions, so, apart from treason, sedition, murder, and a few serious property crimes such as coining or major bank forgery, it was down to the victim or someone acting on his behalf to initiate charges. Clive Emsley, *Crime and Society in England, 1750–1900*, 3rd ed. (Harlow, UK: Pearson, 2005), 183; Peter King, *Crime, Justice, and Discretion in England, 1740–1820* (Oxford: OUP, 2000), 17. Charles Cottu, *On The Administration of Criminal Justice in England; and the Spirit of the English Government* (trans., London, 1822), 37.

3. Isaac Taylor, *Advice to the Teens, or, Practical Helps Towards the Formation of One's Own Character* (Boston: Wells and Lilley, 1820), 171.

4. *Parliamentary Papers* 6 (1828), 12, cited in King, *Crime, Justice, and Discretion*, 360.

5. John H. Langbein, *The Origins of Adversary Criminal Trial* (Oxford: OUP, 2005), 167, n290. V. A. C. Gattrell, *The Hanging Tree: Execution and the English People, 1770–1868* (Oxford: OUP, 1994), 188.

6. Colley Smith to Jackson, October 24, 1812, *FI*, 2: 83–84, TNA, C/106/65.

7. Taylor, *Advice to the Teens*, 173. For earlier eighteenth-century fears, see Margaret Hunt's illuminating discussion of a "generation of vipers" in *The Middling Sort: Commerce, Gender, and the Family in England, 1680–1780* (London: University of California Press, 1996), 46–53. Society for the Suppression of Vice, *Address to the Public* (1803), 92–93, cited in Ben Wilson, *Decency and Disorder: The Age of Cant, 1789–1837* (London: Faber and Faber, 2007), 111. See also his discussion of reforming societies, 106–130.

8. Although the problem of youthful crime had been of concern since at least the middle of the seventeenth century, specific legal procedures and penal institutions for "juvenile delinquents" were developed following parliamentary reports into the apparently dramatic increase in such crime in the early nineteenth century. See Pamela Cox and Heather Shore, eds., *Becoming Delinquent: British and European Youth, 1650–1950* (Aldershot, UK: Ashgate, 2002); and Peter King, "The Rise of Juvenile Delinquency in England, 1780–1840: Changing Patterns of Perception and Prosecution," *Past and Present* 160 (1998): 116–166. For stereotypes of male juvenile delinquency, see Heather Shore, "The

Trouble with Boys: Gender and the Invention of the Juvenile Offender in Early-Nineteenth-Century Britain," in *Gender and Crime in Modern Europe*, ed. by M. Arnot and C. Usborne (London: UCL Press, 1999), 75–92.

9. King, "Rise of Juvenile Delinquency," 121. See also King, *Crime, Justice, and Discretion*, 176–183, on criminal activity in late adolescence and young adulthood that was markedly different from the modern pattern of crime, which tends to decline between the ages of nineteen and twenty-five.

10. Dorothy Davis, *A History of Shopping* (London: Routledge and Kegan Paul, 1966), 196–197.

11. On the functions of shopping, see Maxine Berg, *Luxury and Pleasure in Eighteenth-Century Britain* (Oxford: OUP, 2005), 267–270; Amanda Vickery, *The Gentleman's Daughter: Women's Lives in Georgian England* (London: Yale University Press, 1998), 161–194, on shopping as a form of employment for women; and Margot Finn, "Men's Things: Masculine Consumption in the Consumer Revolution," *Social History* 25, 2 (2000): 133–155, for the male perspective. See Helen Berry, "Polite Consumption: Shopping in Eighteenth-Century England," *Transactions of the Royal Historical Society* 12 (2002): 388–394.

12. I wish to thank John Styles for this information from his "Lodging at the Old Bailey: Lodgings and Their Furnishing in Eighteenth-Century London," paper presented at Britain in the Long Eighteenth Century Seminar, Institute of Historical Research, London, November 2004.

13. James Hardy Vaux, *The Memoirs of James Hardy Vaux*, ed. by Noel McLachlan (London: Heinemann, [1819] 1964), 82. William to Jackson, August 12, 1812, *FI*, 2: 46–47, TNA, C/106/65.

14. William to Jackson, August 12, 1812. Jackson to William, August 13, 1812, *FI*, 2:47, TNA, C/106/65.

15. John Feltham, *The Picture of London for 1802* (1802), 279–280.

16. William to Jackson, August 25, 1812, *FI*, 2:49–50, TNA, C/106/65.

17. Jackson to William, August 26, 1812, *FI*, 2:50–51, TNA, C/106/65.

18. After the success of Bow Street, the Middlesex Justices Act, 1792, created seven more police offices: at Queen's Square, Great Marlborough Street, Worship Street, Lambeth Street, Shadwell, Union Hall, and Hatton Garden. The Thames Police Office was created in 1798.

19. See, for example, Feltham, *Picture of London for 1802*, 10–11; and *Clerk's New Law List*, 16th ed. (London, 1812). On the proliferation of swindling, see Arthur Griffiths, *The Chronicles of Newgate* (1884), 2:38–39. Despite wide discretionary powers, magistrates very rarely bailed prisoners accused of felony; if they believed the evidence was incomplete, a prisoner could be held for up to six days for a further examination and a newspaper advertisement placed to inform the public. John Beattie, *Crime and the Courts in England, 1660–1800* (Oxford: OUP, 1986), 268–283; King, *Crime, Justice, and Discretion*, 89–99.

20. Thomas Fowell Buxton, *An Inquiry whether Crime and Misery are Produced or Prevented, by our Present System of Prison Discipline* (1818), 15.

21. James Neild, *State of the Prisons in England, Scotland, and Wales, Not for the Debtor only, but for Felons also, and other less Criminal Offenders* (1812), 135–138. Vaux, *Memoirs*, 77.

22. Beattie, *Crime and the Courts*, 268–283; William to Jackson, September 8, 1812, *FI*, 2:65, TNA, C/106/65.

23. Charles Day to Jackson, enclosing a copy of a report in the *Morning Post* of September 4, 1812, *FI*, 2:56–57, TNA, C/106/65.

24. Anon to Jackson, nd, *FI,* 2:59, TNA, C/106/65.

25. Cited in Marilyn Morris, "Princely Debt, Public Credit, and Commercial Values in Late Georgian Britain," *Journal of British Studies* 43, 3 (2004): 347, who argues that the prince's supporters highlighted the king's duty as a father to support his son.

26. In Britain "lawyers" was a generic term covering all members of the legal profession. In practice, solicitors (as they are known today) and attorneys acted for individuals or businesses and passed information on to barristers (or counsel), who gave legal advice and actually pleaded cases in court. Penelope J. Corfield, *Power and the Professions in Britain, 1700–1800* (London: Routledge, 1995), 49–52. See Langbein, *Origins of Adversary Criminal Trial,* 111–113, on the rise of solicitors as pretrial fact and evidence gatherers and their displacement of the attorney because of their original association with Chancery practice and hence a wealthier clientele that gave them a "superior cachet"; 143–145. See also Vaux, *Memoirs,* 195, who while in Newgate was himself almost duped by a dishonest attorney.

27. *Westminster Review* 22 (1835): 203–204, cited in Allyson N. May, *The Bar & the Old Bailey, 1750–1850* (London: University of North Carolina Press, 2003), 81. But as early as 1728, a pamphlet set out to expose "the oppressive and dishonest practises" of Newgate solicitors. See Langbein, *Origins of Adversary Criminal Trial,* 124–125. *FI,* 2:58, TNA, C/106/65.

28. Jackson to Colley Smith, September 8, 1812, *FI,* 2:64, TNA, C/106/65.

29. From a report in the *General Evening Post,* September 8–10, 1812. This was probably Robert Barry (d. 1821), listed in appendix of Counsel at the Old Bailey, 1783–1850, in May, *The Bar & the Old Bailey,* 247.

30. On victim negotiation and informal sanctions, see King, *Crime, Justice, and Discretion,* 22–35; and Clive Emsley, *Crime and Society in England,* 183–195. Legislation to pay the expenses of poor prosecutors of convicted felons was introduced in 1752 and extended to all prosecutors in 1778.

31. Silver to Jackson, September 17, 1812, *FI,* 2:69, TNA, C/106/65.

32. Jackson to Silver, September 20, 1812, *FI,* 2:71, TNA, C/106/65. Jackson to Colley Smith, September 8, 1812. Jackson to Silver, September 20, 1812.

33. Jackson to Colley Smith, September 8, 1812.

34. For this discussion of attitudes toward the law, see the "Introduction" to John Brewer and John Styles, eds., *An Ungovernable People: The English and Their Law in the Seventeenth and Eighteenth Centuries* (London: Hutchinson, 1980), 13–18.

35. G. Fitzgerald to Shee, September 22, 1812, *FI,* 2:73, TNA, C/106/65.

36. Shee to Jackson, September 23, 1812, *FI,* 2:72–73, TNA, C/106/65.

37. Jackson to Shee, September 25, 1812, *FI,* 2:74, TNA, C/106/65. The quotation is from a local paper published in Windsor on September 12.

38. Ibid. William to Jackson, September 8, 1812.

CHAPTER 7: A MANSION OF MISERY

1. Michael Ignatieff, *A Just Measure of Pain: The Penitentiary in the Industrial Revolution, 1750–1850* (London: Penguin/Peregrine, 1989), 42. On the design of Newgate, see Harold D. Kalman, "Newgate Prison," *Architectural History* 12 (1969): 50–61. Hansard, *Parliamentary Debates* (London, 1814), 18:74.

2. William to Jackson, September 8, 1812, *FI,* 2:65, TNA, C/106/65.

3. James Neild, *State of the Prisons in England, Scotland, and Wales, not for the Debtor only, but for Felons also, and other less Criminal Offenders* (London, 1812), 415–430,

describes life in the prison and its interior. See also Kalman, "Newgate Prison," 60n40; and W. J. Sheehan, "Finding Solace in Eighteenth-Century Newgate," in *Crime in England, 1550–1800*, ed. by J. S. Cockburn (London: Methuen, 1977), 245.

4. *The Examiner*, September 6, 1812. The anonymous prisoner cited legal sources that noted, "Imprisonment before trial is only for safe custody, and not for punishment; therefore, in the dubious interval between commitment and trial, the prisoner ought to be treated with the utmost humanity, and neither be loaded with useless fetters, nor subject to other hardships, than are absolutely requisite for the purpose of confinement only."

5. Thomas Fowell Buxton, *An Inquiry whether Crime and Misery are Produced or Prevented by our Present System of Prison Discipline* (London, 1818), 48–49.

6. Ignatieff, *Just Measure of Pain*, 71–73. Colley Smith to Jackson, September 12, 1812, *FI*, 2:66–67, TNA, C/106/65.

7. Basil Montagu, *An Inquiry in the Aspersions upon the late Ordinary of Newgate, with some observations upon Newgate and the Punishment of Death* (1815), 15–16. Jackson to Colley Smith, September 13, 1812, *FI*, 2:67–68, TNA, C/106/65.

8. Neild, *State of the Prisons*, 415–430; Hansard, *Parliamentary Debates*, 27:754–755. *The Examiner*, September 6, 1812; Hansard, *Parliamentary Debates*, 18:74. William to Jane Jackson, October 9, 1812, *FI*, 2:77–78, TNA, C/106/65.

9. William to Jackson, September 13, 1812, *FI*, 2:76–77, TNA, C/106/65. On "dying bravely" and the real terror suffered by the condemned, see V. A. C. Gattrell, *The Hanging Tree: Execution and the English People, 1770–1868* (Oxford: OUP, 1994), 32–54. Charles Dickens, "A Visit to Newgate," in *Sketches by Boz* (London, 1836).

10. Allyson N. May, *The Bar & the Old Bailey, 1750–1850* (London: University of North Carolina Press, 2003), 34, 96–97; John Beattie, *Crime and the Courts in England, 1660–1800* (Oxford: OUP, 1986), 333–340.

11. William to Jackson, October 4, 1812, *FI*, 2:75–76, TNA, C/106/65.

12. John H. Langbein, *The Origins of Adversary Criminal Trial* (Oxford: OUP, 2005), 1. William to Jane Jackson, October 9, 1812; William to Colley Smith, October 9, 1812, *FI*, 2:77–78, TNA, C/106/65. William to Jane Jackson, October 9, 1812.

13. Jackson to William, November 6, 1812, *FI*, 2:89–94, TNA, C/106/65, finally admitted that "if it had not been for the prayers and intercessions of your mother, nothing under Heaven would have induced me to employ Counsel in so *bad* a cause."

14. William to Jackson, October 16, 1812, *FI*, 2:78–79, TNA, C/106/65.

15. Jackson to Day, October 23, 1812, *FI*, 2:81–82, TNA, C/106/65.

16. Smith, like many solicitors, remained primarily engaged in dealing with a variety of conveyancing, clerical, and legal duties for landowners, but solicitors "were not registered formally on the rolls of a particular court," even though they did also perform case preparation work for barristers. Fletcher was therefore far more likely to have had more criminal law experience at the Old Bailey. See Gregory Durston, "The Emergence, and Occasional Disappearance, of England's Differing Legal Professions: 1200 to 1900," *Hosei Riron* (Journal of Law and Politics, Japan) 28 (1995): 145–166.

17. Colley Smith to Jackson, October 23, 1812, *FI*, 2: 82–83, TNA, C/106/65. May, *The Bar & the Old Bailey*, 81.

18. "Mr. Adolphus and His Contemporaries at the Old Bailey," *Law Magazine* 35 (1846): 58–59; J. A. Hamilton, "Gurney, Sir John (1768–1845)," rev. by Catherine Pease-Watkin, in *Oxford Dictionary of National Biography* (Oxford: OUP, 2004), http://www

/oxforddnb.com/view/article/11767, accessed August 20, 2007. "Adolphus and His Contemporaries," 59.

19. John Leycester Adolphus, letter to the editor on "The Late John Adolphus," *Fraser's Magazine* 66 (1862): 53. On the characters and careers of Adolphus and Alley, see also "Memoir of the Late Mr. Alley," *Legal Observer* 9, 239 (November 29, 1834): 66–67; and "Adolphus and His Contemporaries," 54–67.

20. "Adolphus and His Contemporaries," 60; May, *The Bar & the Old Bailey*, 107.

21. Colley Smith to Jackson, October 24, 1812, *FI*, 2:83–84, TNA, C/106/65.

22. Jackson to Colley Smith, October 25, 1812, *FI*, 2:84–85, TNA, C/106/65.

23. Colley Smith to Jackson, October 24, 1812.

24. Douglas Hay, "Property, Authority, and the Criminal Law," in Douglas Hay et al., *Albion's Fatal Tree: Crime and Society in Eighteenth-Century England* (Harmondsworth, UK: Penguin, 1975), 41; Peter King, *Crime, Justice, and Discretion in England, 1740–1820* (Oxford: OUP, 2000), 234, 328; May, *The Bar & the Old Bailey*, 108–109. Randall McGowen, "From Pillory to Gallows: The Punishment of Forgery in the Age of the Financial Revolution," *Past and Present* 165 (1999): 138–139.

25. Nearly 70 percent of the verdicts returned at the September sessions were guilty (n = 241). The proportions were similar at the October sessions, with 68.28 percent guilty verdicts (n = 145). Of those convicted, 14.14 percent were sentenced to death and 36.36 percent to be transported (to Australia). OBP, http://www.oldbaileyonline .org/forms/formStats.jsp, searched performed July 5, 2008.

26. Basil Montagu, *Thoughts on the Punishment of Death for Forgery* (London, 1820), 155. Phil Handler, "Forgery and the End of the 'Bloody Code' in Early-Nineteenth-Century England," *Historical Journal* 48, 3 (2005): 683–702. As many as one in three of those executed in London and Middlesex between 1805 and 1818 were forgers. OBP, http://www.oldbaileyonline.org/search.jsp?foo=bar&form=searchHomePage&_offences _offenceCategory_offenceSubcategory=deception%7Cforgery&fromYear=1812&from Month=01&toYear=1812&toMonth=11&start=0, search performed July 5, 2008. Of the twelve forgery cases in 1812, only two did not hire counsel. Gattrell, *Hanging Tree*, 406. Randall McGowen, "Forgery Discovered, or the Perils of Circulation in Eighteenth-Century England," *Angelaki* 1 (1994): 117–118.

27. See, for example, Feltham, *The Picture of London for 1802* (1802).

28. "Adolphus and His Contemporaries," 62.

29. Sessions Rolls, October 28, 1812, London Metropolitan Archives, OB/SR/455, lists names, occupations, and location of jurors. King, *Crime, Justice, and Discretion*, 252–257; Gattrell, *Hanging Tree*, 95.

30. Charles Cottu, *On the Administration of Criminal Justice in England; and the Spirit of the English Government* (trans., London, 1822), 91. The statement also does not reflect the fact that before the advent of lawyers in court and, if the prisoner had no defense counsel, even into the early nineteenth century, judges were expected to guide defendants on points of law to assist their defense.

31. James Oldham, "Chambré, Sir Alan (1739–1823)," in *Oxford Dictionary of National Biography*, www.oxforddnb.com/view/article/5086, accessed April 22, 2008.

32. May, *The Bar & the Old Bailey*, 101. On the limitations of defense counsels' role and how they circumvented them, see Langbein, *Origins of Adversary Criminal Trial*, 296, 301–302. Cottu, *Administration of Criminal Justice*, 89–90.

33. McGowen, "Forgery Discovered," 122–126.

34. October 1812 trial of William Jackson (t18121028–4), OBP, www.oldbailey online.org, accessed January 30, 2008. Jackson to William, November 6, 1812.

35. Allyson N. May, "Silvester, Sir John, First Baronet (1745–1822)," in *Oxford Dictionary of National Biography*, www.oxforddnb.com/view/article/67764, accessed April 22, 2008.

36. October 1812 trial of William Jackson (t18121028–12), OBP, accessed January 30, 2008, shows Colville had reduced the value of the furniture he accused William of stealing to £30 for three mirrors and £1 for two blankets, possibly in the hope of increasing his chances of securing a conviction.

37. Colley Smith to Jackson, October 29, 1812, *FI*, 2:86–87, TNA, C/106/65; October 1812 trial of William Jackson (t18121028–12), OBP, accessed January 30, 2008.

38. Newgate Criminal Registers, TNA, HO26/18; Colley Smith to Jackson, October 29, 1812.

39. Peter King, "The Rise of Juvenile Delinquency in England, 1780–1840: Changing Patterns of Perception and Prosecution," *Past and Present* 160 (1998): 158–161. See H. Shore, *Artful Dodgers: Youth and Crime in Early-Nineteenth-Century London* (Woodbridge, UK: Boydell Press, 1999), 32–33, for an example of a London lord mayor putting juvenile delinquents on remand at parents' request. Cottu, *Administration of Criminal Justice*, 92. Newgate Gaol Delivery Books, London Metropolitan Archives, OB/SB/026–7.

40. Jackson to William, November 6, 1812, *FI*, 2:89, TNA, C/106/65.

41. William to Jackson, November 4, 1812; Jackson to William, and Jane Jackson to William, both November 6, 1812, *FI*, 2:89–94, 94–95, TNA, C/106/65.

CHAPTER 8: CHELTENHAM AND GLOUCESTER UNMASKED

1. Colley Smith to Jackson, November 10, 1812, *FI*, 2:96, TNA, C/106/65.

2. Penelope Corfield, "Georgian Bath: The Magical Meeting Place," *History Today* 40 (1990): 26–33.

3. Sir Robert W. Kennedy to Jackson, December 30, 1812, *FI*, 2:105–106, TNA, C/106/65.

4. Messrs Bally and Bartram to Jackson, November 17, 1812, *FI*, 2:97, TNA, C/106/65. Sigismond to Jackson, December 29, 1812, *FI*, 2:104–105, TNA, C/106/65.

5. Jackson to Bally and Bartram, November 19, 1812, *FI*, 2:97–98, TNA, C/106/65. Jeremy Bentham, cited in Jack Lynch, *Deception and Detection in Eighteenth-Century Britain* (Aldershot, UK: Ashgate, 2008), 185.

6. William to Jackson, November 25, 1812, *FI*, 2:100–101, TNA, C/106/65. William to Jane Jackson, December 19 and 26, 1812, TNA, C/106/69. Jackson to Daniel Powney, December 12, 1812, *FI*, 2:102–103, TNA, C/106/65.

7. William to Jane Jackson, December 19, 1812, TNA, C/106/69.

8. William in Newbury to Jane Jackson, February 7, 1813, TNA, C/106/69. Thomas Frankland to Jackson, February 23, 1812, *FI*, 2:107, TNA, C/106/65.

9. J. K. Griffiths, *A General Cheltenham Guide upon an entirely new plan: comp. from the most authentic sources, and embracing the ancient and modern history, state, and description of that celebrated town and its environs* (Cheltenham, 1818).

10. Gwen Hart, *A History of Cheltenham* (Leicester, UK: Leicester University Press, 1965), 161–170. See, for example, articles by Thomas Newell in the *London Literary Gazette and Journal of the Belle Arts* (1820): 456; and in the *London Medical Gazette* (1829): 576.

11. On discussion and definitions of polite sociability, see, for example, Lawrence E. Klein, "Politeness for Plebes: Consumption and Social Identity in Early-Eighteenth-Century England," in *The Consumption of Culture, 1600–1800: Image, Object, Text*, ed. by Ann Bermingham and John Brewer (London: Routledge, 1995), 362–382; and Paul Langford, *A Polite and Commercial People: England, 1727–1783* (Oxford: Clarendon Press, 1989), 59–122.

12. See David Phillips, "Good Men to Associate and Bad Men to Conspire: Associations for the Prosecution of Felons in England, 1760–1860," in *Policing and Prosecution in Britain, 1650–1850*, ed. by D. Hay and F. Snyder, (Oxford: Clarendon Press, 1989), 113–151; and Peter King, *Crime, Justice, and Discretion in England, 1740–1820* (Oxford: OUP, 2000), 53–57.

13. Colonel W. Caulfield Lennon to Jackson, March 1, 1813, *FI*, 2:109, TNA, C/106/65. Copy of extract from Cheltenham newspaper, March 4, 1813, *FI*, 2:112–113, TNA, C/106/65.

14. Literally *ci-devant* meant "former," but in the eighteenth century it could also refer to the pre-revolutionary French aristocracy or nobility. French was still a symbol of polite learning in elite circles, and its use here probably also reflects both Sir William's nobility and his polite/humane behavior. Jackson to Colonel Lennon, March 2, 1813, *FI*, 2:110, TNA, C/106/65.

15. Victoria County History, "Gloucester, 1720–1835: Social and Cultural Life," in *A History of the County of Gloucester*, vol. 4, *The City of Gloucester*, ed. by N. M. Herbert (1988), 154–159, http://www.british-history.ac.uk/report.aspx?compid=42295, accessed May 7, 2009.

16. Neild, *State of the Prisons in England, Scotland, and Wales, not for the Debtor only, but for Felons also, and other less Criminal Offenders* (London, 1812), 244–245.

17. *General Regulations for Inspection and Controul of all the Prisons, Together with the Rules, Orders and Bye Laws for the Government of the Gaol and Penitentiary House for the County of Gloucester* (Gloucester, 1790, rev. 1808).

18. G. O. Paul, *Considerations on the Defects of Prisons* (1784), cited in Michael Ignatieff, *A Just Measure of Pain: The Penitentiary in the Industrial Revolution, 1750–1850* (London: Penguin/Peregrine, 1989), 100. On prison design, see J. R. S. Whiting, *Prison Reform in Gloucestershire, 1776–1820* (London: Phillimore, 1975), 14–19, 68.

19. Cited in Ignatieff, *Just Measure of Pain*, 101. Surgeon's Journal, March 2, 1813, GA, Q/Gc/32/2. Surgeon's Journal, March 2, 1813, GA, Q/Gc/32/2. Chaplain's Journal, March 3, 1813, GA, Q/Gc/31/1. Whiting, *Prison Reform*, 48. See also *General Regulations for Inspection and Controul of all the Prisons*. Cited in E. A. L. Moir, "Sir George Onesiphorus Paul," in *Gloucestershire Studies*, ed. by H. P. R. Finburg (Leicester, UK: Leicester University Press, 1957), 213. Jackson to Colonel Lennon, March 2, 1813, *FI*, 2, TNA, C/106/05.

20. Chaplain's Journal, May 21, 1813, GA, Q/Gc/31/1. Jackson to Colley Smith, March 24, 1813, *FI*, 2:114, TNA, C/106/65. Jackson, marginalia, March 27, 1813, *FI*, 2, TNA, C/106/65.

21. Jackson marginalia and extract from Cheltenham newspaper, March 4, 1813, *FI*, 2:111–112, TNA, C/106/65. William to Jane Jackson, March 13, 1813, TNA, C/106/69. Philip Rawlings, *Drunks, Whores, and Idle Apprentices: Criminal Biographies of the Eighteenth Century* (London: Routledge, 1992); Michael Harris, "Trials and Criminal Biographies: A Case Study in Distribution," in *The Sale and Distribution of Books from 1700*, ed. by R. Myers and M. Harris (Oxford: Oxford Polytechnic Press, 1982), 1–36; Donna T.

Andrew and Randall McGowan, *The Perreaus and Mrs. Rudd: Forgery and Betrayal in Eighteenth-Century London* (London: University of California Press, 2001), 51–84.

22. Governor's Journal, March 1–May 15, 1813, GA, Q/Gc/3/7.

23. William to Mr. Lewis, March 4, 9, and 19, 1813, enclosed in letter from Mr. and Mrs. Lewis to Jackson, May 23, 1813, *FI*, 2:124–127, TNA, C/106/65.

24. Chaplain's Journal, March 29, 1813, GA, Q/Gc/31/1. Chaplain's Journal, March 24, 1813, GA, Q/Gc/31/1; Whiting, *Prison Reform*, 36. William to Jane Jackson, March 5, 1813, TNA, C/106/69.

25. Sociologists have argued that delinquents effectively "neutralize" legal and moral norms by defining them as inapplicable or unimportant because, in part, these norms are often flexible and not binding under all conditions, as, for example, when a defense of nonage is admissible. Another technique is to transfer blame to others. Thus, while broadly adhering to the dominant value system, a delinquent can provide a rational defense of his behavior. See Gresham M. Sykes and David Matza, "Techniques of Neutralization," *American Sociological Review* 22, 6 (1957): 664–670. For a more recent approach to the theory, see David Downs and Paul Rock, *Understanding Deviance: A Guide to the Sociology of Crime and Rule Breaking*, 2nd ed. (Oxford: Clarendon Press, 1995), 36–37, 156–157, 194. William to Jane Jackson, March 10, 1813, TNA, C/106/69.

26. *Cheltenham Chronicle and Gloucestershire General Advertiser*, April 8, 1813. For additional detail on the entry of judges on assize day, see Charles Cottu, *On the Administration of Criminal Justice in England; and the Spirit of the English Government* (trans., London, 1822), 42–43. *Cheltenham and Glos. Advertiser*; John Beattie, *Crime and the Courts in England, 1660–1800* (Oxford: OUP, 1986), 317.

27. Michael Lobban, "Bayley, Sir John, First Baronet (1753–1841)," in *Oxford Dictionary of National Biography* (Oxford: OUP, 2004), http://www.oxforddnb.com/view/article/1752, accessed May 28, 2009.

28. Governor's Journal, March 31, 1813, GA, Q/Gc/3/7.

29. John H. Langbein, *The Origins of Adversary Criminal Trial* (Oxford: OUP, 2005), 256–257, n16.

30. Cottu, *Administration of Criminal Justice*, 103–104.

31. Thomas Gisborne, *An Enquiry into the Duties of Men In the Higher and Middle Classes of Society in Great Britain*, 6th ed. (London, 1797), 405. Cottu, *Administration of Criminal Justice*, 103. Court proceedings as reported in *Cheltenham and Glos. Advertiser*. Jackson's copy of the newspaper report of court proceedings and his marginalia, *FI*, 2:118, TNA, C/106/65.

32. Jackson's copy of newspaper report.

33. Benefit of clergy was an ancient privilege, allowing anyone who could read a set passage from the Bible (hence originally primarily clergymen) the right to have the death sentence commuted. Its usage gradually came to connote less serious crimes as clergyable offenses not punishable by death. See William Blackstone, *Commentaries on the Laws of England*, 16th ed. (London, 1811), Book 4, chap. 7, http://ebooks.adelaide.edu.au/b/blackstone/william/comment/book4.7.html, accessed November 24, 2011.

34. Cited in Venetia Murray, *High Society in the Regency Period, 1788–1830* (London: Penguin, 1999), 32. Marilyn Morris, "Princely Debt, Public Credit, and Commercial Values in Late Georgian Britain," *Journal of British Studies* 43, 3 (2004): 339–365, http://www.jstor.org/stable/10.1086/383599, accessed December 3, 2012.

35. My thanks to Professor Michael Lobban, the School of Law, Queen Mary College, University of London, for explaining this important legal distinction.

36. Cottu, *Administration of Criminal Justice*, 68. On the exercise of mercy, see also Douglas Hay, "Property, Authority, and the Criminal Law," in Douglas Hay et al., *Albion's Fatal Tree: Crime and Society in Eighteenth-Century England* (Harmondsworth, UK: Penguin, 1975). Blackstone, *Commentaries*, Book 4, chap. 17, http://ebooks.adelaide.edu.au/b /blackstone/william/comment/book4.17.html, accessed November 24, 2011.

37. Jackson's marginalia, *FI*, 2:115–116, TNA, C/106/65.

CHAPTER 9: RETRIBUTION

1. Chaplain's Journal, April 3, 1813, GA, Q/G/c31/1.

2. William to Mr. Lewis, May 2, 1813, *FI*, 2:128, TNA, C/106/65. Jackson to William, May 5, 1813, *FI*, 2:118–119, TNA, C/106/65.

3. Chaplain's Journal, April 15–17, 1813, GA, Q/G/c31/1.

4. Governor's Journal, April 24, 1813, GA, Q/Gc/3/7; J. R. S. Whiting, *Prison Reform in Gloucestershire, 1776–1820: A Study of the Work of Sir George Onesiphorus Paul, Bart* (London: Phillimore, 1975), 36.

5. James Hardy Vaux, *The Memoirs of James Hardy Vaux*, ed. by Noel McLachlan (London; Heinemann, [1819] 1964), 195. Chaplain's Journal, May 4, 1813, GA, Q/Gc/31/1.

6. Thomas R. Forbes, "Coroners Inquisitions on the Deaths of Prisoners in the Hulks at Portsmouth in 1817–27," *Journal of the History of Medicine* 33 (July 1978): 366.

7. PP, *Third Report from the Select Committee on the Laws Relating to Penitentiary Houses* (1812), 165. The table in "Appendix D" shows the next highest rate for the *Prudentia* at eighty-one deaths; the *Captivity* (closest in size to *Retribution*), seventy-three; the *Laurel*, thirty-seven; the *Portland*, thirty-six; and the *Zealand* (only in service for two years), thirteen. See also Vaux, *Memoirs*, 198.

8. "Woolminstone-Woore," in *A Topographical Dictionary of England* (1848), 663– 670, http://www.british-history.ac.uk/report.aspx?compid=51428&strquery=Woolwich Royal Arsenal, accessed June 24, 2009.

9. *Substance of the Speech of George Holford esq. In the House of Commons on Thursday 22nd June 1815 on the Bill "To Amend the law relative to the Transportation of Offenders Containing Provisions Respecting the Confinement of Offenders in the Hulks"* (London, 1815), 4.

10. PP, *Third Report from the Select Committee*, "Appendix B: Instructions to be observed and followed by Captain . . . Superintendant of the Hulk in . . . Harbour," 157.

11. William to Jane Jackson, June 10, 1813, TNA, C/106/69. PP, *Third Report from the Select Committee*, 137; Charles Campbell, *The Intolerable Hulks: British Shipboard Confinement, 1776–1857*, 3rd ed. (Tucson, AZ: Fenestra Books, 2001), 81–82.

12. William to Jackson, May 17, 1813, *FI*, 2:121–122, TNA, C/106/65. William to Jane Jackson, August 1, 1813, TNA, C/106/69.

13. William to Jackson, May 17, 1813.

14. Ibid.; William to Jackson, May 29, 1813, *FI*, 3:1, TNA, C/106/65; Vaux, *Memoirs*, 200. PP, *Third Report from the Select Committee*, 139–140.

15. *Speech of George Holford*, 13. William to Jackson, June 17, 1813, *FI*, 3:3–4, TNA, C/106/65.

16. William to Jackson, May 17 and 29, 1813, *FI*, 2:121–122 and 3:1, TNA, C/106/65. PP, *Third Report from the Select Committee*, 139.

17. William to Jackson and Jackson's marginal comments, May 29, 1813.

18. Ibid.; Jackson's annotation to William's letter, May 29, 1813.

19. William to Jane Jackson, June 10, 1813, TNA, C/106/69.

20. Vaux, *Memoirs,* 199. Pennant, *Journey to the Isle of Wight,* cited in Reg Rigden, *The Floating Prisons of Woolwich and Deptford* (London: Borough of Greenwich, 1976), 13–14.

21. See PP, *Third Report from the Select Committee,* 149–150, Appendix j1, 173–174; *Speech of George Holford,* 27.

22. Jackson to Lewis, May 30, 1813, *FI,* 2:127–128, TNA, C/106/65. Jackson's annotation to a copy of William's letter to Lewis, *FI,* 2:125, March 9, 1813, TNA, C/106/65. Naomi Tadmor, *Family and Friends in Eighteenth-Century England: Household, Kinship, and Patronage* (Cambridge: CUP, 2001), 53–63; Nicola Phillips, *Women in Business, 1700–1850* (Woodbridge, UK: Boydell Press, 2006), 103, 111–112.

23. Jackson to Lewis, May 30, 1813. Jackson's additional notes show he sent a servant with £5 for the Lewises on July 27, 1813, after William contested their claim, *FI,* 3:9, TNA, C/106/65.

24. William to Jackson, June 17, 1813, *FI,* 3:3–4, TNA, C/106/65.

25. William to Jackson, May 17, 1813. Bruce Kercher, "Perish or Prosper: The Law and Convict Transportation in the British Empire, 1700–1850," *Law and History Review* 21 (2003): 536–537. Only a capital felony carried the "attaint" that would make a convicted person dead in law; most of those pardoned by the king whose sentences were commuted to transportation were relieved of this attaint only at the expiration of their sentences. However, attaint was not attached to those convicted of a noncapital felony and sentenced immediately to transportation. William to Jane Jackson, June 10, 1813.

26. Jackson to William, June 7, 1813, *FI,* 3:2, TNA, C/106/65.

27. Ibid.; William to Jackson, June 17, 1813.

28. William to Jackson, July 16, 1813, *FI,* 3:6–7, TNA, C/106/65. Jackson describes the certificate and Huddlestone's visit, *FI,* 3:9, TNA, C/106/65.

29. Ibid., 9.

30. Peter King, *Crime, Justice, and Discretion in England, 1740–1820* (Oxford: OUP, 2000), 318; Douglas Hay, "Property, Authority, and the Criminal Law," in Douglas Hay et al., *Albion's Fatal Tree: Crime and Society in Eighteenth-Century England* (Harmondsworth, UK: Penguin, 1975), 45–47. William to Jackson, May 17, 1813.

31. Christopher Hibbert, "George IV (1762–1830)," in *Oxford Dictionary of National Biography* (Oxford: OUP, 2004), http://www.oxforddnb.com/view/article/10541, accessed July 22, 2009. *A Loyal, but Solemn Expostulation, addressed in a moment of general distress, dismay, and apprehension, to a thoughtless and imprudent young man* (London, 1795), 13–14.

32. Fintan O'Toole, *A Traitor's Kiss: The Life of Richard Brinsley Sheridan* (London: Granta Books, 1997), 58–69, 447–453.

33. William to Jane Jackson, February 17, 1814, TNA, C/106/69.

34. *London Chronicle,* October 25, 1798; Roland Thorne, "Stewart, Robert, Viscount Castlereagh and Second Marquess of Londonderry (1769–1822)," in *Oxford Dictionary of National Biography,* http://www.oxforddnb.com/view/article/26507, accessed July 17, 2009. There was also a connection to Shee and Mr. Jackson via the East India Company— Castlereagh had been appointed to the Board of Control (that took over running the company in 1801).

35. Jackson to Evelyn, March 22, 1814; Colley Smith to Jackson, July 22, 1814, TNA, C/106/69. Dr. John Mitchell to Jackson, October 22, 1813, and December 17, 1813; Jackson to Dr. Mitchell, January 26, 1814, TNA, C/106/69.

36. Charles Bateson, *The Convict Ships, 1787–1868, 4th ed.* (Sydney: Library of Australian History, 1983), 198–199.

CHAPTER 10: THE NATURE OF
A CONTAGIOUS DISTEMPER

1. William at Graves End on board the *Surry* to Jane Jackson, December 29, 1813, TNA, C/106/69. The ship was known at this time as the *Surry*, but there are variant spellings, and later in its long career it became known as the old *Surrey*. Charles Bateson, *The Convict Ships, 1787–1868,* 4th ed. (Sydney: Library of Australian History, 1983), 61–62.

2. PP, *Report of the Commissioner of Enquiry into the State of the Colony of New South Wales* (1822) (448) XX.539, 2, House of Commons Parliamentary Papers Online, http://gateway.proquest.com/openurl?url_ver=Z39.88–2004&res_dat=xri:hcpp&rft _dat=xri:hcpp:rec:1822–007959, accessed March 9, 2013. William to an unknown friend, December 13, 1813, TNA, C/106/69.

3. See, for example, letters from Lt. Fitzgerald to Jane Jackson, August 4, 1813, and January 8 and 10, 1814, TNA, C/106/69. William to Jane Jackson, February 6, 1814, TNA, C/106/69.

4. William to Jane Jackson, February 11, 1814, TNA, C/106/69.

5. Ibid.

6. Stephen Nicholas, ed., *Convict Workers: Reinterpreting Australia's Past* (Cambridge: CUP, 1989), 81, table 5.10. Convict Indent: Convicts Arrived in Sydney from England per Surrey 1, July 28, 1814, SRNSW 4/4004/393.

7. PP, *Report from the Select Committee for Transportation* (1812) (341) II.573, 10, House of Commons Parliamentary Papers Online, http://gateway.proquest.com /openurl?url_ver=Z39.88–2004&res_dat=xri:hcpp&rft_dat=xri:hcpp:rec:1812–002905, accessed March 9, 2013, states that from 1795 to 1801 the death rate of convicts on transport ships was one in ten; from 1801 to 1812 it fell to one in forty-six; 28.

8. Bateson, *Convict Ships,* 18–19.

9. *The Asiatic Journal and Monthly Register for British India and Its Dependencies* 12 (July–December 1821).

10. Asst. Surgeon Redfern to Governor Macquarie, NSW, September 30, 1814, *HRA,* Series 1 (1916), 8:290–291. Brian Lavery, *Nelson's Navy: The Ships, Men, and Organisation, 1793–1815,* (London: Conway Maritime Press, 1989), 271; Bateson, *Convict Ships,* 28. Redfern to Macquarie, September 30, 1814, *HRA,* 8:290–291.

11. William from Rio de Janeiro to Jane Jackson, April 12, 1814, TNA, C/106/69.

12. Redfern to Macquarie, September 30, 1814, *HRA,* 8:284, 287.

13. William from Rio de Janeiro to Jackson, April 12, 1814, TNA, C/106/70.

14. William to Jane Jackson, February 17, 1814, TNA, C/106/70; Lt. G. Fitzgerald to William, January 8, 1814, TNA, C/106/69. Redfern to Macquarie, September 30, 1814, *HRA,* 8:280; Bateson, *Convict Ships,* 195.

15. Alan Brooke and David Brandon, *Bound for Botany Bay: British Convict Voyages to Australia* (Richmond, UK: National Archives, 2005), 142–147.

16. On these methods of navigation, see Dava Sobell, *Longitude: The True Story of a Lone Genius Who Solved the Greatest Scientific Problem of His Time* (London: Fourth Estate, 1996); and Lavery, *Nelson's Navy,* 183–187. Papers Concerning "Surry" in the NSW Court of Vice Admiralty, deposition of Alexander Ross, October 20, 1814, SRNSW, Microfilm 6044, 60–61.

17. Deposition of Alexander Ross. Deposition of Thomas Pitcher, September 13, 1813, Papers Concerning "Surrey."

18. Deposition of Sir John Jamison, October 11, 1814, Papers Concerning "Surrey."

19. Deposition of Joseph Andrews, October 20, 1814, Papers Concerning "Surrey."

20. Deposition of Robert Watson, October 11, 1814; depositions of James Wright and James Reeve Jex, October 18, 1814, Papers Concerning "Surrey."

21. Deposition of Robert Watson, October 11, 1814, Papers Concerning "Surrey."

22. Colonial Secretary: Letters Received, "Government and General Orders," Saturday, July 30, 1814, 513, SRNSW, Microfilm 6038, C2758. *Sydney Gazette*, July 30, 1830.

23. Edward Ford, "Redfern, William (1774–1833)," in *Australian Dictionary of Biography*, http://adbonline.anu.edu.au/biogs/A020324b.htm?hilite=Redfern, accessed March 23, 2010.

24. *Sydney Gazette*, May 21, 1814, http://newspapers.nla.gov.au/ndp/del/article /628916?searchTerm=%22Three+Bees%22, accessed March 23, 2010.

25. Bateson, *Convict Ships*, 198. Statistics taken from Herbert S. Klein and Stanley L. Engerman, "Long-Term Trends in African Mortality in the Transatlantic Slave Trade," in *Routes to Slavery: Direction, Ethnicity, and Mortality in the Transatlantic Slave Trade*, ed. by David Eltis and David Richardson (London: Frank Cass, 1997), 37, 42–43, but mortality rates could vary greatly between voyages.

26. Redfern to Macquarie, September 30, 1814, HRA, 8:285, 287.

27. Ibid., 287, 285.

28. Ibid., 291–293.

29. PP, *Report of the Commissioner of Enquiry*, 1, 7.

30. Ibid., 9; Bateson, *Convict Ships*, 48–50. Edward Eagar, *Letters to The Rt. Hon. Robert Peel, M.P., Secretary of State for the Home Department, On the advantages of New South Wales and Van Diemen's Land as penal settlements for the punishment and reform of offenders, and as colonies for the reception of poor emigrants . . . By A Late Resident in Those Colonies* (London, 1824), 5–7.

CHAPTER 11: OF GENTLEMEN AND CONVICTS

1. This description of Sydney is based on W. C. Wentworth, *A Statistical, Historical, and Political Description of the Colony of New South Wales, and its Dependent Settlements in Van Dieman's Land* (London, 1819), 7, 6, 13; D. D. Mann, *The Present Picture of New South Wales* (London, 1811), 56–57; Peter Cunningham, *Two Years in New South Wales* (London, 1827), 37–45; and pictorial views of Sydney circa 1811–1817 in Tim McCormick, *First Views of Australia, 1788–1825: A History of Early Sydney* (Sydney: Longuevill, 1987), 148–159, 178–187.

2. J. J. Auchmuty, "Wentworth, D'Arcy (1762–1827)," in *Australian Dictionary of Biography*, www.adbonline.anu.edu.au/biogs/A020530, accessed March 5, 2010.

3. John B. Hirst, *Convict Society and Its Enemies: A History of Early New South Wales* (Sydney: Allen and Unwin, 1983), 45.

4. PP, *Report of the Commissioner of Enquiry into the State of the Colony of New South Wales* (1822), 17.

5. Macquarie to Lord Castlereagh, April 1810, cited in Robert Hughes, *The Fatal Shore* (London: Vintage, 2003), 295.

6. William to Jane Jackson, April 12, 1814, TNA, C/106/69.

7. Eagar to Bigge, in John Ritchie, ed., *The Evidence to the Bigge Reports*, vol. 2, *The Written Evidence* (London: Heinemann, 1971), 235–236.

8. Noel McLachlan, "Edward Eagar (1787–1866): A Colonial Spokesman in Sydney and London," *Historical Studies, Australia and New Zealand* 10, 40 (May 1963): 431–456; Kevin Lewis Smith, *Colonial Litigant Extraordinaire: The Edward Eagar Story* (Burrel Creek, Australia: Fast Books, 1996), 20, 119. J. M. Bennett, "Bigge, John Thomas (1780–1843)," in *Australian Dictionary of Biography*, http://www.adb.online.anu.edu.au/biogs/A010093b.htm, accessed May 4, 2010; PP, *Report of the Commissioner of Enquiry*, 104.

9. Colonel O'Connell had been sent to serve in Ceylon just a month after the *Surry* left England. Entries for Joseph Bradley, per the ship *General Hewitt*, 1814, Clerk to the Magistrates, Parramatta; Petition for mitigation of sentence, December 9, 1817, SRNSW, Index to the Colonial Secretary's Papers, 1788–1825, Microfiche 3174; 4/1850, 33. Thomas Campbell letter re: distribution of convicts per "Surry," August 18, 1814, SRNSW, Colonial Secretary's Letters Received, 4/3493, Reel 6004, 255–256S; S. J. Butlin, *Foundations of Australia's Monetary System*, 1778–1851 (Sydney: University Press, 1968), 87.

10. PP, *Report of the Commissioner of Enquiry*, 78, 82.

11. On alternative nomenclature, see Cunningham, *Two Years in New South Wales*, 108–110. Hirst, *Convict Society*, 153, suggests the reluctance to use the term "convict" came from an effort to spare the feelings of ex-convicts, who would otherwise have carried that label as a constant reminder of their former degradation.

12. Hirst, *Convict Society*, 36, 71, 74–75. See also W. Molesworth, notes to *Report of the Select Committee on Transportation* (1838), 76, n22, 227.

13. Fragment of note from Jackson, nd, TNA, C/106/69.

14. PP, *Report of the Commissioner of Enquiry*, 100.

15. This description of Newcastle is primarily drawn from ibid.,114–118. Thomas Campbell to the Secretary's Office, June 10, 1815, SRNSW, Colonial Secretary's Letters, 4/3494, Reel 6004, 91. Wentworth, *Statistical, Historical, and Political Description*, 55.

16. James Hardy Vaux, *The Memoirs of James Hardy Vaux*, ed. by Noel McLachlan (London: Heinemann, [1819] 1964).

17. PP, *Report of the Commissioner of Enquiry*, 100–101; Vaux, *Memoirs*, 217–218. Thomas Campbell to Lieutenant Thompson, Commandant of Newcastle, September 28,1815, SRNSW, 4/3494, Reel 6004, Colonial Secretary's Letters, 212–213. No reason was given for the remittance.

18. Smith, *Colonial Litigant Extraordinaire*, 32.

19. David Neale, *The Rule of Law in a Penal Colony* (Cambridge: CUP, 1991), 102–103; C. H. Currey, "Bent, Jeffery Hart (1781–1852)," in *Australian Dictionary of Biography*, http://www.adb.online.anu.edu.au/biogs/A010546b.htm, accessed May 3, 2010; McLachlan, "Edward Eagar."

20. Smith, *Colonial Litigant Extraordinaire*.

21. Bill of William Collins Burke Jackson and William Collins Jackson (son and infant), in Chancery Pleadings, *Jackson v. Coutts*, TNA, C/13/797/12 (February 1823, amended May 1823). In Jane Jackson's reply, April 14, 1823, to William's Bill of Complaint, she states that she had paid his annuity for five and a half years until March 17, 1820, which means she must have begun doing so in October 1814.

22. On the circulation of information and personnel, see Zoe Laidlaw, *Colonial Connections, 1815–45: The Information Revolution and Colonial Government* (Manchester, UK: MUP, 2005); and Kirsten McKenzie, *Scandal in the Colonies: Sydney and Cape Town, 1820–1850* (Melbourne: University Publishing, 2004). Bill of Edmond Molony, Chancery Pleadings, *Molony v. Coutts*, TNA, C/13/266/25 (1820). A copy of Coutts's accounts

deposed in the Chancery case show that Jane Jackson paid £100 into William's account in July 1816, but that single payment does not seem to relate to his £500 annuity, which William claimed that she had been paying him every six months until 1820. I have assumed that the annuity was also paid into a Coutts account for William. Chancery Pleadings, *Jackson v. Coutts*, TNA, C/13/797/12 (1823).

23. Colonial Secretary's Letters, 21–22, SRNSW 4/1736, Reel 6046, William to Macquarie December 2, 1816, endorsed December 14, 1816. Hirst, *Convict Society*, 53–54, 85. Macquarie had laid down a minimum of three years before a convict could apply for a ticket of leave, but he frequently broke his own rule, and for gentlemen and artists he would often accept an immediate application.

24. Cunningham, *Two Years in New South Wales*, 44, 55, 59.

25. Jane Elliot, "Was There a Convict Dandy? Convict Consumer Interests in Sydney, 1788–1815," *Australian Historical Studies* 104 (1995): 373–392; Margaret Maynard, *Fashioned from Penury: Dress as Cultural Practice in Colonial Australia* (Cambridge: CUP, 1994), 16–20, 41–48.

26. Ibid. Cunningham, *Two Years in New South Wales*, 46–47.

27. On Robert Jones, see OBP, February 1790, trial of Robert Jones (t17900224-56); entries in the Colonial Secretary's index under Jones, Robert, per "Scarborough," 1790; and entries in the *Sydney Gazette*, 1803–1819, Historic Australian Newspapers, 1803 to 1954 Online, http://newspapers.nla.gov.au/ndp/del/home. On Elizabeth Goldsmith/Rayner /Jones, see OBP, June 1788, trial of Elizabeth Goldsmith (t17880625-1); Sian Rees, *The Floating Brothel* (London: Headline, 2001), 85ff; and Michael Flynn, *The Second Fleet: Britain's Grim Convict Armada of 1790* (Sydney: Library of Australian History, 1993). For the voyages of the *Scarborough* and *Lady Julian*, see Charles Bateson, *The Convict Ships, 1787–1868*, 4th ed. (Sydney: Library of Australian History, 1983), 120–131.

28. Cunningham, *Two Years in New South Wales*, 49–50. NSW Marriage Registration, Old Register, vol. 7, Entry 196, December 16, 1815.

29. Will of William Collins Jackson, TNA, PROB 11/1561, image ref. 254/772.

30. D. R. Hainsworth, *The Sydney Traders: Simeon Lord and His Contemporaries, 1788–1821* (Melbourne: University Press, 1981), 107–109. Macquarie to Castlereagh, April 30, 1810, cited in Butlin, *Foundations*, 90. In order to be able to meet the demands of his own creditors, in December 1817 William placed a notice in the *Sydney Gazette* threatening to resort to legal measures against those who owed him money.

31. A Petition of William Collins Burke Jackson, SRNSW, 4/1851, Colonial Secretary's Letters, 186, Microfiche 3178; Conditional Pardon Burke Jackson, January 31, 1818, SRNSW, 4/4430, 120, Reel 774.

32. *Sydney Gazette*, February 14, 1818, and September 1818; letter from Mary Ann to her mother, Sydney, June 19, 1820. My thanks go to Jennie Amos in Tasmania, whose husband is a descendant of Mary Ann's, and who kindly forwarded me this copy.

CHAPTER 12: RUINED SUITORS

1. See an 1877 copy of the now-vanished text from Jane Molony's epitaph that used to grace the walls of St. George's Chapel in Bayswater Road: Robert Pierpoint, "Lady O'Looney's (Mrs. Jane Molony's) Epitaph," *Notes and Queries* S11–111 (1911): 190–191, http://dx.doi.org/10.1093/nq/s11.63.190, accessed June 22, 2012.

2. On married women and the legal effects of coverture and separate property, particularly in the case of remarriage, see Nicola Phillips, *Women in Business, 1700–1850*

(Woodbridge, UK: Boydell Press, 2006), 23–47, 69–91. For case law and the development of separate property, see Susan Staves, *Married Women's Separate Property in England, 1660–1833* (London: Harvard University Press, 1990).

3. Jesse Addams, *Reports of Cases argued and Determined in the Ecclesiastical Courts at Doctors Common and in the High Court of Delegates* (London, 1825), 2:249–253, http:// books.google.co.uk/books/about/Reports_of_cases_argued_and_determined_i.html?id =OpMoAAAAIAAJ, accessed June 25, 2012; Matrimonial Cause in the Consistory Court of London: *Molony v. Molony,* LMA, DL/C/0922. Lawrence Stone, *Road to Divorce: England, 1530–1987* (Oxford: OUP, 1990), 183–184, 194–195.

4. *The Times,* December 10, 1827.

5. Bill of Edmond Molony, December 11, 1820; and answer of Jane Molony, June 22, 1821, TNA, C/13/266/25.

6. Affidavit of Edward Eagar, November 11, 1824, TNA, C/121/129; *The Times,* December 10, 1827.

7. David Neale, The *Rule of Law in a Penal Colony* (Cambridge: CUP, 1991), 178–179; N. D. McLachlan, "Macquarie, Lachlan (1762–1824)," in *Australian Dictionary of Biography,* http://adbonline.anu.edu.au/biogs/A020162b.htm, accessed March 5, 2010; J. M. Bennett, "Bigge, John Thomas (1780–1843)," in *Australian Dictionary of Biography,* http://adbonline .anu.edu.au/biogs/A010093b.htm, accessed May 4, 2010.

8. *Edward Eagar v. William Collins Burke Jackson,* Supreme Court (Civil Jurisdiction) Judgement Book (1821), SRNSW, 9/922; Lewis Smith, *Colonial Litigant Extraordinaire: The Edward Eagar Story* (Burrel Creek, Australia: Fast Books, 1996), 91–97.

9. See witness statements in Colonial Secretary's Correspondence: Re inquest in to the death of Thomas Jones (1821), SRNSW, 4/1819, 363–374. The rough and largely drunken men and women who witnessed Jones's death from a combination of alcohol and physical assault by his stepdaughter's lover, had been laughing about William's misfortune in losing some wine or had purchased some gold trinket from him. SRNSW, entries for Eagar, Edward, in the Index to the Colonial Secretary's Papers, 1788–1825, http://colsec.records.nsw.gov.au/ indexes/colsec/e/F18c_e.htm#Po_o. On Mary Jackson's move to and life in Tasmania, I am grateful for information sent from Laurence Turtle in Australia and Jennifer Amos in Tasmania.

10. Will of William Collins Burke Jackson, TNA, PROB 11/1745, fo. 342v. Online Encyclopaedia of Silvermarks, Hallmarks, and Makers Marks, http://www.925–1000 .com/forum/viewtopic.php?f=38&t=14536, accessed August 18, 2010.

11. Charles Dickens, *Bleak House* (London: Penguin, 2005), 15.

12. E. A. Smith, "Scott, John, First Earl of Eldon (1751–1838)," in *Oxford Dictionary of National Biography* (Oxford: OUP, 2004), http://www.oxforddnb.com/view/article /24897, accessed August 18, 2010.

13. Bill of William Collins Burke Jackson and William Collins Jackson an infant, February 1823 and amended May 1823; answer of Jane Molony, April 14, 1823; and answer of Edmond Molony, April 17, 1823, TNA, C/13/797/12. A supplementary bill to *Jackson v. Molony,* March 8, 1839, summarizes developments of the case over the years, TNA, C/13/1216/11.

14. Noel McLachlan, "Edward Eagar: A Colonial Spokesman in Sydney and London," *Historical Studies, Australia and New Zealand* 10, 40 (1963): 441–443, 446.

15. Supplementary bill, March 8, 1839, TNA, C/13/1216/11; affidavit of Mary Jackson, April 6, 1830, and affidavit of Charles Shee, November 24, 1836, TNA, C/121/129.

16. *The Australian,* March 12, 1828.

17. *The Times*, December 10, 1827.

18. *The Times*, December 14, 1827. McLachlan, "Edward Eagar," 447.

19. Ibid. Several newspapers, including the *Tasmanian Journal*, the *Sydney Monitor*, and the *Sydney Gazette* reported that Eagar was living in Langley Lodge between January and March 1829, but by April that year he was back in London.

20. Peter Cunningham, *Two Years in New South Wales* (London, 1827), 55. *Sydney Monitor*, November 27, 1833, but the report wrongly named a Mr. Joseph Raphael as the sole legatee of the will, an error corrected on November 30.

21. For accounts of the forgery case and execution of Joseph Bradley with his accomplice Patrick Troy, see *Sydney Gazette and New South Wales Advertiser*, October 1, 17, and 22, 1828, http://trove.nla.gov.au/newspaper, accessed June 21, 2012.

22. *Tasmanian Journal*, February 13, 1829, a report reprinted in the *Sydney Monitor*, February 23, 1829.

23. McLachlan, "Edward Eagar," 443–446. Edward Smith Hall, the *Monitor*'s editor, had published a series of letters from Eagar detailing his "frantic, single handed advocacy" of the colonists' rights for trial by jury and taxation by representation. In 1828 Eagar wrote, printed, and personally distributed three hundred copies of a pamphlet to MPs entitled "Remarks and Objections on the part of the Colonists of New South Wales to a Bill, to Provide for the Administration of Justice in New South Wales." *Sydney Gazette*, June 30, 1838. *The Colonist*, January 10, 1838; John B. Hirst, *Convict Society and Its Enemies: A History of Early New South Wales* (Sydney: Allen and Unwin, 1983), 199–200.

24. Lt. Col. Dumaresq, Governor Darling's secretary, cited in McLachlan, "Edward Eagar," 445.

EPILOGUE

1. After marrying James Amos, the son of a free-settler family, Mary Ann moved to a house in Cranbrook, where they raised a large family and her descendant Jennifer Amos still lives. Jennifer kindly contacted me and provided much valuable information about Mary Ann, her brother, and their errant father. Mary Ann died in 1872, and her gravestone can still be seen in Glen Gala, Cranbrook, Tasmania.

2. *Molony v. Molony*, Chancery Masters Accounts, TNA, C/101/2496. The original citation for the cause is marked "nothing prayed 10 November 1826," and no documentation beyond that and the official documents appointing proctors and summoning the litigants exists in the bundle, LMA, DL/C/0922.

3. Robert Pierpoint, "Lady O'Looney's (Mrs. Jane Molony's) Epitaph," *Notes and Queries* S11–111 (1911): 190–191. The argument over the identity of the "lady" whose epitaph this was raged for eight years, from 1907 to 1915, but the details in this account match Jane Jackson's precisely.

4. The will of Jane Molony, formerly Jackson, proved July 15, 1839, TNA, PROB 11/1913, 450. My thanks go to Liz Hore at TNA for tracing George's military records, which show he joined the First Dragoon Guards as a cornet in March 1839, was promoted to lieutenant in June 1840, and became captain in June 1844. He transferred to the Sixteenth Dragoons in June 1845 and to the Seventh Hussars in October 1855, from which he retired with the rank of major in May 1856.

5. See, for example, the 1851 census for Roath, Cardiff, TNA, HO107/2455; the 1861 census for Clifton, Bristol, TNA, RG9/1725; the 1871 census for Kempsey, Worcestershire, TNA, RG10/3057; the 1881 census for Dawlish, Devon, TNA, RG11/2157; and

the 1891 census for Dawlish, Devon, TNA, RG12/1695. Again my thanks go to Liz Hore at TNA for tracing these census records and the value of George's and Catherine Jackson's wills.

6. For an academic attack on Jackson's "characteristic arrogance and rashness," see Kunjukrishnan Nadar Rajayyan, *The Rise and Fall of the Poligars of Tamilnadu* (Madras: University of Madras, 1974), 91, but on 100 the author is less sure Kattobomma should be declared "a patriot." For websites celebrating Kattobomma's life, see, for example, http://wn.com/Veerapandiya_Kattabomman, which includes a clip from the 1959 film depicting the now-famous scene of Jackson's interview with Kattobomma; it is also available on YouTube. See also http://rathnas.wetpaint.com/page/Veera+Pandya+Kattabomma +Naicker+History. For the film *Veerapandiya Kattabomman* (1959), see http://en.wikipedia .org/wiki/Veerapandiya_Kattabomman_(film); and for a download and clips, see http://movies.bollysite.com/movie/veerapandiya-kattabomman-1959.html.

7. Niall Ferguson, "The Human Hive," recorded at the London School of Economics and Political Science and first broadcast on BBC Radio 4 and the BBC World Service on Tuesday, June 19, 2012. Transcript available at http://www.bbc.co.uk/programmes /b01jmxop/features/transcript, accessed June 28, 2012.

8. See http://www.citizensadvice.org.uk/advice4me/youth_debt_advice.htm. PFEG, http://www.pfeg.org/, is the UK's leading financial-education charity; it provides resources, lesson plans, and advice to anyone teaching children and young people about money. See also Audrey Ward, "Lessons to Bank On," *The Times,* July 8, 2012, an interview with moneysavingexpert.com founder, Martin Lewis, who supports financial education to help children and their parents avoid "bad" debt. Advice for students and young people can be found at http://www.moneysavingexpert.com/family/.

9. See, for example, the Law and Parents website advice that "no one wants to see their child with county court judgments, a poor credit history and in the worst cases, facing bankruptcy, so parents are quick to jump to their children's aid, if they can afford to. This, however, does not solve the problem. It merely demonstrates to the child that they are not capable of dealing with issues in the real world and gives them a fall back position," http://www.lawandparents.co.uk/are-parents-responsible-childrens-debt.html.

SELECTED BIBLIOGRAPHY

MANUSCRIPT SOURCES

Australia

State Records of New South Wales, Sidney

Colonial Secretary: Letters Received, Microfilm 6038, 6004, 3178, 774

Papers Concerning "Surry" in the NSW Court of Vice Admiralty, Microfilm 6044

England

British Library, London

MANUSCRIPT ROOM

Add. 60337–60342, Shee Papers: Private, Political, and Diplomatic Correspondence of Sir George Shee, 1st Bart, 1754–1825, and of His Son Sir George Shee, 2nd Bart, 1784–1870

Add. 78555–78559, Evelyn Papers: Letters, Receipts, Account Books, Etc., of John Evelyn, 1743–1827

ASIAN AND AFRICAN STUDIES ROOM

IOR/F/4/12, Records of the Board of Commissioners for the Affairs of India

IOR/H/440, Ramnad, India Office Records and Private Papers, 1797–1799

Gloucestershire Archives, Gloucester

GLOUCESTER GAOL [JAIL] RECORDS:

Q/Gc/1–2, Journal of Visiting Justices

Q/Gc/3/7, Governor's Journal

Q/Gc/31/1, Chaplain's Journal

Q/Gc/32/2, Surgeon's Journal

Q/Gc/38/2, Proceedings, 1799–1816

Q/S/G2, Printed Gaol [Jail] Calendars

London Metropolitan Archives, London

CLA/032/01/043, *Proposed Rules and Orders for Newgate based on those of Gloucester and other Gaols,* 1814

OLD BAILEY RECORDS

OB/CJ/004, Old Bailey Calendar of Indictments

OB/RSB/13, Old Bailey Rough Entry Book, January 1812–April 1815

OB/SB/026–7, Newgate Gaol [Jail] Delivery Books

OB/SR/455, Old Bailey Sessions Rolls

LONDON CONSISTORY COURT RECORDS

DL/C–34, 1823–1824

The National Archives, Kew

ASSI 5, Assizes Oxford Circuit Records

C/13, Court of Chancery, Six Clerks Office: Pleadings, 1801–1842

C/33, Court of Chancery, Entry Books of Decrees and Orders
C/10, Chancery Masters Account Books
C/106/64–70, *Jackson v. Moloway* [*sic*]; papers of William Collins Jackson
(C/106/65 contains the three unpublished volumes of *Filial Ingratitude.*)
C/121, Court of Chancery, Master Richard's Documents
HO/9, Hulk Registers and Letter Books
HO/26/18, Newgate Criminal Registers, 1812
PRIS 1, Fleet Prison Commitment Books, 1686–1842
PRIS 2/104–106, Fleet Prison Commitment Files, 1810–1811
PRIS 3/12, Fleet Prison Discharges and Warrants to Gaolers [Jailers], 1810–1811
PRIS 10/53, Entry Book for Discharges: Fleet Prison, 1805–1815
PRIS 10/191–202, Day Rule Books, 1809–1814
PROB 11, Prerogative Court of Canterbury and Related Probate Jurisdictions,
    Will Registers

Guernsey
THE GREFFE ROYAL COURT ARCHIVES, ST. PETER PORT
X1/74–88; Box 112/25, De Saumarez Family and Estate Papers
Letter Book of Lieutenant General Sir John Doyle, Commander of HM Forces in
    Guernsey and Alderney, 1807–1812

Digital Archives
Clergy of the Church of England Database,
    http://www.theclergydatabase.org.uk/jsp/persons/index.jsp
House of Commons Parliamentary Papers Online, from ProQuest
Nineteenth-Century British Library Newspapers Online, from Gale Cengage Learning
Proceedings of the Old Bailey: London's Central Criminal Court, 1674–1913,
    http://www.oldbaileyonline.org/.
The Times Digital Archive, 1785–2006, from Gale Cengage Learning
Trove Digitised Newspapers, The National Library of Austraila, http://trove.nla.gov.au
    /newspaper

PRINTED PRIMARY SOURCES
Newspapers and Magazines
Asiatic Journal and Monthly Register for British India and Its Dependencies
Britannic Magazine
British Medical Journal
Cheltenham Chronicle and Gloucestershire General Advertiser
Colonist
Evangelical Magazine
Examiner
Fraser's Magazine
General Evening Post

Lancaster Gazette and General Advertiser

Law Magazine

Legal Observer

London Chronicle

London Literary Gazette and Journal of the Belle Arts

London Medical Gazette

New Monthly Magazine

New South Wales Advertiser

Scourge; or, Monthly Expositor of Imposture and Folly

Sydney Gazette

Sydney Monitor

Tasmanian Journal

Times

Westminster Review

Books and Pamphlets

Cheltenham Directory for the Year 1802; giving a succinct account of the nature and use of the waters, description of the well, royal spa, and town of Cheltenham, with the number of houses, population, and rides near the town, a list of the clergy, faculty, law, bankers, etc. Cheltenham, 1802.

The Convict's Complaint; Supposed to be written on board the hulks in the beginning of 1815. London, 1815.

The Debtor and Creditor's Assistant: or, a key to the King's Bench and Fleet Prisons; calculated for the information and benefit of the injured creditor as well as the unfortunate debtor. London, 1793.

Disobedient son and cruel husband, being a full and true account of one Mr. John Jones, a gentleman's son in Wiltshire, whose father left him an estate . . . and married a lady of great fortune . . . but . . . killed his wife and children, and afterwards hanged his mother on a tree in the orchatd [sic]. With the last dying words of this wretch, who was tried and executed this assizes before his mother's door. Ca. 1790.

General Regulations for Inspection and Controul of all the Prisons, Together with the Rules, Orders and Bye Laws for the Government of the Gaol and Penitentiary House for the County of Gloucester. Gloucester, 1790, rev. 1808.

A List of Members of the Society of Guardians for the Protection of Trade against Swindlers and Sharpers. London, 1812.

A Loyal, but Solemn Expostulation, addressed in a moment of general distress, dismay, and apprehension, to a thoughtless and imprudent young man. London, 1795.

"Memoir of the Late Mr. Alley." *Legal Observer* 9, 239 (November 29, 1834).

"Mr. Adolphus and His Contemporaries at the Old Bailey." *Law Magazine* 35 (1846).

Rules and Order of The Guardians: or, Society for the Protection of Trade against Swindlers and Sharpers. London, 1816.

Substance of the Speech of George Holford esq. In the House of Commons on Thursday 22nd June 1815 on the Bill "To Amend the law relative to the Transportation of Offenders Containing Provisions Respecting the Confinement of Offenders in the Hulks." London, 1815.

Addams, J. *Reports of Cases argued and Determined in the Ecclesiastical Courts at Doctors Common and in the High Court of Delegates.* Vol. 2. London, 1825.

Adolphus, John Leycester. "The Late John Adolphus." *Fraser's Magazine* 66 (1862): 49–53.

Barrow, William. *An Essay on Education.* London, 1804 (originally published 1802).

Blackstone, William. *Commentaries on the Laws of England.* 16th ed. London, 1811.

Burke, Edmund. *Correspondence of Edmund Burke,* ed. by Alfred Cobban and Roberta A. Smith. Vol. 6. Cambridge: CUP, 1967.

———. *The Writings and Speeches of Edmund Burke,* ed. by P. J. Marshall. Vol. 6. Oxford: Clarendon Press, 1991.

Buxton, Thomas Fowell. *An Inquiry whether Crime and Misery are Produced or Prevented, by our Present System of Prison Discipline.* London, 1818

Caldwell, Robert. *A political and general history of the District of Tinnevelly, in the Presidency of Madras, from the earliest period to its cession to the English Government in A.D. 1801.* London, 1881. http://www.ebooksread.com/authors-eng/robert-caldwell/a-political -and-general-history-of-the-district-of-tinnevelly-in-the-presidency-hci/1-a-political -and-general-history-of-the-district-of-tinnevelly-in-the-presidency-hci .shtml (accessed March 16, 2011).

Childs, W. M. *The Town of Reading During the Early Part of the Nineteenth Century.* Reading, UK: University College, 1910.

Christian, Theophilus. *The Fashionable World Displayed.* London, 1804. http://www .archive.org/stream/fashionableworlooowengoog#page/no/mode/2up (accessed May 5, 2011).

Clarke's New Law List. 16th ed. London, 1812.

Cleland, John. *Fanny Hill; or, Memoirs of a Woman of Pleasure,* ed. by Peter Wagner. London: Penguin Classics, 1985.

Coleman, George. *The Heir at Law: A Comedy in Five Acts.* London, 1797.

Cottu, Charles. *On the Administration of Criminal Justice in England; and the Spirit of the English Government.* trans. London, 1822.

Cunningham, Peter. *Two Years in New South Wales.* London, 1827.

Dalrymple, Alexander. *A letter to the Court of Directors for the Affairs of the United Company of Merchants of England Trading in the East Indies.* 1769.

Dickens, Charles. *Bleak House,* ed. by Nicola Bradbury. London: Penguin, 2005.

———. "A Visit to Newgate." In *Sketches by Boz.* London, 1836.

Eagar, Edward. *Letters to The Rt. Hon. Robert Peel, M.P., Secretary of State for the Home Department, On the advantages of New South Wales and Van Diemen's Land as penal settlements for the punishment and reform of offenders, and as colonies for the reception of poor emigrants . . . By A Late Resident in Those Colonies.* London, 1824.

East India Company. *East India Lists of Civil Servants.* 1770 and 1790.

———. *The India Calendar: Bengal Establishment.* 1789.

———. *A List of the Names of the Members of the United Company of Merchants of England Trading to the East Indies, who stood qualified to as Voters on the Company's Books on 9th April 1806.*

Egan, Pierce. *Tom & Jerry: Life in London.* London: John Camden Hotten, 1869 ed.

Feltham, John. *The Picture of London for 1802.* London, 1802.

Fleetwood, William. *The Relative Duties of Parents and Children, Husbands and Wives, Masters and Servants, Considered in Sixteen Sermons: with three more upon the case of self-murther.* 16th ed. London, 1811.

Gisborne, Thomas. *An Enquiry into the Duties of Men In the Higher and Middle Classes of Society in Great Britain.* 6th ed. London, 1811.

Goede, C. A. G. *A Stranger in England; or Travels in Great Britain.* London, 1807.

Griffiths, Arthur. *The Chronicles of Newgate.* London, 1884.

Griffiths, J. K. *A General Cheltenham Guide upon an entirely new plan: comp. from the most authentic sources, and embracing the ancient and modern history, state, and description of that celebrated town and its environs.* Cheltenham, UK, 1818.

Gronow, Rees Howell. *Reminiscences of Captain Gronow: Being Anecdotes of the Camp, Court, Clubs and Society, 1810–1860,* abridged and with an introduction by John Raymond. London: Bodley Head, 1964.

Hamilton, Robert. *The Duties of a Regimental Surgeon Considered:; with observations on his general qualifications.* 2nd ed. London, 1794.

Hansard. *Parliamentary Debates.* Vols. 18, 27. London, 1814.

Hickey, William. *Memoirs of William Hickey,* ed. by Peter Quennell. London: Routledge and Kegan Paul, 1975.

Jackson, William Collins. *Memoir of the Public Conduct and Services of William Collins Jackson Esq., Late Senior Merchant of the Company.* 2nd ed. London, 1812.

Johnson, Samuel. *A Dictionary of the English Language.* 4th ed. 1777.

Knox, Vicesimus, *Essays, Moral and Literary.* 11th ed. Vol. 1. London, 1800.

_____. *Liberal Education: or, a practical treatise on the methods of acquiring a useful and polite education.* 7th ed. London, 1785.

Locke, John. *Some Thoughts Concerning Education.* New York: P. F. Collier, [1693] 1909–1914. www.bartleby.com/37/1/ (accessed May 28, 2012).

Mann, D. D. *The Present Picture of New South Wales.* London, 1811.

Minchin, W. R. *The Present State of the Debtor and Creditor Law, Being an essay on the effects of imprisonment: or, a consideration of creditors' rights and debtors' wrongs.* London, 1812.

Molesworth, William. *Report of the Select Committee on Transportation together with a letter from the Archbishop of Dublin on the same subject and some notes.* London, 1838.

Montagu, Basil. *An Inquiry into the Aspersions Upon the late Ordinary of Newgate, with some observations upon Newgate and the Punishment of Death.* London, 1815.

A List of Members of the Society of Guardians for the Protection of Trade against Swindlers and Sharpers. London, 1812.

A Loyal, but Solemn Expostulation, addressed in a moment of general distress, dismay, and apprehension, to a thoughtless and imprudent young man. London, 1795.

Thoughts on the Punishment of Death for Forgery. London, 1820.

Moore, John M. D. *Zeluco: Various Views of Human Nature Taken from Life and Manners Foreign and Domestic.* 2nd ed. 2 vols. London, 1789.

More, Sarah. *The Cheapside Apprentice: or, The History of Mr. Francis H.* London, 1796.

Neale, Robert Dorset. *The Prisoner's Guide; Or, Every Debtor his own Lawyer.* 3rd ed. London, 1813.

Neild, James. *State of the Prisons in England, Scotland, and Wales, not for the Debtor only, but for Felons also, and other less Criminal Offenders.* London, 1812.

Pearce, James. *A Treatise on the Abuses of the Laws, Particularly in Actions by Arrest; Pointing out the numerous hardships and abuses, in the different courts, from the commencement of an action to its conclusion.* London, 1814.

Prior, James. *A visit to Madras: being a sketch of the local and characteristic peculiarities of that presidency in the year 1811.* London, 1821.

Simons, Nicholas. *Reports of Cases Decided in the High Court of Chancery.* Vol. 12. London, 1844.

Stanton, Lt. Samuel. *The Principles of Duelling; with Rules to be Observed in every Particular Respecting It.* London, 1790.

Taylor, Ann. *Reciprocal Duties of Parents and Children.* London: Taylor and Hessey, 1818.

Taylor, Isaac. *Advice to the Teens, or, Practical Helps Towards the Formation of One's Own Character.* Boston: Wells and Lilley, 1820 (originally published in 1818).

Thackeray, William Makepeace. *Vanity Fair,* ed. by John Sutherland. Oxford: OUP World's Classics, 1998.

Vaux, James Hardy. *The Memoirs of James Hardy Vaux,* ed. by Noel McLachlan. London: Heinemann, 1964.

Watson, George. *The Profligate: A Comedy.* London, 1820.

Wentworth, W. C. *A Statistical, Historical, and Political Description of the Colony of New South Wales, and its Dependent Settlements in Van Dieman's Land.* London, 1819.

Winchester School. *The History of the Colleges of Winchester, Eton and Westminster with the Charterhouse, the Schools of St Pauls, Merchant Taylors, Harrow and Rugby and the Free School of Christ's Hospital.* London, 1816.

Woodward, Josiah. *The Soldier's Monitor: Being Serious Advice to Soldiers to Behave themselves with a Just Regard for Religion and True Manhood.* London, 1776.

PRINTED SECONDARY SOURCES
Books

Andrew, Donna T., and Randall McGowan. *The Perreaus and Mrs. Rudd: Forgery and Betrayal in Eighteenth-Century London.* London: University of California Press, 2001.

Australia. Library Committee of Commonwealth Parliament. *Historical Records of Australia.* Series 1. Vol. 8. 1916.

Australian Dictionary of Biography. http://adb.anu.edu.au/.

Bailey, Joanne. *Parenting in England, 1760–1830: Emotion, Identity, and Generation.* Oxford: OUP, 2012.

Bateson, Charles. *The Convict Ships, 1787–1868.* 4th ed. Sydney: Library of Australian History, 1983.

Beattie, John. *Crime and the Courts in England, 1660–1800.* Oxford: OUP, 1986.

Berg, Maxine. *Luxury and Pleasure in Eighteenth-Century Britain.* Oxford: OUP, 2005.

Bowen, H. V. *The Business of Empire: The East India Company and Imperial Britain, 1756–1833.* Cambridge: CUP, 2006.

Brewer, John, and John Styles, eds. *An Ungovernable People: The English and Their Law in the Seventeenth and Eighteenth Centuries.* London: Hutchinson, 1980.

Brooke, Alan, and David Brandon. *Bound for Botany Bay: British Convict Voyages to Australia.* Richmond, UK: National Archives, 2005.

Brown, Roger Lee. *A History of the Fleet Prison, London: The Anatomy of the Fleet.* Lampeter, Wales: Edwin Mellen Press, 1996.

Butlin, J. *Foundations of the Australian Monetary System, 1778–1851.* Sydney: University Press, 1968.

Campbell, Charles. *The Intolerable Hulks: British Shipboard Confinement, 1776–1857.* 3rd ed. Tucson, AZ: Fenestra Books, 2001.

Cannadine, David. *Aspects of Aristocracy: Grandeur and Decline in Modern Britain.* New Haven, CT: Yale University Press, 1994.

Carter, Philip. *Men and the Emergence of Polite Society, 1660–1800*. New York: Pearson Education, 2000.

Colley, Linda. *Britons: Forging the Nation, 1707–1837*. London: Pimlico, 1992.

———. *The Ordeal of Elizabeth Marsh: A Woman in World History*. London: HarperCollins, 2007.

Corfield, Penelope J. *Power and the Professions in Britain, 1700–1800*. London: Routledge, 1995.

Cox, Gregory Stevens. *St. Peter Port, 1680–1830*. Woodbridge, UK: Boydell Press, 1999.

Cox, Pamela, and Heather Shore, eds. *Becoming Delinquent: British and European Youth, 1650–1950*. Aldershot, UK: Ashgate, 2002.

Cruikshank, Dan. *The Secret History of Georgian London: How the Wages of Sin Shaped the Capital*. London: Random House, 2009.

Dalrymple, William. *White Mughals: Love and Betrayal in Eighteenth-Century India*. London: HarperCollins, 2004.

Davis, Dorothy. *A History of Shopping*. London: Routledge and Kegan Paul, 1966.

Dirks, Nicholas B. *The Scandal of Empire: India and the Creation of Imperial Britain*. London: Belknap Press, 2006.

Downs, David, and Paul Rock. *Understanding Deviance: A Guide to the Sociology of Crime and Rule Breaking*. 2nd ed. Oxford: Clarendon Press, 1995.

Emsley, Clive. *Crime and Society in England, 1750–1900*. 3rd ed. Harlow, UK: Pearson, 2005.

Evelyn, Helen. *The History of the Evelyn Family*. London: Eveleigh Nash, 1915. http://archive.org/details/historyofevelynf00eveluoft (accessed May 3, 2012).

Finn, Margot C. *The Character of Credit: Personal Debt in English Culture, 1740–1914*. Cambridge: CUP, 2003.

Fletcher, Anthony. *Gender, Sex, & Subordination in England, 1500–1800*. London: Yale University Press, 1995.

———. *Growing Up in England: The Experience of Childhood, 1600–1914*. London: Yale University Press, 2008.

Flynn, Michael. *The Second Fleet: Britain's Grim Convict Armada of 1790*. Sydney: Library of Australian History, 1993.

Gatrell, V.A.C. *The Hanging Tree: Execution and the English People, 1770–1868*. Oxford: OUP, 1994.

Gatrell, Vic. *City of Laughter: Sex and Satire in Eighteenth-Century London*. London: Atlantic Books, 2006.

Hainsworth, D. R. *The Sydney Traders: Simeon Lord and His Contemporaries, 1788–1821*. Melbourne: University Press, 1981.

Hans, Nicholas. *New Trends in Education in the Eighteenth Century*. London: Routledge, 1951.

Hart, Gwen. *A History of Cheltenham*. Leicester, UK: Leicester University Press, 1965.

Henderson, Tony. *Disorderly Women in Eighteenth-Century London: Prostitution and Control in the Metropolis, 1730–1830*. London: Longman, 1999.

Hilton, Boyd. *A Mad, Bad, & Dangerous People? England, 1783–1846*. Oxford: OUP, 2006.

Hirst, John B. *Convict Society and Its Enemies: A History of Early New South Wales*. Sydney: Allen and Unwin, 1983.

Hostettler, John, and Richard Braby. *Sir William Garrow: His Life, Times, and Fight for Justice*. Hook, UK: Waterside Press, 2010.

Hughes, Robert. *The Fatal Shore*. London: Vintage, 2003.

Hunt, Margaret. *The Middling Sort: Commerce, Gender, and the Family in England, 1680–1780*. London: University of California Press, 1996.

Ignatieff, Michael. *A Just Measure of Pain: The Penitentiary in the Industrial Revolution, 1750–1850*. London: Penguin/Peregrine, 1989.

Kelly, Ian. *Beau Brummell: The Ultimate Dandy*. London: Hodder and Stoughton, 2005.

King, Peter. *Crime, Justice, and Discretion in England, 1740–1820*. Oxford: OUP, 2000.

Laidlaw, Zoe. *Colonial Connections, 1815–45: The Information Revolution and Colonial Government*. Manchester, UK: MUP, 2005.

Langbein, John H. *The Origins of Adversary Criminal Trial*. Oxford: OUP, 2005.

Langford, Paul. *A Polite and Commercial People: England, 1727–1783*. Oxford: Clarendon Press, 1989.

Lavery, Brian. *Nelson's Navy: The Ships, Men, and Organisation, 1793–1815*. London: Conway Maritime Press, 1989.

Lawson, John, and Harold Silver. *A Social History of Education in England*. London: Methuen, 1973.

Lawson, Philip. *The East India Company: A History*. London: Longman, 1993.

Lis, Catharina, and Hugo Soly. *Disordered Lives: Eighteenth-Century Families and Their Unruly Relatives*. Trans. by Alexander Brown. Cambridge: Polity Press, 1996.

Lynch, Jack. *Deception and Detection in Eighteenth-Century Britain*. Aldershot, UK: Ashgate, 2008.

May, Allyson N. *The Bar & the Old Bailey, 1750–1850*. London: University of North Carolina Press, 2003.

Maynard, Margaret. *Fashioned from Penury: Dress as Cultural Practice in Colonial Australia*. Cambridge: CUP, 1994.

McCormick, Tim. *First Views of Australia, 1788–1825: A History of Early Sydney*. Sydney: Longueville, 1987.

McKenzie, Kirsten. *Scandal in the Colonies: Sydney and Cape Town, 1820–1850*. Melbourne: University Publishing, 2004.

———. *A Swindler's Progress: Nobles and Convicts in the Age of Liberty*. London: Harvard University Press, 2010.

Mitchell, Leslie. *The Whig World*. London: Hambledon, 2005.

Muldrew, Craig. *The Economy of Obligation: The Culture of Credit and Social Relations in Early Modern England*. Basingstoke, UK: Palgrave, 1998.

Murray, Venetia. *High Society in the Regency Period, 1788–1830*. London: Penguin, 1999.

Neale, David. *The Rule of Law in a Penal Colony*. Cambridge: CUP, 1991.

Nicholas, Stephen, ed. *Convict Workers: Reinterpreting Australia's Past*. Cambridge: CUP, 1989.

O'Toole, Fintan. *A Traitor's Kiss: The Life of Richard Brinsley Sheridan*. London: Granta Books, 1997.

Oxford Dictionary of National Biography. Oxford: OUP, 2004. http://www.oxforddnb.com.

Peakman, Julie. *Mighty Lewd Books: The Development of Pornography in Eighteenth-Century England*. Basingstoke, UK: Palgrave Macmillan, 2003.

Pearsall, Sarah M. *Atlantic Families: Lives and Letters in the Later Eighteenth Century*. Oxford: OUP, 2008.

Perry, Ruth. *Novel Relations: The Transformation of Kinship in English Literature and Culture, 1748–1818*. Cambridge: CUP, 2006.

Phillips, Nicola. *Women in Business, 1700–1850.* Woodbridge, UK: Boydell Press, 2006.

Porter, Roy. *English Society in the Eighteenth Century.* Rev. ed. London: Penguin, 1990.

———. *London: A Social History.* London: Penguin, 1994.

———. *Quacks: Fakers and Charlatans in Medicine.* Stroud, UK: Tempus, 2003.

Porter, Roy, and Lesley Hall. *The Facts of Life: The Creation of Sexual Knowledge in Britain, 1650–1950.* London: Yale University Press, 1995.

Rajayyan, Kunjukrishnan Nadar. *The Rise and Fall of the Poligars of Tamilnadu.* Madras: University of Madras, 1974.

Rawlings, Philip. *Drunks, Whores, and Idle Apprentices: Criminal Biographies of the Eighteenth Century.* London: Routledge, 1992.

Rees, Sian. *The Floating Brothel.* London: Headline, 2001.

Rendell, Jane. *The Pursuit of Pleasure: Gender, Space, and Architecture in Regency London.* London: Athlone Press, 2002.

Retford, Kate. *The Art of Domestic Life: Family Portraiture in Eighteenth-Century England.* London: Yale University Press, 2006.

Rigden, Reg. *The Floating Prisons of Woolwich and Deptford.* London: Borough of Greenwich, 1976.

Ritchie, John, ed. *The Evidence to the Bigge Reports.* Vol. 2, *The Written Evidence.* London: Heinemann, 1971.

Sharpe, J. A. *Crime in Early Modern England, 1550–1750.* 2nd ed. London: Longman, 1999.

Shore, H. *Artful Dodgers: Youth and Crime in Early-Nineteenth-Century London.* Woodbridge, UK: Boydell Press, 1999.

Smith, E. A. *George IV.* London: Yale University Press, 1999.

Smith, Kevin Lewis. *Colonial Litigant Extraordinaire.* Burrel Creek, Australia: Fast Books, 1996

Sobell, Dava. *Longitude: The True Story of a Lone Genius Who Solved the Greatest Scientific Problem of His Time.* London: Fourth Estate, 1996.

Spear, T. G. P. *The Nabobs: A Study of the English in Eighteenth-Century India.* Oxford: OUP, 1932.

Spierenburg, Pieter. *The Prison Experience: Disciplinary Institutions and Their Inmates in Early Modern Europe.* Amsterdam: Amsterdam University Press, 2007.

Staves, Susan. *Married Women's Separate Property in England, 1660–1833.* London: Harvard University Press, 1990.

Stone, Lawrence. *Road to Divorce: England, 1530–1987.* Oxford: OUP, 1990.

Stott, Anne. *Hannah More: The First Victorian.* Oxford: OUP, 2003.

Tadmor, Naomi. *Family and Friends in Eighteenth-Century England: Household, Kinship, and Patronage.* Cambridge: CUP, 2001.

Tyerman, Christopher L. *A History of Harrow School, 1324–1991.* Oxford: OUP, 2000.

Vickery, Amanda. *Behind Closed Doors: At Home in Georgian England.* London: Yale University Press, 2009.

———. *The Gentleman's Daughter: Women's Lives in Georgian England.* London: Yale University Press, 1998.

Whiting, J. R. S. *Prison Reform in Gloucestershire, 1776–1820: A Study of the Work of Sir George Onesiphorus Paul, Bart.* Andover, UK: Phillimore, 1975.

Whyman, Susan. *The Pen and the People: English Letter Writers, 1660–1800.* Oxford: OUP, 2009.

Wilson, Ben. *Decency and Disorder: The Age of Cant, 1789–1837.* London: Faber and Faber, 2007.

Articles and Essays

Andrew, Donna T. "The Code of Honour and Its Critics: The Opposition to Duelling in England, 1700–1850." *Social History* 5, 3 (1980): 409–434.

Atkinson, Alan, "The Free-Born Englishman Transported: Convict Rights as a Measure of Eighteenth-Century Empire." *Past and Present* 144 (1994): 88–115. http://www.jstor.org/stable/651144 (accessed July 7, 2009).

Banks, Steve. "Dangerous Friends: The Second and the Later English Duel." *Journal for the Society of Eighteenth-Century Studies* 32, 1 (2009): 87–106.

Berry, Helen. "Polite Consumption: Shopping in Eighteenth-Century England." *Transactions of the Royal Historical Society* 12 (2002): 388–394.

Cohen, Michele. "Gender and the Private/Public Debate on Education in the Long Eighteenth Century." In, *Public or Private Education? Lessons from History*, ed. by Richard Aldrich. London: Woburn Press, 2004, 15–35.

Corfield, Penelope J. "Georgian Bath: The Magical Meeting Place." *History Today* 40 (1990): 26–33.

———. "The Rivals: Landed and Other Gentlemen." In *Land and Society in Britain, 1700–1914*, ed. by Negley Harte and Roland Quinault. Manchester, UK: MUP, 1996, 1–33.

Durston, Gregory. "The Emergence, and Occasional Disappearance, of England's Differing Legal Professions: 1200 to 1900." *Hosei Riron* (Journal of Law and Politics, Japan) 28 (1995): 145–166.

Elliot, Jane. "Was There a Convict Dandy? Convict Consumer Interests in Sydney, 1788–1815." *Australian Historical Studies* 104 (1995): 373–392.

Endelman, Todd M. "The Checkered Career of 'Jew' King: A Study in Anglo-Jewish Social History." *Association of Jewish Studies Review* 7–8 (1982–1983): 69–100.

Finn, Margot. "Men's Things: Masculine Consumption in the Consumer Revolution." *Social History* 25, 2 (2000): 133–155.

Forbes, Thomas R. "Coroners' Inquisitions on the Deaths of Prisoners in the Hulks at Portsmouth in 1817–27." *Journal of the History of Medicine* 33 (July 1978): 356–366.

French, Henry, and Mark Rothery. "Upon Your Entry into the World: Masculine Values and the Threshold of Adulthood Among Landed Elites in England, 1600–1800." *Social History* 33, 4 (2008): 402–422.

Gilbert, Arthur N. "Law and Honour Among Eighteenth-Century British Army Officers." *Historical Journal* 19, 1 (1976): 775–787.

Haagen, Paul H. "Eighteenth-Century English Society and the Debt Law." In *Social Control and the State: Historical and Comparative Essays*, ed. by Stanley Cohen and Andrew Scull. Oxford: Robertson, 1983, 222–247.

Handler, Phil. "Forgery and the End of the 'Bloody Code' in Early-Nineteenth-Century England." *Historical Journal* 48, 3 (2005): 683–702.

Harris, Michael. "Trials and Criminal Biographies: A Case Study in Distribution." In *The Sale and Distribution of Books from 1700*, ed. by R. Myers and M. Harris. Oxford: Oxford Polytechnic Press, 1982, 1–36.

Hay, Douglas. "Property, Authority, and the Criminal Law." In Douglas Hay et al., *Albion's Fatal Tree: Crime and Society in Eighteenth-Century England*. Harmondsworth, UK: Penguin, 1975, 17–63.

Innes, Joanna. "The King's Bench Prison in the Later Eighteenth Century: Law, Authority, and Order in a London Debtors' Prison." In *An Ungovernable People: The*

English and Their Law in the Seventeenth and Eighteenth Centuries, ed. by John Brewer and John Styles. London: Hutchinson, 1980, 250–298.

Kalman, Harold D. "Newgate Prison." *Architectural History* 12 (1969): 50–61.

Kercher, Bruce. "Perish or Prosper: The Law and Convict Transportation in the British Empire, 1700–1850." *Law and History Review* 21 (2003): 527–584.

King, Peter. "Newspaper Reporting and Attitudes to Crime and Justice in Late-Eighteenth- and Early-Nineteenth-Century London." *Continuity and Change* 22 (2007): 73–112. http://doi.org/10.1017/S0268416007006194 (accessed June 20, 2011).

———. "The Rise of Juvenile Delinquency in England, 1780–1840: Changing Patterns of Perception and Prosecution." *Past and Present* 160 (1998): 116–166.

Klein, Lawrence E. "Politeness for Plebes: Consumption and Social Identity in Early-Eighteenth-Century England." In *The Consumption of Culture, 1600–1800: Image, Object, Text,* ed. by Ann Bermingham and John Brewer. London: Routledge, 1995, 362–382.

Kopperman, Paul E. "The Cheapest Pay: Alcohol Abuse in the Eighteenth-Century British Army." *Journal of Military History* 60, 3 (1996): 445–470.

Langbein, John H. "Albion's Fatal Flaws." *Past and Present* 98 (1983): 96–120.

McCormack, Matthew. "Married Men and the Fathers of Families: Fatherhood and Franchise Reform in Britain." In *Gender and Fatherhood in the Nineteenth Century,* ed. by Trev Lynn Broughton and Helen Rogers. Basingstoke, UK: Palgrave, 2007, 43–54.

McGowan, Randall, "Forgery Discovered, or the Perils of Circulation in Eighteenth-Century England." *Angelaki* 1 (1994): 113–129.

———. "From Pillory to Gallows: The Punishment of Forgery in the Age of the Financial Revolution." *Past and Present* 165 (1999): 138–139.

McLachlan, Noel. "Edward Eagar (1787–1866): A Colonial Spokesman in Sydney and London." *Historical Studies, Australia and New Zealand* 10, 40 (1963): 431–456.

Moir, E. A. L. "Sir George Onesiphorus Paul." In *Gloucestershire Studies,* ed. by H. P. R. Finburg. Leicester, UK: Leicester University Press, 1957, 195–224.

Morris, Marilyn. "Princely Debt, Public Credit, and Commercial Values in Late Georgian Britain." *Journal of British Studies* 43, 3 (2004): 339–365.

Musgrove, F. "Middle-Class Families and Schools, 1780–1880: Interaction and Exchange of Function Between Institutions." In *Sociology, History, and Education,* ed. by P. W. Musgrave. London: Methuen, 1970, 117–125.

Nechtman, Tillman W. "Nabobs Revisited: A Cultural History of British Imperialism and the Indian Question in Late-Eighteenth-Century Britain." *History Compass* 4, 4 (July 2006): 645–667. doi:10–1111/j.1478–0542.2006.00333.x (accessed December 7, 2006).

Phillips, David. "Good Men to Associate and Bad Men to Conspire: Associations for the Prosecution of Felons in England, 1760–1860." In *Policing and Prosecution in Britain, 1650–1850,* ed. by D. Hay and F. Snyder. Oxford: Clarendon Press, 1989. 113–151.

Phillips, Nicola. "Parenting the Profligate Son: Masculinity, Gentility, and Juvenile Delinquency in England, 1791–1814." *Gender & History* 22, 1 (2010): 92–108.

Pierpoint, Robert. "Lady O'Looney's (Mrs. Jane Molony's) Epitaph." *Notes and Queries* S11-III (1911): 190–191. http://dx.doi.org/10.1093/nq/s11.63.190 (accessed June 22, 2012).

Roberts, Benjamin. "On Not Becoming Delinquent: Raising Adolescent Boys in the Dutch Republic, 1600–1750." In *Becoming Delinquent: British and European Youth, 1650–1950,* ed. by Pamela Cox and Heather Shore. Aldershot, UK: Ashgate, 2002, 41–58.

Roberts, M. J. D. "The Society for the Suppression of Vice and Its Early Critics, 1802–1812." *Historical Journal* 26, 1 (1983): 159–176.

Rogers, Nicholas. "Money, Land, and Lineage: The Big Bourgeoisie of Hanoverian London." *Social History* 4, 3 (1979): 437–454.

Seylon, Raman N. "Study of Poligar Violence in Late 18th Century Tamil Country in South India." *African and Asian Studies* 3, 3–4 (2004): 255–257.

Sheehan, W. J. "Finding Solace in Eighteenth-Century Newgate." In *Crime in England, 1550–1800,* ed. by J. S. Cockburn. London: Methuen, 1977, 229–245.

Shoemaker, Robert. "The Taming of the Duel: Masculinity, Honour, and Ritual Violence in London, 1660–1800." *Historical Journal* 45, 3 (2002): 525–545.

Shore, Heather. "The Trouble with Boys: Gender and the Invention of the Juvenile Offender in Early-Nineteenth-Century Britain." In *Gender and Crime in Modern Europe,* ed. by M. Arnot and C. Usborne. London: UCL Press, 1999, 75–92.

Styles, John. "Print and Policing: Crime Advertising in Eighteenth-Century Provincial England." In *Policing and Prosecution in Britain, 1750–1850,* ed. by D. Hay and F. Snyder. Oxford: Clarendon Press, 1989, 55–111.

Sykes, Gresham M., and David Matza. "Techniques of Neutralization." *American Sociological Review* 22, 6 (1957): 664–670.

Victoria County History. "Gloucester, 1720–1835: Social and Cultural Life." In *A History of the County of Gloucester.* Vol. 4, *The City of Gloucester.* Ed. by N. M. Herbert. 1988, 154–159. http://www.british-history.ac.uk/report.aspx?compid=42295 (accessed May 27, 2009).

Unpublished Papers
Dille, Catherine. "Lessons in Liberty: Schoolboy Rebellions in the English Great Public Schools, 1770–1820." Paper presented at the Institute for Historical Research, London, May 5, 2012.

Durston, Gregory. "Vignettes from the Eighteenth-Century Old Bailey Trial Jury." Conference paper from the Metropolis on Trial, Open University, Milton Keynes, July 2008.

Styles, John. "Lodging at the Old Bailey: Lodgings and Their Furnishing in Eighteenth-Century London." Paper presented at the Long Eighteenth Century Seminar, Institute of Historical Research, London, November 2004.

INDEX

This index covers the introduction, chapters 1 through 12, the epilogue, the notes, and the art insert. Titles of works are shown in *italics*. Illustrations are also indicated in *italics*. The locator *Fig.* followed by a number refers to the images in the art insert. A locator consisting of a page number with the suffix *n* refers to a note. William Jackson and his father have the same name, except for the addition of *Burke* to the son's. To avoid confusion, the precedent adopted in the text of referring to the father as *Jackson* and the son as *William* has also been used here when referring to them in subheadings.